From Privileges to Rights

EARLY AMERICAN STUDIES

Daniel K. Richter and Kathleen M. Brown, Series Editors

Exploring neglected aspects of our colonial, revolutionary, and early national history and culture, Early American Studies reinterprets familiar themes and events in fresh ways. Interdisciplinary in character, and with a special emphasis on the period from about 1600 to 1850, the series is published in partnership with the McNeil Center for Early American Studies.

A complete list of books in the series is available from the publisher.

From Privileges to Rights

Work and Politics in
Colonial New York City

Simon Middleton

PENN

University of Pennsylvania Press
Philadelphia

10   9   8   7   6   5   4   3   2   1

Published by
University of Pennsylvania Press
Philadelphia, Pennsylvania 19104-4112

Library of Congress Cataloging-in-Publication Data

Middleton, Simon (Simon David).
   From privileges to rights : work and politics in colonial New York City / Simon Middleton.
      p.   cm. — (Early American studies)
   Includes bibliographical references and index.
   ISBN-13: 978-0-8122-3915-7
   ISBN 10: 0-8122-3915-6 (cloth : alk. paper)
1. Artisans—New York (State)—New York—History. 2. Entrepreneurship—New York (State)—
New York—History. 3. Working class—New York (State)—New York—History.
4. New York (N.Y.)—History—Colonial period, ca. 1600–1775. I. Title. II. Series.
HD2346.U52N545 2006
331.7'94'0974109033—dc22

                                                        2005042441

For Carolyn, Betsy, and Rosie

Contents

Illustrations

Introduction

When I began the research for this book, I had a fairly clear idea about where my project might fit within an established historiography. Three decades of social and labor history had provided a persuasive account of the transformation of colonial American artisans into waged workers during a contested transition to capitalism. Building on the work of European scholars, American historians traced the rise of a market society and the decline of customary practices, craft pride, and workshop traditions that were thought to have once forged a powerful social bond between masters, journeymen, and apprentices. This decline was accompanied by a worsening of artisanal working conditions and material fortunes that fostered novel forms of republican political protest and ultimately class struggle. It would be difficult to exaggerate the influence of this view in labor and social history in the last four decades.[1] However, there were also gaps in the literature and—lacking the late medieval and early modern research that underpinned the work of their European peers—the most noticeable gap in colonial American history was the surprising dearth of studies of urban skilled workers in the seventeenth and early eighteenth centuries.[2]

With this in mind I set out to examine the artisanal trades in early New York City, suspending my inquiries at 1760 so as to avoid the gravitational pull of the American Revolution that already held so many excellent studies in its orbit. After several, mostly unsuccessful, forays into the archives I began to appreciate why we knew so little about artisanal work in the earlier colonial period: court minutes and published sources frequently mentioned tradesmen who brought disputes before the magistrates, registered as freemen, paid taxes, or served in the militia; these registers and lists provided the raw data for several sociological analyses of the distribution of wealth, ethnic composition, and occupational structure of New York's skilled workforce.[3] But these snapshots revealed a static picture at best, little concerning the ups and downs of daily trade, and still less of the social and political import of artisanal work in the early city. A chance discovery provided an opportunity to investigate in greater detail the activities of a larger and, I came to believe, more representative sample of city tradesmen. Following a reference to a set of uncatalogued papers, I discovered a substantial collection of miscellaneous legal documents comprising several thousand complaints filed to initiate civil suits in the city's Mayor's Court. The complaints provided a wealth of detail concerning prices, wages, and the exchanges that constituted the everyday concerns of tradesmen and their customers. As luck would have it, the records were particularly rich for the late seventeenth and early eighteenth centuries—the period about which so little was known and so much inferred.[4]

The Mayor's Court Papers revealed that city artisans served a local market and that labor shortages made gainful employment generally easy to find. However, the complaints and related documents—bonds, promissory notes, bail agreements, and witness depositions—also disclosed that as early as the third quarter of the seventeenth century the fortunes of ordinary working men and women were intimately bound up with the Atlantic trade and the commercial development of the city's rural hinterland. Tradesmen divided their energies between skilled work and all manner of commercial enterprise, relying on credit to pursue whatever opportunity offered the best return. They participated in the export of furs, tobacco, and plantation supplies and purchased imported cloth and household goods for resale in the city and its environs. They financed speculative ventures, and bought, sold, and rented property; they farmed—raising crops and livestock for local and export markets—and provided food, drink, and lodging for paying guests. In these and other endeavors, tradesmen were far from independent. They relied on wives, family members, slaves, and waged workers for labor and on partners and patrons for credit, capital, and access to customers for their finished goods and services. Indeed, the closer one looked, the more interdependent and impermanent artisans' fortunes appeared. Skilled practitioners working in all areas experienced success and failure, and their commercial strategies seemed to be directed more toward the short-term opportunism of the economy of a bazaar than the orderly pace of craft work usually associated with preindustrial colonial towns.[5] Indeed, by the early eighteenth century the commercial logic of the city's trading economy encouraged artisans to undertake the reverse of what has previously been considered their usual working practice: rather than mastering one trade in a workshop dedicated to the production of bespoke products for local customers, artisans participated in whatever enterprises and markets promised profits with a minimum of risk.

From the Mayor's Court Papers, it seemed increasingly likely that the view of a general and fundamental shift from independent, amenable, and reasonably rewarded craft work to dependent, alienated, and penurious wage work, which had long figured in studies of early industrialization and class formation, had mischaracterized the experience of earlier skilled workers and overestimated the transformative effects of the late eighteenth and early nineteenth centuries.[6] Moreover, if the uncertainties of the market—the rise and fall of individual fortunes, subcontracting, wage work, and cyclical debt dependency—were already common in New York in the late seventeenth and early eighteenth centuries, then their long-supposed intrusion a generation or two later could not adequately account for the form taken by republican and class protests—protests that contrasted the harsh and unyielding temper of a "new" market society with a more affable era of craft work: a lost world of customary mores and workshop practices that was memorialized in countless speeches, banners, and songs, but for which there was little or no evidence in the sources.[7] Rather than continuing to take late eighteenth-century tradesmen at their word, giving credence to their representations of a collective past, my task became the recovery of the world of New York City artisans that preceded the association between skilled work, independence, and virtue that informed the small-producer, republican tradition in the era of the American Revolution and subsequently.

The investigation of this earlier urban scene required that I broaden my focus beyond artisans' commercial activities to consider the relationship between the practice and perception of skilled work, artisanal status, and community rights in New Amsterdam and early New York City. As a wealth of historical and anthropological studies have shown, work has ever been more than a material and technical pursuit bounded by considerations of location and resource. The organization of productive capacities and employment of skills is also a social process that requires the justification of authority and interests in terms of norms and expectations that change over time, norms and expectations that are only fully intelligible when set within the wider context of contemporary political and legal discourses. Moreover, the universality and mundanity of work affords it a particular significance in the determination of social and cultural meanings for ordinary men and women: the daily repetition of simple tasks and replaying of social roles relieves individual doubts and uncertainties regarding the arbitrary assignment of political and cultural meanings by making such meanings appear routine, normal, and even natural. Above all, the function of work as the source of basic material provision in some cases and of comfort and considerable wealth in others grants it a defining role as *the* human activity in which aspirations confront possibilities and, once tempered in light of perceived limitations, quickly harden into realities.[8]

*   *   *

My study of the linkage between skilled work and political culture in New Amsterdam and early New York has benefited from the continuing renaissance in New Netherland history and New World Dutch studies.[9] Scholars have demonstrated that towns such as Beverwijck (later Albany) and New Amsterdam were more than fur-trading outposts of the West India Company's far-flung commercial empire. Communities in early New Netherland sustained diverse economic activities and settler groups who were keen to replicate their orderly Old World origins.

Beginning in the late 1640s, a merchant pressure group in New Amsterdam conducted a successful campaign in the name of ancient Dutch freedoms for a municipal government that could manage local trade in the residential or "burgher" interest.[10] The justification for this campaign drew upon the Dutch tradition of autonomous urban government and protectionism that aimed to provide for community needs through civic, charitable, and commercial institutions—for example, local courts of justice, orphanages, and weigh-houses—and the distribution of municipal privileges and liberties including occupational protections and monopolies to nurture local trade. In large Dutch cities such as Amsterdam, Leiden, and Utrecht, occupational privileges and liberties were overseen by guilds, themselves regulated by the city government, which monitored standards of workmanship and training, pricing and membership and assisted members during sickness or old age. In smaller towns, where there were too few practitioners to require guilds and elaborate regulations, citizenship and trade privileges were nevertheless deeply imbricated in popular conceptions of social and moral order and exerted a symbolic significance far beyond the commercial advantage they afforded holders: privileges and liberties constituted and regulated local relations of production and ensured community well-being; they provided for an individual's public identity (as citizen and craft practitioner) and for the absorption of newcomers and exclusion of dissidents from the municipal space. Most important of all, by indicating the limits of authoritarian government, privileges and liberties also served as guarantees of individual and community freedoms.[11] Thus attacks on local privileges, whether real or imagined, were often construed as threats to fundamental liberties and the common good. These privileges, liberties, and freedoms were frequently referred to as rights, but only in the sense that their holders exercised them with or by right. The social and political implications of this objective conception of rights (and what distinguished it from the modern subjective form) provided for the distinctiveness of colonial New York's and arguably much of early modern European and American political culture. This requires an explanatory note before we proceed further.

In their early modern and objective form, rights were powers granted for a purpose, broadly speaking the promotion of moral and political order and the common good. Objective rights conveyed the idea that an individual may do something because it was right or, as in the case of early New York, because it accorded with divine and natural law or metropolitan and local custom. The first thing to note is the close affinity between the objective conception of rights—a term I will use interchangeably with privileges and liberties—and considerations of status or rank. For, as Richard Dagger has argued, to say within this schema that one was a burgher or a baker was also to say that one held rights—for example to residential and legal preferment or to the product of one's labor—that accorded with one's place and function in society. In this sense, rights served as the means by which individuals contributed to an orderly moral and social life that accorded with the injunction of divine and natural law and the purpose of just and legitimate government.[12]

The function of early modern objective rights as the means to an orderly moral and social end meant that they were always accompanied by obligations that required holders to employ their powers in the service of the common good. As we shall see, it was in these terms that New Amsterdam's bakers were granted protective privileges for their trade in return for meeting their duty to bake bread at a regulated weight and price. In this respect, objective rights afforded individuals a justifiable (or rightful) claim to acts that they were under an obligation to perform. Equally importantly, however, they also afforded holders a concomitant right to what others were obliged to render unto them. Thus city bakers invoked their obligation to provide bread for the burghers when justifying demands for regulations that ensured they received their just desserts and when they insisted on the exclusion of unregistered itinerants from baking and selling bread and cakes in the town.

The political and commercial reciprocities bound up with the objective conception of rights bore noteworthy social consequences. For inasmuch as obligations and duties bearing upon rights and privileges specified an individual's public behavior—whether a baker, a burgher, or a burgomaster—they also sustained assumptions concerning the normativity of a prescriptive social hierarchy in which individuals arrayed in their various ranks served different and unequal functions. In so doing, the objective form of rights met particularistic and conservative ends by making hierarchical social arrangements both intelligible and justifiable. It is in this sense that objective rights were distinct from the modern notion of subjective rights, which rose to prominence with the late eighteenth-century revolutions.

In the objective form, the idea of right implied a claim, usually considered part of an individual's property, to act in accordance with a known and accepted standard of behavior that held others in its thrall. In the subjective form, the themes of property and propriety were united in a self-justifying claim that recognizes that an individual *has a right* to act in a certain way, a claim in which the concept of rights has become synonymous with the conception of what is right. With the development of this subjective conception, rights are perceived as a primary feature of humanity and provide for the radical claims concerning equality and liberty of the sort advanced during and after the era of the American Revolution. However, and herein lies this study's key claim, before the modern conception of subjective rights could gain purchase in the everyday world of ordinary men and women, the idea that individuals were fundamentally alike and entitled to possess universal and equal rights had to supplant the view that differences in rank, culture, and nationality were rooted in immemorial and natural differences. This is the incremental transformation that I shall examine from the perspective of the practice and status of artisanal work in colonial New York City.

In the first part of the book I consider the creation of a batavianized civic community based on objective rights and privileges on the southern-most tip of Manhattan Island and the implications of the administrative priorities of this civic community for the status and fortunes of resident artisans. Chapter 1 investigates how, beginning in the late 1640s, tradesmen settled in increasing numbers and pursued all manner of opportunities, especially the fur trade, in addition to their skilled occupations. In doing so, they established a commitment to commercial ambition and diversity that characterized artisanal trade for the remainder of the colonial period. However, when tradesmen came before the city they did so not only as *homo economicus*, or individuals involved in manufacturing, the provision of services, and petty dealing. They also appeared as freeborn subjects and resident burghers who claimed commercial and legal privileges and as practitioners of occupations deemed essential for the provision of the common good. It was this bundle of identifications that provided for the status of tradesmen in local society and differentiated them from the strangers, women, slaves, and indentured servants who occupied different, and mostly subordinate, positions within the municipal scheme. Although trade skill was an important part of an individual's civic identity, it was not the only component. The urban Dutch republican tradition upon which New Amsterdammers drew also emphasized the obligation of residents to undertake militia duty and defend their communities, to conduct their commerce according to the formalities of the Roman-Dutch law, and to defer to the judgment of burgomasters drawn from a local elite who possessed the necessary virtues to qualify for a position in the municipal government.

In the late 1650s and early 1660s, the town's prosperity rested on the deference of middling burghers to civic leaders, who rationalized their administration by the claim that it provided for the common good.[13] Chapter 2 examines how, following the conquest in 1664, the defense of this civic order figured in the protracted transition to English rule. Thinly resourced and faced with the government of a dispersed and alien population, the English were initially content to maintain the city as an administrative and protected commercial center. The fact that the continuity of municipal privileges and Dutch legal practice was taken by many to indicate the nondespotic character of English rule was a fortunate (if unintended) consequence of English flexibility and ensured a painless administrative transfer. Trouble flared, however, in the 1670s and 1680s when the pace of English reforms quickened and the exploitation of local trade and residents by the governors and their merchant cronies was perceived to sacrifice the common good in the interests of a narrow clique. City tradesmen increasingly feared that their local rights and privileges were imperiled by a conspiratorial and arbitrary ruling elite. When these fears became entwined with antipopery sentiment whipped up by a cadre of Calvinist zealots responding to local and international threats to the Reformed Protestant religion, tradesmen took to the streets as armed militiamen to defend the city and inhabitants from popery and slavery.

The militiamen's revolt—which was only later identified with its zealous German leader, Jacob Leisler—signaled the beginning of the end of the batavian civic order. In the ensuing four decades amendments in the practice of city government and the law undermined these earlier commitments and provided for changes in the status of local tradesmen. The second half of the book considers these changes and begins with a chapter examining the artisanal trading economy. The decline of the fur business drew city artisans away from dealings with upriver Amerindian traders and concentrated their commerce in urban credit networks spawned by the import of European goods and the export of colonial products. Labor shortages encouraged the shift to slave labor, and the opportunities presented by commercial expansion discouraged the city from limiting access to its markets, prompting the decline of freemanship and apprenticeship restrictions. The introduction of the common law erased all vestige of earlier, Dutch legal practice. As the tolerance of the Mayor's Court for claims concerning idiosyncratic privileges and duties diminished, assertions concerning rights to property in labor were also obscured by complex and costly common law pleadings. In the process, claims and practices that had once been the subject of local political and legal debate were increasingly viewed as archaic traditions, with a consequent reduction in their purchase on the public's attention.

The direction and ultimate outcome of this sequence of discursive shifts was hidden from those experiencing the incremental changes. However, the diminishing significance of claims for particularistic rights and liberties associated with artisanal work undermined assumptions concerning their place within the broader prescriptive social hierarchy. This muddling, if not yet leveling, of public perceptions of social status had important consequences for the role of artisans in city politics. The establishment of a provincial assembly in the aftermath of Leisler's Rebellion sapped the authority and influence of the municipal government and drew city artisans into English-style election contests in which politicians alternated between competing for gubernatorial patronage and challenging the royal prerogative power in the name of "popular rights." The potential for instability in partisan politics was limited by the internal coherence and shared values of the provincial oligarchy and the initial disinterest of the predominantly non-English voting population. However, in the 1730s, the competition for spoils among the provincial elite broke beyond previous constraints, prompting a constitutional crisis that marked a watershed in the city's political history. Against the backdrop of a severe economic recession, political leaders imported the radical republican ideas of the English "country" opposition. Thereafter, provincial politicians championed consent as the foundation of legitimate government and appealed to the equality of interests that united all property-owning men. It was in this context that the figure of the craft-proud and virtuous artisan, familiar from the late eighteenth-century urban scene, first appeared in New York City politics.

The story told here is of the contribution of early New York artisans and the perception of the work they did to the process of political innovation and conceptual change that produced an artisanal subject who came to play a prominent role in radical republican politics. This book's central proposition is that the demise of the idea that city tradesmen occupied a particular and privileged place undermined long-held assumptions concerning the natural inequality of man and in so doing provided for the expression of novel conceptions of the social and political status of city tradesmen that figured in the development of a subjective rights based politics in eighteenth-century America. Or, put more simply, before New York City tradesmen could take on the role of free men possessed of equal rights, they first had to jettison an earlier, late medieval political culture that secured their status and rights on the basis of their privileged place within a prescriptive local hierarchy. Before we can understand how New York artisans shed their privileged civic status, then, we must first investigate how they came to possess it in New Amsterdam. And so we begin with Henry Hudson and his fractious crew, as they edged their way down the Atlantic seaboard late in the summer of 1609.

Chapter 1
"Earning a beaver":
Tradesmen in New Amsterdam

On 11 September 1609 Henry Hudson guided the *Half Moon* from the open sea, through the narrows dividing present-day Staten Island and Long Island, and into the large bay that lay beyond. He had set sail from Holland in April, intending to explore the Arctic seas north of Norway for a possible eastern route to the Indies. When ice floes barred the way, Hudson journeyed five thousand miles west to North America and followed the eastern seaboard southward before reaching the Long Island coastline late in August. The captain and his crew spent a week or so exploring the coast around Sandy Hook before preparing to navigate the great river that separated the island of Manhattan from the mainland and which Hudson hoped might yet lead them to the Indies via a western route.

The *Half Moon* was a small vessel, measuring sixty-three feet from stem to stern, and was designed to negotiate the difficult approaches through the Zuider Zee to Amsterdam. As such, it was ideally suited for the cautious navigation that lay ahead. For five days the explorers edged their way up as "fine a river as can be found, wide and deep, with good anchoring ground on both sides." Robert Juet, an officer under Hudson's command who wrote an account of the journey upriver, described how the crew traded "Bevers skinnes, and Otters skinnes, which wee bought for Beades, Knives, and Hatchets" with the Amerindians. However, while some of the Indians seemed "very glad of our coming," the mariners suspected that others wanted "to betray us" and took hostages and preemptive attacks against some of the locals they encountered. The exploration ended approximately ninety miles upriver, when Hudson encountered dangerous shallows. The passage to the Indies had eluded him, but Hudson had seen enough to know that he had stumbled across a territory rich in furs and timber, which would please his Dutch backers in Amsterdam. Within a year news of the discovery had fired the ambitions of Dutch merchants and traders, who dispatched vessels seeking opportunities in the new land.[1]

In spite of their role in Hudson's momentous voyage, little is known of the crew of eighteen or so Dutch and English sailors who accompanied him, although we can glean something of their attitude toward the voyage from surviving accounts. Whether because of the conditions on the cramped vessel or nervousness given the challenges they faced, the crew were an unruly lot and given to misbehavior that influenced the voyage at critical points. It was the crew's mutinous mutterings that prompted Hudson's decision to go west when only a few weeks out of Amsterdam after encountering the ice floes to the north of Novaya Zemlya. When the expedition reached New France in mid-July, Hudson anchored to take on water, replace a missing foremast, and trade with the Indians for skins. However, his crew antagonized the locals, "taking their property by force out of which there arose quarrels among themselves" and the Indians. Fearing a fight in which his crew would be "outnumbered and worsted," Hudson could only pack up and head south. The continued lack of "good-will among the crew" and their insistence on the need to find a suitable seaberth for the winter also figured in Hudson's decision to cut short his navigation upriver and head back across the Atlantic. Detecting a suspicious lack of enthusiasm for his favored option of a return to Holland, Hudson elected to sail for Ireland, eventually putting in at Dartmouth, on the south coast of England, on 7 November 1609.[2]

Hudson's dependence on his crew was clearest in his fourth and final voyage in search of a northwest passage to Asia undertaken at the behest of a group of London merchants. Once again disputes between captain and crew plagued the expedition. A few weeks out, Hudson demoted his mate, Robert Juet, and then angered the ship's surgeon by refusing to auction off the belongings of a deceased crew member in keeping with maritime custom. When the explorers reached North America's wintry coast, Hudson ordered the ship's carpenter ashore in freezing conditions to build a shelter, but the man refused, declaring that the "snow and frost were such as hee neither could nor would goe in hand with such worke." Hudson berated the carpenter, calling him "many foule names" and threatening to have him hanged when they returned. But the tradesman stood firm, countering that "hee knew what belonged to his place better than himselfe [Hudson] and that hee was no house carpenter." The argument petered out, but when the expedition ran short of provisions and lost its way a few weeks later, the crew mutinied. Incited by Juet and the disaffected carpenter, the mariners resolved to set their captain, his son, and seven sickly seamen adrift in an open boat in the icy waters of Hudson Bay.[3]

The relationship between Hudson and his crew captures the interdependence, mutual scrutiny, and occasional (and sometimes bloody) conflict that characterized relations between ordinary settlers and the colonial authorities in New Netherland. Visitors regularly commented on the colony's fertility and prodigious flora and fauna. However, New Netherland needed settlers—and particularly farmers and tradesmen—to realize its commercial potential, and this need afforded ordinary men and women a measure of influence over their New World circumstances.[4] Just as Hudson's crew acknowledged their captain's command while grabbing opportunities to profit and finding ways to nudge the ship in the direction they favored, so New Netherland's tradesmen deferred to their colonial overseers even as they pursued their individual interests and sought to realize the protections and benefits of what Hudson's carpenter termed his "place" in their New World communities.

In the early years, harsh conditions and the paucity of commercial opportunities made New Netherland an unattractive destination for skilled workers or migrants of any sort. The West India Company tried various schemes to profit from its monopoly on the colony's trade but with little success. The population remained small and dependent on the supplies dispatched annually from Amsterdam. In 1640, the Company relinquished control of New Netherland's trade in the hope that economic freedom would attract private capital and migrants to settle the colony and expand its commerce. The strategy worked, and independent settlers—farmers, artisans, and fur traders—came to seek their fortunes. However, the directors appointed to administer New Netherland soon faced calls from merchants and tradesmen for a municipal government that would administer the town's affairs in the residential interest and in accordance with the laws and customs of the United Provinces. Thereafter, in the years leading up to the English conquest in 1664, tradesmen in New Amsterdam secured civic privileges protecting their occupations from competition by strangers and accepted duties to pay taxes, work on public projects, and defend the city as members of the militia. In this respect, changes in attitudes toward craft work and in the status and fortunes of skilled artisans marked time for the process by which the settlers transformed their ramshackle frontier community into a colonial facsimile of a Dutch republican and municipal community worthy of the name New Amsterdam.

* * *

In 1621, the West India Company secured a charter from the States General granting a twenty-four-year monopoly of the trade between Holland and Africa and the Americas between Newfoundland and the Straits of Magellan. Initially the Company concentrated on advancing Dutch geopolitical interests and the Protestant cause by fighting the Spanish and Portuguese for control of northeastern Brazil, largely ignoring the territory discovered by Hudson which became known as New Netherland.[5] It was not until the summer of 1624 that the *Nieu Nederlandt* brought thirty Walloon families to establish a community at Fort Orange, the site of modern-day Albany. The Lenape Indians were soon trading furs and the shell currency seawan, or wampum as it was known in New England, with the settlers for duffels, kettles, and axes. In the fall of 1626, the *Arms of Amsterdam* returned to Holland with 7,246 beaver, 853 otter, 81 mink, 36, wildcat, and 24 muskrat skins, encouraging the shareholders to dispatch several more ships with a hundred or so colonists provided with wagons, ploughs, clothing, food, and firearms. Under the guidance of Willem Verhulst, the director-general, and the engineer Cryn Fredrick, the settlers cleared land for farming on Manhattan and selected the southernmost tip of the island as the site for Fort Amsterdam, which quickly became the major port of entry for New Netherland.[6]

The West India Company's charter granted extensive rights, but it also imposed obligations upon the board of major shareholders who sat as the Assembly of the Nineteen to administer New Netherland. The Assembly oversaw the monopoly of the West Africa slave trade and all other commercial ventures in the New World; they were charged with making alliances with local rulers, building forts, appointing and discharging officers, administering civil government, and dispensing justice. The Assembly delegated their "supreme and all power" over New Netherland to a provincial director-general who governed with a handpicked local council. However, the Assembly had to make regular reports on its affairs to the States General, which approved the appointment and instruction of superior officers. The charter also required that the Assembly administer its territories according to the "Dutch Roman Law, the imperial statutes of Charles V, and edicts, customs, and resolutions of the United Netherlands."[7] As long as New Netherland was thinly populated by Company employees and a handful of independent migrants, the potential for disaffection prompted by the contradictions between Company policies and metropolitan laws and customs was limited. It was only following the arrival of free and independent settlers that claims for municipal rights and privileges sparked years of intermittent dispute concerning the administration of New Amsterdam.

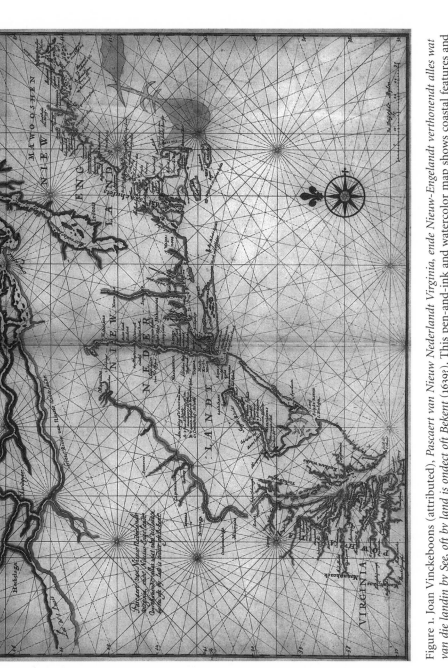

Figure 1. Joan Vinckeboons (attributed), *Pascaert van Nieuw Nederlandt Virginia, ende Nieuw-Engelandt verthonendt alles wat van die landin by See, oft by land is ondect oft Bekent* (1639?). This pen-and-ink and watercolor map shows coastal features and geographical entities on the northeastern coast of the United States. It captures the precarious placement of the Dutch colony of New Netherland, sandwiched between its more populous English neighbors.

The earliest settlers were subjects of the Company's fiat and endured harsh conditions regardless of their skills and status. The Provisional Orders, issued in 1624, provided free transportation and land for those willing to migrate, but required that all the colonists swear an oath of allegiance to the States General and the Company and agree "to obey and carry out without any contradiction the orders of the Company in regard to matters of administration and justice." The majority of settlers were Company employees who had signed indentures agreeing to serve up to seven years. Their work assignments and conditions were indistinguishable from those of the first African slaves in New Netherland, who were purchased from a passing pirate ship in 1626.[8] A prohibition on independent fur trading and exorbitant prices for supplies charged at the Company store offered few incentives for New Netherland's early settlers. Dominie Johannes Michaelius, who arrived in 1628 to take up his post as minister in the Dutch Reformed Church, wrote of the "hard and scanty food" and lack of "proper sustenance for want of bread and other necessaries." He also captured the mood among company employees who admitted that "they had not come to work . . . and that it was all the same what one did or how much one did, if only in the service of the company." Michaelius called on the Assembly to "send out good laborers and exercise all care that they be maintained as well as possible." However, by the late 1620s, as thousands of English Puritans prepared to depart for the territory to the north, the population of New Amsterdam stood at a meager two hundred and seventy souls.[9]

The dearth of tradesmen in early New Amsterdam reflected a variety of factors, not least the Company's determination to manage the colony's trade in its own interests. One group of shareholders favored a permanent and self-sufficient settlement to cement relations with the Indian fur traders and reduce the expense of importing provisions, but others viewed the migration of skilled workers with mixed emotions.[10] Most could agree on the need for settlers with core skills such as carpentry and boatbuilding; as early as 1636, David de Vries had little difficulty finding skilled shipwrights who went "into the woods and cut a good oak tree" to refit the keel of his sixty-foot vessel, which had been "entirely eaten by worms."[11] However, the shareholders' determination to profit from the supply of trade goods and provisions to New Netherland prompted restrictions on skilled workers. The Assembly prohibited weavers and dyers from working in New Netherland and forbade others from taking apprentices and passing on their "handicrafts upon which trade is dependent." Regardless of the Company's attitude, the employment opportunities available in the steadily expanding Dutch towns made New Netherland a less than attractive option for skilled work-ers from the Low Countries. As the Assembly ruefully observed in 1629, the chief difficulty in settling "such wild and uncleared lands . . . [lay] not so much for want of population, with which our provinces swarm, as because all those who will labor in anyway here, can easily obtain support, and therefore, are disinclined to go far from home on uncertainty."[12] Those who went found that the rates of pay were often not much better than could be found at home when one factored in the inflated local price of household necessaries. To make matters worse, the Company was a bad payer, and tradesmen in New Netherland had to rely on family members to dun the Assembly in Amsterdam for their wages.[13]

Even if the Company had been more committed to the recruitment of tradesmen, the uncertainty of the local market for craft skills and the lure of more profitable opportunities discouraged craftsmen from their trades. Some worked for the Company or as agents for wealthier investors back in Holland, others settled on small farms. Cornelius van Vorst traveled to Italy as a young man to train as a wood-carver before establishing himself in Holland. Following his arrival in New Netherland in 1625, he quit carving to farm and subsequently served as agent and chief administrative officer for Pavonia, amassing a substantial estate by his death in 1638. The baker Barent Dircksen came to New Netherland in the 1630s and leased one of the Company's farms, subsequently acquiring several plots on Manhattan which he sublet to others to fund his participation in the fur and tobacco trade. Hans Hansen came to work as a ships carpenter but was soon farming his own land and managing a tobacco plantation belonging to Andries Hudde. Abraham Pietersen served as the official miller at the Company's windmill and reinvested his profits in a New Amsterdam tavern. Speculation and diver-sification ended badly for some: Hendrick Jansen, a tailor, acquired several farms near New Amsterdam and established a brewery, but fell into diffi-culties when he was unable to pay his debts and had his credit cut off at the Company store.[14]

However, the greatest single check on the early development of arti-sanal enterprise in New Amsterdam was the fur trade, the ubiquity of which was such that "earning a beaver" soon became idiomatic for engaging in commerce of any kind. The trade depended on bands of Indian hunters who supplied Europeans with pelts, and it was ideally suited for petty dealers who found willing customers among the mariners and passengers who brought small parcels of duffel, broadcloth, axes, pins, kettles, and adzes on ships from Holland. A settler who garnered even a handful of pelts realized considerable benefits. In the 1650s, a single skin provided for an adult's bread needs for approximately three months; ten pelts would purchase enough wheat to keep a family fed for a year. The authorities in Holland and New Netherland tried to curtail the illicit dealings and the evasion of duties levied at the Company's counting house, but with little success.[15]

The settlers' devotion to the fur trade also undermined the Company's scheme to attract new immigrants and private capital by providing sizable land grants (patroonships) to handpicked investors who agreed to transport twenty families to New Netherland. The scheme promised the Company a profit from imposts and freight charges on goods and furs shipped to and from New Amsterdam.[16] In 1630, Killaen van Rensselaer became the most important patroon when he acquired approximately 700,000 acres around Fort Orange. Van Rensselaer hoped to control the supply of furs and profit from the sale of supplies within the colony. With this in mind, he hired artisans and farmers in Holland to establish a settler community. However, the employees refused to stick to their occupations and were soon trading furs on their own and joining others in land speculation. The story of thirty-three-year-old Claes Jansen, a house carpenter from Naerden, was typical. In August 1636, Jansen agreed to go to New Netherland with his wife, Piertke Jans, and supervise the construction of a mill and a church. Soon after arriving, however, Jansen and his wife left Rensselaerswyck for New Amsterdam, promising to compensate their ex-employer with half their future earnings.[17]

By the late 1630s, the failure to establish a sustainable community threatened the Dutch presence in North America. A decade of English immigration to the north and a series of bloody victories over the Pequots had brought Puritan farming communities to the Connecticut Valley and eastern tip of Long Island. The self-sufficient population of almost two thousand settled at the mouth of the Charles River easily outnumbered the four hundred or so gathered at New Amsterdam who depended on the shipment of supplies from the United Provinces.[18] Fearing that the English might soon force the Dutch out of their northern American niche, the States General in Holland instructed the Company to offer whatever "inducements and pre-eminences" were necessary to increase immigration and encourage settlement. In 1640, the Assembly relinquished its trade monopoly and undertook to govern the colony "according to the style and order of the province of Holland and the cities and manors thereof . . . [and] as far as possible, the ordinances received here in Amsterdam." The revised freedoms and exemptions—and the granting of charters to the English towns on Long Island and outlying Dutch communities—made it clear that the Company expected the provision of local rights and privileges to attract badly needed colonists while the shareholders retained overall control of the colony.[19]

The scheme worked, and the liberalization of trade and promise of local rights transformed New Amsterdam into a bustling seaport and center for a seasonal fur trade. Each spring the Indian traders came to Fort Orange to exchange pelts for European goods and seawan; in midsummer the private traders took their furs downriver to New Amsterdam for resale or transshipment aboard the vessels that arrived from Holland in August.[20] The settlement on Manhattan's tip grew, and the Company finally realized a moderate income from supplies sold to the expanding population and the duties levied on furs received in Amsterdam. Unfortunately, New Netherland's improved trade rested on an uncertain foundation: two decades of European competition for Iroquois and Algonquian furs had sponsored the mass production of seawan in Algonquian villages along Long Island Sound leading to oversupply and inflation. In response to the diminishing value of the shell currency—and in the same year in which the West India Company relinquished its trade monopoly—the Massachusetts General Court demonetized wampum and coined the pine tree shilling. New England traders proceeded to dump their accumulated stores of wampum on New Netherland, giving the Dutch an inflation problem that plagued local commerce for the next twenty years.

Even as the effects of seawan/wampum inflation took hold, the expansion of New Amsterdam provided customers for skilled workers who begun to spend at least part of the time working at their trades. During his visit in 1643, the Jesuit Isaac Jogues noted the presence of "some mechanics . . . who ply their trades [and] are ranged under the fort." As the colony's total population crept up to twenty-five hundred, masons, carpenters, and bricklayers undertook work for private customers in New Amsterdam: Abraham Clock and Peter Cornelissen's contract to build a house and barn for Abraham Winckelman was one of several such agreements indicating the intention of some to establish firmer roots in the community. A handful of indentures—such as the one binding Cornelius Janszen Jonker to Evert Duycking, a master glazier and glass painter from Westphalia—signaled the beginnings of local apprenticeships.[21] By the mid 1640s New Amsterdam boasted a growing number of bakers, wheelwrights, brickmakers, and five surgeons. Ever eager to reduce its costs, the Company recommended that the "carpenters, masons, smiths, and such like" in its employ "ought to be discharged and left to work for whomever will pay them."[22]

In 1639, the Amsterdam Board dispatched Willem Kieft to implement its free-trade policy and secure the settlement in New Amsterdam.[23] The new director-general introduced a series of measures consistent with the Company's undertaking to govern New Amsterdam in accordance with Dutch urban practice and insisted that innkeepers, or tappers, use "the measures common in Holland" and that "Mechanics and laborers in the Company's service" begin and end their labors at the ringing of a bell on pain of a hefty fine payable to the newly appointed commissary of workmen, Gillis Voocht.[24] However, Kieft's approximation of a Dutch urban administration did not go far enough for leading free settlers, who used the opportunity presented by his requests for help in fighting local Indians to try and establish themselves as if they were a "council of a small village in Fatherland [that] consists of five burgomasters [and] seven Schepens." When Kieft suspended their meetings, the reformers denounced the director-general for behaving as if "he was Sovereign and that it was absolutely in his power to do or to permit, everything . . . [heeding] little that the safety of the People was the supreme law."[25]

The core of the dispute between Kieft and the independent settlers derived from the competing claims for local administrative authority in New Amsterdam. The regulation of labor provided a particular point of contest between the two sides. Part of the problem was the lack of clarity concerning the status of Company employees and free settlers, who considered themselves independent burghers within the "commonalty" of New Amsterdam. The majority of New Amsterdam's residents had been beholden to the Company at one time or another: all journeyed to New Netherland aboard Company ships, some as employees; others depended on Company patents for the security of land tenure or on credit and trade goods from the store for their start in the fur trade. Oloff Stevenson van Cortlandt came to New Netherland as a soldier and held several administrative posts under Kieft, before setting himself up as a brewer and fur trader. Hendrick Pieterse worked as a contract carpenter for the Company; Sibout Claessen, a master carpenter from Hoorn on the Zuider Zee, operated the Company's sawmill on Nutten Island under a three-year lease. Still others depended on informal but no less essential support for their ventures: the farrier Burger Joris and blacksmith Hendrick Jansen relied on the loan of the Company's bellows, anvil, and "half of the smith's house" for their trades.[26] Given the Company's support for local enterprise, it is easy to see why the distinctions drawn by settlers between the status of employees and freeborn Dutch burghers were lost on Kieft—a man who considered himself a "divinely appointed magistrate" governing unquestioning subjects. Moreover, the social standing of some of those elected by the commonalty—mariners, illiterates, and tradesmen of low birth—hardly qualified them for office in the provincial administration. Yet the settlers' sense of their right to a say in their own affairs is clear in their challenges to Kieft's authority ranging from petty vandalism to public confrontations.

Two incidents illustrate the potential for disagreements surrounding the regulation of labor and skills to mushroom into disputes concerning general rights and obligations to obey authority in New Amsterdam. By 1644, Kieft's Indian wars had all but bankrupted his administration and the director-general introduced a new excise on wine and beer, payable by brewers and tappers, to bolster his diminishing government funds. In August, the Company's fiscal, or sheriff, charged a group identified only as "the brewers of New Amsterdam" with nonpayment of the excise. Yet when the offending brewers were summoned to explain themselves, they stood their ground, declaring that "if they voluntarily pay the excise they will have the . . . commonalty about their ears." In the same year, Kieft's decision to free eleven Company slaves in recognition of their contribution to the defense of the city during the Indian hostilities also inflamed residential passions. The director-general manumitted the slaves on condition that they pay an annual tribute and that their children "already in existence or hereafter born shall be slaves." Kieft's intention was to reduce his administrative costs by freeing the slaves, who would provide for their own upkeep thereafter, while retaining title to the fruits of their children's labor. However, his critics considered the conditional manumission further evidence of the director-general's arbitrary abuse of power and "contrary to all public law that any one born of a free Christian mother should, notwithstanding, be a slave."[27]

What was at stake in these disputes had less to do with the monetary value of the liquor excise and the fate of the freed slaves' children and more with a challenge to Kieft's authority over the independent brewers and status of newly freed slave laborers. What the settlers contested was Kieft's right to establish precedents concerning the regulation of skilled occupations and the fate of a free subject's children that contradicted metropolitan practices, residential privileges, and the fundamental rights of freeborn subjects. Although the details are unclear, the settlers appear to have won concessions: local excises remained a source of disagreement until establishment of a burgher government in 1653, and in the matter of the manumissions, the authorities in Amsterdam amended Kieft's order so that the children of the former slaves were born free. From early on, then, the regulation of labor and skills proved a contentious issue in New Amsterdam. In these early skirmishes one glimpses the outlines of disagreements and struggles that informed the campaign for municipal government in the 1650s and early 1660s.

Not long after these disputes, and following another disastrous offensive against the Indian settlement at Pavonia that united almost the entire native population of the lower Hudson Valley against the colonists, Kieft was ordered home to account for his administration.[28] Despite the havoc wrought by Kieft's Indian conflicts, by the mid-1640s a more settled community was developing in New Amsterdam. Increasing numbers of vessels from Dutch ports carried to New Netherland family groups who clustered around Fort Amsterdam or spread out in search of new areas for cultivation.[29] Although agricultural productivity remained low, there were signs that the settlement had attained a sufficient size and stability for the rising price of imported necessaries to distract a few from the fur business and toward artisanal trades.[30] A growing number of local skilled workers supplemented their fur trading, farming, and land dealing by working at their trades. As they did so, New Amsterdam's tradesmen faced competition from outsiders and unstable prices owing to seawan inflation for which transplanted Dutch protectionist practices offered a solution. However, the regulation of local trade in the residential interest flew in the face of the Company's declared commitment to free trade which the shareholders believed was responsible for the recent expansion and trickle of revenue via imposts on imported supplies and exported furs.[31] In the 1650s the Company and its colonists would workout a compromise that went someway toward meeting the needs and objectives of both sides.

*   *   *

In 1645, the Company tightened its control of New Netherland, replacing the indecisive administration of the Assembly of Nineteen with the Amsterdam Chamber. One of the Chamber's earliest acts was to appoint Peter Stuyvesant as the colony's director-general.[32] The thirty-five-year-old Stuyvesant and his handpicked council set about reforming the administration of New Netherland with a flurry of orders dealing with matters ranging from compulsory church attendance to fire prevention and the fencing of hogs and goats. The provincial government also prohibited brewers from selling in small measures, licensed tavern keepers, and forbade brewing or tapping before two o'clock on the Sabbath under "penalty of [offenders'] being deprived of their occupation." Endeavoring to protect New Amsterdam's currency from the inflation caused by nonresident merchant traders who "spoil[ed] trade and business by giving 11 or 12 guilders in loose Seawan for one Beaver" and then leaving without paying local taxes, Stuyvesant prohibited itinerants from trading unless "they take up their abode here in New Netherland for three consecutive years and . . . build in this city New Amsterdam a decent citizen dwelling." However, the Amsterdam Chamber disallowed these and similar orders, which, it argued, contravened the free-trade policy and discouraged commercial expansion. By limiting the provincial government's reforms to measures that protected local consumers and encouraged immigration while leaving the colonists at the mercy of unregulated trade, the Company adopted a contradictory approach to New Netherland—affirming the duty of artisans and other settlers to obey the director-general and work for the common good, while offering little in the way of reciprocal and compensatory rights and privileges in return.[33]

The consequences of the Company's approach were clearest in the case of the city's bakers, whose skills were critical to Stuyvesant's efforts to create a stable and harmonious community in New Amsterdam. Bread was an essential part of the seventeenth-century diet, and residents of Amsterdam consumed an estimated two to two and a half pounds per day.[34] However, aside from the kitchens of the better-off, domestic baking of ordinary bread was uncommon in the Netherlands. Families relied on bread made at bakeries or took homemade dough to cook in the ovens of local bakers. In the 1620s and 1630s the Company had ordered the construction of a windmill and a bakery to supply its store with bread.[35] Given this provision, and as long as the population remained scattered, it was difficult for independent bakers to establish a viable customer base. For example, the passenger lists identifying 174 immigrants who came to the Rensselaerswijck patroonship between 1630 and 1644 mentioned thirty-two different occupations but only one baker. However, by the mid-1640s, there were signs that independent bakers had begun to supplement the provisions offered at the Company store: Hendrick Jansen ran a bakery and sold bread; Frederick Lubbertsen's contract to build a house for Lourens Cornelissen included mention of "stone enough to build an oven capable of baking a skepel and a half of wheat"; in 1644, Nicholas Jansen agreed to provide the ship *Wapen van Rensselaers* with bread for its voyage to Europe; and, by 1649, bakers such as Joost Teunissen had developed contacts with provincial farmers from whom he secured wheat for his bakery in New Amsterdam.[36] Residential complaints concerning the shortage of good loaves in the same year suggest that private bakers had become the key providers of the town's much-needed bread supply.

Figure 2. Governor Peter Stuyvesant, painted in New Amsterdam by Hendrick Couturier (c. 1660). Accession number 1909.2, Collection of the New-York Historical Society. Peter Stuyvesant was the son of a clergyman from Friesland and served the West India Company as governor of Curaçoa, losing a leg during an ill-fated attack on the Portuguese island of St. Martin, before being appointed director-general of New Netherland in 1645.

In November 1649, the townspeople complained regarding the scarcity of coarse bread, the light weight of white bread, and the fact that "the savages or natives of this country take the white bread from the bakers without inquiry for or scrutiny of the black bread or price in seawan." It is worth pausing to consider the cultural implications of the complaint regarding the disproportionate supply of white and black bread as it points up developing concerns for civic responsibilities in New Amsterdam. Throughout early modern Europe, white bread was considered purer and possessed a higher status than darker varieties, which served as everyday household bread. In part this was because the local authorities kept the price of dark bread low to prevent bakers from exploiting the needs of the poor. Although well intentioned, this regulation of the price of ordinary bread motivated bakers to bake as little household bread as possible, and that little nasty, confirming popular views of the inherent differences between dark and white bread and the higher status of the latter.[37] Thus, in 1649, New Amsterdam's residents were complaining not only about the shortage of dark or household bread, but also of the cultural slur implied by the bakers' indiscriminate provisioning of the Indians with white and underweight bread. Pressing home their demand for local supply, the petitioners complained that the bakers' "greed and the desire for profits . . . cause[d] the savage and barbarous natives to be accommodated with the best before the Christian nation."[38]

Stuyvesant wasted no time in responding: he established standards for bread baked in the colony and, so that the "inhabitants and natives might not be inconvenienced," he commanded the bakers to use clean wheat or rye flour to bake loaves weighing eight, four, or two pounds. Instructing the bakers to sell their bread at prices "which the Honble Court shall from time to time fix," the director-general permitted the baking of finer bread for "grand entertainments" but forbade "the wanton consumption and general sale of white bread and cakes to inhabitants as well as to natives."[39] Stuyvesant's orders were familiar to residents, as similar measures regulated bakers and ensured local supplies of coarse bread throughout the United Provinces and early modern Europe. However, whereas Old World price regulations and the imposition of occupational duties were reckoned in relation to the costs of vital ingredients and counterbalanced with protectionist privileges, Stuyvesant's action constituted a leap in the dark in a community where the uncertainty of grain supplies and yearly devaluation of seawan made it difficult to determine what constituted a fair price for bread.[40] To make matters worse, the Company's free-trade policy prevented worthwhile protection of the bakers' commerce and, in the absence of compensatory privileges,

Stuyvesant's orders inspired subtle changes in the bakers' marketing strategy the following year.

In April 1650, the townspeople complained to the provincial government again, but this time they accused the bakers of baking insufficient household bread and oversized and ergo prohibitively expensive white loaves.[41] The director-general amended his earlier ordinance, permitting the bakers

Figure 3. Job Berckhetde, *The Baker* (c. 1681). The baker, dressed in his work clothes and cap, blows a horn to announce the arrival of freshly made loaves of different sizes as well as pretzels and assorted rolls.

to offer white bread, "but not cakes or cracknels, provided that the said white bread conform in weight with the rules of the Fatherland." The bakers were again instructed to bake loaves from clean wheat and rye flour to prevent complaints concerning "the thinness and meagerness of the common bread." In May, Stuyvesant identified part of problem when he noted, as Kieft had in his time, that New Amsterdam was awash with low-grade seawan, much of which was "unpierced and only half-finished, made of stone, bone, glas, shells, horn, nay even of wood, and broken, [and] which causes many inhabitants to complain, that with it they cannot go to market and buy any commodities, not even a little white bread or a mug of beer." The director-general addressed the currency problem by clarifying the distinctions between merchantable seawan, strung on wire or thread, and poorer quality, unstrung seawan and establishing exchange rates for each in the upcoming season. However, the following year there were more complaints of profiteering by the bakers who reportedly refused "to bake rye bread, and do not hesitate to give as the reason that they derive more profit from the white and wheaten bread." The bakers' decision to pursue profits from the better margins on white loaves left many hungry and threatened the development of local agriculture as "the farmers cannot sell the rye they have raised." Once again, Stuyvesant ordered the bakers to bake eight-pound loaves of wheat and rye bread, setting prices of fourteen and twelve stivers respectively. He also commanded them to bake white bread according to its "correct weight" of one pound, one half pound, and one quarter pound and not to sell it "for more than three stivers a pound . . . on pain of being excluded from their business and fined 25 guilders."[42]

Stuyvesant's efforts to compromise between the town's need for a reliable supply of fresh bread and the bakers' commercial fortunes were hampered by two problems that lay beyond his control: the seasonal and mostly unregulated trade in furs that intensified the competition within baking each year and motivated the bakers to bake white bread and cakes rather than household bread, and the Company's refusal to countenance protectionist privileges for local trade that restricted Stuyvesant's policy options.[43] The first problem centered on the annual influx of nonresident traders and poor quality seawan and the activities of part-time bakers. Seawan and beavers were "current money" in New Amsterdam, meaning that they were acceptable as payment of taxes and in trade. As the lowest denomination available in the town, seawan was also the currency commonly used for everyday purchases such as bread, and the bakers had to accept it when tendered in payment. Each year traders from the United Provinces and neighboring

New England descended on New Netherland in search of furs, flooding the market with seawan and devaluing local stocks.[44] Bakers who had bought flour with seawan or beavers valued at earlier and higher rates found themselves having to sell bread at fixed prices for the devalued currency and losing out on each loaf sold. To make matters worse, the influx of traders to the city called forth part-time bakers who cashed in on short-term demand and peddled their wares on the streets to seawan-rich fur traders. The competition from part-timers was particularly grievous given that New Amsterdam's bakers served a relatively narrow customer base.[45] In these circumstances, the temptation to switch from dark to white bread proved too great for some, leading to a shortage of household bread and customer complaints.

The second problem derived from the Company's mixed feelings regarding the protection of local commerce and its determination to maintain the freedom of New Netherland's trade. The Amsterdam Board censured restrictions on the activities of nonresident fur traders and never wavered from the view that "the trade should be open to everybody." When it came to artisanal occupations, however, the Amsterdam Board was less consistent, allowing some measures deemed essential to local order and censuring others. Thus the Board assented to regulations restraining brewers from also tapping, regulating the butchering of cattle and the size of barrels made by coopers, and restricting the use of grain in times of dearth.[46] But the Amsterdam shareholders balked at measures they felt limited the possibilities for individual enterprise. For example, upon hearing of Stuyvesant's introduction of local monopolies for the production of bricks and salt, the Board counseled against further "very pernicious and impracticable" grants "in a new country, which . . . must be peopled and made prosperous by general benefits and liberties . . . to everybody, who desires to settle there with this or that profession or handicraft."[47]

That Stuyvesant might have managed the town's affairs better if left to his own devices is suggested by his response to a 1652 petition by New Amsterdam's surgeons seeking a monopoly of public shaving. In support of their petition, the surgeons pointed to the damaging competition, and occasionally hazardous service, offered by ship-based and transient practitioners. Stuyvesant accepted the public health argument and prohibited any persons other than the recognized surgeons from "keeping a shop" in New Amsterdam. However, because "shaving is properly not in the province of the surgeons but is only an appendix to their calling," the director-general refused to prohibit residents from shaving each other "for friendship's sake, [or] out of courtesy and without receiving payment." Had Stuyvesant and his council been free to adopt a similarly sensitive approach to baking, innkeeping, carpentry, and other trades, a measure of stability and residential harmony might have accrued in New Amsterdam. However, the Company struck down orders fixing prices charged by bakers and tavern keepers and the wages set for carpenters and masons arguing that "in the infancy of a newly opened country . . . growth must be promoted . . . by encouraging and unlimited privileges, [rather] than by prohibitions and restrictions."[48] In so doing, the absentee board of shareholders almost certainly nurtured the campaign for local government reform in New Netherland and New Amsterdam.

As the settlement's population grew, demand for food outstripped local production, and the infant export trade between New Netherland and the mid-Atlantic and West Indian colonies intensified the competition for local grain. Bakers looked farther afield for their ingredients and fell out with customers and suppliers of raw materials. In August 1653, the baker Andries de Haas refused to accept the seawan that Daniel Litschoe, a local tavern keeper, offered in payment for his bread. Late in 1655 Joost Teunissen assaulted Francois Fyn after a disagreement over firewood supplies; the following spring, Teunissen was in court again, this time suing the English merchant Samuel Mayhew for failure to deliver 730 florins' worth of prepaid grain. Even as the market value of grain and demand for baked goods increased, inflation diminished the value of seawan while prices remain fixed by regulations introduced in 1650. Rising costs and diminishing returns squeezed the bakers' profits, and a few found themselves in court answering creditors.[49] In 1656, a boom year for the fur trade, the increase in commerce merely exaggerated the problems within baking: traders flooded the town with seawan, bakers produced insufficient coarse loaves, and residents complained. However, this time residents' complaints were countered by the bakers' protests against the damaging competition of part-timers and non-residents and calls for restrictions on those allowed to bake and sell bread in New Amsterdam.[50]

In October, Stuyvesant acknowledged the bakers' complaints and accepted that the good order of baking required protective privileges such as regulations on entry to the trade. He compared the problems in baking with "tapping," or innkeeping, as another trade plagued with difficulties, "since there is as yet no guild nor certain body known." Accordingly, and "for the advantage of Christians as for the sake of the profits arising from it," Stuyvesant ordered that "no person shall be allowed to do business as a tapster or baker" unless they first register and pay one Flemish pound for a license renewable every three months. However, the new regulatory structure focused more on ensuring that bakers fulfilled their duty to bake rather than protecting their trade interests. The director-general ordered registered bakers to bake good and wholesome bread at least once or twice a week and established fines ranging from twenty-five to six hundred florins for breaches of the regulations; those guilty of three transgressions were threatened with the suspension of baking privileges and "absolute closing of business." The Company's schout enforced the regulations and claimed a third of fines levied; Frederick Barents, a man with no discernible experience of baking, was appointed to supervise the trade.[51] Stuyvesant had established the principle that baking should be a closed affair limited to registered practitioners, but he required the bakers to pay a quarterly tax equivalent and insisted they bake even in unfavorable circumstances: in spite of the inflationary pressure on seawan and the growing demand for bread, the prices of different loaves remained fixed at the level set six years previously.[52]

The regulation of tradesmen and their commerce in New Amsterdam was ultimately a question of political economy: how to allocate scarce resources among competing groups with differing ends in mind. However, Stuyvesant's effort to ensure the community's bread supply while remaining within the limits on local regulation set by the Amsterdam Board generated contradictions that fueled discontent within the ranks of the bakers and their customers. Prior to the director-general's order requiring city bakers to bake sufficient household bread and white loaves at the "correct weight," the trade had been open, and no one practitioner bore any duty or enjoyed any advantage over another. However, by affirming the bakers' civic duty to bake for the town, Stuyvesant articulated a public distinction that highlighted their contribution to the community's well-being. He also provoked more specific demands by consumers for dark and white bread at various weights and by the bakers, who made strategic changes in their marketing practices and called for the regulation of prices and restrictions on access to the trade. In this respect, Stuyvesant's attempt to regulate baking through the assignment of public duties called forward demands for compensatory privileges whose implementation was prevented by the Amsterdam Board's refusal to countenance the protection of residential trade.

The bread supply—and urban trade in general—would remain uncertain until the view that the local economy should be managed in the interests of residents supplanted the Company's policy on free trade in New Amsterdam. This change came gradually and as part of a broader campaign for local rights and privileges in accordance with Dutch practice. To understand the multiple meanings of these rights and privileges for New Amsterdam artisans and their resonances and tenacity in the later seventeenth century, it is necessary to consider the campaign for municipal government and the republican political theory from which it derived.

*   *   *

Following his arrival, Stuyvesant continued Kieft's practice of periodically assembling boards of advisors to consult on local affairs and consent to the levying of taxes. In 1648 he selected a board of Nine Men, who quickly became the focus for criticism of the director-general and a campaign in favor of regulations to protect residential interests. Stuyvesant was no more tolerant of dissent than his predecessor and denounced his critics as "rascals, liars, [and] rebels," for whom "hanging was almost too good."[53] When he suspended their meetings, the Nine took to gathering in each others' houses, where they drew up a record of administrative abuses dating back to Kieft's time. This record became the foundation for a remonstrance charging the Company with failing to defend and nurture New Netherland and calling for reforms likely to increase immigration from the United Provinces. More important, for our purposes, the remonstrance and related documents provide an ideal source for insight into the New Amsterdammers reading of the subtleties of mid-seventeenth-century Dutch republican political thought.

The reformers made their case in three documents: a *Petition*, to which was attached some *Additional Observations*, and the *Remonstrance of New Netherland*, the longest and most elaborate of the three texts. In the summer of 1649, the Nine dispatched delegates to the States General in Holland to present their case for a "suitable municipal (*borgerlycke*) government . . . resembling the laudable Government of our Fatherland."[54] The Nine were all long-term city residents whose investment in local trade doubtless added a self-interested edge to their calls for good government and residential privileges: the reformers railed against excessive taxes, itinerant traders, and Stuyvesant's partial enforcement of customs regulations so that "scarce a ship comes in or near this place that he does not look on as a prize, unless it be the property of [his] friends." Yet the men who challenged the West India Company's charter rights mostly came from modest backgrounds, lacked the status for a prima facie claim for inclusion in the local administration, and had to justify their case with something more compelling than their individual interests.[55] Close inspection reveals that the New Amsterdam merchants' campaign for local autonomy and commercial privileges chimed with recent constitutional arguments that championed individual and community liberties in the face of centralizing and arbitrary forces.

The sophistication of the Nine's presentation reflected the influence of political savants such as Cornelius Melyn and, in particular, Adriaen van der Donck, who served as the lead delegate from New Netherland to the States General.[56] Whoever was the primary author of New Netherland's *Petition* and *Remonstrance*, they were clearly a devotee of the jurist and political theorist, Hugo Grotius (1583–1645), whose republican and constitutional opinions were returning to prominence as the New Netherland delegates set sail for Amsterdam in the spring of 1649. Grotius's "true republican" view combined the resistance theories of European Calvinists with humanist principles inspired by admiration for the Venetian and Florentine republics in advocacy of an aristocratic republican government dedicated to expansion of commerce and the preservation of liberty. The vitality of the republic was thought to depend on two crucial, but in many ways contradictory, variables: the preservation of the decentralized authority of oligarchic groups of provincial landowners and urban regents and the militaristic pursuit of an overseas empire that, it was hoped, would bind together and enrich the state. The former was essential because it was widely believed that the cultivation of rulers with the virtues necessary to devote themselves to public affairs could only flourish in a republic in which provincial communities and towns retained their constitutional independence and administrative autonomy. However, the need for a well-organized and militarily powerful state called for centralized authority and institutions such as the Dutch East and West India Companies with the capital and martial force necessary to prosecute the republic's overseas endeavors.[57]

A fully worked-out division of authority between the federal and centralized elements of the Dutch constitution eluded the finest thinkers and provided for a struggle for mastery between urban oligarchs, particularly in Holland, and the stadholder throughout the seventeenth century. Even Grotius had to satisfy himself with an optimistic appeal to the Batavi: a mythic Germanic tribe credited with the establishment of ancient Dutch liberties whose spirit he hoped would prevail and save the republic from tyranny. However others—such as Grotius's contemporary Piet van der Cun, who was an instructor at Leiden around the time of Van der Donck's undergraduate years—were less sanguine about threats to Dutch liberties. Van der Cun's writings warned of the corrupting effects of wealth and overly powerful central institutions and advocated the creation of a republic of egalitarian and independent landowners to guard against the rise of tyrants—a vision

Figure 4. Jacobus G. Strycker, *Adriaen van der Donck* (n.d.). Negative number 19849a, Collection of the New-York Historical Society. Adriaen van der Donck (c. 1618–55), who was dispatched to protect the interests of his patron and employer, Kiliaen Van Rennselaer, became a champion of republican political liberties and municipal reform in New Netherland and New Amsterdam.

that would fascinate many more republican thinkers and politicoes over the course of the seventeenth and eighteenth centuries.[58]

The delegates who traveled from New Amsterdam to present the settlers' case clearly courted metropolitan republican lobbies. The first half of the *Remonstrance* established the settlers fair and legal title to their farms and homes and thereafter extolled the prodigious flora and fauna that, the Nine Men argued, offered Dutch immigrants to New Netherland a "fine country, which alone is of greater extent than the Seventeen Dutch Provinces." However, instead of a burgeoning community of free and landowning Dutch citizens who could provide vital support for the republic's New World geopolitical interests, the Company's "bad government with its attendants and consequences" stifled New Netherland's prosperity and threatened its survival. The Company interfered with the weighing and packing of goods, impeded the expansion of the port, and denied the townspeople access to a properly constituted and fair-minded court. Indeed, far from providing for fair and impartial hearings, the director-general carried himself as if he were a "Prince in the Netherlands." Consequently, "a man in that country is not sure of either his life or property, if he but say anything displeasing or otherwise offensive to the Governors who comport themselves like sovereign tyrants." Assuming the guise of regents from a Dutch town, the delegates styled themselves the "burgomasters" and (in Van der Donck's case) "President of the Commonalty" of New Amsterdam and urged the States General to grant "what we consider to be the mother of population, good Privileges and Exemptions, which could encourage the inhabitants."[59]

The delegates presented their case as the republic was recovering from its severest constitutional crisis in thirty years. A contest for power between the stadholder, William II, and Holland, the most powerful of the United Provinces, had revived arguments regarding the rights and privileges of autonomous states and towns within the federal structure of the Dutch constitution. Indeed, 1650 has been identified alongside 1618 and 1672 as one of the three most important years in the history of Dutch republicanism for the quality and vehemence of the tracts that issued forth from urban presses.[60] The emergence of Holland as the victorious party in this dispute favored the New Amsterdam burgomasters' challenge to what they characterized as the Company's arbitrary administration. The New Amsterdammers' invocation of the republican shibboleths of fundamental liberties, urban privileges, and local representation played directly into this true republican revival. In addition, the Nine's account of the Company's unjust and unnatural administration offered in the *Remonstrance* and other pamphlets picked out themes that were the stock in trade of contemporary tracts that aimed at inflaming popular spirits against official corruption and abuses of power and charged the West India Company with tyranny and enslavement of freeborn subjects.[61]

The hyperbolic terms in which the delegates described their condition highlights what they perceived as the critical nexus between individual and community liberty and the proper balance between rights and privileges and the obligation of subjects to obey legitimate authority. In this view, liberty and slavery were considered the best and worst conditions possible for individuals and the states in which they lived. However, slaves were unfree not only because they could be coerced into acting by physical force or the threat of it but also because they had lost control over their fates and lived under the authority of another.[62] In a similar fashion, free citizens of an independent state could find their liberty endangered and be subjected to slavish conditions when powerful elements within the state ignored customary rights and privileges, assumed discretionary authority, and determined the fates of citizens without due process or the assent of their representatives. Experience taught liberty-loving republicans that the threat of arbitrary government was more or less constant. But the liberty of Dutch citizens remained secure as long as they lived under their own authority as expressed through their representatives and the sovereignty of the republic: the ancient network of councils, colleges, estates, and urban governing institutions that embodied the social bond that united freeborn Dutch subjects around the Republic and—at least according to the delegates from New Netherland— in the New World. In this respect, the rights and privileges of individual citizens and the different communities in which they lived were intimately related to one another. Thus, an attack on any part of the Dutch Atlantic structure, the delegates argued, constituted a threat to the whole.[63]

To bolster and explicate the case for an independent municipal government in New Amsterdam, the Nine drew connections between their high-blown critique of the Company's administration and the misfortunes of individual settlers. They offered case studies describing the unjust treatment meted out to prominent merchants such as Cornelius Melyn and Arnoldus van Hardenbergh. The arguments highlighting the need for local representation were most telling when they focused on less prominent residents such as the carpenter Sibout Classen and the baker Joost Teunissen, tradesmen who were prevented from pursuing their lawful callings and who were powerless to defend themselves without the protection afforded by a municipal government of private citizens. Teunissen—whom the delegates accounted "an honest Burgher . . . of good repute, though moderate means"—was imprisoned in New Amsterdam following charges "raked up against him" that he had sold weapons to neighboring Indians. When the baker appealed to the Nine for assistance as the "organ of the Commonalty," their requests for a fair trial were met with "injurious language" by the Company schout who behaved like a "hideous monster." Teunissen journeyed to Amsterdam with the delegates and presented a petition confirming the Nine's account and adding that he had been prevented from traveling "hither and thither through the country to purchase his wheat and grain, which his business required for bread for the use of the burghers."[64]

As far as the delegates were concerned, the prevention of Teunissen and others for pursuing their rightful callings provided proof "as palpable as the sun at clear noon" of the need for reform. In their view it was vital that "those interested in the country may also attend to its government and keep a watchful eye over it, without its being entrusted to a set of hairbrained people, such as the Company flings thither." In his personal petition Teunissen implored the States General for protection from Stuyvesant, "who is too powerful for your petitioner," and asked that he be allowed to "earn his living honestly and honorably for himself and family, both by his daily labor and trade." The delegates finished by urging the States General to favor New Amsterdam "with a good civil government, composed of those interested in the country; [and] unalterable Privileges . . . To the end that the worthy patriots . . . [may be] entirely relieved and released from oppression and slavery."[65]

In the view of the Nine Men and their supporters, then, the West India Company's administration of New Netherland was not simply bad for business. It also denied the inhabitants their rights and privileges as freeborn subjects and thereby threatened Dutch geopolitical interests and the foundations of republican government at home and abroad. Fortunately for New Amsterdam's reformers, developments on the international scene favored their cause. In 1650, England's Protectorate Parliament introduced the first Navigation Act designed to push the Dutch out of the American trade. The emerging Anglo-Dutch maritime conflict discouraged the States General from undermining the West India Company's charter rights. However, the same threat also made the security of the Dutch presence in North America imperative. Following an inquiry into the New Amsterdam delegates' case, the States General pressured the Company into redrafting the freedoms and exemptions applicable to New Netherland in order to attract new immigrants.

In the spring of 1652, the Company instructed Stuyvesant to placate his critics and equip New Amsterdam with "a Burgher Government," a schout, two burgomasters, and five schepens.[66]

Stuyvesant did not implement the order until the following February, and even then he made his own appointments to the newly established Court of Burgomasters and Schepens and refused to consider a list of candidates nominated by the commonalty. Yet the director-general soon found himself having to compromise with the burgomasters, who enjoyed the support of leading business interests and the commonalty, and who added incrementally to their administrative authority over the town's affairs. The new municipal governors presided over biweekly court days that heard civil cases up to the value of one hundred guilders; they took charge of the school, docks, piers and a newly established public weigh house where controls over the quality of tobacco packed for export were enforced by municipal inspectors; they fixed the prices for the transport of passengers, livestock, and goods on the ferry between Manhattan and Long Island and were granted the authority to levy "any new small excise or impost with the consent of the commonality."[67] Stuyvesant remained head of the provincial government, as the representative of the West India Company, and retained executive authority and the right of approval over measures introduced by the burgomasters. The Swedish threat to the Dutch presence on the Delaware and the short but bloody Peach Tree War emphasized the New Amsterdammers' continued reliance on Stuyvesant's protection. Yet by the mid-1650s, the reformers had realized their ambition of a burgher government in New Amsterdam, or the "City of Amsterdam in New Netherland" as they took to calling their diminutive New World settlement.[68]

*   *   *

It was in the context of their broadening municipal remit, and in response to difficulties thrown up by the boom fur-trading year of 1656, that the burgomasters sought new protective privileges to address the problem of itinerant traders and the inflationary oversupply of seawan. Residential trading privileges and a monopoly of local commerce had been key demands for almost a decade, and in the months following the end of the 1656 season, New Amsterdam's municipal leaders once again debated plans for the regulation of local citizenship.[69] However, it was not until the following February—in the wake of another bakers' protest provoked by currency inflation and declining margins—that the burgomasters took steps to address the problem. The burgomasters reiterated familiar protests against the seasonal traders' violation of the city's staple privileges whereby "this good Commonalty suffers . . . great injury." Then, calling for special "consideration for the good and voluntary services, expeditions, watches, and other burdens which the Burghers have hitherto done and borne," they petitioned the director-general for "the establishment of burgher right or citizenship and that none be allowed to keep store except resident freemen."[70]

Stuyvesant acceded to the burgomasters' request and established a two-tier "Great or Small Burgher Right" modeled on the practice introduced in Amsterdam five years previously. All native-born residents and anybody who had lived in the town for a year and six weeks, married "native born daughters of Burghers," or paid twenty guilders were eligible for the small or lesser burgher right. Residents who were or ever had been "in the High or Supreme government of the Country," former and present burgomasters and schepens, ministers of the gospel, military officers, and persons of high status who paid fifty guilders (and the male descendants of all these ranks) were entitled to register for the great burgher right. The order required burghers to establish residence by owning or renting real property and to pay the necessary taxes. This granted holders the freedom of the city and the privilege of engaging in local commerce. In addition to trade privileges, great burghers also qualified for administrative preferences and were deemed appropriate candidates for the "offices and dignities within this City, and consequently to be nominated thereto."[71]

It was little wonder that the magistrates considered the burgher right "one of the most important privileges in a well governed city." The two-tier civic status bolstered the status of Manhattan's aspirant merchant oligarchy of twenty or thirty leading individuals and enhanced their influence over New Amsterdam's commercial life. The key concern of this group and their partners remained the control of the import and local retail trade and the export of colonial products such as grain and flour. The burgher right ensured that only those with premises in New Amsterdam would be permitted to trade at Fort Orange. It enhanced the city's management and quality control of the export trade. The burgomasters established new municipal inspectorates to monitor the sale of grain and lime and to inspect weights, cans, ells, and barrels used in the city to ensure that they were "according to [the] measure and custom of Old Amsterdam." Shortly thereafter, the burgomasters added the office of vendue master, or overseer of public auctions and land sales, and the long-coveted position of schout to their appointive authority.[72]

NIEUW AMSTERDAM ofte NUE NIEUW IORX op't TEYLANT MAN

Figure 5. *The Prototype View* (after 1664). Facsimile of original in The Hague, Museum of the City of New York, The J. Clarence Davies Collection. This watercolor of New Amsterdam dates from after the 1664 conquest but is most likely a copy of a sketch made between 1650 and 1653. It shows the church and a block of buildings on the Strand on the right and the settlement gathered before the fort and windmill on the left.

Enhanced authority over the city and its trade also meant increased control over lesser burghers and artisans. The oath sworn by those registering for the lesser right nicely captured the deference owed by ordinary residents to the newly elevated great burgher oligarchy. The oath replicated the text of the earlier loyalty pledge to the West India Company and the States General, but added an undertaking to obey "the burgomasters and Rulers of this city, present and future" and to show them "all respect and reverence and to obey them in all honest and just matters as a faithful Subject and good Burgher is bound."[73] When Jan Martyn was disrespectful toward Pieter van Couwenhoven "in his capacity of Schepen on the public street," the lesser burgher was warned not "to insult either Burgomasters or Schepens any more on certain penalty." On another occasion, Saartje Steendam was called to appear before the magistrates and fined for ridiculing the municipal fire wardens as "Brick Sweeps . . . with a laughing mouth," because "such words must not be spoken to public servants," even lowly fire wardens.[74]

In addition to showing due respect to municipal officers, lesser burghers were also required to serve in the militia, maintain their property in accordance with city regulations, pay municipal fees when required, contribute either financially or with labor to public works, and conduct their commercial affairs according to official weights, measures, and prices. When the butcher Egbert Meydertsen failed to comply with this latter order, he had his butchering privileges withdrawn for six weeks and was only restored to his trade after undertaking to "demean himself for the future as an honorable burgher." The summer following the introduction of the burgher right, the magistrates sought to enhance their control of tradesmen and laborers still further, resolving to "fix certain hours of the day when working-people should go to their work and come from their work, as well also their recess for meals" and to "draft a petition to the Director-general General and Council to establish Guilds."[75] Following the trading season that year, the spiraling costs of local necessaries prompted the municipal leaders to petition Stuyvesant again, this time recommending that "all bakers, brewers, shopkeepers and merchants should sell their goods at reasonable prices to the people." Stuyvesant obliged them with revised rates for seawan exchange and an order requiring brewers, bakers, tapsters, shopkeepers, and ships chandlers to sell "daily household commodities" at fixed prices.[76]

Given these and similar orders, it is perhaps not surprising that scholars have tended to consider the burgher right as a tool of social control wielded by Stuyvesant and an increasingly confident merchant elite.[77] However, the fragility of social distinctions and the popularity of the civic privilege among ordinary residents belie this impression. As we have seen, the members of New Amsterdam's emerging elite were mostly self-made men whose material wealth and status fell well below the level of the Dutch urban regents they aped. Moreover, social status in New Amsterdam remained fluid, and the clear-cut distinction implied in the two-tier civic status was more aspired to than real. For example, the ranks of the great burghers included the erratically successful tailor and fur trader Hendrick Kip, who secured his place as a veteran of the campaign for municipal government. The lesser burghers counted the aspiring carpenter Fredrick Flipzen, who would one day be the richest merchant in New York, among their numbers. Furthermore, ordinary residents' enthusiasm for the burgher right was such that the magistrates initially had to manage with a hastily penned oath and issue the privilege and "certificates to persons demanding it and having paid the fees." A few weeks later, the court introduced the formal oath and began to register all those living and working in New Amsterdam, warning that those who did "not make known their names shall be deprived of their right to such privileges." Over the ensuing months, almost the entire male population of New Amsterdam trooped to court to claim the privileged civic status.[78]

The introduction of the burgher right capped almost ten years of municipal activism by merchant reformers, but the administration of New Amsterdam remained a far from top-down affair. Whatever authority the burgher right afforded the merchant elite depended to a great extent on the cooperation of local residents. For example, Stuyvesant's support for the burgomasters' proposals to regulate local workers and prices did nothing to guarantee their success: the plan to establish guilds came to naught and the year following his orders concerning working practices and rates, Stuyvesant lamented that "the expected reduction of prices for necessary commodities and labor did not follow . . . for everything remains as dear as formerly."[79] Ordinary residents and tradesmen in particular considered the various orders concerning civic behavior less as unswervable dictates and more as acceptable duties whose authority resided in the republican tradition of active-citizen participation in public life. In this respect, the heterogeneous schedule of municipal ordinances and regulations that directed the lives and commerce of local tradesmen also provided residents with a measure of comfort: municipal regulations and the obedience they commanded (most of the time) offered a routine demonstration that the settlers' government lay in the hands of their own representatives rather than a quasi-military Company administration.

*   *   *

In the 1650s and 1660s the burgomasters' delimitation of residential and occupational duties stimulated claims for protective privileges from the ranks of ordinary residents. In the regulation of artisanal working practices one discerns a dialogue between municipal governors and craft practitioners that figured in the articulation of a local identity that drew on two additional aspects of urban life imported from the United Provinces: the Roman-Dutch law and the requirement that adult male residents serve in the local militia. The first provided a forum in which ordinary residents settled their grievances in accordance with locally established notions of equity. The second promoted solidarity and civic harmony among men who were divided in terms of rank and property but who shared a commitment to the preservation of patriarchal priorities and community defense. Considered together, the three elements of residential and occupational privileges, legal practice, and militia service provided for the articulation of an artisanal identity that drew upon Dutch traditions to address colonial questions concerning social order, female commercial activities, and the superior status of free and skilled workers in comparison to the increasing numbers of African slaves in New Amsterdam.

The burgher right confirmed resident artisans' preferential position in local trade and before the law, granting privileges that skilled workers invoked and were quick to defend from encroachment. Registered burghers claimed exclusive access to the handicraft and retail trades and were also were protected from seizure of goods for debt providing they appeared in court when required. Thus David Wessels and Fredrick Arenzen, a turner and chair maker, complained to the burgomasters that some country people came to the city "asking for work or [to] make chair matting" and were "allowed to earn the wages" that the two men protested deprived resident burghers of "support for themselves and their families."[80] However, in addition to this general prohibition against strangers trading in the city, artisans working at particular trades sought supplementary privileges and liberties. For just as the burgomasters held city tradesmen to occupation-specific duties—to bake bread at a certain weight and fashion barrels of the requisite dimensions—so skilled workers claimed particular privileges above and beyond the general preferences enjoyed by all.

Following the introduction of the burgher right, the burgomasters refined the privileges and duties of those who worked as bakers, porters, and butchers. The bakers won the repeal of Stuyvesant's licensing scheme, and

some secured lucrative municipal contracts and offices in the administration.[81] From their new vantage point, the bakers now considered their trade
interests within a provincial context and sought more precise assessments of
the costs of ingredients and their relation to the regulations setting the price
and weight of different loaves.[82] In 1659, the bakers secured the first increase
in their margins on household bread since the prices set by Stuyvesant nine
years earlier. By the following year they were claiming a right to link the
price of bread to provincial expenses, indicating a maturing sense of local
and trade identity that was matched by developments in other occupations.
For example, following the introduction of the burgher right, the magistrates upheld the licensing of innkeepers who agreed to pay the excise and
to sell beer at the regulated price as long as they were permitted to charge
what they pleased for wine and strong liquor, "as the price and pay for wines
are different and not so necessary for the common people." Next the burgomasters expanded the city's force of public porters, modeling the trades'
duties and privileges on the practice of Amsterdam. After the city established a twice-yearly cattle fair and constructed a new meat market with a
tiled roof, six local men came forward "requesting to be sworn butchers."
The six secured a monopoly on local slaughtering in return for an undertaking to work at regulated rates, supervise the quality of meat offered for
local consumption and export, and collect a municipal excise calculated on
the value of slaughtered beasts "in accordance with the laudable custom of
our Fatherland and for the accommodation of the Burghers."[83]

The emerging sense of New Amsterdam as a distinctive provincial community also reflected the influence of the Court of Burgomasters and Schepens, which adhered to the principles and formalities of Roman-Dutch law.
The court offered various modes of settlement. In many cases the magistrates
simply issued a judgment following a hearing of the facts of the case. They
also directed disputants to attempt a private settlement before pursuing a
public remedy. Alternatively, litigants relied on court-appointed or mutually
agreed-upon arbitrators, who were directed to "examine the a/c and hear the
parties' arguments and reconcile them in this regard if possible, and if not to
report their award to the court." Once the arbitrators had met and reported,
the magistrates would give their decision and set out procedures for the remedy of the dispute. While the arbitrators met to decide the case, they were
provisioned with food and drink at the litigant's expense, and this encouraged the parties to have their books straight before the arbitrators met.[84]

New Amsterdammers were careful and deliberate traders and mindful
of legal formalities and the customs and litigation practices of Amsterdam

courts.[85] However, not all agreements were amenable to formal written terms, and this was particularly the case for contracts between tradesmen and their patrons, which frequently involved quibbles over customer satisfaction and payment. When a tradesman failed to complete the work on time or did a shoddy job, or when customers withheld payment, the parties looked to the magistrates and knowledgeable arbitrators to settle arguments and restore public reputations. Once submitted, the arbitrators' report informed the magistrates' judgment, thereby receiving the imprimatur of the court and the law for their assessment of what constituted reasonable customer expectations and reward. Thus, in 1653, when the carpenter Auken Jansen demanded wages of twenty-four florins from the wife of Juryaen Andriesen, she refused declaring that he had "damaged the work and the building more than he has earned and . . . therefore nothing is due to him." The court appointed the carpenters Gillis Pietersen and Abram Clock to inspect the work and report their findings. Alternatively, when Willem Albersten sued the cooper Claes Terhaer for the balance outstanding of the seventy-five florins he had advanced in payment for casks, Terhaer claimed to have "earned 90 fl. in casks," and the court directed Jan Jansen and Tomas Fredricksen "both coopers here . . . to appraise the work done by the deft as to its value *here* and to make parties agree or else make a written report."[86] In this fashion, city tradesmen and their customers figured in the establishment of notions of equitable exchange and contributed to New Amsterdam's sense of itself as a distinct trading community.

Residential militias (schutterijen) had long played a central role in the civic life of Dutch towns, and service in New Amsterdam's local defense force assumed similar significance in the 1650s and 1660s. In the United Provinces, the militias organized shooting festivals, male clubs, and parades in celebration of their role in the defense of fundamental liberties against the Spanish during the sixteenth-century Dutch Revolt. They were also charged with defending the town from external threats and internal disorder during times of rebellion among the lower orders. This internal police function, and the fact that militia members were responsible for kitting themselves out with the necessary uniforms and weaponry, meant that the militia was generally drawn from the ranks of the better and middling sorts. In New Amsterdam, however, the paucity of population and ubiquity and imminence of English and Indian hostilities required that all able-bodied men between sixteen and sixty serve in the militia; indeed, in the wake of the Peach Tree War Stuyvesant even ordered those "who live by sailing sloops up and down the river and have no fixed place of residence" to register for service.[87]

Notwithstanding their motley appearance, at least in comparison to metropolitan peers, the New Netherland militia played an important role in the defense and civic life of New Amsterdam. In 1653, when the newly established burgher government and the director-general were jockeying for administrative authority in the town, the burgomasters' threat to suspend nightly patrols left Stuyvesant no choice but to compromise on the question of control over the excise of wine and beer.[88] It is also likely that the militia observed ceremonial formalities when mustering and dispatching their duties: following the introduction of the burgher right, the burgomasters petitioned the Amsterdam Board for "three new standards with their appurtenances, as the General [Stuyvesant] intends to divide the two Burgher Companies into three." A few months later, the directors obliged the city and dispatched "three flags, the partisans, halberds, and drums required for the trainbands . . . also some drumskins, snares and strings to be used when necessary." The bond that developed between militiamen was negatively expressed in an anti-Semitic petition submitted to Stuyvesant seeking the exclusion of Jews on the grounds that they "be not admitted and counted among the militia in the renown mercantile city of Amsterdam or (to our knowledge) any other city of the Netherlands." Whatever the prejudices of its members, the militia's defensive function was never in doubt. In 1662, and to Stuyvesant's horror, the Amsterdam Chamber even considered abolishing the Company's garrison and relying "on the inhabitants alone for the offensive and defensive maintenance" of the city.[89]

In just over a decade New Amsterdam was transformed from a fractious frontier settlement to an increasingly orderly and prosperous seaport town. The success of this commercial community rested to a great extent on the achievement of a balance between private commercial pursuits and civic-minded deference to a burgher government and municipal regulatory order that the Company's administration had conspicuously failed to inspire. The daily work and lives of New Amsterdam residents increasingly resembled those of their peers among the urban Dutch brede middenstand—roughly translated to the English middling sort—who combined commercial pursuits with civic life under the watchful gaze of a local burgher government: bakers who provided for the public bread supply, also served as municipal inspectors; residents engaged in the fur trade also dedicated time and effort to repairing fortifications and digging out the Heere Gracht, a canal that allowed merchants to deliver goods into the heart of the city; tappers such as Lourens Cornelisen van der Wel also sought out the position of gunner in the artillery post mounted on the city's north wall; the cabinetmaker

Lodowyck Pos, who ran a tavern with his wife, served as a captain of the watch and patrolled the streets at night.[90] By 1659, even the Company's shareholders in Amsterdam had realized the benefits of a measure of municipal autonomy. Presumably intending to head off any future disagreements between provincial and municipal governments, the Board dispatched "twelve copies of a little book, called 'Ordinances and Code of Procedure before the Courts of the City of *Amsterdam*,'" instructing Stuyvesant to distribute them among the burgomasters and schepens, "who must strictly govern themselves accordingly."[91]

The establishment of an urban order based on prescriptive privileges and duties had important consequences for race and gender relations in the city. As we have seen, in the earliest days, most of New Netherland's settlers were bonded laborers of one kind or another, and the Africans who worked as slaves shared the working conditions and servile status of Company servants. The Company owned almost all of the city's earliest slave workers, who retained rights to work on their own behalf when not employed by the Company.[92] In the 1630s and 1640s, slaves bore arms during Kieft's War, married and baptized children in the Dutch Church, and owned land and—in a few cases—slaves. A handful were manumitted on condition that they pay an annual tribute in goods or services to the provincial authorities. This half-freedom afforded holders rights to own land and work for themselves, but it also picked out freed slave workers as distinct from white settlers whose post-indenture service was not subject to similar restrictions.[93] In the 1650s, the campaign for municipal rights and privileges elaborated further on the distinctions between black and white residents by excluding the former from the privileges and duties of the burgher right. Orders commanding the townspeople to donate their time to working on the city's fortifications required a reduced commitment from black residents, and although free and enslaved blacks were called to bear arms when the city was under threat, it is unlikely that they served as regulars in the city's militia.[94]

The articulation of these distinctions at a time when a change in the Company's fortunes augured the possible substitution of slave for freeborn workers may indicate a connection between artisans' claims for local rights and trade privileges and the delineation of the city's early racial boundaries. Following the sacking of Pernambuco and the loss of Brazil in 1654, the West India Company looked to New Amsterdam as an alternative entrepôt for its Atlantic commerce and opened up the slave trade to private merchants. The Company had long used slaves for farm work and laboring in an effort to reduce its costs, and in the mid-1650s, more private citizens purchased slaves with a view to setting them to work in the city. In 1657, a proposal to further increase the city and colony's reliance on slave labor threatened to undermine local efforts to establish an adapted Dutch civic order of free burghers. In April, the Amsterdam Board directed Stuyvesant to assess the feasibility of training slaves to "Trades such as carpentering, bricklaying, blacksmithing . . . as it was formerly done in Brazil and is now done in Guinea and other Colonies." The use of slaves in occupations coveted by free tradesmen threatened to transform the town from an aspiring "City of Amsterdam in New Netherland" to a miserable trading depot along the lines of Pernambuco. Replying to the Company's instruction a few months later, Stuyvesant discouraged further exploration of the proposal and reported that he could find "no able negroes fit to learn a trade."[95] The introduction of the burgher right limiting artisanal and retail trades to registered residents just weeks before may have been entirely coincidental, but by affirming the exclusion of blacks from civic and trade privileges, New Amsterdam's municipal order provided for new and powerful distinctions between residents of African and European descent living in the city.

The consequences of the introduction of civic privileges for gender relations are a little harder to gauge: women were entitled to register for the burgher right, but, although the names of a handful of female Dutch traders do appear on the list of registered burghers, most inherited the privilege from fathers or shared in their husbands' right. There is no shortage of evidence that women of all ages and stations engaged in commerce and worked at skilled trades, but public recognition of women's work and female skills was limited to a handful of activities such as midwifery and housekeeping whose character was related to enduring assumptions concerning female nature.[96] Moreover, where women labored under the same licensing conditions as men—such as baking, tavern keeping, or butchery—they never appeared as public representatives of the trade. Civic and trade identities were limited to male household heads and excluded strangers, women, and others whose status marked them as dependents. In this respect, civic and trade privileges bolstered masculine identities and enforced patriarchal boundaries. To understand how, and perhaps why, we first have to consider the attitude of the Roman-Dutch law to New Netherland's female traders.

Despite including provisions that clearly discriminated in terms of gender, the Roman-Dutch law equipped women to survive in a commercial society, and New Netherland's female traders took advantage of opportunities whenever possible.[97] The law treated women of all ages as minors under the guardianship of their fathers or husbands, and married women could only appear in court with their husbands' approval; without this permission, wives could neither engage in trade nor initiate and defend an action in their own name. In addition, although Dutch wives held property and enjoyed joint ownership with their husbands over marital and communal goods, a male household head was free to sell his wife's portion without her prior agreement or consent. However, notwithstanding these gendered inequalities, spousal permission was commonly granted, and Dutch women played an active role in the management of the household economy. Thus, despite the potential for legal limitations, married women retained a legal right to property, engaged in trade, and regularly appeared in court on their own and their husbands' behalf.

New Amsterdam's court records reveal that provincial marriages followed the prevailing Dutch model of a companionate union that treated the household economy as a joint venture.[98] Once married women entered the world of commerce they were subject to the same laws as men except in one respect: a "gender-related protection" that prevented women from binding their estate as surety in their own exchanges or as the principal debtor for a third party, for example, as wives and guarantors of their husbands' debts. Unless they renounced this safeguard or were deemed public traders, the protection afforded single and married women a form of limited liability, and this seems to have rankled the men with whom they traded in New Netherland: although there is little evidence of disputes between married partners, the records suggest that a disproportionate number of men slandered or broke contractual agreements with female trading partners, forcing them to seek redress in court.[99]

Conclusions remain tentative until further research provides a fuller picture of gender relations in early New Netherland. However, the components of the burgher right and the public persona it afforded its artisanal holders were likely bound up with the affirmation of masculinity in New Amsterdam. In the 1640s and early 1650s increasing numbers of families settled in the town and faced Indian attacks, commercial uncertainties, and struggles against the West India Company for municipal rights. In the ensuing years, New Amsterdammers constructed a civic order that culminated with the securing of the burgher right in 1657. Thereafter, the provision of local government and rights sustained male residents' sense of themselves as bearers of civic privileges and duties, militiamen, and freeborn and independent subjects living under the government of their own representatives. The municipal order and burgher right provided a transplanted context within which men took up their role as household heads and defenders of the community, thereby articulating their social and cultural domination over women and, in particular, over female traders who competed with and frequently bettered their male counterparts in New Netherland's unpredictable trading economy. In this fashion, masculine rights, privileges, obligations, and duties affirmed the endurance of Old World patriarchal norms and sensibilities that were critical to seventeenth-century notions of familial and community order and governance.[100]

*   *   *

By the 1660s, then, the Nine Men's assertion that "privileges and exemptions" would be the "mother of population" and prosperity was borne out by the success of New Amsterdam. The city's population had swollen to fifteen hundred, as increasing numbers of settlers made the eight-week voyage from the United Provinces and established themselves as artisans and traders in the town. The dock bustled with activity as porters, carters, and boatmen unloaded cargoes of grain and furs from upriver and tobacco from Virginia and Maryland and, following inspection and packing in locally manufactured barrels, reloaded the colonial products for the voyage to Holland.[101] New Amsterdam's merchant leaders could scarcely contain their satisfaction at the progress of their "capital" city, whose "many fine houses" built by local carpenters and bricklayers were the envy of their English neighbors and "surpassed nearly every other place in these parts of North America." The three militia companies of artisans and farmers ensured that the town was "properly fortified" and "formidable to evil-minded neighbours and savages."[102] Ten years after settling in New Amsterdam, Jacob Steendam was inspired to pen his *Spurring Verses*:

Communities the groundwork are of every state
They first the hamlet, village and the city make
From whence proceeds the commonwealth; whose members, great
Become, an interest in the common welfare take
T'is no Utopia; it rests on principles
Which for true liberty, prescribes you settled rules.

Little did the burgomasters and commonalty realize that their success was about to become the source of their undoing and that the city's defenses would shortly be called to repel an English invasion force. In the late 1650s the colony's newfound prosperity attracted the attention of powerful English interests who were jealous of the Dutch imperial success.[103] Within

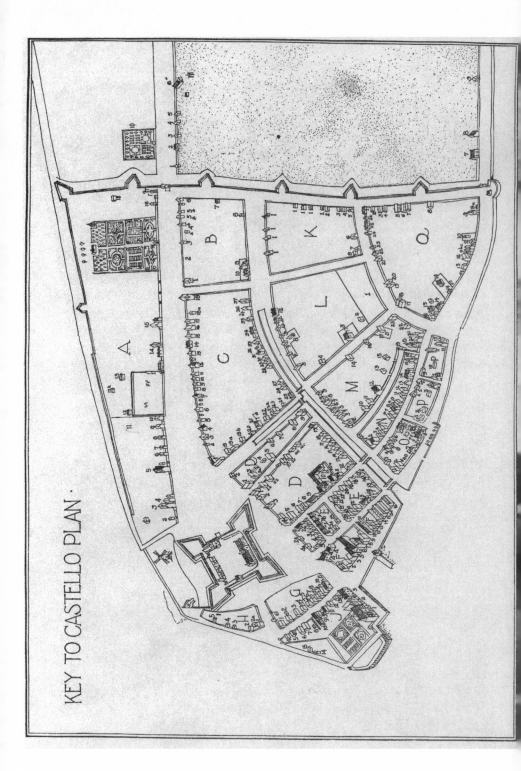

KEY TO CASTELLO PLAN .

Block/house number/name/occupation

A1. Lodowyck Pos, cabinet maker/tavern keeper
A9. Lucas Dircksen, tavern keeper
A10. Pieter Sinam, tailor
A11. Lucas Dircksen, tavern keeper
A13. Laurens Andriessen, turner
A14. Paulus Leendertsen van der Grift, burgomaster
A18. Jacob Swart, carpenter/porter
B1. Augustine Herman, merchant
B3. Pieter Schaefbanck, court messenger/jailor
C1. Jan Jansen van Bresteede, cooper
C3. Abraham Pietersen, miller/tavern keeper
C8. Jan Hendricksen van Gunst, butcher/glazier
C9. Thomas Fransen
C13&14. Cornelius Janssen

Cloppenborgh, tavern keeper
C17. Jan Gerritsen, mason
C18. Coenraet Ten Eyck, shoemaker
C24. Toussaint Briel, porter
C25. Cornelis Barentsen van der Cuyl, baker/lime measurer
C28. Coenraet Ten Eyck, shoemaker
C29. Coenraet Ten Eyck, shoemaker
C30. Coenraet Ten Eyck, shoemaker
C31. Coenraet Ten Eyck, shoemaker
C32. Jacob Mensen, tailor
C32a. Thomas Verdon, carter
C33. Jan Cornelissen, porter
D1. Frederick Arenzen, turner/cabinet maker
D3. Jacob Teunissen de Kay, baker
D4. Fredrick Philipse, carpenter

D5. Joost Teunissen, baker
D7. Jeronimus Ebbingh, merchant
D15. Garret Jansen Roos, carpenter/butcher
D16. Reynout Reynoutsen, shoemaker
D17. Pieter Winster, hatter
D18. Coenraet Ten Eyck (residence), shoemaker
D19. Pieter van Naerden, carter.
D19. David Wessels, turner
E1. Hendrick Willemsen, baker
E14. Hendrick Willemsen, baker
E15. Hendrick Willemsen, baker
E17. Teunis Cray, porter/tavern keeper
F1. Cornelis Steenwyck
F2. Cornelis Steenwyck
F3. Cornelis Steenwyck
F13. Samuel Edsall, hatter

F14. Nicholas Jansen, baker
F15. Franse Jansen van Hooghten, carpenter
G8. Claes Jansen, baker
G9. Gillis Pietersen van der Gouw, carpenter
J1. Peter Stuvesant, director-general
J3. Issac Grevenraet, merchant/schepen
J5. Pieter Jacobsen Marius, ships carpenter/merchant
J7. Claes Jansen de Ruyter, carpenter
J10. William Kock, carter
K5. Cornelis Hendricksen, drummer/weighhouse laborer
K7. Thomas Verdon, carter and porter
L2. Pieter Pietersen, carpenter/brewer?

M1. Adriaen Vincent, porter/tapper
M5&6. Abraham Jansen, carpenter
M9. Jochem Beeckman, shoemaker
M10. House of the Company's slaves
M11. Joost Goderis, porter
M14. Robert Roelantsen, carpenter
M17. Michael Jansen, brewer
M21. Dirck Jansen, smith
M22&23. Meindert Barentsen, cooper
N3&4. Cales Karstensen, porter
N5. Jochem Backer, baker
N15. Asser Levy, butcher/trader
O2. Sibout Classen, carpenter
O4. Adolph Pietersen, carpenter

O6. Sybrant Jansen de Galma, carpenter
P11. Evert Duyckingh, glazier/merchant
P12. Abraham Martens Clock, carpenter
P13. Marten Clock, cooper
Q1. Mathys Muller, watchman
Q8. Lambert Huybertsen Mol, ships carpenter
Q9&8a. Daniel Litschoe, tavern keeper
Q11. John Lawrence, merchant
Q12a. Andries Jochemsen, sail maker/tavern keeper
Q14. Govert Loockermans, merchant
Q16&17. Burger Jorrisen, blacksmith
Q18. Marten Jansen Meyer, blacksmith

Figure 6. Plan of 1660 by Jacques Cortelyou (the Castello Plan). The sale and rental of city properties make it difficult to say for sure who lived where when Jacques Cortelyou drew up his 1660 plan in what proved to be the final years of Dutch rule. The chart and residencies given here provide a partial identification of city property holders based on I. N. Phelps Stokes's "Key to the Castello Plan" in *The Iconography of Manhattan Island*, 2: 215–341, and give an impression of occupancy in the late 1650s and early 1660s. We can see that the holdings of the shoemaker and tanner Coenraet Ten Eyck (C18 and C28–31) and the baker Hendrick Willemsen (E1 and E14–15) meant they were well positioned to take advantage of the increase in trade and urban property values in the 1670s and 1680s, while poorer tradesmen, such as the turner David Wessels and the carter Pieter van Naerden (D19), shared smaller lots. What is particularly striking is the dispersal of occupations and residencies of different social ranks across the city. This contrasts with the increasing concentration of trades and wealthy (and poorer) residents in distinct neighborhoods beginning in the early eighteenth century (see Chapter 3, 120–21).

months of the restoration of Charles II in 1660, Parliament adopted a second Navigation Act confirming England's intention to drive the Dutch from the American trade. The keenest advocates of England's commercial empire gathered around the king's younger brother, James, Duke of York. By March 1664, James and his counselors had succeeded in persuading the king to grant his brother part of present-day Maine and a handful of islands near its shores. In an act of superlative aggrandizement, the most substantial part of James's grant awarded him control of all the territory lying between the Delaware and Connecticut rivers—the territory comprising New Netherland.

"Like a child in their debt and consequently their slave": The Transition to English Rule, 1664–1691

In May 1664 James Duke of York dispatched Colonel Richard Nicolls with four ships and three hundred soldiers to secure the "entrye submission and obedience" of England's newest colonial American subjects. In mid-August, the invaders disembarked from vessels anchored off Long Island in Gravesend Bay and moved west to Brooklyn, where they secured the ferry station across from the fort at New Amsterdam. Nicolls's strategy combined demonstrations of superior force with the offer of lenient terms: he enlisted residential militias from the English towns on Long Island, dispatched two ships up the Hudson within sight of Manhattan's eastern shore, and ordered local farmers "not to furnish any provisions to the city"; he then distributed handbills ahead of the advancing troops offering fair treatment for those who surrendered. The English commander reiterated his terms in a letter written to Stuyvesant, promising that in return for capitulation the settlers would "peaceably enjoy whatsoever God's blessing and their own honest industry have furnished them with and all other privileges with his majesty's English subjects."[1]

Stuyvesant was prepared to make a fight of it, but the burgomasters and commonalty refused to support his defense of the city. Rumors reached New Amsterdam "from divers country people who daily noticed the growing and increasing strength of the English" that the invaders' "business was not only with New Netherland but with booty and plunder." Residents were no safer within the city, where elements of the Company's garrison were heard to declare that they were "fixed more on plunder than on defence . . . [and knew] well where booty is to be got and where the young women reside who wear chains of gold." In one alleged incident, a group of Company soldiers intent on mischief gathered in front of a house owned by the merchant Nicholas Meyer and were only persuaded to withdraw by members of the burgher militia. When Stuyvesant tried to convince New Amsterdam's leaders to keep news of the surrender terms and reports of the fort's limited supply of good gunpowder from the inhabitants, the burgomasters left the meeting "greatly disgusted and dissatisfied." Furious at their defiance, the director-general tore up Nicolls's letter. Within hours work, on the city's fortifications ceased, and a delegation of the "inhabitants of the place assisted by their wives and children crying and praying" confronted Stuyvesant and demanded that he reassemble the letter and negotiate terms. The following day ninety-three prominent burghers—including the director-general's own seventeen-year-old son—presented a remonstrance denouncing resistance as a folly that would not save "the smallest portion of our entire city, our property and (what is dearer to us), our wives and children, from total ruin." Stuyvesant relented, and merchant leaders Oloff Stevenson van Cortlandt, Cornelius Steenwyck, Nicholas Varleth, and Jacques Cousseau met with Nicolls and his officers to draft the Articles of Capitulation under which New Netherland and New Amsterdam became New York, New York.[2]

Facing a superior English military force and Stuyvesant's perceived inability to control the garrison, let alone guarantee the security of the town, New Amsterdam's residents elected to agree to the Articles of Capitulation. For a time these terms provided for the continuity of the city's civic order. Nicolls and his successors were military men charged with the command of the largest English garrison in the North American colonies. They devoted their attention to the French and Indian threat to the northwest, and they relied on the city's business leaders to administer local trade, collect taxes, and provide for the soldiers in the newly renamed Fort James. In return for their cooperation, New York's merchants secured recognition of the city's staple right and related privileges that enabled them to supplement the diminishing fur trade with a profitable business exporting primary products and importing supplies and trade goods.[3] The only threat to the mutually beneficial partnership that developed between New York's governors and their commerce-minded subjects came from a group of English merchants who established themselves in the city following the end of the Third Anglo-Dutch War in 1674. The Englishmen resented the advantages enjoyed by their Dutch rivals and launched a protest that momentarily threw the colony into turmoil. However, the competition for patronage and spoils within the merchant oligarchy soon passed and a powerful Anglo-Dutch clique of traders who worked closely with the governors assumed control of the city's import and export trade.

Unfortunately, the New York merchants' pursuit of privileges and profits failed to foster the general welfare of the town. The residents' united front in the face of conquest in 1664 was sorely tested in a protracted transition to English rule. Initially, tradesmen and their families were content to submit to the new imperial authorities that confirmed and in some cases extended local rights and trade privileges. The respect shown by the conquerors for the municipal government's regulatory regime, occupational privileges, and established legal practices affirmed the English undertakings given in the Articles of Capitulation. However, following the brief reconquest of the colony by the Dutch in 1672–74, the administrations of Edmund Andros and Thomas Dongan introduced commercial and governmental reforms that fell particularly hard on middling residents: new taxes to pay for improvements in the city's infrastructure and regulations intended to promote commerce seemed to many to favor the interests of a narrow clique of merchants at the expense of the community at large. Civic and commercial regulations that had once served as symbolic guarantees of individual and community freedoms were increasingly suspected as measures designed to advance the interests of a few at the expense of the many. In the late 1680s the fears of city artisans for the security of privileges and liberty became bound up with antipopery sentiment whipped up by Calvinist zealots. Forty years after the campaign against the West India Company on behalf of municipal rights, New Yorkers once again feared that they had fallen under the sway of an arbitrary and tyrannical government. In 1689, when news of the Glorious Revolution and the accession of William and Mary reached New York, city tradesmen mustered as the militia rose up to defend their privileges and liberty from a suspected papist plot to deliver the city into the hands of its French and Indian enemies.

*   *   *

New Amsterdam's burghers agreed to the Articles of Capitulation to prevent not only bloodshed and the destruction of property but also the political consequences of English conquest. Following his recall to Amsterdam to account for the colony's surrender, Stuyvesant argued that unsuccessful resistance would have granted the English conquerors *jure belli*, or a right of war, to have "attacked, overwhelmed, [and] plundered us and the good inhabitants." To support his case, Stuyvesant pointed to the fate of the Dutch defenders at New Amstel and the settlements on the Delaware River. Nicolls had dispatched one of his junior officers, Robert Carr, to secure the area, and when Carr met with resistance, his men plundered New Amstel down "to a very nail" and sold the defenders into slavery in Virginia. The Articles saved New Amsterdammers from such a fate and bespoke their determination to establish individual and community rights on a new but, in their view, no less certain foundation. The agreement provided those who wished to leave six months in which to dispose of their land and goods. For those who remained, it also guaranteed property rights, freedom of religious observance, inheritance customs, and the adjudication of existing contracts according to Dutch law. Nicolls also promised to allow new settlers to come from the United Provinces and to permit residents to maintain their trade with Dutch vessels for an additional six months. For those wishing to travel within or beyond the colony, he issued passports certifying their status as a "free denizen of this place." The Articles also guaranteed that New Amsterdammers would not be pressed into English military service, although the city's defensive needs continued to require militia duty of male residents between the ages of sixteen and sixty. Finally, the Articles guaranteed that the "town of Manhatans shall choose Deputies, and those Deputies shall have free voices in all public affairs." In a world where the security of rights and privileges rested on the sanction of past practice continued into the present, there was much to assuage city residents' concerns in the conquest settlement and early years of English rule.[4]

Nicolls's leniency is an indication of the value he set upon maintaining order in New York City. The governor had approximately two hundred troops to guard a colony of eight thousand or more, fifteen hundred of whom lived in the province's urban center. Moreover, the duke's financial difficulties meant that neither Nicolls nor his successors received much support from England and had to rely on local cooperation to provision the garrison. York's decision to grant the area between the Hudson and Delaware rivers to Lord John Berkeley of Stratton and Sir George Carteret soon after the conquest further diminished the tax base upon which his governors might draw. With colonial revenues expected to cover administrative costs, the ducal income, and the governors' emoluments, Nicolls and his peers looked to support and encourage rather than oppress their Dutch charges. The diffiulty of raising taxes on settlements scattered around the colony made it logical to focus revenue collection on the port of New York. Directing provincial trade through the city also benefited local merchants and tradesmen and encouraged them to collaborate with the English administration. The strategy depended on the success of the city in provincial trade, and, as the burgomasters had demonstrated in the 1650s, this depended on the presence of a municipal authority that could enforce commercial regulations and collect the duties payable by city residents.[5]

The governor nurtured the city's municipal autonomy by omitting it from the provision of laws that he freely admitted were intended to curb local rights and privileges elsewhere in the colony. In 1665, Long Island, Staten Island, and Westchester were incorporated under a civil and criminal code known as the Duke's Laws. Ignoring the Long Islanders' petitions— and notwithstanding his earlier undertakings when securing their support for the invasion—Nicolls made no provision for local freemanship privileges or a representative assembly. The English towns came under the direct supervision of the governor and his council, who regulated all manner of civil and commercial activity and sat annually with the high sheriff and justices of the peace as the Court of Assizes. In a letter to York, Nicholls explained that the Duke's Laws were "not contrived so Democratically" as in other colonies. His aim was to establish the "foundation of Kingly Government in these parts," and he confessed to the duke that this "truly is grievous to some Republicans."[6] The Long Islanders repaid Nicolls and his Stuart patrons with thirty years of intermittent protest against what they considered an arbitrary government that rode roughshod over local rights and favored the interests of an urban minority. In the city, by contrast, Nicolls satisfied himself with minor reforms designed to make the municipal government more amenable to English ways: he replaced the incumbent burgomasters, schepens, and schout with English appointees who administered affairs as a mayor, five aldermen, and a sherriff "according to the Custome of England in other of his Maties Corporacons"; he stifled opposition by appointing Englishmen such as Thomas Willet as mayor, a trader well-known and respected by local Dutch merchants; finally, Nicolls confirmed the municipality's continued "full power and auth500tye to Rule & Governe as well all the Inhabitants of this Corporacon, as any Strangers, according to the Generall Lawes of this Governmt and such peculiar Lawes as are, or shall be thought convenient & necessary." Shortly after the conquest, the city's merchant magistrates were pleased to write to the duke thanking him for sending "so gentle, wise, and intelligent a gentlemen" to administer their affairs.[7]

Nicolls was bullish regarding the city's prospects, and he wrote to the duke declaring his belief that New York might one day be "the best of all His Majties Townes in America."[8] To encourage the city's fortunes, the governor confirmed its status as the province's staple port and tolerated breaches of the Navigation Acts by permitting Dutch merchants to import goods from Amsterdam beyond the six-month deadline agreed to in the Articles of

Capitulation. When the authorities in London prohibited further imports from the United Provinces, New York's canny Dutch merchants invoked their status as English subjects and used locally owned vessels to bring in cargoes from Amsterdam. Francis Lovelace, who succeeded Nicolls as governor in 1668, endorsed the city's Dutch commerce by joining it: Lovelace and his brother Thomas invested in the Amsterdam trade in partnership with local merchants Cornelius Steenwyck, Francis Hooghlandt, Nicholas Gouvernor, and Isaac Bedloe. Lovelace further advanced the city merchants' interest by cutting import taxes and lowering the duties payable on goods reexported up the Hudson to Albany. When Frederick Philipse complained that strangers were trading illegally at Esopus and Albany, Lovelace obliged him and his peers with an order requiring that goods bound upriver had to be first brought to New York and unloaded for inspection and duty payment before being reloaded onto vessels owned by the city's freemen. Strangers who wanted to travel to Albany were only given "leave to negotiate there having first obteyned the Privilege of being free burghers of this Citty." In 1671 the order was renewed and made binding forever, thereby ensuring city merchants a monopoly of the Hudson River trade as far as Albany.[9]

The merchants who secured lucrative concessions in provincial and international trade continued to regulate the quality of exported goods and collect taxes, duties, and fees to meet the costs of local government. Magistrates farmed the inspection of tobacco, slaughtered animals, grain and barrels and casks to a handful of peers and trusted lesser traders. Selected city artisans and middling residents secured positions on the lower rungs of the municipal ladder: Teunis Cray worked as a beer porter and tavern keeper in New Amsterdam for almost thirty years before being appointed public measurer of apples, onions and turnips in 1667. In January 1670, Jan Langestraat and Adriaen Cornelissen, a farmer and an innkeeper (tapper) living north of the city wall at Fresh Pond, were appointed as branders of horses and cattle and charged with ensuring that only beasts bearing the town's mark graze upon the public common. The more important and lucrative offices—such as vendue master, weighmaster, and collectors of liquor and burgher right excises—remained in the hands of the circle gathered around the merchant oligarchy. The municipal authorities monitored changes in city trade and amended regulations and appointed inspectors accordingly: when a shortage of wine prompted a rise in cider consumption, the court quickly added cider to the excise schedule; following Lovelace's order requiring provincial farmers to transport live hogs to the city for slaughter, the municipal government appointed Jan Jansen van Brestede and Pieter Abrahamsen as sworn packers and viewers of all meat dispatched from the city.[10]

By the late 1660s, the city's population was becoming increasingly skewed in favor of skilled artisans who constituted between one-fourth to one-half of white male residents. For these 130 or so skilled tradesmen who worked at twenty different occupations, the burden of duties, fees, and inspections was mitigated by the assurances these measures provided concerning the continuity of established municipal practices.[11] Trades such as baking, carting, tavern keeping, coopering, carpentry, and shoemaking all employed ten or more practitioners. The prominence of artisans in city life was reflected in the regulation of working practices that continued virtually unchanged from the Dutch era: tavern keepers still paid one florin per quarter—the rate established in 1656—and were required to renew their licenses "on pain of being deprived of the privilege of tapping." As the magistrates extended their regulatory purview, tradesmen in the city came forward to claim new privileges or refine earlier grants.[12] In October 1665, the butchers requested an increase in their slaughtering fees and measures against "diverse persons . . . [who] undertake to slaughter in this City without first having obtained proper consent." The magistrates duly confirmed the number of sworn butchers at eleven—allowing the registered men six guilders for large beasts and maintaining the fees for smaller cattle at the 1662 rate—and forbade all others from slaughtering livestock. In return, the sworn butchers undertook to "Kill noe Cattle hoggs etz. Without a Ticket of Consent from the Collector of the Major and Aldermen, except it be for the Right Honble Governr Richard Nicolls."[13]

The regulation of urban trade affirmed the burghers' duty to work to acceptable standards and contribute to the costs of local government, but it also implied the continuity of trade privileges and a commitment to administer commerce in the residential interest. As the targets and low-level enforcers of orders regulating local commerce, tradesmen were particularly well-placed to assess the efficacy of city ordinances and to estimate monies taken in and spent on municipal projects. Butchers monitored the enforcement of their slaughter monopoly, and tavern keepers knew how much they paid in excise and could have made a fair estimate of the amount taken in across the city. Sworn butchers such as Egbert Meyndertsen kept a tally of slaughter permits issued and an account of excise monies collected.[14] Even the motley crew of weigh-house porters and beer carriers who assembled at their station as dawn broke each morning had a role in the regulation of local trade: the five sworn porters were granted the privilege of working for set rates and contributed a portion of their pay to a fund to provide sick benefits of six guilders a week in the event of illness. In return, the porters promised to conduct themselves in a civil manner, not drink on the job, and not carry wine and beer without first obtaining a permit; they also under-took to gather up the permits at the end of each day and deliver them to Nicholas Bayard, the municipal officer in charge.[15] In these and other ways, local tradesmen participated in the administration of local commerce and gained insights into the costs of the municipal administration to which they contributed as residents and taxpayers.

City tradesmen's continuing sense of their place within the civic order was also reinforced by the maintenance of the burgher right restrictions, apprenticeship regulations, and established legal practice in court. Shortly after the conquest, New York's magistrates refused Gerrit Hendricksen van Rys's request for an exemption from the burgher right on the grounds that "he has not brought any goods for himself" to the city; the court decreed that "the petitioner shall have to pay his Burgher right." A few days later Hendrick Aarsen the Spaniard was told that "he must pay for his Burger Right" and was required to nominate Nicholas Verbraack as surety, as "he can pay nothing for the present time." Registered burghers continued to enjoy privileges over strangers in court and could not be arrested for debt unless the court show that they intended to leave the city.[16] The Duke's Laws also encouraged the reproduction of a skilled labor force by instructing parents and masters to "bring up their Children and Apprentices in some honest and Lawful Calling, Labour, or Employment." The municipal authorities enforced the regulations, returning those who ran away before the end of their indenture and requiring masters to provide adequate training.[17]

For a decade or so following the conquest, the structure and procedure in the city's court remained virtually unchanged. Once again, this likely re-flected pragmatism rather than magnanimity on the part of the new author-ities. The dearth of English legal talent and the ramified network of local credit relations extending over many years made an abrupt change in civil law impracticable and potentially hugely damaging to business confidence.[18] Nicolls and Lovelace were intent on preserving the stability and smooth operation of trade and were content to rename the city's busiest tribunal the Mayor's Court and insisted on the provision of jury trials at litigants' re-quest. However, the Mayor's Court heard cases in much the same way it had as the Court of Burgomasters and Schepens since 1653 and, for all intents and purposes, according to the Roman-Dutch law. Residents continued to rely on the magistrates' summary judgment or arbitrators to establish the quality or value of skilled work under dispute, and, just as before the con-quest, litigation remained a face-to-face affair. The court made allowances for the nonappearance of tradesmen, if a reasonable excuse was offered, and litigators enjoyed inexpensive access to arbitration.[19] Wealthier Dutch litigators occasionally took advantage of their newly established right as English subjects to appeal decisions to a jury trial. However, for most, the expense of providing food and drink for two or three arbitrators was burdensome enough, and the cost of provisioning twelve jurors likely dissuaded them from similar appeals.[20]

By continuing to provide a forum in which residents could settle their differences concerning the value and quality of skilled work, the court also sustained tradesmen's views of themselves as free, independent practitioners and the idea of locally prevailing rates of return. For example, when Goert Olphertsen, a carpenter, sued Annatie Gerrits for 106 florins in seawan— wages for carpentry work and lime delivered "as per account"—Gerrits's son-in-law claimed that Olphertsen work "is not properly done," although he offered to pay "in linen." The magistrates appointed Sanders Stulther and William Churcher to inspect the work. Following their assessment, the arbitrators recommended that Olphertsen make the job "good and tight" providing that Gerrits "furnished the materials at a proper season." If the materials failed to appear, Stulther and Churcher were ordered to make a second inspection to establish the value Olphertsen's work so far and propose a figure to be subtracted from the sum originally agreed upon. On occasion tradesmen anticipated the arbitration process and volunteered their work for inspection: when Mistress Anthonie sued Jan Harmensen for the return of twenty-five florins she had paid for a churn she considered badly made, Harmensen offered "to submit himself to the decision of two impartial coopers." The court appointed the gauger of barrels, Jan Jansen van Briested and Evert Wessels, to inspect the churn, which they subsequently declared merchantable.[21] In cases involving simple services or exchanges where rates were well-known, the court bypassed the arbitrators and invoked accepted practice—further enhancing the sense of continuity from Dutch to English eras: when Adam Onckelbach sued Frederick Philipse, who had promised to pay his wife, Neeltje Jans, "as much wages as she gets from others" for stringing seawan, Philipse countered that he had specified payment at four guilders per hundred for white wampum and two guilders per hundred for black. In court Neeltje Jans Onckelbach denied this arrangement, adding that she usually received five guilders for white and two guilders and ten stivers for black from her brother. Faced with conflicting accounts, "as the one says that they had agreed with the other and the other denies it," the magistrates ordered Philipse to pay Onckelbach "as wages for stringing wampum according to the custom heretofore" and at the higher rate.[22]

In 1664, the burgomaster and residents of New Amsterdam surrendered to the English invaders in order to preserve not only their lives and property but also the civic order and urban privileges that served as guarantees of their individual and community liberties. In the first decade after the conquest, city tradesmen could be forgiven for thinking that the Articles of Capitulation provided a solid foundation for these privileges and liberties. The English needed security and stability if they were to consolidate the imperial gains made in the wake of the Restoration. In New York this implied support for the city's staple right and the continuity of Dutch municipal and legal practices, which, by allaying fears of repression and plunder, ensured a local acquiescence to English rule. Just as Stuyvesant and the burgomasters had discovered in the late 1650s, civic harmony and the enforcement of regulations concerning the production, packing, retail, and movement of goods and provision of skilled services depended to a great extent on the willingness of residents to fulfill their duty to work to acceptable standards and for reasonable rates. Apart from an understandable reluctance to pay the costs of quartering the garrison, Anglo-Dutch tensions in the city were limited to sporadic confrontations between residents and unruly (and often drunken) soldiers.[23]

Scholars have long noted the surprisingly harmonious transition from Dutch to English rule, although opinions on the source of this cordiality differ: some point to the settlers' dissatisfaction with the West India Company; others stress the gains made by ambitious merchant collaborators. However, the stability of postconquest New Amsterdam reflected more than long standing antipathy toward the West India Company's Amsterdam Chamber and the advantages secured by a minority of resident merchants. It also depended on the continued deference of the city artisans and petty traders to municipal mercantile governance. The meaning of deference is notoriously difficult to pin down, but it has usually been associated with a society consisting of an elite and a nonelite in which the latter regard the former, without noticeable resentment, as being of superior status and naturally suited to rule.[24] What is noted less frequently is that, while a deferential order necessarily precludes sections of the population from claims upon leadership positions, it does not release those who hold these positions from critical scrutiny by the governed, who retain a capacity to evaluate the performance of their "betters" in accordance with accepted and expected community norms and rights. Considered thus, deference freely rendered indicates less the tacit acceptance of subservience and more an express statement of confidence in the governing elite, as long as they remain within the bounds of expected terms and conditions. In the later years of New Amsterdam and the early years of New York these terms and conditions—at least as far as city artisans were concerned—comprised the continued enjoyment of individual and community rights and occupational privileges established in the 1650s and 1660s that had been secured, or so it was believed, by the Articles of Capitulation. In this respect, artisanal deference to English rule in post-conquest New York was as much a sign of their optimism for the future as it was of their dislike for the West India Company or their fear of the garrison holed up in Fort James. But this optimism and the confidence it bespoke had its limits. From early on, one can discern the signs of future stresses and strains in the preparedness of the governors and their supporters to manipulate local rights and privileges in order to secure what they considered the interests of the town. This much was clear from the differing treatment accorded the city's bakers and carters during the first decade after the conquest.

* * *

New York's bakers waited until the trading season of 1666 before testing their position with the new English authorities. On 9 August, the magistrates heard reports that the bakers "dared to deal out and sell both brown and white bread" that was not of "due quantity and quality." In mitigation the bakers argued that strangers were baking and selling bread in the city and others were carrying their loaves beyond the fortifications for sale to the Indians. The magistrates appointed Christoffer Hooglandt and Hendrick Willemsen as inspectors, authorizing them to visit bakers within the city "as often as they shall deem necessary" and to "enquire if the bread has its due quantity and quality." The court also ordered that "all . . . are forbidden to peddle bread or cakes . . . but they may only sell in form at retail in their houses" and prohibited "all bakers or any other person or Indian" from transporting "bread and cakes from this city to the Indian plantations in order to expose for sale and sell the same there." The refinement of bread regulations revealed that the authorities and the bakers shared an interest in the bread supply and established a pattern for the future. The bakers secured continued recognition for their right to exclude outsiders, and the city's leaders guaranteed the community bread supply. The new regulations also ensured that the Indians came to town to make their purchases.[25]

The grant of denizen status to the Dutch in New York opened up the Caribbean market for provincial grain, flour, and supplies of ship biscuit or tack. However, the still limited amount of improved agricultural land barely provided for the city's needs and left precious little for export. The importance of bakers in the emerging provincial flour trade is evident from their partnerships with exporting merchants and the municipal authority's reliance on them for reports on city grain supplies. Thus, in April 1667, the magistrates sent for Hendrick Willemsen, Jacob Teunissen, Reynier Willemsen, and Lourens van der Spiegel to ask that they make a report on "what grain they have in store and how much they ordinarily consume." Bakers such as Cornelius Pluvier worked closely with merchant exporters providing bolted flour and bread, and he was not averse to adulterating his flour to maximize profits from scarce supplies of ingredients. In September 1667, Captain Morisen complained that Pluvier had twice delivered parcels of bread "on the accompt of Mr Steenwyck" for sale in Barbados that was "soo far from marchandable, that it was not fit for men to eat." The magistrates fined Pluvier ten guilders wampum and warned him against producing such poor quality bread in the future "upon forfiture of the Trade of baking." As the plantation owners' demand for New York's flour and bread increased, the authorities tightened up quality controls, replacing Hendrick Willemsen with the Huguenot merchant, and future mayor, Francis Rombouts as municipal bread inspector. By 1670, the increasing supply of grain to the city prompted the baker and grain measurer Cornelius Barentsen to request that Jan van Gelder be appointed as a second official measurer "for the convenience of the Burghers."[26]

Although the bakers worked closely with merchant exporters, the charge against Pluvier suggests that they retained a keen eye for their own fortunes: but for Morisen's careful sampling of the bread delivered on account, Pluvier might have succeeded in selling poor quality product with impunity—risking Steenwyck's reputation as a merchant in Barbados rather than his own as a baker in New York City. On other occasions, bakers invoked their duty to provide bread for the town in order to secure special protection for their interests. In March 1671, following concerns for shortages, Lovelace and his council sent for the bakers to ask "whether they thought it convenient that the corne might be transported from hence to forraigne parts." The bakers declared their fear that if "exportation be permitted," it might not be "possible that the town can be supplyed by them this next summer with bread." However, rather than a total suspension of exports, the bakers recommended that provincial grain supplies be directed through the city and "made into flower or bread" before being dispatched. Careful to identify their interests with the common good, the bakers pointed out that in this fashion the export of grain as flour and bread would provide for the city's needs and ensure that "coopers and other mechanics and other laborers kan in some part gett their livelihood." The proposal limited the freedom of up-river farmers and exporters based outside the city, but it sat well with the governor's desire to direct provincial trade through the city. New York merchants enhanced their control over the grain supply, but only by first accepting a regulatory niche market for city bakers as flour bolters and bread producers. Following the bakers' report, and omitting any reference to bread and bolted flour, the council ordered "no wheat *in grain* to be exported for a year." When the council renewed the order the following year, it acknowledged that the bakers' surplus production was now being exported when it instructed the bread inspector, Christoffel Hooglandt, to make sure that he "view the Floure and Bread that is to bee transported in Caske out of this City, that it bee good and merchantable."[27]

The bakers' role as providers of the local bread supply and a valuable export commodity and their connections to higher authorities provided for their commercial success and rising wealth and status in the town. Tax assessments indicate that the fortunes of leading bakers rapidly improved during the first decade of English rule: in 1655 Andries D'Haas, Hendrick Willemsen, and Joost Teunissen contributed twenty, twenty-five, and twenty-five florins respectively to a means-tested assessment for contributions to public works; nine years later, Hendrick Willemsen was assessed at 250 florins, Reynier Willemsen at 100 florins, and the bakers Clas Jansen and Anthony De Milt at 150, and 100 florins. By 1674, fortunes of 2,000, 5,000, 5,000, and 8,000 florins respectively warranted the inclusion of four bakers among the sixty-two "best and most affluent inhabitants of the city."[28] The bakers' increasing prosperity rested on the municipal support for their privileges and the enforcement of regulations excluding strangers, suspending exports of unprocessed grain, and setting profitable prices for bread sold in the town. This recognition of the bakers' privileges in their role as providers of the public bread supply extended, in principle, to all residential tradesmen who employed their various skills in the interests of the common good. However, the experience of the carters—who also provided a service that was vital for the smooth operation of the city's trade—reveals that the governor and his merchant supporters were prepared to compromise this principle in the service of what they considered the city's greater good.

Carting attracted men from poorer backgrounds and provided additional employment for those experiencing difficulties in other trades. Customers and municipal officers routinely complained of the carters' abusive manner, and subsequent historians have generally concurred with the assessment of the carters as unskilled men whose coarse manners reflected their lowly origins. In the years leading up to the English conquest and shortly thereafter, there is evidence that the carters disdained local regulations, particularly the prohibition against riding on their wagons and driving recklessly through the city's streets. In 1659, the schout Rosevelt Waldron charged Romein Servein "one Sunday riding with his car on the strand" and Thomas Verdon for "sitting on his cart whilst riding along the street." The magistrates refused Verdon's defense that he had only sat on the cart "whilst riding through the mud and until he should have time to drive up the hill" and fined both men six guilders for breaching the regulations and Servein six more for working on the Sabbath. The need for some sort of regulation of the carters' activities was amply demonstrated one day shortly after the conquest, when Jan Smede's horse bolted and killed a child. But riding on carts remained a bone of contention, and the carters proved surly when confronted by public officials on this and other matters. When Sheriff Allard Anthony complained that William Kock's cart horse had kicked his son, the carter's laconic defense scarcely qualified as an apology: "it is his [the horse's] custom and many persons complained against him on that account."[29]

Yet the carters were not all, or even mostly, rough and uncouth laborers. Some were connected to rising local families, and most were no different from the majority of middling residents who pursued a variety of commercial opportunities to provide for their households. Sigismundus Lucas and John Coursen were shoemakers; Thomas Verdon had worked as a registered beer carrier and weigh-house porter in the city before taking up carting.[30] Wolphert Webber ran a small farm and kept a tavern at Fresh Water and carted off and on with his son Arnou in the 1660s and 1680s. Webber senior was father-in-law to the baker and aspiring trader Laurens van der Spiegel, who married his daughter Sarah in April 1661.[31] Like others among the city's middling sort, the carters had families to support, and occupational mobility and residence patterns suggest a struggle to find security. In the years following the conquest, carters such as Thomas Verdon, John Coursen, and Jan Smedes congregated in one of the city's poorer neighborhoods around Smith Street, but such residential clumping also reflected shared occupational interests and anticipated a pattern common in most trades by the turn of eighteenth century. Moreover, the 1677 four-shilling assessment on the value of Smede's house, smallholding, and orchard placed him on a par with respectable householders such as a Captain Lockwood, who lived on Broadway, and the turner Jacob Smyth, who resided at The Walls.[32]

The carters' unsavory historical reputation perhaps tells us as much about enduring negative attitudes toward laborers and menial work as it does about these workers' character and manners. Indeed, the carters' notoriously boorish behavior might provide the best guide we have to how they experienced and viewed their work in postconquest New York City. Carting was physically demanding, difficult, and, given the endless possibilities for ricked backs and jammed fingers, most likely painful work. Carters lifted heavy goods and building materials—barrels of beer, hogsheads of tobacco and liquor, stones and timber—onto and off wagons and guided their loads to and from the dock and around the city's muddy and narrow streets. They also brought essential firewood supplies along the rutted tracks around Fresh Water, which connected the city with the farms and forests to the northwest. The fees and profit margins for carting were modest, and because servants and adolescent boys could guide a horse and wagon through the street the carters' occupation was susceptible to encroachment by outsiders. In addition, the prohibition on riding on wagons lengthened the carters' already tiring workdays by requiring them to walk alongside their wagons when passing through the city.[33] It was in the context of this poorly paid and arduous work that we can understand the carters, ill-mannered outbursts, particularly following a dispute concerning trade privileges and the responsibility for repairing the roads and other public duties within the city.

In March 1666, the magistrates invited the farmers at Fresh Water to nominate two of their neighbors to serve as overseers of roads and fences. The overseers were instructed to ensure that residents maintained the roads and fences adjacent to their property and received a share of any fines levied on those failing to comply. The following year, on the morning of 16 April 1667, the overseers Dirck Sicken and Jan Langestraat charged the carter Jan Smedes with nonpayment of charges relating to road repairs.[34] The magistrates ordered Smedes to pay a fifty-guilder fine and added two more of Fresh Water's residents, Kier Wolterson and Thomas Hall, to the roster of overseers. The Fresh Water farmers' determination to force a duty on the carters to assist in the repair of the road prompted the tradesmen to seek compensatory privileges. When the court reconvened that afternoon, eight carters including Smedes petitioned the magistrates that they "may be confirmed in their actual number and no more, in form of a Guild like the Weighhouse labourers and that all newcomers may be forbid to cart within this City." The court assented to the request and confirmed the eight as privileged city carters, in return for which the men were ordered to be ready to come to the city's assistance when the fire bell rang.[35]

Two months later, the carters invoked their recently secured privilege in a challenge aimed at the overseers for roads and fences. In June, the carters complained that the tanner Stoffel van Laer had hired Kier Wolterson's wagon "by the day to ride his tan from the bush to the scow at the shore and again from the shore to his house," in "direct contravention to the privilege accorded by the W.[orshipful] court." The magistrates accepted the complaint and ordered that, while individuals could continue to cart their own goods, "no one except the appointed carmen shall be privileged to cart any goods within the city, whether for Burghers or merchants." The court also fixed the carters' rate at ten stivers per load and established stiff fines and penalties for overcharging. The carters' petition had clarified the scope of their earlier privilege and denied Wolterson the opportunity to subcontract the use of his wagon. In October, Wolterson and his fellow overseers struck back and charged the carters, "being ten in number," with damaging the road around Fresh Water and recommending a fine of six guilders or the loss of "one day's time in repairing the highway." The carters—whose numbers had increased by two since the April order restricting the trade to eight—countered that because they did not live by Fresh Water, "they are not included in this instruction." Acknowledging the justice of the carters' defense by waiving the fees and fines associated with the overseers' charge, the magistrates nevertheless ordered the carters to assist in "any just and necessary work" needed to repair the road. A few weeks later the court compensated the trade in a noteworthy reversal of long-standing practice and declared that the carters be "set at Liberty to Ride in their Karts in the streets." However the revised privilege was granted on the condition that the carters drove their carts with care and agreed "to Keepe in Repaire the streets & highways," not just around Fresh Water but "Within this Citty."[36]

The court had acknowledged the carters' claims for trade protection, but they had also demonstrated that they were prepared to manipulate the terms of their trade privileges to ensure the availability of men for hire, firefighting, and road repairs. When the magistrates received complaints that "several of the Karrmen of this Citty do not perform their duty in takeing good care of the goods" and "many times use ill and bad Language to the Burghers," they threatened the offenders with dismissal. Thereafter the court enforced rate restrictions and took advantage of the carters' annual application for confirmation of their privileges to add to their duties. In September 1670, the magistrates confirmed the existing ten men as carters, held their rates at ten stivers per load, and added garbage collection to their duties. City carters were required to turn out on Saturday afternoons, remove the garbage set out by householders from the streets, and transport it outside the city. Two years later, although some new faces had appeared, the carters' numbers remained fixed at ten, but their duties were broadened beyond express definition to encompass all "such public work as they are commanded by the magistrates GRATIS." Emphasizing their determination to control the trade, the magistrates appointed Charles Floyd as overseer of the carters—one of three Englishmen carting in the city and new to the trade in the previous two years. When Thomas Fransen—a Dutch carter with ten years in the trade—objected to Floyd's orders, the court warned him to do as he was bid or "he shall not be suffered to be a Carman any Longer in this Towne."[37]

In the first decade after the conquest the city witnessed intermittent tensions but it remained a generally harmonious and far from divided community. Daniel Denton's promotional brochure published after his visit to the city in 1670 may have been more reliable than similar exhortations of colonial life that aimed to increase immigration from the Old World: "For tradesmen there is none but live happily there, as Carpenters, Blacksmiths, Masons, Tailors, Weavers, Shoomakers, Tanners, Brickmakers, and so many other Trades."[38] However, and notwithstanding Denton's optimism, from early on, different groups around the city enjoyed varying levels of respect for their rights and privileges, depending on the extent to which their interests matched the interests of the more powerful governing merchant group: the bakers' fortunes improved while the carters continued to struggle in a difficult line of work. As long as the municipal authorities were dealing with representatives of a single trade with an unsavory reputation, disputes could be managed through the manipulation of privileges and duties and a stern word or two from the magisterial bench. It was only when individual instances of discontent became sufficiently widespread that an accumulation of threats to particularist rights and privileges, whether real or perceived, created a more general sense of alarm regarding the security of individual and community liberties and presented the authorities with a less tractable collective protest.

*   *   *

In 1672, the Third Anglo-Dutch War brought a Dutch invasion force to New York that easily overpowered the English garrison and retook the colony for the States General in Holland. The settlers who had made do with a government based on the Articles of Capitulation were thrilled with the prospect of a return of Dutch rule. City residents greeted the Dutch forces with "demonstrations of joy" and worked with the military commanders to re-construct a provincial and municipal government "conformably to the laws and statutes of our Fatherland." The militia labored with "zeal and industry" to repair the dilapidated defenses of the renamed New Orange in readiness for the anticipated English counterattack. When the English assault failed to materialize and the Dutch forces prepared to quit the city and engage the enemy elsewhere, the burgomasters and schepens begged the commander to leave behind "at least one superior officer and two ships of war," without which they feared that they would be "prey to be destroyed or to be sold as slaves to the English plantations." In the end, it was diplomacy rather than the Eng-lish navy that did for New Orange. In 1674, the Treaty of Westminster estab-lished a lasting Anglo-Dutch peace and returned the colony to the Duke of York. When news of the treaty reached New Orange, residents hurled "curses and execrations" at the deal struck in London, threatening to "fyre the Towne, Pluck downe the ffortifications [and] tear out the Governours throats, who had compelled them to slave soe contrary to their priveledges."[39]

The inhabitants' rage is understandable given their hard work building defenses that would now benefit the enemy they were intended to repel. The implications of the peace treaty for the city's privileges and liberties were even more disturbing: when the colonists welcomed their Dutch liberators, they had broken faith with their earlier loyalty oaths to the duke, and the regranting of the colony to York under the Treaty of Westminster brought the status of the 1664 Articles into question. Some among the duke's advisors suggested expelling the ungrateful colonists from the colony once and for all or forcing them to relocate to Albany and settle the inhospitable frontier. In the end, York settled for the appointment of Edmund Andros as governor— an autocratic and quick-tempered military man who could be relied upon to guard his patron's prerogative and bring the inconstant colonists into line.

Andros introduced reforms intended to secure the duke's revenue and to reform New York's institutions in accordance with English practice.[40] How-ever, the governor's determination to tighten his grip on provincial trade and legal and religious practices sharpened the distinctions between the Eng-lish administration and the predominantly non-English settler group. While some in the city, especially among the leading merchants, could see advantages in Andros's reforms others feared for the security of local rights and privi-leges and Old World ethnic practices. Thus merchants such as Nicholas Bayard and Johannes de Peyster, who had initially refused to take a loyalty oath fol-lowing Andros's arrival, joined Frederick Philipse, Stephen van Cortlandt, and others within English-identified ranks.[41] However, even as the governor affirmed the force of English laws governing married women's commerce, primogeniture inheritance, and the use of weights and measures, Dutch wives conducted business in their own (rather than their husbands') names, Dutch parents bequested equal portions of their estates to male and female progeny, and residents persisted with the use of Dutch cans and ells.[42] Between the ranks of anglicizing Dutch merchants and ordinary Dutch residents whose ethnicity had become a de facto bone of public contention, a third group of settlers from diverse backgrounds also becomes visible. This group included Englishmen such as Benjamin Blagge and William Churcher and French Huguenots such as Johannes de Bruyn and Daniel de Klercke, who became batavianized—marrying Dutch women and joining the Dutch Reformed Church—and found common cause with their neighbours' fears for the security of local rights and privileges and the independence of religious practice.[43]

In the late 1670s, the governor introduced new procedures and fees into the city's Mayor's Court and ordered that "no more papers . . . [were] to be brought in the Dutch language."[44] Although scholarly opinion regarding the impact of this intervention remains divided, there is a broad consensus that, while sophisticated players such as Frederick Philipse and Stephen van Cortlandt continued to use the city's Mayor's Court, artisanal and middling residents were less likely to bring their disputes to court, perhaps preferring to settle their differences through informal arbitration.[45] The reform of earlier legal practice fell hardest on independent female traders, whose commercial ventures and gendered protections had compensated for their subordinate civic status in the burgher community. In the 1670s and 1680s the number of independent female fur traders and tavern keepers in Albany and New York fell precipitously, as did the number of cases in which women appeared as lone litigants. The long-term impact of this marginalization of female traders can be inferred from the growing number of women counted among the criminally accused in the early eighteenth century.[46]

The governor's intervention in the Dutch Church and his appointment of Nicholas van Rensselaer as a minister in Albany led to a schism whose effects figured mightily in events over the next two decades.[47] New York's Reformed ministers had previously welcomed the English authorities' intervention in the enforcement of salary payments, but they balked at the imposition of a minister not ordained by the Classis of Amsterdam. A bitter struggle ensued between Andros and supporters of the "English" Domine and orthodox ministers and leading lay congregants—including Jacob Leisler and Jacob Milbourne. Although Van Rensselaer emerged victorious, Andros's meddling raised fears of the administration's popish tendencies among a small but vocal group of ardent Calvinists who increasingly regarded the Dutch Church as a tool of English rule.

The anglicized Dutch merchant collaborators were more sanguine about Andros's interventions in local affairs, and those who supported the governor during the Van Rensselaer dispute were rewarded with readmission to positions on the provincial council and municipal government.[48] One indication of the rising confidence of this leading merchant group was their acquiescence in the narrowing of the burgher right privilege that was restyled as the English freemanship following Andros's arrival. In 1675, when a shoemaker, a tailor, and a carpenter sought admittance "to the Burgery of this Citty to the end that they may follow their trades and calling," the magistrates took the opportunity to remind "all persons whatsoever that live in this city or that come from other parts to trade or exercise their profession" to apply for "their burgership or freedom." Just as before, freemen were required to "keepe fire and Candle Light and pay Scot and Lot," or maintain a local residence and pay taxes, and the right entitled holders to a share in the monopoly of handicraft and retail trade. However, the exclusive right to import goods to the city was suspended in the freemanship's revised form. This refinement would have likely provoked a protest among leading city merchants had they not already been confident of their controlling influence over the import trade.[49]

Andros's intervention in the city was part of a broader program of imperial reform and adjustments in Anglo-Indian relations and economic regulations intended to secure the empire's strategic and commercial interests. Indeed, the reforms introduced in the 1670s anticipated the integration attempted under the Dominion of New England following the James II's accession to the throne in 1685. The governor renewed English alliances with neighboring anti-French Mohawks and secured their support for the New Englanders fighting Metacom's (King Philip's) War to the north. These negotiations also provided the foundations for the Covenant Chain, which thereafter afforded the Iroquois advantages as brokers between the English and Indians nations.[50] The governor also revised the regulation of provincial commerce. Albany received a closely regulated monopoly of the diminishing fur trade and was required to import its trade goods through New York City. Boats leaving the city to travel upriver had to secure the governor's permission. Beginning in 1676, three years of good harvests lowered the price of winter and summer wheat and enlivened the export trade in grain. Andros responded by prohibiting the bolting of flour and the packing of wheat for export outside the city, directing provincial grain supplies through the port. The governor subsequently extended the regulation to include the slaughtering and packing of beef and pork for retail and export. The favoring of city trade was accompanied by improvements in local infrastructure. In 1676, the Common Council ordered the filling in of the canal, dug twenty years previously, and the erection of a new market house. However, the most ambitious project by far was the construction of a huge stone breakwater designed to accommodate oceangoing vessels with a new pier extending from the city's east side. To pay for the work, Andros and the Common Council levied additional taxes, exacted public labor, and sold vacant land—even dividing "the old grave-yarde or late burying-place in the Broadwaye," which was "layed out in foure lots of twenty-five foot front [for] auction to the highest bidder." There were moments of confrontation between the governor and his merchant supporters, but with the city's staple right and their commercial advantages restored, mercantile fortunes improved and relations were generally cordial.[51]

Tax records and the levies for public works permit some insight into the financial condition of individuals and groups in the two decades following the English takeover. These records suggest that while the fortunes of city artisans and other middling residents stagnated or declined, the estates of leading merchants and selected associates such as bakers improved, in some cases spectacularly. In 1664, a means-tested tax levied to pay for the quartering of English troops revealed that the richest 10 percent of taxpayers, some twenty-five merchants, accounted for just over one-fourth of the city's assessed wealth while the poorest 80 percent shared almost one third. Eleven years later, a similar levy, this time to raise funds for the construction of the breakwater, disclosed that the richest 10 percent of the city's taxpayers—now thirty merchants—had doubled their holding, while the share of the city's middling sort had been halved.[52] Indeed, by 1676, three merchants—Stephen van Cortlandt, Cornelius Steenwyck, and Frederick Philipse—had amassed personal estates of between three and thirteen thousand pounds, amounting to 20 percent of the city's total taxable wealth; all three held influential offices within the provincial and city government and had also joined commercial alliances with the English governors.[53] Further down the social scale, some tradesmen did well, but there were also growing disparities in middling fortunes. For example, in 1664, the tanners Arian and Stoffel van Laer, the hatter Warner Wessels, and glazier Evert Duykinge were all assessed at two florins per week—indicating more or less equal levels of personal wealth. Twelve years later, however, the Van Laers were assessed at the fifty-pound minimum, and Wessels and Duykinge at two hundred pounds. Aggregate figures emphasize the extent to which many in the city were left behind in the commercial expansion of the late 1670s and early 1680s: although the proportion of taxpayers gathered in the lowest four percentiles remained constant at approximately 80 percent, the number in the lowest rank of all doubled to a quarter of all those assessed, while more than half the city's white male population failed to meet the fifty-pound minimum. The sharpening of local inequalities and the precariousness of personal fortunes did not go unnoticed on New York's narrow and winding streets.

Beneficiaries of English rule such as the bakers continued their climb up the social and economic scale. By 1676, Reynier Willemsen and Laurens van der Spiegel—who, along with Van Laer, Wessels, and Duykinge, had been assessed at two florins per week in 1664—had amassed fortunes of five and eight hundred pounds respectively. The bakers' success was tied to the rising grain trade, and the extent to which they had refined their organization of the city's flour and bread trade to meet the demands of exporters was evident from a meeting convened by Andros to consider a proposal from Samuel Griffeth, captain of the *Diamond*. Griffeth had conveyed the governor from England in 1674 and by the following spring he was making ready to return to London. He proposed that his ship be "specially supplied with . . . Bisquit for his voyage," for which he offered to pay fifty-one shillings "in silver or beaver" for each hundred weight, presumably on the duke's account. The meeting requested that four of the bakers "goe and consult about the matter and bring their report to the Mayor at 2 of the clock." When the four returned, they undertook to supply Griffeth with fifteen thousand pounds of ship biscuit at the agreed rate—a gross return of some 340 pounds sterling. The deal demonstrated that the bakers had access to either reliable suppliers or extensive flour reserves and that the collaboration with merchant exporters had stimulated further organization of the baking and flour trade since the struggle for privileges in the 1650s.[54] Over the next decade or so leading bakers confirmed their social position and local influence by marrying into rising merchant families within the Anglo-Dutch elite and securing lesser municipal posts. Jacob de Kay wed Helena van Brugh, daughter of prominent merchant Johannes van Brugh; Hendrick Willemsen's daughter, Griete, married the English merchant John Robinson, whose personal wealth was estimated at twenty-five hundred pounds in the assessment for work on breakwater; Laurens van der Spiegel's daughter, Sarah, married Rip van Dam, an aspiring trader recently arrived from his native Albany, who was destined to play a leading role in the city's future.[55]

The municipal government continued to keep a close eye on the bakers: following complaints about bread shortages in the summer of 1676, the Common Council ordered all those who "Use or Exercise the trade mistery or occupacon of a baker shall bake . . . [and] sell to the inhabitants and strangers both bisket and house bread according to the Lawes of England or not sell anything at all." However, by 1680, local merchants were exporting sixty-thousand bushels of grain each year and gristing an equivalent amount for Newfoundland fisheries and West Indian plantations, resulting in complaints from local residents. In 1681, "several inhabitants" complained of "the scarcity of bread and corne occasioned chiefly by the transportation thereof," and the following year the provincial government once again prohibited the export of unbolted grain, providing a boon to the city's bolting and baking sector.[56] In 1685, the Common Council appointed Anthony De Milt, Teunis de Key, and Reynier Williamson to be supervisors of bread: "That at any time when they shall be thereunto required . . . they will give their judgement (upon the view of any bread baked in this city) wither the same be according to the city or no." Three years later the supervisors were charged with bringing a list of "what bakers are necessary and fitt for employment within this city" and to organize a daily schedule of recognized bakers. Thereafter the bakers were required to "bring in a report of the price and waight and goodness as bread ought to be according to the prices of wheat as it rises and falls."[57] The bakers' success in securing influence within the city's ruling group had ensured that their trade would enjoy a privileged place in the city for decades to come.

The most vociferous critics of Andros's partnership with local Dutch merchants were the English traders who came to New York following the Treaty of Westminster in 1674. The group included Englishmen with New York trade experience, such as John Darvall from Boston and John Lawrence from Long Island, and established Atlantic players, such as Richard and Lewis Morris from Barbados, as well as newcomers such as Robert Livingston from Edinburgh, and George Heathcote from London. What these men lacked in local contacts they made up for with powerful friends in London, to whom they complained of Andros's favoritism of Dutch merchants who offered cheap—and, under the Navigation Acts, illegal—Dutch goods for sale in the colony.[58] This protest resulted in Andros's recall and a tax strike that took advantage of the duke's problems in England to secure a "Charter of Libertyes and Priviledges." In 1683, the charter provided for a short-lived local assembly overseen by Andros's successor, Thomas Dongan. From the little that we know of the assembly debates, it appears to have been dominated by

English merchants whose political affinities lay with conservative Whigs who were opposed the Stuarts' absolutist pretentions but who remained committed to monarchical ideals and a government of appropriately qualified men.[59]

The controversy surrounding Andros's recall and the assembly marked the integration of English merchants into the local oligarchy that administered the city and its trade. Shortly after the assembly adjourned in December 1683, a reconstituted Anglo-Dutch ruling group successfully petitioned Dongan for a new city charter that would divide the city into six wards, each having an elected alderman, constable, and two assessors to serve with the mayor, coroner, sheriff, and clerk appointed by the governor. During the administrative disruption, provincial towns and farmers had ceased bringing their flour to the city for bolting and packing according to the regulations established by Andros. The Anglo-Dutch merchant elite sought confirmation of recently established monopolies, which they counted as one of the city's "ancient Customes, Priviledges and Libertyes" and rights as "the Staple porte of the whole Province where all merchandize was Shipped and unloaden." Dongan acknowledged the merchants' claims for New York as an "Antient City" and "body Politick and Corporate" and confirmed all the "liberties, privileges, franchises, rights, royalties, free Customs Jurisdictions and Immunities which they . . . antiently held." Shortly thereafter, the governor introduced the Bolting Act, which prohibited the "Packing of flower [sic] and makeing bread for Exportation att any Other Place then att the Citty of New Yorke." The Common Council showed their appreciation with a "free and voluntary gift" of three hundred pounds.[60]

It is tempting to characterize Andros, Dongan, and their merchant supporters as unprincipled fortune seekers who rarely missed an opportunity to line their own pockets. However, such an assessment fails to appreciate the peculiar challenges that confronted New York's English governors. They were military men better suited to planning naval landings and expeditions against the French than managing the day-to-day administration of the civic and commercial affairs of a polyglot community. Moreover, the governors were charged with raising rather than consuming the duke's revenue, and all the costs of provincial government had to be met with local taxes. Relying on leading merchants to administer the city and its commerce proved the most effective means to achieve this end: in the two decades following Andros's arrival, shipping and grain export revenues doubled, city land values trebled, and the stock of urban housing grew from around three hundred to nearly one thousand dwellings—almost two-thirds of which were involved in the flour trade. By 1685 New York boasted some eighty locally owned vessels that sheltered behind the new dock, including nine ocean-going ships, two forty-ton ketches, and twenty-seven smaller sloops. Anglo-Dutch city merchants such as Robert Livingston, Frederick Philipse, and Stephen van Cortlandt exacted profitable privileges in return for their successful management of the provincial economy, which also benefited sections of the city's artisanal community such as the bakers.[61] Nevertheless, the rising tide of urban prosperity left other tradesmen behind and excluded a handful of well-to-do merchants, who remained outside the governor's clique. By the mid-1680s, the combination of ethnic tensions, religious divisions, and the stagnation of fortunes led increasing numbers of city residents to suspect that their trade privileges and the common good were being elided by an influential and self-interested minority. Once roused, such suspicions proved difficult to dispel in the uncertain and volatile circumstances of the late seventeenth-century Atlantic world.

* * *

Any scheme of commercial regulation designed to direct surpluses in a particular direction will generate losers as well as winners. In the 1650s, New Amsterdam's campaign for privileges rested on the promotion of residential interests over the ambitions of itinerant fur traders and peddlers. The English conquerors maintained the town's municipal government and nurtured a local Dutch, and subsequently Anglo-Dutch, merchant oligarchy in order to secure the benefits of a similarly well-managed commerce. However, in the 1680s the English administration provoked discontent among two broad and overlapping groups: merchants outside the governor's circle and middling artisans whose fortunes took a downward turn, and orthodox Calvinists who were still smarting from the clash over the Van Rensselaer affair and who rankled under the administration of the catholic Dongan. In 1688, the Glorious Revolution in England and the consequent crisis in imperial authority prompted a revolt of city artisans and farmers mustered in their militia companies. The revolt deposed the royal officials and their merchant cronies in favor of a committee of well-organized Protestant zealots who were committed to rooting out papist conspiracies within the town.[62]

The intensity and rapid spread of antipopery in the late 1680s—and its equally abrupt disappearance following the return of royal rule in 1691—has long presented New York historians with something of a conundrum. While there can be no disputing the importance of doctrinal differences for the cadre of orthodox Calvinists who whipped up fears of a papist conspiracy in the years leading up to the revolt, it is questionable whether a majority of those who joined the rebellion would have been counted, under normal circumstances, among the godly in the city. Although the Dutch Reformed Church enjoyed widespread support among settler families in the two decades following the English conquest, less than half of the city's male population were members, and contemporary commentators noted the heterogeneity of faiths and popular religious indifference more often than they did the adherence to orthodox Calvinist strictures. When Captain William Byrd visited New York in 1685, he observed that the residents "seemed not concerned what religion their neighbour is, or whether he hath any or none"; two years later, Dongan, admittedly a Catholic with a partial view, noted that "Here be not many of the Church of England; a few Roman Catholics, aboundance of Quakers preachers men and women especially; Singing Quakers; Ranting Quakers; Sabbatarians; Anti Sabbatarians; Some Anabaptists; some Jews; in short of all sort of opinions there are some, and the most part, of none at all." And in the 1690s Benjamin Bullivant reported that Dutch New Yorkers generally ignored the Sabbath, "some shelling peas at theyr doors children playing at theyr usuall games in the streets & the taverns filled."[63]

Unsure what to make of the upsurge of antipopery sentiment among such previously inconstant congregants, scholars have tended to stress economic, familial, and ethnic Dutch causes for the revolt or, in one case, to attribute the vehement anti-Catholicism to a paranoid reaction to the collapse of the Stuart dynasty.[64] The latter approach considers the fears of a papist conspiracy to enslave the town as an anxiety-induced and delusional social spasm similar to that which afflicted the villagers of Salem, Massachusetts, and their Essex County neighbors during the witch hunts of 1692.[65] However, if we bear in mind that antipopery (much like beliefs about witches) meant different things to different people, it is possible to combine the city's theological and secular discontents in a more compelling fashion. Seventeenth-century antipopery ranged from complex doctrinal disputes between godly initiates to simple bigotry that ascribed all manner of negative characteristics—from sexual promiscuity and indolence to tyrannical government—to Catholics, in contrast to the positive attributes of those living in Protestant states. Antipopery's capacity to inflame popular sentiment lay in its ability to relate all manner of social strife and deviant behavior to the pope and his papist agents. Once reduced to a unitary and evil force, the cause of general concern—whether it be an overbearing colonial governor or a merchant who set his own interest ahead of the common good—became a legitimate target for resistance in the name of defending the Protestant faith. In this form, as popular prejudice rather than cerebral doctrinal dispute, anti-popery was able to deliver massive support at times of crisis, momentarily thrusting into leadership positions theological zealots whose rigid and uncompromising stance ensured that they remained on the margins of political life at other times.[66]

It is in these terms that we can understand the rapid spread of antipopery sentiment among New York City artisans and others that culminated in charges of papist disaffection being leveled at stalwarts of the Dutch Reformed Church such as the Nicholas Bayard, Stephen van Cortlandt, and even Domine Henricus Selyns. Antipopery flourished in New York City because it provided an explanation for the breakdown in civic harmony, prescribed and legitimated resistance to tyrannical leaders, and held out the prospect of a return to order and prosperity once the corrupting papist influences were eradicated. Of course, fears of a papist conspiracy and even enslavement were not based entirely on misperception and rabble-rousing by zealots: correspondence between French commanders to the north made mention of plans to acquire New York and even schemes to enslave the inhabitants. However, the condemnation of leading anti-Leislerians as crypto-papist conspirators soon after the revolt had an apocryphal ring derived from their origins in prejudice and fear: in July 1689, within weeks of the collapse of royal rule, Peter Godfrey and Henry Carmer reported hearing the Anglican chaplain Alexander Innis "commend several in Canada and Jesuits . . . and [say] that the Catholick Romish Religion was the best and true Religion and that . . . Common people should not be suffered to read scripture nor dispute about religion because they were unlearned." In September, Daniel Clarke testified that when faced with an appeal against a tax that the people protested they could ill-afford, Mayor Van Cortlandt was heard to declare then "let them be sold for it." Whether or not Innis or Van Cortlandt ever uttered the incriminating remarks, the accusations are indications of the extent to which the imperial administration had become associated in the popular mind with tyranny and the designs of papist conspirators and corrupt "grandees."[67]

Two more elements were required before the flickering flame of antipopery would catch in New York: a series of provocations that brought provincial Calvinists into open defiance of the Stuart-appointed administration and the defense of the "one true religion" and the emergence of a constituency of local disaffection broad enough to transform the opposition of a group of Calvinist extremists into a popular revolt—the only full-scale revolt in the colony's history prior to the American Revolution. The former was provided by the accession of pro-Catholic James II; the revocation of the Edict of Nantes, which brought hundreds of Huguenot refugees to the city with tales of the persecution of French Protestants; and the insensitivity of the Catholic governor, Thomas Dongan. The latter developed gradually during the Andros and Dongan administrations and grew out of resentment of the municipal government and encroachments on local rights and privileges that had previously served as guarantees of individual and community liberties. By the late 1680s, city artisans had become convinced that the machinations of the ruling merchant group and their disregard for established practices signaled a conspiracy that "in a most arbitrary way subverted our ancient privileges making us in effect slaves to their will."[68]

*   *   *

The beginning of the end of the Stuart-appointed administration came in the turbulent decade of the 1680s as the *arriviste* merchant leaders began to enjoy their recently acquired fortunes.[69] Tradesmen wandering the city's streets could scarcely fail to notice the development of city lots snapped up by wealthy traders, often at public sales held to raise money to repay debts owed to the purchasers who were also the major municipal creditors. In the early 1680s, Abraham de Peyster, Thomas Coker, and others bought lots along Wall Street on the site of the city's dilapidated defenses; William Pinhorne paid forty pounds for a garden house on lower Broadway. Other New York merchants erected fancy houses and indulged themselves with imported manufactured goods: Cornelius Steenwyck's house on the corner of Bridge and Stone streets boasted a two-story kitchen and cellar, elegant Russian leather chairs with silver lace coverings, a French nutwood cabinet, and imported tapestries and curtains. Anyone peeking through the fine white calico curtains that dressed Francis Rombout's windows would spy Holland cupboards filled with earthenware and porcelain dishes, chairs bedecked with cushions, and a brass hearthstead adorning the iron-back fireplace. In 1686, and shortly before the granting of the charter that ceded all vacant land to the municipal corporation, Dongan scooped up a piece of prime real estate, set in two acres of landscaped grounds, for the construction of a pied à terre. The Common Council repaid the governor's magnanimous grant with a two-hundred-pound gift—monies the councilmen raised by the sale of land along the newly laid out Dock Street and Queen Street to the likes of John West, William Cox, George Heathcote, Ebeneezer Willson, Frederick Philipse, and the Van Cortlandt brothers, who built residences and established the city's first wealthy enclave.[70]

The beautification of sought-after city neighborhoods contrasted with the conditions of many tradesmen, laborers, and free blacks who clustered together on poorer lanes and inhabited hastily constructed shacks on the side of the road heading north out of the city to Fresh Water and beyond.[71] Jasper Danckearts's account of his visit to New York in 1679–80 adds to the impression of a city in which the interests of merchant importers had become paramount. Danckearts and his companion Peter Sluyter were members of a Labadist sect and came to the province in search of a possible location for the settlement of their coreligionists. When the two arrived in New York City in January 1680, they were summoned to meet with Edmund Andros and Mayor Francis Rombouts, who demanded to know their "trade or business, condition and purpose" as was the "custom in Europe." The Labadists challenged the request, arguing that "it is not so in any of the United Provinces . . . except upon frontiers." But Rombouts was adamant and insisted that they declare whether the two men wanted to be considered as citizens, and so pay the freemanship excise, or as strangers and therefore be "forbidden to carry on trade, particularly with the inhabitants, that is, to sell anything to private persons, but you may dispose of it to merchants who sell to private individuals." Electing to be considered strangers, Danckearts and Sluyter traveled upriver to Albany before returning to New York the following May.[72]

Danckearts's journal is particularly valuable for the insights it offers into the perception of Andros's administration and his merchant supporters among middling city artisans with whom Danckearts and Sluyter spent most of their time: men such as the carpenters Gerrit Evertsen van Dun and his aging father-in-law, Jacob Swarts, and Arnoldus de la Grange who "had a small shop, as almost all the people here have, who gain their living by trade, namely in tobacco, liquours, thread and pins, and other knick knacks."[73] The views of these petty traders and artisans are most clear in comments penned toward the end of Danckearts's stay, as he prepared to leave for Boston in June 1680. Noting that his imminent departure presented an opportunity to address topics about which he had previously "thought it was not well to write," Danckearts launched into a scathing account of the administration of Andros and his merchant associates, whom the Labadist considered "if not worse, at least usurers and cheats."[74] His reliance on contacts among the middling sort is especially evident in his discussion of long-term trends in the grain and alcohol trade and local frustrations that predated his arrival in New York.

Prior to the 1664 conquest, Danckearts reported, city dwellers had brewed their own liquor from local grain or bought cheap supplies of strong drink from Boston merchants. However, because "this country yields in abundance everything most essential for life . . . the exports and imports were not so much, and produced few customs or duties, in which profit consists." In addition, local brewers threatened the merchants' margins by bidding up the price of provincial grain supplies and supplying city taverns with liquor. Beginning in 1676, the combination of improved harvests and regulations prohibiting the use of good quality, exportable grain in distilling reduced demand for provincial grain supplies, driving down the price of wheat. Cheaper grain undermined the credit of New York's "poor boors," who used it "in payment for their debts" to merchant creditors. The decision to suspend exports of unbolted grain in 1682 precipitated a 25 percent drop in the price of local product, from four shillings and six pence to three shillings, devastating upriver farmers and debtors with outstanding loans now repayable with devalued commodity money. To add insult to injury, city merchants shipped cheaper New York wheat to the West Indies, where they traded it for Barbadian rum, which they imported back into New York for sale at premium prices.[75]

The perceived manipulation of the grain and alcohol trade and Danckearts's informants' nostalgic longing for the better days when they were free to brew their own drink underlay suspicions concerning the intentions behind other commercial regulations and the disbursement of local taxes.[76] As the Labadist reported, the city had been transformed from a community wherein the residents "have everything at home" to one that depended on merchant importers who "charged so dreadfully dear for what the common man had to buy from them that he could hardly ever pay them off and remained like a child in their debt and consequently their slave." Not surprisingly, Danckearts further noted, "It is considered at New York a great treasure and liberty, not to be indebted to the merchants for any one who is will never be able to pay them." That Danckearts treated his informants' complaints as more than idle grumbles is suggested by his decision to wait until the end of his visit before writing down his observations and by the amendments he made to his plans just before leaving the city. Having asked Frederick Philipse to forward any mail that might arrive following his departure, Danckearts became concerned after hearing that Andros has "people everywhere to spy and listen to everything and carry what they hear to him." Noting his concern that "he [Philipse] and the governor were one," Danckearts feared that "it might be that our letters . . . had been withheld . . . as some persons had absolutely declared and others had half insinuated." There is no way of knowing for sure who tipped Danckearts off, but just before leaving, he released Philipse from the favor and asked Arnoldus de la Grange to forward his mail instead.[77]

Dissatisfaction with the regulatory regime and suspicions concerning the intentions behind municipal orders were also evident in the coopering, shoemaking, and carting trades. As we have seen, city coopers had been closely regulated since the Dutch era: barrel making was a precise craft requiring specialist tools and superlative skills, not least because the need for uniformity in the manufacture of casks was critical to ensuring the fairness of exchanges and quality of exported goods. In 1678, the confirmation of the city's flour-bolting monopoly ensured that provincial grain supplies flowed into the port to be processed and packed in barrels made by city coopers. However, the rising demand for barrels prompted a shortage of materials, increased competition, and a decline in trade standards. Following complaints concerning the quality of barrels, the Common Council ordered the sworn packers and cullers Richard Elliot and Andries Brestede to ensure that "there be a burnt marke sett upon Every Pticular Coopers caske" and to "cull all Such pipe and other Staues as you shall be Called to or have Notice of and see yt [that] they be of good Tymber fitt and Sizeable both for Length and breadth and Thickness."[78] In December 1679, seemingly intending to bolster the common councilmen's concern for manufacturing standards, twenty-one city coopers drew up a "paper of combination" setting rates for work of good quality and establishing a fifty-shilling fine, to be given "for the use of the poor," for those who broke the agreement. The coopers' combination aimed to stabilize conditions within the trade, securing a reasonable reward for their labors while maintaining manufacturing standards. As if to emphasize the orderliness of the proceedings, the coopers secured the signatures of past municipal cullers of staves, viewers and packers of barrels, and the current inspectors, Richard Elliot and Andries Brestede, for their "combination." Little did these tradesmen imagine the offense they caused.[79]

When news of the coopers' agreement reached Andros and the Common Council, their response was swift and severe. The governor convened a special tribunal, comprised of himself, the council, and the mayor, and summoned the signers to account for their dealings. The coopers "acknowledge[d] their subscription, but pretend[ed] no ill intent." The tribunal then sent them out and, after conferring, called each man back for individual questioning. Only a handful of sentences describing this inquiry have survived, but even these scraps suggest a withering encounter in which the coopers sought sanctuary in evasion and dissimulation. Richard Elliot was called in first. When asked to account for his subscription, he "first pretends great Ignorance [and then] saith nothing to the purpose." Evert Wessels was next. He declared that the agreement "was writt at Peter Stevesen['s]"; then came William Waldron, who reported "that Crookes['s] bro[ther]: (a seaman) writte it." When Cornelius Wynante and Marten Clock added "nothing more," the tribunal terminated its investigation and recalled all the offenders to proclaim their collective guilt. Levying the coopers' own punishment for members' infractions against their combination, the court ordered the subscribers to each pay fifty shillings to "the Church for pious uses." Then the magistrates dismissed Elliot and Brestede from their municipal posts, declaring them "incapable of being packers, Cullers etc. hereafter."[80]

A subsequent municipal order requiring coopers, carpenters, and other skilled tradesmen to serve five-year apprenticeships before setting up business for themselves acknowledged that the coopers' concern for standards in the trade was well-founded. However, the reaction of Andros and his advisors to the combination—especially when compared to the more even-handed dialogue between tradesmen and burgomasters in New Amsterdam—indicates the appearance of divisions between the city and its skilled workforce. It is worth pausing to consider the status of some of those the governor and his council of advisors dealt with in such a summary fashion that day. The group included Englishmen such as John Crooke, William Waldron, and the disgraced municipal culler Richard Elliot. There were also men of Dutch and German descent and sons of families who traced their history back to the earliest days of New Amsterdam. Evert Wessels had lived in the city since the 1650s, had served as an arbitrator in court, and was assessed for taxes with property of one hundred pounds in 1676. He had also worked intermittently with Jan Jansen Brestede, who passed on his coopering skills and post as municipal culler to his son, Andries Brestede. Jan Vinsent, Hendryck Kermer, and Marten Clock were also native born sons of preconquest families. In addition to their shared occupational interest, these men were conjoined in other civic contexts as church members and privates in the same militia company. The coopers, in short, were not recent arrivals or anonymous day laborers, but long-term residents and creditable fathers and sons of established families who constituted the core of respectable late seventeenth-century middling society.[81]

In the 1680s, New York's butchers and shoemakers also felt they had reasons for concern. For almost thirty years, sworn butchers had slaughtered cattle brought in from Long Island within the confines of the city's narrow streets and sold the hides to nearby tanners who prepared the skins in malodorous pits. As New York City became more densely populated, such obnoxious practices presented greater difficulties, and, in the summer of 1676, the butchers, tanners, and shoemakers became the focus of a municipal drive to clean up the city. Such was the climate of mistrust, however, that even sensible measures in response to changing urban needs were construed as suspicious. After ordering the butchers and tanners to suspend their activities within the city walls, the Common Council directed the shoemakers and tanners to nominate four of their number from whom it would select two to fill the newly established posts of city tanners.[82] The meeting proposed four ambitious shoemakers—Coenraet Ten Eyck, Jacob Abrahamson, Kaertsen Leursen and Jan Harberdingh—who had recently, and as it transpired fortuitously, purchased land to the north of the city where the authorities now directed the establishment of new tanning pits.[83] The Common Council selected Harberdingh and Abrahamson as tanners and nominated the Englishman Peter Pangborne as a currier; the council then declared that henceforth "Noe Butchers bee Permitted to bee Curriers Shoomakers Or Tanners Nor shall any Tanner bee Either Currier Shoomaker or Butcher."[84]

The new regulations were a reasonable response to the needs of a growing city, or so it seemed. But they were accompanied by restrictions that raised suspicions among anonymous commentators. At a subsequent meeting, the Common Council appointed Ten Eyck and William Boyle, an English shoemaker not nominated at the original meeting, as inspectors and instructed them to "Search all & Euery Tann Pitts & take an accompt of all and Euery Person & Persons of what Hides be in Eurey Tann Pitt." Following this inspection, the councilmen further ordered that "noe Tanner or Shoomaker . . . shall take any Leather Hide or Hides out of the Pitts to sell or worke Vpp" without first presenting it for examination by the inspectors and receiving their permission. This latter measure may have been intended as a quality control check on the standard of leather produced for sale or export. However, when coupled with an increase in the duties on exported hides and reports that Frederick Philipse was shipping large numbers of skins to England, the new regulations prompted rumors that there were plans afoot to curtail tanning in New York and compel residents to buy more expensive imported shoes made from colonial tan exported to England. As Danckearts noted in his journal, although this plan "had not yet gone into effect when we left . . . the intention however is evident."[85]

The group that suffered the severest encroachments on their privileges and liberties in the 1670s and 1680s was the city's carters. Soon after the return of English rule in 1674, the Common Council revoked the carters' privilege of riding on their carts through the city that had been granted seven years earlier. Sigismundo Lucas's refusal to cart a load "for the governor nor nobody else" following the revocation earned him a court appearance and a warning. However, relations between the city and the carters worsened still further following the start of work on the new breakwater in 1676. The carters were crucial to the project, which required an estimated eighteen thousand loads of stone and was finished in just under two years—in time for Jasper Danckearts to sketch it during his visit in December 1679.[86] At the start of the work, the council confirmed the ten carters in their places and held the rates at ten stivers per load except for difficult loads such as lime, wine, and bricks, for which the carters could charge sixpence. The following October, however, the court charged twelve carters with contempt and ordered the "discharge of all and every of the above said persons to be cartmen within this city or liberties thereof until further order." The precise cause of the dispute is unclear, but it likely revolved around the carters' dissatisfaction with the pace of forced work on the dock construction and the jump in their numbers which increased competition for other jobs within the city.[87] Of the twelve carters removed from the roster in October, five either were new to the trade or had returned after an absence. When the dismissed carters apologized and "prayed to be [re]admitted" they were allowed to return to work, but only after agreeing to pay a three-shilling fine or carry fifteen free loads to the dock; the council also took the opportunity to reduce the carters' rates "for the public use of this citty . . . [to] eight stivers a load."[88] Before the end of the dock construction the council had added seven more carters to the roster; some were required to carry thirty loads for the city free of charge, and others had to provide sponsors and ten-pound bonds guaranteeing their good behavior.[89]

The construction of the breakwater doubled the number of carters from ten to twenty, and once the public building project was completed, these twenty or so competed for work at rates that were 20 percent lower than those agreed upon a decade earlier. The increase in competition made the carters' already straitened circumstances even more difficult, and some tried to profit by offering short supplies of firewood to local residents. This tactic prompted the Common Council to appoint official corders to measure out bundles offered for sale.[90] In March 1684, reports of disagreements between the carters, boatmen, and residents regarding the size of a one-shilling bundle of corded firewood resulted in the establishment of a regulated "place of cording." The carters were ordered to deliver their wood to the porters, who were to settle "Any Difference therein that Arise between the buyer and the seller" for a fee of fourpence halfpenny. After this inspection, the carters were instructed to deliver the wood to the purchasers. The inhabitants had to pay an extra sixpence for the corded wood, but the carters were the real losers because they made extra trips to and from the "place of cording" and received a paltry onepence halfpenny in return. The compromise failed, and the authorities received more residents' complaints concerning the "Sale of firewood by the stick being of uncertaine and unequall length, and Bigness, and Often tymes seurall notches put on a stick whereby they are defrauded of their due (itt being only att the pleasure of the boatmen and carmen what they will call one hundred sticks)."[91] The magistrates ordered the carters to comply, and when fifteen men went on strike, they were dismissed for refusing to obey the "lawes and Orders of this city." Determined to break the carters' protest, the Common Council declared that "all and every person or persons within this city have hereby free lyberty and lycence to serue for hyre or wages as Carmen (the said carmen now discharged and slaves excepted)." The authorities refused to readmit the strikers "without first acknowledging their fault" and paying a six-shilling fine, and the carters' ignominious drift back to work was not considered worthy of reporting in the Common Council minutes.[92]

By the mid-1680s, then, the city was divided, and new legal and municipal reforms merely added to the pervading sense of unease that had supplanted the earlier, more harmonious negotiated civic life.[93] The common councilmen kept a watchful eye on movement into and out of the city: at night, the gates were locked from nine o'clock until daylight; innkeepers were required to report the arrival of strangers on pain of a ten-shilling fine. The appointment of a new clerk in the market house increased supervision over what had been relatively relaxed, twice-weekly gatherings of country people and city residents. Periodic prohibitions on the distilling of good quality grain were unpopular, as were new limits on the number of individuals licensed to tap.[94] Following the reorganization of the city into wards, the common councilmen instructed each of the constables to hire eight additional watchmen at twelve pence per night, giving New York City a bigger police force than English towns four times its size. The authorities also stiffened already severe sabbath laws, prohibiting working, card playing, sporting activities, visiting taverns, or congregating in the streets. These orders were accompanied by new regulations for the disciplining of unruly laborers, apprentices, servants, and slaves and the outlawing of "Pockett Pistols" and concealed weapons.[95] Protests against new taxes became increasingly common within and beyond the city's walls: in 1684, the Common Council's decision to raise a further two hundred pounds in taxes to pay for repairs to the wharf and market house provoked resistance from William Graverad, a tax collector, who refused "further to collect the Assessmts" and was dismissed. The following meeting, the Common Council introduced fines for those refusing to meet their municipal duties as directed. Out of the city, James II's decision to require the colonists to register new patents and pay additional quitrents provoked an uprising on Long Island.[96]

In the midst of these heightening urban and provincial tensions, the city's maritime trade suffered a series of body blows leading to a recession that wiped out the finely balanced fortunes of middling and lesser traders. Competition from Pennsylvania for New York's trade in tobacco and flour undermined city exporters, while the renewal of Anglo-French hostilities and a rise in piracy and privateering further sapped confidence in colonial maritime trade.[97] In response to the French threat Dongan launched a military expedition comprising the garrison and 10 percent of the provincial militia against French forces in Canada. The expedition was an abysmal and costly failure. Merchant suppliers such as Robert Livingston realized staggering profits, emptying provincial coffers and leaving Dongan short of the funds needed to pay the allowances promised to the militiamen who had slogged up the Hudson in the icy winter months.[98] In 1687, the governor confessed that "when I come to New York to impose another tax on the people I am afraid they will desert the province." Dongan appealed to London for the construction of more forts, "the people growing every day more numerous [and] they generaly of the turbulent disposition," but to no avail. A few months later he wrote again, this time of his fear that "there are so few of his Maty's natural born subjects, the greater part being Dutch, who if occasion were, I fear would not be very fitt for [militia] service."[99] The city was primed for rebellion.

*   *   *

In August 1688, Edmund Andros returned to the colonies as head of the Dominion of New England that was designed to curtial colonial autonomy especially in the Puritan colonies to the north. Arriving in New York, Andros found the city "very much unhinged by Coll Dongans remis[s]nes[s]: the walls of the Citty and Gates ruind: the fort much out of repair: [and] the inhabitants opressed by heavy taxes." Gathering up the city's vital records, Andros departed for Massachusetts and left Lieutenant Governor Francis Nicholson in charge of the unsettled province. The removal of the imperial administration and city records to Boston increased the disaffection among

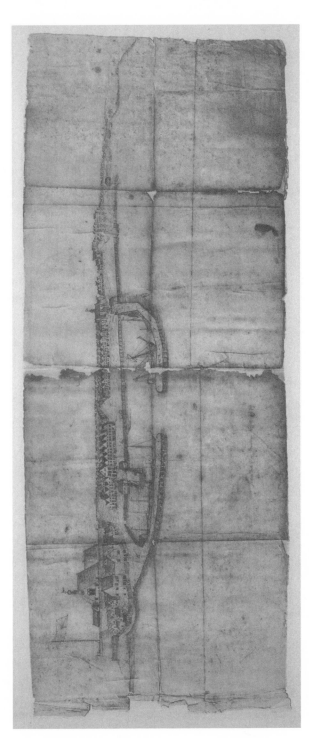

Figure 7. Jasper Danckaerts's sketch showing the great dock in 1679. Courtesy of the New York Public Library. The new dock offered a powerful symbol of emerging urban divisions. In the following decade, some would make their fortunes in the city's expanding maritime trade, while others found their conditions worsening and feared that their liberties were under threat.

sections of the city's merchants, not least because of the diminished oppor-tunities for office seekers based in New York. But the merchants' discon-tented mutterings were nothing compared to the unease that followed the news of James II's flight to France and William of Orange's successful inva-sion of England. Mindful of their allegiance to the defunct Stuart monarch, Nicholson and his counselors tried to keep the news of James's troubles and the likelihood of renewed Anglo-French conflict from the townspeople. How-ever, by 25 April 1689, the council were forced to admit that they "culd not so easily beat it out of the peoples minds, being so possest with jealousyes and feares of being sold [and] betrayed."[100] When reports of the collapse of the Dominion in Boston and Andros's arrest reached New York the follow-ing day, the royal government edged closer toward collapse.

It is fitting that the revolt that defended residential and occupational privileges grew out of the ranks of the militia, the only institution to remain virtually intact from the city's earlier Dutch republican civic order. Although the Articles of Capitulation, agreed to in 1664, and reaffirmed in 1674, guar-anteed that New Yorkers would not be pressed into English military duties, financial constraints and provincial defensive needs continued to require militia service of men aged between sixteen and sixty.[101] By 1689, the city's militia comprised some four hundred men organized in six companies, captained by Jacob Leisler, Charles Lodwick, Abraham de Peyster, Gabriel Minvielle, Nicholas Stuyvesant, and Johannes de Bruyn, all of whom served under the command of Colonel Nicholas Bayard. In addition to the usual undertakings of loyalty to the king and his governor, militia captains also undertook to "apply ourselves earnestly to the welfare and peace of the . . . city and its inhabitants" and committed themselves "to the utmost of our ability [to] defend . . . [the city] against all its enemies."[102] The captaincies of relative political outsiders, such as Leisler and De Bruyn, emphasize the extent to which the militia's chain of command remained distinct from the provincial governing structure. The militia oath was also sworn by the arti-sans and farmers who served as junior officers—lieutenants, sergeants, cor-porals, and ensigns—in each company and by those serving as privates.[103] It was from these lower ranks that the spirit of rebellion emanated in the spring of 1689.

Given a decade or more of civic discontent, the activities of well-orga-nized Calvinist agitators, and the uncertain international situation, it may already have been too late for Nicholson and his council to revive con-fidence in their administration. However, their continued dithering and perceived lackluster commitment to the defense of the city in the final days of May precipitated the final collapse of royal authority. As the lieutenant governor deliberated on the news of Andros's arrest in Boston, rumors that the French "were coming over from Cadaraqua with a thousand men and a great number of Indians" spread through the province. The fear of an imminent French attack and the government's seeming lack of preparedness prompted the mobilization of the Long Island town militias, who marched on the city intent upon freeing the province from the "heavy burdens imposed upon us by an arbitrary power" and defending their "English nations liberties and properties from Popery and Slavery." The march petered out at Jamaica, fourteen miles east of New York City, but the Long Islanders' fury raised questions concerning the loyalties of Stuart appointees and heightened fears for the security of the town.[104]

Nicholson and his council sprang into action, dispatching lookouts to Sandy Hook to watch for French ships, posting additional militia sentries in the fort, and delegating a committee to assess the condition of the city's batteries and palisade and plan repairs. However, in the critical days and weeks that followed, the lieutenant governor and his supporters were unable to throw off the taint of suspicion concerning their loyalties. Early in May, a group of disaffected city merchants (which included Leisler) denounced the customs collector Mathew Plowman as a "notorious papist" and refused to pay further duties unless the funds were put toward the cost of defenses. A few days later a second disagreement regarding the location of the defenses recommended by a subcommittee of the provincial council prompted a petition from the middling militiamen who had been directed to work on the fortifications. The roots of the dispute lay in the dealing in city properties during Dongan's time that had muddled the boundaries between private lots and the public ground containing the defenses. As Stephen van Cortlandt observed, "the common people being very willing to work and fortifye the towne and seeing a difference amongst ourselves . . . did chuse 15 men who presented a petition unsigned and ill penned" calling for the proper fortification of the city.[105] The dispute took nearly three weeks to resolve, and the authorities had no sooner settled the location of the city's defenses than Nicholson gave permission for Jervis Baxter—the Catholic commander of the fort at Albany which stood between the northern French forces and New York City—to withdraw in the face of local antipopery sentiment; shortly thereafter, the lieutenant governor welcomed six Irish soldiers who had fled from Boston following Andros's arrest to the fort in New York, raising fears of an attempt to reinforce the city's papists ranks. Finally, on Thursday, 30 May, sometime between ten and eleven o'clock at night,

Nicholson clashed with a respected militiaman, Hendrick Cuyler, to whom he was later alleged to have declared his intention to fire the town.[106]

News of Nicholson's abuse of Cuyler, who was considered by locals to be "a very civill man," fostered "such a noise and jealousy all that night & especially next morning through the Towne that," as Van Cortlandt reported, "all what wee could say would not satisfy" the commonalty. Rumors circulated that Nicholson had described the townsfolk as a conquered people who "could not so much claim Rights and Privileges as English men . . . but that the Prince might lawfully govern . . . by his own will." Seeming to confirm the inhabitants' suspicions, Nicholson convened a special court the following day and stripped Cuyler of his militia commission. Cuyler's dismissal prompted an angry exchange between Abraham de Peyster (his militia captain) and the lieutenant governor that culminated with De Peyster and his brother, Johannes, joining the steadily forming opposition camp. When efforts to persuade the De Peysters to return failed, leading English settlers John Lawrence, William Merrit, and Gabriel Minvielle denounced "the factiousness and rebelliousness of divers the Inhabitants" and declared that they would "stand up for the good of the Government and the Crowne of England." However, soon after, as Van Cortlandt later wrote to Andros, "we heard the drums beat and the Towne full of noise, and seeing the people rise and run together in armes . . . in ½ hour's time the fort was full of men armed and inraged, no word could be heard but they were sold betrayed and to be murdered, it was time to look for themselves."[107]

There is no way of knowing for sure whether the seizure of the fort was orchestrated by a conspiratorial group of shadowy opposition figures or followed a spontaneous uprising by middling militiamen driven to distraction by a decade of arbitrary government and fears of a papist conspiracy to enslave the town. In the weeks and months that followed the collapse of royal authority, the rebellion became identified with the man who emerged as its leader, Jacob Leisler, and this identification has been accepted by many historians. However, the most recent and exhaustive study of Leisler's role argues that it is unlikely that he masterminded the revolt.[108] Prior to the emergence of Leisler and his Calvinist associates on the committee of safety that assumed authority in the town, the balance of evidence suggests that events were driven on by ordinary militiamen and their junior officers who acted in accordance with Old World precedents and assumed stylized political roles. In retrospect, the submission of the petition protesting the condition of the defenses was an important indication of popular discontent. The petition declared the militiamen's dissatisfaction with Nicholson and implicitly invited Bayard, as their colonel, to meet his sworn obligation to defend the town. The authorities failure to respond as required, and their concern to identify and in all probability chastise the petitioners proved decisive. For it was at that moment that the militiamen feared "the ill intentions of those [leading] persons and their adherents and resolved to make ourselves masters of the fort." When the militia were unable to persuade either Captain Leisler or Colonel Bayard to lead them, the ranks took matters into their own hands and, seizing the fort, issued a declaration proclaiming "that notwithstanding our severall pressures and griviences thes many years under a wicked arbirtarie Power execissed by our Late popish governr," they had been resolved to "Expect with great patience our Redemption from England." But fearing that "delay [would be] Dangerous and so we haue animously Resolved to Live no Longer in Such a Danger but to secure the fort . . . In the Behalf of the Power that now governeth In England."[109]

In these terms, Donna Merwick is surely right to characterize the revolt as a *burgeroorlog,* or townspeople's war, in defense of civic privileges and liberties that echoed the Low Countries' sixteenth-century stand against Spain.[110] Indeed, the New York militia's seizure of the fort scarcely qualifies for the title "rebellion," compared to populist demagoguery whipped up by Nathaniel Bacon in Virginia a decade or so earlier and the crowds of Bostonians that threw Andros and his associates in jail and attacked royal property and persons.[111] But it would not do to overemphasize the orderliness and ethnic Dutch characteristics of New York's revolt, which was prosecuted by a polyglot citizenry who picked out targets for retribution on various occasions. Both sides of the revolt included residents of Dutch descent— although the well-to-do were far more likely to support the anti-Leislerians— and in some cases divided families. Moreover, in the wake of the fort's seizure, the Leislerians organized a multiethnic defense force that drew upon city companies and militias from outlying towns in an effort to bind together the provincial anti-Stuart forces. The introduction of punitive fines for "railing at anyone or make any distinction in Nationality" indicates the determination of the officers and men to counteract ethnic chauvinism.[112] What united this group of rebels—which included veterans of the coopers' and carters' combinations in the preceding decade and of the ill-fated Albany expedition—was less a shared Dutch heritage and more their commitment to the preservation of local rights and privileges that they feared were threatened by an arbitrary and tyrannical government. For all its Old World allusions, this was a New World struggle.

Thus began the train of events that would lead Leisler to the gallows in

April 1691. What began as a dramaturgical act of civil disobedience by the residential militia was transformed into a Calvinist coup d'etat during which Leisler found himself thrust onto the political stage as the unlikeliest of rebel leaders: one of the five wealthiest men in the city connected by marriage or commercial ties to the other four—all of whom stood against him and formed the core of the anti-Leislerian opposition; an orthodox Calvinist with a legalistic and aristocratic mien who disdained popular politics and demagoguery.[113] Had the English relief forces been a few days or weeks away, Leisler might have remained in the background of a short-lived colonial disturbance or shared responsibility with other prominent Calvinist and merchant supporters such as Samuel Edsall, Abraham de Peyster, or Peter Delanoy. However, troubles in England meant that it was eighteen months before Henry Sloughter arrived with a commission to reestablish royal rule in New York. Therein lay the seeds of Leisler's undoing and of his historiographical longevity.

The crisis provoked by the Glorious Revolution in England provided the context within which disparate discontents regarding the encroachment on residential and artisanal privileges and liberties coalesced into a revolt in defense of fundamental rights to liberty and property. In the critical days and weeks that followed the collapse of the Dominion of New England, many feared that the city was imperiled and it became an open question to whom deference was due. It was at this moment that the specter of a papist conspiracy held sway over residents' hearts and minds by alleviating their fears and providing answers to difficult questions. The sources of anxiety were real enough, and Andros's intervention in church affairs, Dongan's appointment of Catholics to influential positions, and the arrival of Huguenot refugees had been more than sufficient to keep the Calvinists' antipopery pots boiling through the 1670s and 1680s.[114] However, the strength of antipopery feeling among artisanal and other middling residents of New York City derived from its ability to provide an explanation for the discontent arising from the subversion of residential and occupational privileges and liberties and to recommend a course of action to restore community harmony. Thus a group of orthodox Calvinists, united by a commitment to doctrinal truths, found themselves at the head of a popular revolt dominated by artisans and farmers whose unity derived from their shared opposition to a rapacious class of "grandees" who had conspired "in a most arbitrary way [and] subverted our ancient privileges making us in effect slaves to their will."

*   *   *

At the close of the revolt, Leisler and his supporters took one more opportunity to demonstrate that theirs was a revolt in defense of particularist
rights and privileges and the established order and in search of the restoration of "Loyall and faithfull persons fit for Government." In January 1691,
Major Richard Ingoldsby arrived in New York with orders to secure the city
ahead of the newly appointed governor Henry Sloughter. The anti-Leislerians
welcomed Ingoldsby and encouraged him to demand the fort's immediate
surrender. But Leisler refused to yield, on the grounds that Ingoldsby's commission as commander of the troops did not afford him the authority to
assume control of the city. The two sides traded letters and denunciations
for two months before clashing in an inconclusive armed encounter. In the
midst of this standoff, on 19 March, Sloughter arrived and, urged on by the
anti-Leislerians, dispatched Lieutenant Ingoldsby to demand the fort's surrender. However, Leisler refused, declaring that he could not be sure whether
or not Sloughter had actually arrived and dispatching Joost Stol to verify
Ingoldsby's claim. When Stol returned and confirmed the governor's arrival,
Leisler denied a second command to yield, on the grounds that it was not
customary to surrender forts at night.[115]

The following morning, a furious Sloughter secured the fort and the city
and arraigned the rebel leaders before a hastily convened Court of Oyer and
Terminur. Leisler and his son-in-law and stalwart lieutenant, Jacob Milbourne,
refused to respond to the indictments, maintaining that as officeholders under
the king's commission they were answerable only to the monarch. However,
the time for appeals to imperial protocols was long past, and a court packed
with anti-Leislerians and English officials convicted Leisler, Milbourne, and
six others of high treason and sentenced them to death. Sloughter subsequently reprieved the lesser defendants, but the anti-Leislerian foes would not
tolerate mercy for Leisler and Milbourne: on 16 May, the rebel leader and his
lieutenant were hanged, drawn, and quartered, and their bodies were buried
in unconsecrated ground near the gallows.[116] Leisler's unwavering commitment to imperial proprieties and military custom, which at the last appears
almost comical to the modern eye, was a fitting coda to the city's revolt, his
gruesome fate a bloody indication of the extent to which his pedantry mis-
read the mood of his opponents and governor.

Chapter 3

"Diverse necessaries and conveniences work found and provided": Trading in a Craft Economy, 1691–1730

The accession of William and Mary delivered a mortal blow to the Stuarts' absolutist ambitions and affirmed the force of parliamentary sovereignty and English liberties over the claims of hereditary succession. Yet few in Parliament tolerated the philosophical abstractions and leveling sentiments of radical Whigs, such as the notion that all Englishmen possessed a natural right to found their political order anew. Parliamentarians justified the Glorious Revolution with claims to ancient rights and customs that gave the 1688 settlement a Janus face: Englishmen looked to an immemorial past and the conservation of ancient liberties to legitimate a novel constitutional monarchy and radical departure in the nation's political life.[1] The security of English rights henceforth depended on the trust vested in the king and Parliament and on the constitution's capacity to check and balance the authority and interests of royalty, nobility, and the commons. Above all it rested on obedience to the rule of law. As the eighteenth-century oracle of Whig political thought, Edward Blackstone, had it, the constitution required "that the community should guard the rights of each individual member, and that . . . each individual should submit to the laws of the community . . . [for] without which submission of all it was impossible that protection be certainly extended to any."[2]

The metropolitan mood and the pressure of a new war with France guided the revision of imperial government in post-Leislerian New York City. In March 1691, Henry Sloughter assumed command of the colony for the crown, assembled an advisory council, and arranged elections for a provincial assembly.[3] The arrival of Benjamin Fletcher the following year signaled a return to gubernatorial graft and cronyism: "To recount all his [Fletcher's] arts of squeezing money both out of the publick and private purses," the

Leislerian Peter Delanoy averred, "would make a volume." The Tory governor took "a particular delight in having presents made to him declaring [that] he looks upon 'em as marks of their esteem of him, and he keeps a catalogue of the persons who show that good manners, as men most worthy of his favor." The men Fletcher favored most were the anglicized Dutch, English, and French anti-Leislerian merchants, such as the Stephen van Cortlandt, Frederick Philipse, Nicholas Bayard, and Lewis Morris, who received lavish grants of millions of acres of land in return for their loyalty and service as counselors and business partners.[4]

Fletcher's administration was disturbed by two controversies that exhibited the themes of conservative restoration and radical departure that informed metropolitan political debates: the campaign to restore the city's flour-bolting monopoly (which the Leislerians had suspended) and the establishment of the Anglican Church in New York. Following the return of royal rule, the municipal government appealed for the restoration of the bolting monopoly in petitions bristling with justifications that drew upon precedents dating back to the Dutch era, city charters and laws issued since the English conquest, and evidence of urban prosperity gleaned from shipping and tax records.[5] The mayor and aldermen identified the city's commercial fortunes with the provincial common good and asserted what they believed to be a customary—and, ergo, morally justifiable and legally enforceable— right to the bolting monopoly. Unfortunately, the defenders of the city's "antient rights and privileges" did not reckon with the lobbying of the manorial landlords who had been favored by Fletcher's largesse and who now secured the governor's support for a campaign against the monopoly. As merchants and crop shippers, Van Cortlandt, Philipse, and others had benefited from urban privileges; as landowners and crop growers, they joined established upriver families such as the Schuylers and Livingstons in denouncing the bolting monopoly as "a grievance and a violation of the people's property."[6] In return for Fletcher's support against the bolting monopoly, the upriver landowners fell into line behind the governor's establishment of the Anglican Church under the 1692 Ministry Act. When sections of the Assembly objected to the governor's plans to appropriate public funds for the construction of an Anglican church, Fletcher denounced his critics, invoking long-standing rights and privileges: "There are none of you but are big with the privileges of Englishmen and Magna Charta which is your right" growled the governor, but "the same law doth provide for the Religion of the Church of England [and] against sabbath breaking and other profanities."[7] The argument over funding rolled on, but when the construction of

Trinity Church commenced in 1697, the charter traced its establishment to the original Ministry Act.

The debates concerning the bolting monopoly and the Ministry Act indicate the extent to which convention required that public encounters continued to be conducted within an idiom informed by an objective conception of rights that championed the authority of past practice and particularistic privileges and liberties. The municipal government's defense of the bolting monopoly rested on the assertion that the satisfactory fulfillment of a function or office imposed an obligation on others to respect whatever action was conducive to the common good. In a similar fashion Fletcher asserted—and a generation later, Blackstone concurred—that the colonists' ancient rights and privileges were balanced by obligations and duties that they respect the constitution, their sovereign, and the law. This emphasis on precedent and the rights, obligations, privileges, and duties of subjects arrayed in their various ranks made intelligible and justified conservative social arrangements derived (or so it was believed) from a morally well-ordered universe structured and lent certainty by the laws of God and nature.[8] By the turn of the eighteenth century, however, this prescriptive language of rights and privileges was becoming increasingly detached from colonial social practice and political realities. The city's defense of its "antient rights and privileges," for example, was entirely reasonable in light of past practice, legal grants, and the provincial prosperity that followed the rise of the port of New York. However, given the shift in the balance of political and commercial power from city to province, it was naïve of the common councilmen to expect a return to pre-1689 arrangements in post-Leislerian New York. Similarly, Fletcher's caustic response to local dissenters—intended as an imperious assertion of the authority of the royal prerogative and the established church—masked the failure of New York's Anglicans to achieve religious hegemony in a city where religious pluralism would mark the boundaries of imperial authority for the remainder of the colonial period.[9]

Further down the social scale, similar discrepancies between the things said about tradesmen and skilled labor and the realities of their daily work and life in the city were also increasingly evident. The Common Council remained committed to the regulation of local commerce and the exclusion of nonregistered tradesmen. In 1692, for example, the Council reinstituted the requirement that tradesmen register for their freemanships with the city or face a fine. When bread shortages prompted customer complaints regarding the quality of local bread available for sale, the council reaffirmed the bakers' duties to provide for the town's bread supply.[10] We shall explore the early eighteenth-century fate of the freemanship and other occupational privileges and liberties in more detail in the next chapter. For now, suffice it to say that even as public talk of local rights accentuated the distinctions between resident artisans and freemen and strangers and itinerants, it masked the growing similarities in their respective conditions and commercial prospects. In particular, the assertion of static civic privileges and duties obscured the increasing fluidity and impermanence of artisanal fortunes and the extent to which economic success and failure depended on variables that lay beyond the purchase of municipal orders, civic conventions, and the prescriptive social hierarchy ideal.

By the late seventeenth century, the opportunity to "earn a beaver" was fading fast, and the rise of the Atlantic trade drew city tradesmen away from exchanges with the Indians and into ramified networks of credit and exchange run out of merchant counting houses. Artisanal fortunes increasingly depended on securing all manner of commodities and consumer goods —on credit and in exchange for the use of their skills—that could be used to satisfy household needs or traded for a little profit. Artisanal reliance on local credit and trade networks for access to raw materials, working capital, and customers required them to combine craft employment with petty trading. In seeming defiance of the singularity of occupational titles that identified individuals as a butcher, a baker, or a carpenter on tax lists and the register of freemen, artisans ran taverns, farmed plots of land, raised livestock, owned and operated sloops, hired out slaves, sought minor municipal office and participated in whatever enterprises and markets promised profits with a minimum of risk. A fortunate few rose from the ranks to enjoy greater prosperity and security than their peers. However, for most, the network of credit and exchange ensured that they remained at work but in debt to financiers who relied on increasingly formal legal proceedings for the administration of debtors and cash collection.

∗ ∗ ∗

In the four decades after Leisler's Rebellion, New York's rise as a leading port sponsored the expansion of the city's dynamic market economy that connected the rural hinterland with the Atlantic trade. New York City's commerce grew in fits and starts: warfare between 1689 and 1697 produced economic stagnation; recessions followed a devastating outbreak of yellow fever in 1702 and the renewal of Anglo-French hostilities in Queen Anne's War; hard times hit shipbuilding and city trade again in the early 1720s.

However, in spite of these difficulties, the port of New York expanded in response to the growth of the European market for West Indian sugar and the consequent increase in the demand of southern and Caribbean plantations for foodstuffs, clothing, and timber to provision their slaves. Prompted by the diminishing supply of furs and the growth of colonial markets, New York merchants and middling traders increasingly focused their energies on exporting wheat, flour, lumber, pork, pig iron, and whale oil; an enterprising few experimented with sugar refineries and the production of naval stores. The introduction of duties on goods shipped from Boston fostered New York City's commercial autonomy and the expansion of its merchant community. An influx of English and French traders augmented second- and third- generation merchant families, enhancing local contacts in London, Amsterdam, and Barbados. Englishmen such as Richard Willet and Caleb Heathcote and French Huguenots such as Stephen Delancey, Benjamin Faneuil, and Elias Boudinot rubbed shoulders with sons of established merchant families including Adolph Philipse, Jacobus van Cortlandt, Isaac de Peyster, and Jeremiah Tothill. These were the men who predominated in provincial trade and politics in the next three decades, relying on networks of family and commercial contacts to run cargoes to and from Europe, the West Indies, West Africa, and beyond to Madagascar and the Indian Ocean.[11]

New York merchant importers supplied the city and expanding rural hinterland and southern plantation markets with a dizzying array of imported household goods.[12] The changing focus of New York's trade is evident in the shipping lists of goods dispatched from and delivered to city merchants and in local traders' stock inventories. Elizabeth Bancker's 1694 inventory of the goods in the city store she ran until well into her seventies made mention of a handful of personal items, trade goods, a stock of wampum, and a male slave named Toby. However, the deceased widow's premises were also a veritable charnel house of skins and pelts: 103 beaver, eighteen otters, nine fishers, eight minks, two cats, eighteen water rats, a wolf, nine grey and one red squirrel. Two decades later, however, the trader Robert Benson's papers listed a female slave named Betty but made no mention of wampum or furs. Instead, Benson's inventory boasted an impressive inventory of colonial products and imported luxury goods: firkins of butter and soap, bushels of salt, thirty-five gallons of molasses, and unquantified amounts of flour, bricks, sugar, and rice; fabrics—including drugget, calico, muslin, garlix, osnaburgh, silks, and thread—buttons, and cotton wool; household goods and furniture comprising seventy pint mugs, three "iron potts," earthenware, tobacco pipes, coffee, frying pans, silver spoons, silver tankards, candlesticks, six chairs, cupboards, and assorted pictures.[13]

The expanding maritime trade attracted settlers who established families in the city, increasing the population from 4,937 in 1698—the year of the first official census—to 8,664 in 1737. By 1701, skilled tradesmen constituted 60 percent of the white male urban population of approximately one thousand and worked at seventy different trades, including fifteen core occupations that employed at least ten local practitioners. These major occupations included carters, tailors, blacksmiths, silversmiths, brickmakers, joiners, carpenters, mariners, coopers, and cordwainers.[14] The city's workforce also employed a growing number of slaves imported from Africa and the plantation colonies in the Chesapeake and West Indies. In 1698 40 percent of city households owned at least one of New York's seven hundred slaves, although the spread of ownership was uneven and slave owners were concentrated in the wealthier areas of town: whereas almost one-half of the households in the well-to-do South Ward owned slaves, only one-fifth of households in the artisan-dominated North and West Wards did so. Slave ownership was also ethnically skewed, with a greater proportion of English and Jewish than Dutch households owning slaves—perhaps indicating the diminishing fortunes of the majority Dutch population relative to other ethnic groups. Slave ownership within the artisan community was concentrated in the more lucrative trades: in 1703, bakers, bolters, brewers, and butchers owned thirty-seven of the sixty-seven male slaves who worked for city tradesmen.[15]

The growth in urban population also reflected natural increase and the arrival of English and French immigrants who congregated in ethnic enclaves around the city. English mariners such as Benjamin Bill, Nicholas Tinmouth, and John Searle challenged for positions in the maritime trades whose fortunes were closely connected to imperial concerns. Others went into victualing and tavern keeping, occupations increasingly attuned to the needs of the city's pluralistic ethnic clientele. For those with a shrewd eye, there were good profits to be made in the smallest of trades. In 1710, Robert Hunter reckoned that a 100 percent advance over London prices on goods was "reckoned cheap . . . in the shops" of New York and as the city grew its inhabitants developed a keen eye for metropolitan fashions. In 1720, Cadwallader Colden complained to his London partners that the latest shipment of goods included a "mixture of your mens stockings . . . [that were] soe very odd that noe body will Look on them." "There was not aboue a pair in a doz of any colour that any body would wear," Colden went on, "and the shopekeeper that bought them was forced to dye them black" before they would sell.[16]

While the Philipses, Van Cortlandts, Delanceys and Schuylers controlled the commanding heights of city commerce, the middling majority of traders forged connections between hinterland and seaboard and coastal settlements. Recent arrivals such as Gabriel Ludlow from Somerset and Walter Thong from Hertfordshire competed with second-generation New Yorkers such as Jacob de Kay—son of the New Amsterdam baker—in urban and regional markets subject only to the limitations of the availability of that most vital of ingredients in a trading economy: credit.[17]

In an economy starved of specie, or coined money, credit was the lifeblood of local trade. The empire operated on the assumption that England was locked in a struggle for military and commercial ascendancy with other European states. New York, no less than the other American colonies, was supposed to enrich the empire by importing English manufactured goods and exporting raw materials and specie. London merchants with interests in the colonial trade provided credit for New York partners and insisted on payment in specie whenever possible. Throughout the late seventeenth and early eighteenth centuries, New Yorkers consistently imported more in goods and credit from England than they exported in colonial products and cash resulting in a balance of payments deficit.[18] In the 1690s, merchants tried to make up the difference with booty earned from financing buccaneers such as Captain Kidd and the gold and silver brought in by their export trade. However, the English campaign against piracy after 1700 and a decline in the price of West Indian sugar exacerbated the drawing off of cash from New York. In 1704, a handful of retail sales held by nonresidents was sufficient to have "drayned not only the City but the whole Province of the Currant Cash." Twenty years later, the province's surveyor general, Cadwallader Colden, lamented that "whatever advantage we have with the West Indies it is hard to make it even with England, so that the money imported from the West Indies seldom remains six months in the Province before it is exported to England." To make matters worse, lobbying by local merchant creditors opposed to issuing paper money ensured that the Assembly emitted a limited amount of bonds and bills of credit in the first half of the eighteenth century.[19]

The specie shortage was compounded by the demise of the two widely used forms of commodity currency: beaver skins—owing to diminishing Indian supplies—and wampum, which was demonetized in 1701. In the absence of a reliable supply of coined money tradesmen depended on money substitutes, barter, and whatever specie or precious metals were available. Shipmasters paid mariners in tobacco; the city's carters subcontracted work to free black drivers for liquor; residents paid artisans (and artisans paid each other) with trade goods ranging from linen to slaves and grain. On other occasions, artisans paid in kind. Thus Jonathon Gleaves, a carpenter, agreed to make a chest of drawers and a table for Jacob Hayes, who promised to supply him with a bed, including curtains, rods, and a valance in return. City tradesmen also worked with a bewildering array of metallic currencies requiring complex calculations concerning values and rates of exchange, for example, gold "pistoles," spanish "pieces" and pieces of eight, doubloons, Dutch guilders and stivers, and even buttons and buckles made from precious metals. These calculations were further complicated by the need to reckon differences between "current money" of New York and exchange rates in disparate localities from East and West New Jersey to the Carolinas, Ireland, and Curaçao. When exchange of any kind proved impossible, artisans secured commodities and much-needed raw materials on account: thus, in the summers of 1697 and 1699, the bricklayer and aspiring building contractor Dirck van der Burgh took delivery of two lots of timber boards and borrowed two pounds fourteen shillings, and fourpence from Stephen van Cortlandt but did not settle the debt until late 1701.[20]

To further compensate for the shortage of specie, New York's merchants and tradesmen relied on financial instruments such as promissory notes, bills of exchange, and bonds. A promissory note was a written promise by one person to pay another a certain sum of money: when Andries Barhyt sued Joost Sooy (a fellow shoemaker) for debt in 1724, he demanded repayment for shoemaker's work and for a note wherein Sooy promised to pay Barhyt three pounds five shillings.[21] A bill of exchange was a written order from one person directing a second to pay a third. Bonds were written agreements witnessed and signed under seal that gave details of a loan or a promise to undertake action and the terms and timing of repayment or penalties in the event of nonperformance.

Under the 1665 Duke's Laws, and in accordance with mercantile custom and English common law, written instruments witnessed and formally executed under seal were assignable and could circulate to third or more parties. A 1684 amendment to local New York law extended assignability to any "other note in writing." This relaxation of the rules doubtless improved the flow of notes and credit and explains why mason John Marsh thought it worthwhile to steal the widow De Hart's "bank books and other bills bonds and credits" when he burgled her house in 1690.[22] But the increase in financial liquidity came at a price: the assignee of an obligation took it subject to all defenses that may be raised against the note at a future time. This greater vulnerability seems to have encouraged lenders to opt for the use of penal

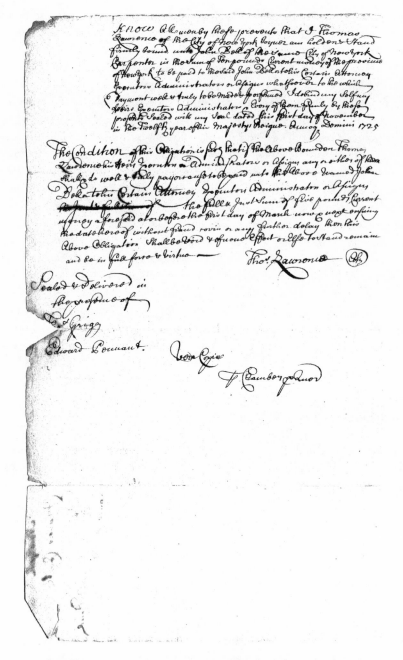

Figure 8. Conditional bond. Under the terms of this bond, drawn up on
1 November 1725, the carpenter Thomas Lawrence agreed to pay for his fellow
carpenter, John Bell, five pounds by the following March or be liable for a debt of
ten pounds.

bonds, which carried hefty penalties of double the amount for failing to repay on time. Penal bonds were also attractive to creditors because they provided for the circumvention of English usury statutes and the maximization of profits from lending in New York's cash-poor economy.[23] This assignment and reassignment of bonds and debtor obligations facilitated the flow of credit and commodities around the city and connected merchants and tradesmen to the wider Atlantic world.[24] By the mid-1720s, the use of paper bills and the problem of wear and tear as they passed from hand to hand prompted legislation that provided for their exchange with new notes issue by a public treasury. As Governor William Burnet reported to the Lords of Trade, "The constant use of these Bills in the Market, and among common people, had destroyed so many of them that it was necessary in common justice to find away to exchange them when they were no longer fit to pass"[25]

In the absence of a sufficient supply of coined money, credit was an unavoidable and defining characteristic of New York City's early eighteenth-century commerce. Merchants eager to secure access to the small amounts of specie that found its way into the hands of city artisans conducted from

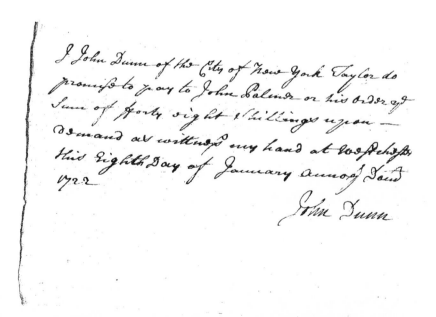

Figure 9. Promissory note. A promissory note provided credit on a less formal basis than a bond. In this note, the New York City tailor John Dunn promises to pay John Palmer forty-eight shillings upon demand following an agreement made in Westchester on 8 January 1722.

one-half to three-fourths of their trade on credit. Artisans relied on easily available credit for household necessaries and working capital; a sample of one hundred agreements involving artisanal borrowers reveals that more than two-thirds were for less than twenty pounds and fewer than 10 percent were for more than fifty pounds. Robert Benson's accounts provide a glimpse of the ties that bound merchants to tradesmen, and to middling dealers further down the financial food chain. When he died in 1716, Benson's estate of 1, 946 pounds compromised three roughly equal parts: 612 pounds for his house and possessions; 665 pounds in bonds and mortgages with merchants such as Isaac Verplanck, Adolph Degrove, and Jacobus Provoost; and 669 pounds in cash and debts on account. Thus two-thirds of Benson's net worth were tied up in property, stock, and written obligations bearing fixed terms and conditions. The remaining third, which was subdivided into 400 pounds "ready money" and 269 pounds in debts on account, constituted Benson's liquid assets: value he could realize at short notice to pay a debt or invest in a profitable opportunity. The schedule of Benson's debtors on account identified 105 men and women whose debts ranged from a few shillings to twenty four-pounds owed by his largest debtor, Abraham de Peyster. What is noteworthy is that eighty of Benson's one hundred or so local debtors owed him less than three pounds, and almost half owed less than twenty shillings. Thus, a substantial amount of Benson's liquid capital in the form of debtor obligations was owed by middling borrowers. Within a decade or so, Benson's merchant peers were advertising their financial services in the city's first newspaper: "Whereas many Persons in this Province have often Occasion to borrow Money at Interest, and others have Sums of Money lying by, which they want to put out," loans were offered upon an application and demonstration of "good Personal Security."[26]

City artisans depended on merchants and each other for the credit, employment, and commodity exchanges that underpinned their individual commercial success or failure. Single and terminal exchanges for cash were far from the norm and punctuated the usual course of commerce underwritten by promises to pay at a future date. The appearance of cash frequently marked the beginning of new trading relationships, a settling of accounts following an agreed term, the death or relocation of a business partner, a difference of opinion, or the winding up of a collaborative project. In time, the provision of credit promoted the development of a network of client-patron financial relations that ramified between resellers and borrowers within and beyond the city. Merchants and artisans at all levels of New York society carried a burden of debt, and to this extent success was more often attained through the effective management of creditor obligations rather than by amassing fortunes unencumbered by liabilities and debts. The ability to defer final payment offered opportunities to those who could balance their commercial ambitions and debts with compensating obligations and cash reserves to meet unforeseen civil suits or circumstances. If New York's artisans had been able to rely on working consistently at their chosen trades, this equilibrium might have been relatively easy to maintain. However, the specie shortage, the need for credit, and the exchange of artisanal skills for commodities meant that such a narrowly defined and limited engagement with the local market was not always possible or even advisable.

*   *   *

The career of John Dunn illustrates the interdependence, diversity, and uncertainty that characterized early eighteenth-century artisanal trade. Dunn identified himself as a tailor when he registered for his freemanship in New York in 1713. He also owned two slaves, Wan and Tom, whom he hired out to work for the shipwrights Samuel Pell and Joseph Latham and used to slaughter the cattle he raised and most likely traded with local butchers. Dunn borrowed from merchants and tradesmen to buy livestock and a boat, the *Mary*, with which he joined the Hudson River carrying trade. Dunn also provided credit for his customers and others who were unable to meet their obligations in court.[27] In November 1721, Dunn filed a complaint against John Deprees to recover a debt of fourteen pounds, five shillings, and twopence owed "for diverse necessaries and conveniences . . . work found and provided." This phrase appears in hundreds of complaints submitted to the Mayor's Court, and there is usually no way of knowing to what it refers. However, Dunn included a copy of the disputed account in his complaint against Deprees, thereby providing a glimpse of their dealings over the preceding three years. The account discloses that Dunn made a "waistcoat and breeches" for Deprees late in 1720 and charged him for the thread, buttons, and tailored clothes. Dunn also supplied Deprees with stockings, hats, and several pairs of shoes that he had acquired from John Dunlap, a local shoemaker. In addition, Dunn provided Deprees with food and lodging, arranged for the care of his horse, ran his errands, ferried his wife and family around the colony, and settled some of his debts — giving Captain Blagg six shillings' worth of rum in December 1718 and lending Deprees a shilling at Hopper's Mill in January 1719. When Deprees was unable to repay the cumulative debt for all these services, he turned to Thomas Slow, a victualler, who endorsed a bailpiece providing Dunn with surety for repayment of the amount owed and damages totaling thirty-eight pounds.[28]

Dunn's dealings with others were no less diverse in subsequent years, and business appeared to pick up: in the early 1720s, Dunn added sheep and hogs to his livestock interests and, in partnership with John Salnave and the glover Roger Groves, he borrowed 108 pounds from Samuel Weaver, a local merchant; a year later, Dunn was considered sufficiently creditworthy to stand bail for Daniel Ponton, with whom he was negotiating the purchase of a house, when Stephen Mileman sued Ponton for slander. On other occasions, the enterprising tailor struggled to meet his obligations and resorted to illicit activities to turn a profit. In 1720, the formidable merchant partnership of Francis Harrison and Gilbert Livingston sued Dunn for a paltry three pounds. In 1721, and notwithstanding his appointment as a tax collector in the North Ward, Dunn was fined for attempting to smuggle a hogshead of molasses into the city. When Dunn's neighbors charged him with keeping a disorderly pig-sty in 1726, he turned to Alexander Moore, a saddler, for bail of ten pounds. The following year, John Hybon sued Dunn for nonpayment of wages and damages relating to unfinished carpentry work. When John Dunn died in 1729, he left the house acquired from Ponton and the family home to his wife and daughter.[29]

John Dunn's career was unique only in the details of his various deal-ings, the diversity of which emphasizes the fluidity of artisanal fortunes, which often depended on exchanges unrelated to the occupation with which an individual might be formally identified on tax lists and other civic regis-ters. The entries in Abraham de Peyster and Elizabeth Schuyler's account books confirm the evidence of court records that artisans took tradeable commodities and household goods on credit and subsequently paid with the use of their skills and small amounts of cash. The pattern of transactions suggests that city trade picked up each spring and summer as sloops and brigs arrived from the southern colonies, the West Indies, and the Atlantic Islands seeking the imported goods brought by European vessels during the winter months. In 1724, De Peyster exchanged commodities for credit and cash with more than sixty people, including the pewterer Francis Basset and the glazier Hendrick van der Spiegel and merchants such as Richard Ash-field and Frederick Philipse.[30] In the spring of 1737, the baker Coenraet Ten Eyck took nine yards of shaloon, a rug, and some red cloth, velvet, and other assorted fabrics worth a total of twenty pounds from Elizabeth Schuyler. In June, Ten Eyck provided Schuyler with a cask of flour, charging for the cask and the nails; on 16 August he delivered a batch of "milk bread" that

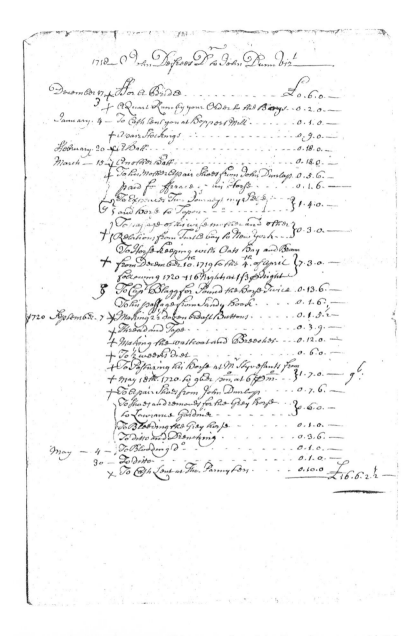

Figure 10. John Dunn's account. This extract from John Dunn's account with John Deprees indicates that the ambitious tailor provided his customer with more services than those of a tailor.

Schuyler traded three days later to William Walton, the shipwright. The following March, Ten Eyck supplied a batch of brown bread, and in September he settled the remainder of the account with cash. In the same summer that Elizabeth Schuyler traded with Ten Eyck, she supplied the gunsmith John Vangelder with some iron, tea, china, sugar, and house cloth. He settled his account over the ensuing twelve months by mending a gun, a key, and some iron implements and paying the balance in cash.[31]

Taking commodities on credit in return for the future employment of skills diversified artisanal interest, drawing them away from craft occupations and into petty trading on their own account. This diversification accounts for why so many artisans appeared in court as litigants in cases dealing with nonpayment for "diverse goods and merchandize" and commodities unconnected with craft interests. Thus, in 1699, the vintner Jeremiah King took delivery of "sundry parcells of hats and other goods" valued at nine pounds twelve shillings from Lancaster Simms; in 1701, Moses Levy sued Edward Cole, another vintner, for nonpayment for fabrics, including ten yards of drugget and a piece of bengal. Alternatively, one finds Ralph Potter, a tailor, securing two hogsheads of molasses from the flour bolter Gerrit van Horne; on another occasion, the same Ralph Potter provided a promissory note guaranteeing future payment of three pounds in return for three barrels of beer from Thomas Noxon, a distiller. In 1710, the cooper Samuel Benson agreed to work aboard Nicholas Evertsen's sloop if Evertsen agreed "to buy merchandizes at Surinam and deliver them to New York." The following year, Johannes Tiebout, a turner, petitioned the court to recover three hundred coco nuts from John Marshall. The New York City blacksmith Nicholas Matthieson undertook metal work for Thomas Day, but he also supplied him with "diverse barrels of beer" valued at twenty pounds. Peter Jay's accounts for the 1720s detail the sale of seventy-two hats (of various sizes and styles) to Cornelius Clopper, a cordwainer-cum-tailor. And in 1724 the blacksmith James Leach and his partner Jonathon Gilbur, both of Elizabethtown, New Jersey, and the victualler Joseph Jackson were so keen to trade that they left the specifics of exchange open: Leach and Gilbur accepted ninety-five casks of molasses from Jackson, who asked for eight pounds and fourteen shillings in "iron, or coine or any other specific at the market price" in return.[32]

In this fashion commodities and trade goods passed from hand to hand before being consumed, sold, or reexported. The pace of the trade was such that it occasionally prompted uncertainties concerning the proper legal title of trade goods. In May 1700, when creditors secured a court order to seize John Righton's goods in place of payment for debt, Bastian DeWitt and Joseph Smith came to court to recover two hats that each claimed as his own.[33] New York artisans operated within uncertain and often narrow margins and had to cut deals that worked in their favor. In 1701, the innkeeper Carter Liersen informed a merchant for whom the mariner Jacob van Tilborough "carried" that his associate had taken four gallons of rum out of a cask and refilled it with sand, "cut of four pieces of cloth each of four yards," and helped himself to some sugar. In 1719, Benjamin D'harriette sued Jeremiah Chardavine, a tailor, for damages, recounting how he had delivered "three yards of good fine black cloath" to be used in the tailoring of "a good and fashionable coat." However, Chardavine did not use all the cloth "but a greate parte thereof out of the coat aforesaid did detaine" and "so inartificially did cut out and make the same coat . . . [that] the body of him the said Benjamin D'harriette it doth not fitt but is so scanty and was by him the said Jeremiah so pieced and patched up that the same coat became of no use."[34] Tradesmen also sought advantages by delaying payment, insisting on the precise terms of a deal or picking out ambiguities in agreements and throwing up obtuse legal challenges. When Thomas Willis sued Peter Adolph, a carpenter, for four pounds owed for twenty bushels of wheat in December 1701, Adolph invoked the terms of the original covenant in which Willis had agreed that payment would only following delivery of the complete order of one hundred bushels.[35]

Once we appreciate the extent to which tradesmen operated within a network of local commodity exchange and credit, rather than in an isolated and male-centered workshop economy, it is easier to understand how well-to-do and working women earned their livings and turned a profit. Women worked as laborers and as butchers and bakers, often following the death of their husbands, or as seamstresses and milliners, occasionally taking on young girls as apprentices, and as petty dealers and traders in their own right.[36] Robert Crannel's accounts for 1720 include the "hire of two women to cleane the city hall." Peter Willemse Roome, a carpenter who built a ferry house for the city, supplied bread for resale to Mary Thompson, giving her a commission of six shillings for every fifty-shillings' worth sold. Wealthy widows and the "better sort" traded on their own account and secured access to the fruits of the local economy by renting houses or land and providing raw materials and investment for artisanal enterprises.[37] The many tradesmen who were also identified as innkeepers likely relied on their families to run the tapping business: artisans such as Thomas Grigg and Johannes van Zandt, who sued others for "diet and drink" and "washing," were likely recovering monies owed for services rendered by wives, children, and household servants or slaves. The grandest example of a woman working in this capacity is Elizabeth Jordain's petition to the Common Council claiming her expenses for organizing the municipal feast attended by 150 of the city's notables to celebrate the arrival of Richard Coote, Earl of Bellomont, as governor of New York in 1698. Jordain's account of thirty-four pounds, four shillings, and threepence included the cost of six geese, ducks, pork, gammon, sausage, butter, capers, anchovies, eggs, cloves, cinnamon, sugar, lamb, pastry, oyster pie, lamb pie, cranberry tart, apple tart, and four days' labor of a male slave and a female slave.[38]

Artisans moved within and between trades and into and out of commercial collaboration in pursuit of opportunities. Partnerships permitted tradesmen to combine their respective skills, sources of credit, or market knowledge and improve their chances in the local economy. In February 1700, the brickmakers John Ackerson and Edmond Heynes agreed to work "in firm partnership joyntly . . . on the one half parte of a certain brick work . . . at the brickyard of Richard Moore." Two men working together could make more bricks than individuals toiling apart, but Ackerson and Heynes's partnership was aimed at more than maximizing their productivity in Richard Moore's yard. The two also agreed to work together on "any other brickwork or brickmaking . . . for one summer season either working together or apart" and "to render and pay unto each other y one moyely or half parte of all such net gaynes and gettings as should be so by them gained and gotten."[39] Occupational titles often depended more on expertise with raw materials or manufacturing processes than identification with a particular craft: hatters were also known as feltmakers, bakers as bolters; carpenters skilled at using lathes worked as turners, shipwrights as joiners; brickmakers turned to bricklaying, mariners to boating, and cordwainers worked as tailors. Changes of title likely reflected the fortunes of tradesmen working in different areas, or the efforts of some to claim expertise in a variety of occupational guises, thereby improving their chances of gainful employment. Innkeeping and the liquor business were also popular sidelines: goldsmiths, hatters, carpenters, mariners, bricklayers, and coopers all appeared in court as vintners and purveyors of food and drink.[40] Mariners, shipmasters, and land-based tradesmen were also frequent investors in merchant enterprise and supplied tradesmen with raw materials and slaves; a few quit the sea for more profitable and probably less physically demanding land-based occupations. The bolter Gerrit van Horne owned slaves and had part share in a brigantine that sailed between New York and the West Indies. In 1706, a group identified only as "several merchants and inhabitants" from New York City loaded the *Rachel* with fifteen hundred pounds' worth of horses, flour, candles, and tobacco for a voyage to Surinam.[41]

The entry of skilled workers into and out of credit arrangements and partnerships and their participation in commodity exchange belies the enduring view of independent colonial artisans at work in workshops dedicated to bespoke craft production. The concentration of commerce in local networks meant that tradesmen were pushed by the search for capital and customers and pulled by the choice of items offered for exchange and the promise of opportunities into accepting a range of commodities. Diversification required tradesmen to act as buyers and sellers and creditors and debtors in a variety of markets, in addition to offering services as practitioners of their respective occupations. City tradesmen worked in a competitive environment in which all kinds of adjustments factored in success or failure: capital, credit, industriousness, good fortune, and skill all played a part. Yet they did so less by increasing the efficiency or quality of an individual's craft work and more by improving his or her position relative to others within a constantly shifting network of credit and exchange. In this process, vintners appeared in court buying and selling fabrics and tailors traded beer, and artisanal commercial strategies seemed more focused on the short-run opportunism characteristic of the economy of a bazaar rather than the steady pace of craft work usually associated with preindustrial colonial towns.[42] Those who worked more or less consistently at skilled occupations did so less because of pride in their craft skills and a commitment to traditional ways of working and more because a favorable family background, municipal privileges, or political and financial patronage ensured access to credit and consumers, affording them advantageous influence in local markets for subcontracted labor and the raw materials and finished goods associated with their trades. To be a successful craftsman in eighteenth-century New York, one had to secure a position of influence within, rather than remain outside, the market.

* * *

Realizing the competitive and frequently hectic nature of urban commerce begs the question of how—aside from an advantageous marriage or a fortuitous investment—one got ahead in early eighteenth-century artisanal trade. During the transition to English rule, favorable municipal regulations and well-placed contacts had allowed a leading group of city bakers to clamber up the commercial and social ladder, and tax data suggests that a middling strata of successful artisans in other occupations also managed to distinguish themselves from their peers. An assessment of 1,005 New York taxables in 1701 revealed that the hundred or so wealthiest taxpayers owned 46 percent of the seaport's taxable assets while the poorest five hundred shared just under 10 percent. This distribution of urban property remained more or less constant until the third quarter of the eighteenth century, when inequalities increased markedly and placed New York on a par with other mainland colonial towns such as Boston. Unsurprisingly, the city's merchants and a handful of spectacularly successful artisans dominated the upper ranks, while tailors, carters, shoemakers, and brickmakers were more likely to be found at the lower end of the taxable scale. However, the middle ranks included representatives from almost every major occupational group in the city: bakers such as Leonard Lewis, John Varvarick, and Coenraet Ten Eyck, Albert Clock the cordwainer, and Arent Blom the block maker paid taxes in the middle and upper brackets and counted wealthy merchants such as Stephen Delancy and Robert Lurting among their neighbors on Queen and Dock streets in the city's prosperous East and Dock Wards.[43]

Municipal regulation of occupations such as baking, butchery, and the liquor trade—which included tavern keepers, brewers, and victuallers—afforded these occupations advantages by mitigating the uncertainties of local commerce. By the early eighteenth century, the setting of bread prices in accordance with the costs of local wheat had become accepted practice. The Common Council revised its assize of bread on a quarterly basis or sooner, when circumstances demanded, and the town crier gave notification of public weights and prices; beginning in 1725, official weights and prices were also posted in the New York Gazette. Excise fees for the slaughter of beasts, the sale of liquor, and the provision of tavern licenses continued to limit access to the butchery and innkeeping trades, in addition to providing the municipal government with revenue. A handful of operators enhanced their position within an already closely regulated local market: in 1705, the butcher Jeremiah Callcutt secured the exclusive right to sell at the Broadway shamble; three years later, George Norton was granted permission to open a new butcher's shop in the market at Burghers Path.[44] A more or less predictable market enabled city butchers to order livestock a year in advance and to slaughter just enough for weekly needs.[45] Commercial success brought local status and influence, and bakers and innkeepers dominated the upper ranks of artisanal taxpayers who were also more likely to hold influential municipal offices.[46] Overall, municipal protection, the refinements of privileged individual positions, and the reliability of local demand for food and drink afforded some a marginal advantage by providing a surer foundation for skilled occupations, on the basis of which they could diversify into other areas.

Beginning in the 1690s, an upsurge in city building projects and municipal protection even benefited the city's long-suffering carters. In the decade following Leisler's Rebellion, city builders enjoyed a boom prompted by several large projects, including extensions and repairs to the fort and docks, a new Dutch Reformed Church on Garden Street, completed in 1694, and (three years later) the construction of Trinity Church. During his visit to the city in 1697, Benjamin Bullivant reported that Governor Fletcher "was . . . pleased to walk the town with me and shew me the multitude of greate and Costly buildings erected since his arrivall about 4 years since to be their Gouvernour." Two years later, Bellomont described New York as the "growingest town in America. Since my coming hither there are not fewer than a 100 fair brick houses built, and a very noble Town-house".[47] To cope with the demand for their services supplying sites with materials, carters subcontracted work to day laborers and free black workers, who were prohibited from owning and operating carts. In a practice that became common in ensuing decades, registered carters agreed on contracts at a daily rate of three shillings and paid half that to white workers or gave a few pennies or a measure of liquor to black laborers. As New York's commerce grew, carters were able to hold their numbers down, realize a better return for their labor, and even secure low-level municipal appointments as corn measurers and overseers of the public drains. During the business downturns in 1718 and 1719, the Common Council raised the regulated rates to cushion the trade. In 1729, the authorities published a detailed schedule of the carters' privileges and duties, enumerating carting weights and rates for more than a hundred commodities, establishing a standard for the dimensions of city carts, and requiring the carters to paint their registration number in red on the vehicle's side.[48] In this fashion, the city authorities and its previously lowest-esteemed tradesmen reached a compromise on the backs of slave laborers and ensured the provision of badly needed transportation services in an era of commercial expansion.

In addition to the handful of trades regulated as providers of essential services, the Common Council continued to lease or "farm" lucrative offices and franchises. Applicants for the opportunities were frequently required to provide substantial bonds to guarantee the corporation's income; once a franchise was awarded, the holder was bound to provide the service and pay the rent, even when what might have seemed a sound commercial opportunity realized a meager return. For its part, the city gained a self-sustaining municipal workforce and the prospect of a regular income from those who leased municipal liberties and privileges.[49] The Council also granted monopolies and special privileges to encourage the production of sought-after commodities and the provision of essential services.[50] In 1699, the baker Jasper Nessepot, in partnership with the mason John Marsh, petitioned "for liberty to build a mill at Kings Bridge." Their petition was granted, on condition that Marsh construct the mill and Nessepot provide for a channel and allow boats to pass through "upon reasonable request." A municipal privilege was intended to protect the holder from the damaging competition of others. Thus, in July 1721, Josiah Quincy applied for a grant of land and "liberty to fish in the river [at Kings Bridge] and that no other person have liberty to sett up or carry on any other fishery contiguous to him or so near to him as may prejudice the fishery." Petitioners routinely justified their requests by appealing to the provision for the common good. Josiah Quincy highlighted the benefits of having a regular supply of fish available daily and undertook to provide the Common Council with an annual donation of a "good dish of fresh fish." Similarly, in 1718, William Dugdale and John Searle petitioned the city for a long, narrow strip of land upon which to construct a ropewalk, arguing that "it will very obviously appear to your worships to tend a publick as well as a private advantage by giving encouragement to the raising of hemp tarr as also by imploying of journeymen and laborers and bringing up of boys."[51]

Holders of municipal franchises and privileges secured a number of advantages—most notably the profits that accrued from municipal recognition, in the form of a prime site for a mill or retail pitch—in a particular occupation. To secure this recognition, applicants presented themselves and their petition in as favorable a light as possible. In their application for the establishment of a ropewalk, Dugdale and Searle made much of their expertise in the trade, gained from an English apprenticeship, although they were more likely better known as a merchant and a mariner and master of the ship *Content* that sailed between New York and the West Indies.[52] In addition, a privilege-enhanced business provided the ideal foundation for more speculative ventures in the wider trading economy. The summer following the setting up of the ropewalk, Dugdale and Searle appeared before the aldermen again, but this time as "reapers," when they registered the apprenticeship of John Galloway, whom they intended to set to work harvesting a crop. In July 1721, they appeared again, this time as merchants whose reputations had been ruined in the Barbadian market by the quality of flour consigned to them by Thomas Kearney in New York.

Perhaps the greatest advantage gained by the possession of a municipal office or franchise was the purchasing power it afforded the holder and, ergo, their increased prominence as a consumer and provider of credit within local networks of exchange. Thus the cooper James Harding's tenure as ferry master provided him with a fee income from ferry charges but also with access to the public purse for the costs of "sweeping the chimneys" and repairs that required "45 days eating and drinking . . . liquor for the workmen" and "for the glazier's diet," which Harding purchased from local suppliers.[53] City officials spending from the municipal purse secured a similar advantage. For example, aldermen regularly purchased the services of carpenters, carters, and laborers on behalf of the city and were remunerated from municipal coffers. On the evidence of rates charged for the hire of their personal slaves, these municipal officials were generally honest and charged the city at a reasonable rate.[54] Their commercial advantage accrued from having access to spending power that enabled them to redress trading imbalances with others by using public funds. Of course, not all trades benefited from municipal regulation or enjoyed access to the city's coffers, but the principle was the same throughout the city: the combination of a reliable line of credit, customers for products or services, and investment in projects that facilitated the subcontracting of work to others provided one of the surest routes to success. This is clear when we consider the fortunes of a bricklayer, a carpenter, and a shipwright in the early eighteenth-century city.

*   *   *

The bricklayer Dirck van der Burgh came to the city from Albany on the eve of Leisler's Rebellion intending to establish himself in trade. Van der Burgh's move followed in the footsteps of his elder brother, Cornelius, who worked as a silversmith and was appointed one of the city's two official keepers of gold and silver weights in 1684. Dirck van der Burgh's membership in the Lutheran Church—and possibly Cornelius's connection with the incumbent city government—prompted him to take the side of the deposed English authorities during the revolt, and he later served on one of juries impanelled to try leading Leislerians.[55] Shortly thereafter, Van der Burgh was rewarded with a municipal sinecure and, appointed to a four-person committee, instructed to "goe round the Town and View each fire place and Chimney that they be Sufficient and Clean Swept"; the following year he was charged with the office of tax collector for the West Ward; the year after that he became the "sole Overseer and Viewer of hearths and chimneys." Before coming to New

York, Dirck van der Burgh had invested a small legacy in parcels of land in partnership with the felter and family friend, Bay Crosevelt. Thereafter, the aspiring bricklayer dedicated himself to property development and parleyed his connections within the Lutheran Church into a piece of the biggest construction contract in late seventeenth-century New York.[56]

In 1695, the leaders of the Anglican community chose a plot of land as the site for the new Trinity Church chartered by Benjamin Fletcher three years earlier. The plot was owned by the Lutherans and, as an elder in the congregation, Dirck van der Burgh assisted in the conveyancing and was subsequently awarded the contract to oversee the bricklaying and masonry work. Van der Burgh arranged for the supply of materials and subcontracted the work to a team of eight to ten masons and their laborers, who worked for more than a year to complete the job. Thereafter, he edged his way up the commercial scale, securing lucrative government contracts and mingling in social ranks far above his familial roots in tavern keeping and itinerant preaching. As the new century dawned, Van der Burgh used his contacts and capital to diversify into land deals. In 1702, along with local notables such as Henry Beekman and the attorney Barne Cosens, he was granted a special license for the purchase of Indian lands in Dutchess County. In 1704, he was made a justice of the peace and, in 1705, he was elected as an alderman and appointed to his most senior post as surveyor of the city. When he died in 1710, Dirck van der Burgh left a house and land in Dutchess County and an estate valued at 350 pounds.[57]

If membership in the Lutheran congregation and the good fortune to emerge on the winning side in post-Leislerian New York worked for Dirck van der Burgh, deep roots in the city's Dutch and Leislerian community did not unduly handicap Teunis Tiebout's prospects as a carpenter. Tiebout's father, Johannes Tiebout, was a native of New York and served in the hand-picked company selected to guard the fort during the 1689 militia revolt. Following the rebellion, Tiebout senior settled down as a wood turner in the city's North Ward but remained active in politics: in 1696, during the Fletcher administration, he was charged with seditious speech and fined fifteen shillings at the Quarter Sessions. The return of the Leislerians to municipal influence following the arrival of Bellomont in 1698 saw Tiebout elected to the Common Council as an assistant from the North Ward. When the common councilmen planned the construction of the new city hall, they included Tiebout on the committee charged with "Calling to their Assistance Such Carpenters & Bricklayers as they Shall think Convenient to make an Estimate of What Stone, Bricks, Lime Timber and Other Materials will be

Necessary." Johannes served intermittent terms as an assistant for the next ten years, and his contacts provided for the employment of his son, Teunis Tiebout, and grandson, Hendrick Tiebout, on municipal repair jobs.[58]

Teunis Tiebout's big break came when he was hired to carry out repairs on city properties and graduated from submitting accounts through third parties to filing his accounts directly with the Common Council. In 1719, the Council directed Alderman Jansen to arrange for the repair of a bridge and an area of the dock, and he used Tiebout for the job. Following completion of the work, Tiebout submitted his accounts to the council through Jansen, claiming twenty pounds and five shillings for carpenter's work, carting expense, and for monies owed to Jacobus van Cortlandt, Martyn Creiger, and Harevell Matyse for nails, boards, blacksmith's work, as well as the cost of "1 negro for 2 days work." Tiebout's choice of suppliers suggests that he had secured a place within an influential group: Van Cortlandt, Crieger, and Matyse were all municipal officers who regularly supplied materials to the city. By the following year, Tiebout submitted his accounts directly to the Common Council and included expenses for nails, timber, locks, hinges, and glass bought from a wider circle of suppliers, as well as wages for himself and family members, including Henry Tiebout, Albartus Tiebout, Johannes Tiebout Jr., and John Tiebout. The jobs were not always pleasant: in 1723, Tiebout undertook the unenviable task of altering the course of the common sewer at the end of Broad Street. However, his work on the city hall, bridge, docks, and ferry stations in Brooklyn and Nassau Island made Tiebout a significant purchaser of local materials and labor. Over time he diversified beyond carpentry—securing the contract to supervise iron work at the ferry house—and subcontracted work to others, including his son Hendrick, who also undertook contracts as an independent contractor and submitted his accounts to the city.[59]

Family background and a reliable source of credit also featured in the success of the Latham brothers, Joseph and John Jr. The brothers were the third generation of Lathams to work as shipwrights in the city, and their dynastic background in trade likely afforded them access to tools and local contacts.[60] The first John Latham had learned his craft in England before coming to New York, were he worked as a master shipwright in the 1690s. Governor Bellomont considered Latham "the Shipwright of best skill and experience here" and, in 1699, dispatched him upriver to conduct a "survey of all the woods" and report back on the viability of producing "Naval Stores and Masts for the Kings ships."[61] John's son, Daniel Latham, trained as shipwright and followed in his father's footsteps, operating a yard on the East

River north of Wall Street until his death in 1719, when his sons took over the family firm.

Shipbuilding was a community enterprise involving not only shipwrights and related trades but also carters, cabinetmakers, tanners, bricklayers, bakers, butchers, and brewers who provisioned the workforce. Investments in materials of twenty or thirty pounds and up indicate that shipbuilding was not for the fainthearted, but the returns for those with access to working capital and customers were proportionate to the risks.[62] Successful ships carpenters, such as Dennis Riche, invested their profits in slaves and the West India trade; the Lathams concentrated their efforts on the purchase and resale of desirable waterfront lots and fine houses in the city.[63] When a group of investors hired Joseph Latham to build a seagoing vessel, the *Dolphin*, in 1729, they provided him with credit of 280 pounds and trade goods —pork, sugar, rum, osnaburgh linen, fine white holland thread, and cambric—worth a further 100 pounds to secure the necessary labor and materials to commence work. Latham's accounts display his disbursements over the ensuing year as the 122-ton vessel took shape in dry dock: timber cutting, carting, the labor of slaves hired from their owners and "Philip and Walter two saylors," liquor and wine to mark "setting y mast" and the eventual launch. Building a vessel to order ensured that Latham avoided the fate of John Parlie, a shipwright from nearby Richmond County, who came to the city sometime in 1717 and "built a ship for sale." When recession hit the city, Parlie was unable to find a buyer or pay the mounting dockage fees for the ship, which he was ultimately forced to sell at a loss to the "absolute ruine of myself and poor family."[64]

Artisans with sufficient credit and customers could expect to work more or less consistently at their trade, supplementing their earnings with petty dealing and speculative ventures. They also benefited from subcontracting work to others and, on the evidence of a sample of carpenters' contracts, the stability of wage rates suggests an established market for subcontracted skilled work. Throughout the early eighteenth century, master craftsmen could be had at six shillings per day, journeymen between three and five shillings, and servants, apprentices, and slaves from two to three shillings.[65] The subcontracting of work by leading figures in different occupations explains why artisans working in similar trades tended to cluster in certain wards around the city. It made sense for mariners and ship's captains to congregate in the Dock Ward close to the City's wharf and in some cases ethno-religious concerns encouraged artisans practicing the same trade to live in close proximity. However, tailors, coopers, carpenters, and brickmakers who catered for local demand and who one might assume would benefit from locating apart from one another gathered together in different wards. Each of these occupational clusters included artisans who enjoyed varying levels of success and local prominence within their trades. In 1701, John Croche, an Englishman, resided in the North Ward but was rated in the sixth tax rank ahead of neighboring Dutch coopers Simon Breadsteade and Peter Burger on Broad Street. Peter Williamse Roome lived in the North Ward, but enjoyed greater success than neighboring English and French carpenters Edward Burling and Francis Cowenhoven on Broadway. The occupational clusters were never absolute, and representatives of different trades could be found across the city. However, the pattern in 1701 remained evident thirty years later, when nine of New York's fifteen major occupational groups remained concentrated in one ward.[66]

Tradesmen such as Van der Burgh, Tiebout, and Latham were the success stories of early eighteenth-century artisanal commerce. They are more likely to appear in the records because their commercial fortunes permitted them to hold public office, enter into lucrative partnerships, and acquire wealth and land that they bequeathed to heirs. Their careers suggest that artisans were most successful when they worked in regulated trades, benefited from contacts from within ethno-religious and kinship circles, and secured influential positions as purchasers and employers in local networks of credit and exchange.[67] Those who lacked these advantages and contacts worked independently or for wages paid by others and pursued whatever occupations or ventures promised the best return.

*   *   *

One could read the occupational mobility, diversification, and constant reckoning of returns that characterized artisanal trade as indicative of an early eighteenth-century spirit of enterprise and commercial ambition. However, considering the financial circumstances of the majority of the city's laboring and middling residents, artisans' energetic commerce is just as likely to indicate an unremitting search for security and a modicum of comfort in an uncertain trading economy. Whichever position one takes, the evidence concerning the material fortunes of the less successful among the middling and lower sort in the early eighteenth-century city is ambiguous. Some studies stress the early appearance of urban indigents and point to the rising cost of poor relief as a percentage of municipal expenditure after 1691. However, others argue that without underestimating the difficult conditions experienced by the needy, the numbers of people seeking relief between 1690 and 1740 remained small in a population that grew from just under five to almost nine thousand.[68] Contemporary testimony seems to confirm the more optimistic view. Thus, in 1699, when Bellomont proposed the construction of a workhouse for the poor, the Assembly "smiled at it, because indeed there is no such thing as a beggar in this town or country." As Bellomont subsequently informed the Lords of Trade, "I believe there is not a richer populace anywhere in the King's dominions than is in this Towne."[69] Moreover, as late as 1734, the churchwarden's accounts listed fewer than fifty adults on permanent relief, and the city lacked a dedicated poorhouse until two years later. The limited numbers of men and women seeking relief— and the comparatively gloomier conditions facing working men and women after 1740, especially in the later eighteenth century—have encouraged scholars to conclude that urban workers fared reasonably well in the four decades after Leisler's Rebellion.[70]

More recent studies qualify this favorable impression and suggest that while the numbers on relief rolls remained small, working families struggled to make ends meet. The limited information we have on the distribution of local wealth points to steadily worsening conditions for middling and laboring folk. The 1701 assessment that identifies the successful from among middling ranks also reveals that the poorest five hundred taxables— or roughly half of the adult white male population—shared just 10 percent of the city's wealth. Thirty years later, the assessments disclose that almost 50 percent of New York's taxable residents were assessed at the lowest rate of ten pounds or less. Assuming that those who paid no taxes in 1730 were no better off than the poorest taxables, it is likely that as many as 60 to 70 percent of working men and women possessed taxable assets of ten pounds or less and lived at or very near a subsistence level by the third decade of the eighteenth century.[71] There are also indications of a growing burden of debt among middling residents, who were more likely to be tenants than homeowners in the city as the eighteenth century progressed. Whenever the city's economic fortunes took a turn for the worse, nervous lenders called in debts, forcing periodic peaks in the number of cases heard in the Mayor's Court and doubling the per capita rate of debt litigation in the five decades following Leisler's Rebellion.[72] With minimal taxable assets, it would have been difficult for an individual, much less a family, to weather financial crises ranging from a failed investment to health care costs or a creditor's inexpected demand for payment.

The evidence of limited municipal relief and difficult conditions faced by middling and laboring residents suggests the need to reconsider early eighteenth-century urban poverty less in terms of absolute numbers of the destitute and more with a less visible but no less worrisome concern for financial insecurity in mind. Prior to 1712 a handful of measures suggest the presence of a small number of paupers who relied on public relief: in February 1700, the Common Council rented a house owned by Abraham de Peyster on the corner of Broad and Princes streets to use as a house of correction and poorhouse; four years later, the city engaged a physician, Dr. Viele, to care for the needy; three years after that, the common councilmen instructed churchwardens to put a badge "upon the Clothes of such poor as are Cloathed by this City With this Mark N;Y in blew or Red Cloath." This latter instruction indicates an attempt to distinguish between real and feigned seekers of charity and an effort to stigmatize the poor as people who had no alternative to public relief. These concerns are confirmed by the increasingly detailed records describing the provision of welfare after 1712–13, in which poor relief officials regularly reviewed recipients' circumstances with a view to moving them off the public charge as soon as was practicably possible: when Thomas Clifton lost his eyesight and was "unable to gain a living for himself and his wife," the wardens recommended that "his wife be provided with a flax wheel and pair of wool cards for their better support"; ten-year-old Richard Blanck from Bristol, who had been abandoned by his uncle, was bound out to John Guest, a saddler and currier, for ten years; Samuell Carratt was to be maintained "until able to work"; Darby Connel was granted eleven shillings on condition that he leave the city.[73]

Public relief, then, provided a safety net for the defenseless and infirm and those who had lost or failed to secure a place within the local network of credit and exchange. Municipal charity was only extended to those who were clearly incapacitated; everyone else was expected to find local means to support themselves, and this invariably meant finding creditors who would provide the financial wherewithal to purchase household necessaries and trade goods with which to enter the speculative economy. Life without credit was all but impossible in the early eighteenth-century city, but finding a place within local networks of borrowing and exchange also meant entering into exploitative relations of dependency. For while some contemporary commentators were struck by the absence of beggars on the streets, others remarked on the difficulties of getting a start in New York, which led many to move on in search of more amenable surroundings. In 1701, Robert Livingston bemoaned the lack of available labor in New York, which he described as "a nursery of people both for the West Indies and the neighboring

Provinces." To the first "they goe being in hast to get rich," and to the second, "young men brought up in husbandry remove in flocks to settle . . . where they are free from taxes, and . . . detacht in time of war."[74] Following a visit to the city two years later, Colonel Robert Quarry wrote to the Lords of Trade concerning the "labourers and tradesmen . . . [who were] quitting the Queen's Government to go and settle in the Propriety Governments on the bare name of great wages." In 1714, Governor Robert Hunter observed that the "one hardship which I have observed ever since I came into this country, which fall chiefly upon the poorer sorts . . . that there being no currency but of silver and bills of credit, the smallest of which is of two shillings, they have not the same relief from the ordinary markets as in other places."[75]

Those who lacked the contacts and advantages of a Tiebout or Latham relied on credit and subcontracted employment to negotiate daily difficulties. For the most part, lenders were pleased to offer financing for those who asked, because rich and poor shared an interest in maintaining the ties of debt dependency that provided for the continuity of trade. Forcing settlements that sundered commercial relationships that had previously benefited both sides served no one's interests in an economy built on speculation and trust. Creditors assumed that debtors would pay in the fullness of time, and debtors expected to be allowed to settle their accounts at an appropriate juncture. Benjamin Kiersted attended to Moses Hart's barbering and periwig needs for more than five years before suing him for repayment in 1725, and many of the complaints filed with the Mayor's Court indicate a similar willingness to extend credit to regular customers and clients for lengthy periods.[76] In November 1725, Hugh Mosier of Brookhaven provided the yeoman Daniel Sexton and his city-based partner William Golding, a bricklayer, with four pounds on a penal bond, which gave them until the following June to repay, after which time they would owe him eight pounds. However, he gave the pair a further two years before finally seeking redress in court in 1728. In other cases creditors placed borrowers on payment plans to spread the burden. When Richard Tinker sold John de Forest a house and land in Princes Street for eighty pounds, the two agreed to repayment in six installments ranging from five to twenty pounds. Similar arrangements were made for much smaller amounts: in 1689, the mason John Marsh provided John Mulliner of Westchester with five pounds, agreeing to accept fifty shillings in two months and the remaining fifty the following year.[77]

Scholars have long been struck by the willingness of residents of early American communities to provide credit for one another and to defer payment until borrowers were ready and able to repay. Some have read these liberal terms as evidence of a sense of neighborliness and social cohesiveness that sprang from early settlers' physical proximity and shared sense of the need to resolve rather than exacerbate disputes in their wilderness communities. For others, it is indicative of the influence of a complex and nuanced cultural framework within which credit was offered: a framework in which a concern for reputation and relations over the longer term frequently took precedence over the impersonal calculation of profit and loss.[78] One can find similar evidence of a willingness to lend and resolve disputes in an amicable fashion in early eighteenth-century New York, where the provision of credit made commercial sense for those who were in a position to lend. As we have seen, New York City traders conducted a substantial amount of their business on account, and without these arrangements trade would have been sluggish and less profitable. Acquiring debtor obligations provided an alternate route for investment in the local economy. Thus, in 1712, the mariners Thomas Hicks and Edward Mackeny relied on the assistance of John Elsworth, a shipwright, to satisfy John Cure, to whom they each owed a few pounds. Elsworth considered the mariners an acceptable risk and assumed responsibility for their debt to Cure, whom he promised to pay once he had received "what is remaining due to the two for their shares of the prizes lately brought into the port by captain Charles Ropinkthman."[79] Debtors also provided a form of insurance and could be assigned to another person in payment of an unanticipated suit. In 1706, Elizabeth Jordain sued Thomas Williams for a debt of nine pounds, and Williams ordered his own debtor Ralph Astin to meet the obligation with money advanced him in a note. Astin in his turn instructed Evert Garner, a mariner, to whom he had assigned the note, to pay Jordain. Garner could not meet the debt and, having no one indebted to him, found himself being sued by Jordain for nonpayment of nine pounds.[80] The off-setting of debtor obligations in this way was also formalized in the use of penal bonds in which a borrower secured funds for a specified period of time on condition of a financial penalty (usually twice the principal sum) that came into play if the lender lost an antagonistic and anticipated civil suit.[81]

Although credit was relatively easy to come by, all manner of adjustments in the local order prompted suits for debt and created ripples in the interconnected and sensitive credit economy. Recently married husbands commenced suits against their new wives' debtors and were liable for whatever obligations their spouses carried forward from earlier marriages or periods as *feme sole*.[82] Merchant financiers came to court to recoup small and large sums provided as working capital for local artisans, and for butchers, bakers, and innkeepers who retailed goods on credit, periodically purging their accounts, bringing multiple suits for debt to court.[83] The death of local merchants and tradesmen required the settlement of estates or trading relationships with multiple partners, which often ended up in court. A breakdown in neighborly relations could also lead to civil suits. In 1700, Vincient Delamontagne sued George Sydenham following the latter's complaint of the damage to his fences by Delamontagne's horse and wagons. No sooner had Delamontagne filed his suit, than Sydenham countersued for money owed to him, and the case rolled on for the remainder of the summer before ending in a victory for Delamontagne in the Supreme Court.[84] Those planning to leave the city, even for a temporary period, might also face calls to settle their affairs before departing: when news of John Guest's plans to send his wife and children to Philadelphia leaked out in 1710, three of his creditors filed suits to recover debts; Peter van Tilburgh's decision to begin working as the post rider between New York and Philadelphia, a job requiring frequent absences from the city, made his creditors similarly skittish.[85]

Assuming that one could meet one's obligations, a suit for debt need not necessarily present a problem. Unfortunately, a badly managed debt might cause a ripple effect resulting in the greatest threat to an individual's commercial future—a run on their credit. Default on even a small amount could lead to more damaging suits. In 1727, the tailor John Munro's failure to repay a promissory note of two pounds to the glover Thomas Dobson resulted in actions by his more significant merchant creditors, Samuel Sharmar, John Scot, and William and Joseph Haynes, for the recovery of more than fifty pounds in outstanding loans and monies owed for the supply of "garlix," "droget," "holland" muslin, one green rug, three double capes, two rose blankets, and two striped blankets.[86] The fear of dissatisfied creditors explains the petition of Daniel Ebbits, a bricklayer, following his work on repairs to the fort in 1704. City contracts could be lucrative, but the municipal government was a notoriously slow payer. Ebbits completed the repairs in May but, although his account for forty-one pounds was "auditted and found Just," he was still waiting for payment in October. The delay placed Ebbits in a difficult position, for having procured "materials for the said work on his promise to pay for them in a very short time," his creditors now threatened to have him "arrested and putt in prison for the Victuals he and his family eat while he was working on the said Garrison." The bricklayer feared that without payment "he shall inevitably Starve in Goale this winter and his family perish for want of Sustenance."[87]

Those who were unable to pay what they owed faced a dismal set of alternatives. Creditors could subject debtors to the ignominious attachment, or seizure and public auction, of their goods and personal property.[88] Such was the fate of John Righton, a hatter, following Gabriel Minvielle's suit for nonpayment of a bond worth 117 pounds and fifteen shillings in January 1700. Righton's inability to pay Minvielle prompted other creditors to come forward and secure an order attaching his goods for resale. Debtors who were suspected of concealing their assets or planning to leave the city could be arrested and imprisoned at their own charge.[89] Although a creditor who elected to imprison a debtor could not subsequently attach their goods, they could have the court order the nonpayer to work off his or her debt. Those pressed into service surrendered their independence and risked mistreatment at the hands of resentful creditors who had to not only accept nonpayment but also assume responsibility for the debtor as servant within their household.[90] If a creditor did not take the option of enforced servitude, the law required the release of a debtor by the following court session. Nonpayers were routinely imprisoned prior to court proceedings, and court delays and complications, especially in cases involving large amounts, meant that an unlucky few spent many weeks in jail following judgments against them.

The final option open to debtors was to seek assistance from others and either settle out of court or find bondsmen to stand surety for the repayment of the debt following a judgment against them. This was the most popular alternative and further indicates the willingness of lenders and debtors to compromise their affairs if they possessed the wherewithal to do so. Almost half of all cases commenced in the Mayor's Court in the early eighteenth-century ended in default, following the failure of one or other of the parties to appear or comply with a court order. The available evidence suggests that most of these disputes were resolved out of court by the parties concerned.[91] Settling out of court enabled a creditor to recoup some or all of what they were owed from debtors who returned to work and trade, albeit in debt to their redeemers. It also saved both sides the inconvenience and expense of lengthy trial proceedings, which, as we shall see in a subsequent chapter, increased steadily following the rise of professional attorneys and the beginnings of a recognized legal bar after 1729. It is in the nature of out-of-court agreements that they remain mostly hidden from view. However, papers accompanying cases that subsequently came to court offer glimpses of the kinds of calculation and speculation involved in efforts to reach agreement. Thus, in the summer of 1700, William Wasset and William Toble, members of the crew of the *Newnham*, relied on the support of their captain, William Norman, to avoid arrest for a debt of seven pounds they owed Elizabeth Jarrat, a local housekeeper. Norman gave Jarrat two pounds and promised the rest when he had completed his business with Rip van Dam, a prominent New York merchant. Faced with two penniless mariners, Jarrat accepted the promise of a captain of a vessel recently arrived from the West Indies who had business in the city. Unfortunately, when the *Newnham* sailed for London the following week, Norman's debt remained unpaid, and Jarrat's five pounds was lost.[92]

In other cases, tradesmen attempted to settle disputes before court proceedings advanced too far. In August 1719, Wynaut Van Zandt sued Johannes Ten Eyck for eight pounds, five shillings, and sixpence and damages of ten pounds "for the work as a turner and blockmaker and . . . for diverse wares and merchandises provided." Ten Eyck came to court and offered "six pounds and five shillings and six pence" and pleaded "discount as to the residue." Merchants and artisans occasionally took advantage of debtors facing difficulties in court and offered relief on stringent terms. On 5 July 1719, John Dunn—the tailor with whom we opened our discussion of artisanal trade—provided the mariner Kenneth Cowan with a penal bond worth nine pounds two shillings that carried a penalty of double the amount if Cowan failed to repay Dunn within one year. When the luckless seaman failed to pay on time, Dunn invoked the conditions of the penal bond and sued him for the full amount on the first available court day.[93] If the judgment went against them, debtors could avoid a spell in jail and the possibility of servitude by securing the support of bondsmen, who provided surety for a debtor's intention to meet the creditor's demands in accordance with the decision of the court. In some cases, family members and tradesmen who worked in similar areas acted as bondsmen for relations and artisanal peers.[94] However, a sample of the bail agreements drawn up in the Mayor's Court reveals that merchants and artisans from different trades, including men and women of limited means, most often provided support.[95]

The motives for this financial munificence and the obligation owed by debtors to their bondsmen are not always entirely clear. It is likely that debtors received assistance from creditors who had an interest in maintaining the solvency of a valued trading partner. However, restricting our notion of interest to a concern for the possible profits from future trade obscures the other benefits that accrued to the providers of bail. Providing bail at public hearings held in the city's busiest tribunal also increased an individual trader's store of symbolic capital by demonstrating their own creditworthiness. Given the importance of trust and reputation in the everyday operation of New York's credit economy and the dangers of a run on one's credit, this could be no mean gain. Bearing in mind that, throughout the eighteenth century New York City traded with a balance of payments deficit, and both merchants and tradesmen suffered from chronic indebtedness, such symbolic displays performed in the theater of the court provided a more reliable guide to individual success and failure than the account books listing trading details whose real and realizable value would not bear close scrutiny.[96] Unfortunately, as New Yorkers would discover in the crippling recession of the 1730s, cultural capital is a poor substitute for specie when it comes to maintaining the levels of investment necessary to drive forward a speculative trading economy.

*   *   *

In the forty years after Leisler's Rebellion, merchants and artisans contributed to the formation of client-patron credit relations that held sway in New York City until the emergence of larger-scale manufacturing in the late eighteenth and early nineteenth centuries. Where once the port town looked inward, endeavoring to protect its finite local commerce from strangers and incomers, by the early eighteenth century, city artisans and others looked outward to farmers from the rural hinterland, plantation customers in the Chesapeake and Caribbean, and financiers and investment houses in London and elsewhere. In the city, the advantages enjoyed by selected trades and hierarchies within occupations meant that some rose to positions of wealth and influence using subcontracting, debtor obligations, and political and family contacts during periods of prosperity. Others relied on credit or worked for wages—negotiating seasonal and subcontracted employment at daily, monthly, and yearly rates—and managed at the margins of city commerce. The increasing use of slave labor permitted white workers to avoid the most arduous and unpleasant work and provided for the economic growth that afforded free white and skilled workers a wage of six shillings a day. During difficult times, creditors provided white workers with a financial safety net until economic stability and prosperity returned.

This picture of earlier eighteenth-century artisanal work is at odds with the image of craft employment memorialized in protests raised in the era of the American Revolution. The dependency on creditors and the labor of wage workers, family members, and slaves undermines later claims regarding the independence and self-reliance of skilled hands as they moved from apprentice to journeyman to master in an all-male workshop economy. Moreover, the dissemination of ordinary abilities and the limited range of materials used in many urban crafts provided for continual movement within and between occupations in a manner that made it difficult to develop a sense of craft pride or occupational tradition. The participation of tradesmen in elaborate trading networks and the scramble of many to keep their financial heads above water also sits uneasily with later celebrations of community ideals and the intimacy of artisanal production in a workshop economy organized according to customary practices and communitarian values. If it is difficult to locate the origins of these claims in everyday life and work, it is easier to do so in the rhetoric of midcentury republican politics, within which the figure of the virtuous and craft-proud artisan first appeared in New York City. Before considering this debut, however, we have to first consider the demise of city artisans' earlier civic rights and privileges and the impact of the rise of slavery on the urban economy and the perception of free and skilled workers.

"The only obstruction at this present is our want of people": The Labor Problem, 1691–1730

In 1705, the governor of New York, Edward Hyde, Lord Cornbury, wrote to the Board of Trade in London regarding the colony's commerce. Routine reports on commercial comings and goings were a key administrative duty for England's colonial governors, and in most respects Cornbury's memorandum was no different from previous communications. The governor described the regional exchange of colonial products for Caribbean commodities and the trade with England: New York exporters exchanged "flower [*sic*] and biskett" for plantation-produced rum and sugar, which they dispatched—along with furs, whale oil, and timber—to England in return for imported cloth, cooking pots, china, nails, medicine, tools, and other household and luxury goods. In this fashion, New York played its part in the mercantilist scheme whereby the colonies provided goods and services for one another and raw materials and markets for metropolitan manufacturers. This maintained the principle "that all these Colloneys . . . are but twigs belonging to the Main Tree [and as such] ought to be Kept entirely dependent upon and subservient to England." Lord Cornbury was devoted to this imperial system, which, he believed deserved the colonists' unqualified allegiance. However, in this particular report, he informed the Board of local efforts to manufacture hemp, cloth, and clay pipes that he feared would "hurt England in a little time." Worse still, there were artisans in New York who declared that "as they are Englishmen, soe they may set up the same manufactures here as people may do in England." This portended dire consequences, for "once they can cloath themselves, not only comfortably but handsomely too, without the help of England," Cornbury feared that "they who are already not fond of submitting to Government would soon think of putting in Execution designs that they had long harbored in their breasts."[1]

Cornbury's memorandum reminds us of the intimate relation between the organization, practice, and perception of skilled work and notions of individual and community rights that lay at the core of eighteenth-century imperial political economy. It also reveals that this relationship was far from immutable, that it was linked to discussions of local conditions and loyalties, and that it was subject to contest and change over time. A half-century or so earlier, the protection and express *encouragement* of local manufactures provided New Amsterdam's skilled workers with a vested interest in the establishment of a prosperous and stable community. The ambitions and ideals that underpinned the settling of this burgher community accorded with contemporary assumptions regarding Dutch republican precedents and the view that a prescriptive local hierarchy was the sine qua non of order and prosperity. By Cornbury's time, however, this earlier civic and regulatory order was on the wane, and artisanal work was considered within an English imperial rather than Dutch republican frame of reference. New York City was transformed from the idealized closed corporate community imagined by its Dutch founders to a more lightly regulated Atlantic entrepôt. In the process, the imposition of political and legal reforms and the increasing reliance on slave labor transformed artisanal working conditions and the perception of their occupations and place in local society.

We will consider the consequences of legal change on artisanal trade and status in the next chapter. This chapter examines the impact of early eighteenth-century labor shortages and political developments on artisanal status and working conditions in the four decades after Leisler's Rebellion. In the 1690s, the leading landowners and merchants drawn from the province's ten counties who served as assemblymen endeavored to secure their interests by competing for the governor's favor.[2] By the turn of the eighteenth century, these provincial politicoes had concluded that it was essential to bolster the status of the provincial assembly as a counter-weight against uncooperative or inept governors. As early as 1703, Colonel Robert Quary, a visiting justice from Pennsylvania's Admiralty Court, observed that New York's "Assembly were for asserting rights which never any of their predecessors ever pretended to." By 1711, Robert Hunter was complaining that "the Assembly . . . claim[s] . . . all the privileges of a House of Commons and stretch[es] . . . them even beyond what they were ever imagined to be."[3] Hunter's protest notwithstanding, the Assembly's influence remained subordinate to that of the governor and his council until the late 1730s and 1740s.[4] Nevertheless, the right of approval over legislative bills and participation in provincial administration afforded the representatives influence that largely eclipsed the municipal government as the talking shop for local affairs. The focus of regional policy contests in the provincial assembly ushered in an era of relative political quiescence in the city, where municipal elections were lackluster affairs that returned the same men to office as aldermen and assistants year after year. Those elected dedicated themselves to the management of city properties and prosperity, and it was in the service of the latter aim that the Common Council presided over a loosening of commercial and civic regulations and the gradual demise of the freemanship and apprenticeship in the city.

New York City wanted for one factor that threatened to obstruct its rise as one of the leading coastal towns in colonial British America: labor. The growth of the city's fleet ensured that city merchants held their own in the competition for export markets with Philadelphia and frequently bettered their Boston-based competitors. But the rise of Atlantic commerce did not translate to more immigrants, and, for all its prosperity, New York failed to attract settlers in the kinds of numbers that went to Philadelphia.[5] The low levels of immigration meant that the labor shortages routinely complained of in neighboring colonies were particularly acute in New York. It was in response to this problem, and following the demise of the Royal Africa Company and the opening up of the Atlantic slave trade, that city residents turned more and more to slave workers. The increasing reliance on slave workers and the diminution of freemanship and other civic privileges did not trouble city artisans while there was credit, skilled employment, and trading opportunities. But the distinction between free and slave labor did introduce subtle alterations to local perceptions of work and workers by supplanting the earlier distinction between residents and strangers and stigmatizing hard labor as menial, slavish, and only fitting for those whose bondage precluded all other possibilities. In time the distinctions between residents and strangers and the salience of particularistic civic and trade privileges yielded to a more stark differentiation between free and enslaved and, ultimately, "white" and "black." When a crippling economic recession and competition for employment with slave workers again raised the question of artisanal rights and status, free white city workers were attracted to a new kind republican politics that championed their qualities as electors and honest and virtuous workingmen. Before considering the beginnings of artisanal republicanism in the economic crisis of the 1730s, however, we first have to examine the demise of residential and occupational privileges and the rise of a new racialized labor market in the early eighteenth-century city.

*   *   *

In the late 1690s, Bellomont's scheme to manufacture naval stores cast a revealing light on the nature of New York's labor problem. Following his arrival, Bellomont was kept busy reviewing his predecessor's accounts and introducing measures to combat piracy. However, in February 1698, the Board of Trade urged its governor to heed other parts of his commission and to apply himself "to the promoting of the production of whatever sort may be most suitable and best brought to perfection in any of your Government."[6] Bellomont first investigated the possibilities for production of ships' masts, pitch, turpentine, and tar in New Hampshire and Massachusetts, noting, disapprovingly, that Fletcher had failed to exploit the region's rich natural resources. But the difficulties of organizing the venture at a distance and the supplementary benefits of upriver locations soon encouraged Bellomont to focus his energies closer to home.

Over the ensuing months, Bellomont devised a scheme to employ soldiers in the production of naval stores on the banks of the Hudson and Mohawk rivers around Albany and Schenectady, where the governor's scouts told him there were "an infinite number of pines" and easy "water carriage [to New York City] which will mightily conduce to their cheapness." The endeavor fulfilled a number of objectives: placing an English military force in the path of any future French attack ensured "the defence of this and all the rest of the Colonies," in addition to "furnishing of his Majesty and the Nation of England with Naval Stores." Because many of the "good pines for masts of ships" were situated on land granted away by Fletcher to his supporters, the project also offered the governor an opportunity to harry his provincial opponents. Given that all the necessary skills could easily be passed on to the soldiers, Bellomont advised the Board that "the only obstruction at this present is our want of people."[7] In fact, what the governor's "great and usefull designe" lacked was not simply "people," but laborers who could be compelled to stick to the grueling task of clearing land and hauling lumber in the province's inhospitable backcountry. Bellomont's failure to locate a viable source of dependent and compellable labor ensured the failure of his scheme for the production of naval stores.

Early on in the proceedings Bellomont realized that he faced two difficulties. In the first place, the city and colony of New York suffered from a chronic shortage of laborers who could be set to hard manual labor. As chapter three discussed, even those who struggled to keep their financial heads above water participated in the trading economy, often relying on creditors eager to invest in debtor obligations. This situation left Bellomont lamenting that there are "not a 100 labouring men possibly to be had in this Province at 3 shills pr day" and that "their labour here is performed mostly by negroes, and the others have trades or keep sloops by which they earn much more than 3 shillings per day."[8] It was this shortage of local labor, and the provincial government's lack of a slave workforce, that encouraged Bellomont to think of employing his garrison. In addition to the strategic advantages gained by keeping a force to the north on the banks of the Hudson, the enlisted men shared two important qualities: they were unable to pursue independent commercial opportunities as were other skilled residents, and they were subject to military discipline—in addition, their basic pay and provisions were so niggardly that the soldiers were likely to respond positively to the offer of additional means of support. As Robert Livingston noted, "a laboring man at New York has 3s [shillings] a day and a soldier's weeks subsistence is but 3s 6d [sixpence] which with ease they consume in two days." Moreover, Livingston went on, given that "Cloathing and drink are double the price of that in England [and] a pot of beer cost 4 ½ d . . . to keep the soldiers from working [for hire] and to [their military] duty is a hardship next to starving."[9]

Unfortunately, Bellomont's second major problem was that by the time he arrived in New York the garrison's morale was at an all-time low, and desertions had left the ranks dangerously depleted. Two years previously, Benjamin Fletcher had reported difficulties recruiting for the ranks because the "Rate of Laborers runs high in this Country, that most necessitous Men rather choose to earn their bread by the Spade than the Sword." He also notified the Lords of Trade regarding the growing problem of desertion and those who were lured away "by the great wages given to labourers in the neighboring Colonies where the people protected and concealed them." Fletcher neglected to mention, however, the various scams that he and his officers had introduced to redirect military expenditures to their own pockets and that had likely exacerbated the rate of desertions. Following his investigation of the accounts, Bellomont reported that Fletcher had shaved a penny a day off the enlisted men's miserable subsistence, returned full muster rolls to London "when there hath not been half the number effective men," and pocketed additional monies raised locally to pay for the garrison's needs; in one noteworthy sting that drew the garrison into a controversy surrounding the 1701 municipal elections, Fletcher demanded payment before granting permission to soldiers who sought "liberty to exercise their Trades" in the city. As a consequence of these and other dodges, one of the companies of approximately one hundred men had been reduced to thirty-five, and the garrison was so weakened that Bellomont feared that "should a war breake out our fronteers not being guarded this province will be in great danger."[10]

The governor knew he needed fresh hands and incentives to launch his plan to produce naval stores, and he worked hard to convince the Lords of Trade of the value of his scheme. The project's success depended on the payment of a four-penny supplement to new recruits who agreed to undertake the work. Pegging his labor costs to the commodity prices published in a recent copy of the "Merchants' Weekly Remembrance," Bellomont calculated that at this price military labor would not only "furnish the King with these stores in a sufficient quantity, but also at as cheap a rate." In May 1698, he wrote to the Board of Trade proposing the recruitment of four additional companies and the "keeping [of] a 1000 men in the King's pay in this Province, to manufacture the severall species of stores."[11] Unfortunately, Bellomont had not counted on the parsimony of the Lords of Trade, who rejected his applications for additional funding and troops. The consultation dragged on for two years, but at the outset the Board was opposed to an increase in spending and suggested that Bellomont reward his soldier workers by "allow[ing] them a proportion out of the produce of their own labour."[12] In October 1699, and in anticipation of the repossession of lands granted by Fletcher, Bellomont tried a different tack, proposing the investment of a portion of the pay for soldiers who worked on the naval stores project and the granting of a lump sum and forty acres of land at the end of their seven-year terms.[13] However, the Lords were unmoved, and by December 1700, Bellomont declared himself "quite tyr'd out with taking pains for the publick, without any profit to myselfe" and "in a place where my predecessor Fletcher got a great deal of money." In April 1701, the Lords wrote to Bellomont recommending, once again, that he find a way to resource his scheme locally instead of looking to London for support. But the governor had died before the letter arrived, and the plan for naval stores died with him—at least for the time being.[14]

One can speculate that even if Bellomont had been able to survive the rigors of office and convince the Board of Trade to fund his scheme, it was still unlikely that it would have succeeded. In addition to the Lords' stinginess, progress on the naval stores scheme was delayed by the glacial-like passage through Parliament of legislation to deny Fletcher's lavish land grants.[15] The governor and his scheme were also handicapped by the corruption of his own appointees to the project, who took the best timber samples for themselves and sent poorer quality product to London. However, even without all of these difficulties, it is likely that Bellomont's greatest difficulty would have remained his want of labor. For even with a four-penny supplement, his proposal only offered members of the garrison work at a shilling a day, well below the three-shilling rate commanded by local free laborers in New York. Moreover, although the soldiers in New York City needed to supplement their allowances, they were choosy about the work they would accept. As Robert Livingston observed, allowing soldiers to "work hiring their duty spoils there discipline and manners" because "tho' they are willing to work when they please and can have liberty, yet [they] will not like to be compelled thereunto, especially for one third part of the wages which a Negroe slave receives every day in New York for splitting of fire wood and carrying the hodd."[16] When Livingston revived Bellomont's scheme some twenty years later, he found that forty or so families of German Palatinate refugees were no more amenable to hard and compelled labor than were English soldiers. Abandoning their allotted land and tasks, the Palatinates squatted on more fertile ground near Albany, from whence they launched a decade-long protest in defense of their rights and liberty as freeborn subjects.[17]

The refusal of soldiers and the Palatinates to undertake hard labor emphasizes the extent to which such work had already become identified with the conditions of those trapped by involuntary servitude and the determination of freeborn Europeans, even refugees, to refuse the work imposed on slave workers. Bellomont had noted this predisposition when he considered other labor alternatives early on in his planning for the project. At one point, the governor had looked into the possibilities of using Native American workers. However, he quickly discounted this option, arguing that "the Indians are so proud and lazy that 'tis to be feared they will not be prevail'd with to work."[18] On another occasion, he proposed the use of a slave labor force, which offered even greater savings than military labor. Writing to the Board of Trade in April 1699, Bellomont suggested that rather than employing the garrison "(for I confess I grudge our parting with people out of England) I should advise the sending for negroes to Guinea," who could be had for "£10 a piece New Yorke mony [and] cloath and feed 'em very comfortably for 9 d a piece p day . . . 3d p day lesse than I require for the soldiers."[19] However, the Lords of Trade, who had balked at a four-penny daily supplement, were unlikely to be swayed by Bellomont's proposal, which would have required a substantial initial investment in a slave workforce. What is also noteworthy about this unsuccessful proposal, however, is Bellomont's parenthetic confession to a preference for African rather than soldier laborers. Although both soldiers and slaves endured harsh discipline and meager means of support, slaves were forced rather than recruited into servitude, and severe treatment did not diminish their numbers. Thus the need to maintain muster rolls for the colony's defensive needs made Bellomont reluctant to employ soldiers whom he realized would in all probability desert at the earliest opportunity.

But it was not only soldiers but all "people out of England" that Bellomont was loath to use, and his reluctance disclosed a distinction between freeborn European laborers and enslaved African workers which was arguably even more critical to the colony's immigration and future prosperity than its defensive needs—a distinction between those who could be forced to work at arduous tasks and those who could not. The refusal of European laborers to accept dependent employment in grueling work was a constant complaint of ambitious investors interested in the possibilities for the production of naval stores, potash, iron, salt, and other exportable products. As the merchant and royal official Francis Harrison observed, freeborn European laborers were "so used to property and to Command . . . that they will rather starve than serve under any roof but their own." In 1723, Cadwallader Colden similarly bemoaned the disinclination of laboring men and women to "work for hire" that made "labor continue very dear a common laborer usually earning 3 shillings by the day." In Colden's view, this single expense "overballances all the advantages which the country naturally affords & is the hardest to overcome." Moreover, he went on, this coveted independence was not something with which the imperial authorities should trifle as it constituted the "surest tye she [England] has upon the affections of the people in the Plantations where the native English are less in number than Foreigners French and Dutch." For the moment at least, Colden observed, New Yorkers "think themselves happy under the English Liberty," and this was an impression the imperial authorities would do well to preserve: "for the maxim that free subjects are more usefull to their Prince than Slaves will be found as true in America as in Europe."[20]

In the two decades that separated the failure of Bellomont's scheme from Colden's observations on the priorities of freeborn laboring men and women, New York City solved its labor problem by honing discriminatory practices aimed at black workers and committing itself to the importation of slaves from Africa and the plantation colonies to the south. In this respect, the commitment to slavery reflected political as well as economic considerations. The instability in the city in the decade or so following Leisler's Rebellion, the continuing hostilities with the French, and the lamentable condition of the garrison in New York all underscored the fragility of English rule. Almost forty years after the conquest, English residents comprised a mere quarter of the city's population, and Anglican churchwardens likened their surroundings to "a conquered Foreign Province held by the terrour of a Garrison."[21] The most effective way to bind the city's heterogeneous population was through a shared language of rights and privileges and appeals to the settlers' desire for security and commercial opportunities. Thus the reliance on African slave laborers provided for the rise of a prosperous community of British subjects who reveled in their membership in an empire dedicated to the preservation of liberty and property. Little did New York City tradesmen suspect that the same administrative and legal recategorization that designated black workers as slaves would in time also undermine their own privileged status and working conditions.

*   *   *

The origins and development of slavery and its identification with African workers in colonial British America has long fascinated historians. For many years, discussions focused on whether white racial antipathy preceded and inspired the negative categorization of black workers or whether such feelings emerged as a post hoc justification for human chattel slavery in the Chesapeake's plantation economy. More recent studies have enhanced earlier insights into the interconnections between black enslavement and white power relations by demonstrating that the degradation of black labor varied considerably across time and space, as did the kinds of African American communities and culture that emerged in different regions. In particular, Kathleen Brown's rendering of the discursive and legal processes that figured in the establishment of slavery's critical components—lifelong servitude, inheritable status, and association with perceived "racial" characteristics such as skin color—indicates considerations that can assist in the examination of the formation of the slave system in New York City. First, the manner in which knowledge or awareness of racial difference is bound up with the simultaneous articulation of related notions of difference, which acquire social force when expressed through legal and institutional mechanisms that delimit appropriate (and inappropriate) modes of behavior and social life. Second, the setting of this discursive construction within the context of daily life and work wherein its totalizing effects are reinforced by their expression in everyday practice—for example, the identification of servility with dark skin color following the association of these two elements over time.[22]

As we have seen, the earliest demarcation between European and African settlers along the lines of color or race came in the 1650s under the auspices of the campaign for municipal rights: orders commanding the townspeople to donate their time to working on the city's fortifications required a reduced commitment from free blacks; even as the city pressed every available male resident into service, blacks were exempted, or more likely excluded, from the militia's musters and parades. The introduction of the burgher right in 1657 institutionalized the racial distinction between blacks and whites by excluding free black residents from the civic privilege. The right doubly discriminated against free black residents. First, they were denied the privileges of residents and effectively treated as strangers. Second they were refused the facility of establishing residency and registering as a freeman in the future in the manner of a newly arrived European settler. By excluding blacks and affirming the freeborn condition of independent burghers who owed duties to the city and enjoyed a privileged monopoly of local trade, the burgher right called forth a new and powerful distinction between residents of African and European descent living in New Amsterdam just as the city's slave population increased sharply.[23]

The continuity of New Amsterdam's municipal order following the English conquest maintained black workers in a racially discriminated-against but not yet fully degraded state. The English authorities did not require the free blacks to swear loyalty oaths to the Duke of York or to serve in the militia, but they respected the slave manumissions and freedmen's property rights. Free blacks remained marginalized in a civic half-world and beyond the remit of municipal duties and privileges. In the late 1670s Jasper Danckearts described the liminal condition of New York's free black community in his comments on the ramshackle community of twenty-four or so men and women living in what had become known as "negro land"—a patch of ground lying beyond the city's fortified wall and close to Stuyvesant's Bowery plantation and its labor force of forty or so slaves. Although it is difficult to make definite connections, as the turbulent 1680s approached, the insecurity felt by sections of the city's laboring men and women prompted them to distinguish white from black work, and the association of blackness with civic exclusion and servility became increasingly matter-of-fact. Thus, in 1684, the Common Council agreed to the carters' petition regarding the exclusivity of their trade and affirmed that "Noe Negroe or other slave doe drive any Carte within the Citty"; three years later, when Elsie Leisler petitioned the court for permission to use her slave to cart their corn, as they had trouble finding a registered carter, the court ruled that Leisler could move her own goods "but the cart must be driven by a white man."[24]

By the 1690s there were seven hundred African Americans living in New York, almost double the number identified at the time of the English conquest, and the city depended on them to undertake menial and laborious work. Yet if black workers already occupied a degraded civic position and were routinely lumped together with slaves in a racialized category of servile labor, the synonymity between blackness and bondage that would serve as the defining marker of American slavery would not develop for another twenty years.[25] This raises the question of how we account for the lag in what, with hindsight, appears as an inexorable progression from racially discriminatory civic codes and labor regulation to racial slavery in New York City.

The slow drift toward slavery reflected the intractability of the problems thrown up by efforts to justify slavery in a free community and the determination of black New Yorkers to resist degradation as mean and servile laborers. In the 1640s and 1650s New Amsterdammers' concern for their own republican liberties made them acutely sensitive to the setting down of dangerous precedents regarding the treatment of slaves and freedmen in their midst. In addition, Dutch anxieties regarding the enslavement of men and women who had been baptized required tortuous and self-serving interpretations of Christian theology and ultimately discouraged whites from admitting their slaves as congregants in the Reformed Church. In this respect, notions of whiteness and blackness—of essentialized and irreducible differences between people of distinct "colors"—were initially called forth to shield revered political and theological principles from the contamination of slavery, a status that was the focus of universal fear and opprobrium in the early modern world. In response to their exclusion from white society, free and enslaved Africans established their own community, maintaining family ties across three seventeenth-century generations, observing traditional burial practices, and adapting European liturgical celebrations to their own religious mores. Indeed, by the time of Bellomont's arrival the prevalence and tenacity of African religious practices prompted the Board of Trade to direct the governor "to facilitate and encourage the conversion of Negroes and Indians to the Christian Religion." Finally, the willingness of free and enslaved blacks to resist discrimination and the efforts by whites to cast them in the role of servile and slavish laborers, frequently with force on the city's streets and surrounding fields and forests, slowed the process of social degradation that led to bondage.[26]

That free and enslaved Africans retained and prosecuted claims to fundamental rights until late in the seventeenth century is clear from the case of

Cresee, which came before the Mayor's Court in the winter of 1691. Cresee had been a slave in the family of Asser Levy, a Jewish merchant who rose from impecunious beginnings to become a wealthy and respected trader with diverse business interests including the franchise for the public slaughterhouse before his demise in 1682. When his widow, Maria Levy, died in November 1691, her estate was attached by her creditors, who included Frederick Philipse, the city's wealthiest merchant who claimed Cresee as his own. On 22 December, Cresee appeared in court accompanied by Jansen Rose, Levy's erstwhile partner in the slaughterhouse, and three other city butchers and proclaimed his freedom. Cresee's butcher witnesses, "being sworn vouching the freedom of . . . Cresee," deposed that "his master and mistress had often declared that after her decease the said Cresee should be free." The magistrates postponed judgment until their next court day, giving time for James Emmot to present "his evidence on behalf of Mr Frederick Philipse." However, when the magistrates reconvened on 3 January, they declared that "Cresee a negroo man formerly belonging to Ashur Levy deceased is adjudged and allowed to bee a free man by this Court according to the Deposicions given unto them the last court day."[27]

Cresee's case indicates that, as late as 1691, slaves retained a fundamental right to their liberty beyond the boundary set by their current but not necessarily permanent condition. Cresee's claim rested on the assumption that because of a promise made before reliable witnesses his bondage ended on the day his mistress died. Regardless of Maria Levy's indebtedness, a slave who belonged to nobody ceased to be a slave and—in the absence of any other legal title or restraint—Cresee was free. We can only speculate about the butchers' reasons for supporting Cresee's case: given the timing of the suit, the winter following Jacob Leisler's summer execution, it is possible that their testimony implied a protest at the claim of Frederick Philipse —an erstwhile "grandee" and beneficiary of the discredited Stuart administration. Alternatively, given the rebellion in defense of individual and community liberty, the restored English authorities might have been cautious about denying such a well-supported suit and breathing new life into local fears of arbitrary imperial governance. Whatever their motives, the butchers' court appearance is one indication of the intimate connections between free tradesmen and black and enslaved workers. Moreover, although manumissions remained few in number, Cresee's case also demonstrates that in the late seventeenth century whites and blacks continued to share much as legal subjects who could pass from freedom to slavery and vice versa.

Had Cresee brought his case twenty-five years later, the supporting cast in his personal drama would have been required to play very different roles to achieve the same denouement. In the two decades after Cresee's case, the city's black population swelled to more than fifteen hundred, with new arrivals coming from Africa, the West Indies, and the French and Spanish territories acquired following Queen Anne's War (1702–13).[28] In 1711 the establishment of a daily hiring fair for bond people at the Meal Market on the city's east side indicated the integration of slave workers into the city's labor market. From here locals such as printer William Bradford, widow Elizabeth Berton, and shipwright Dennis Riche hired out their slaves to a joiner, a blacksmith, and a baker for terms ranging from a few weeks to a year or more. As the private importation of slaves continued, manumissions declined, and the free black community was dwarfed by the slave presence in the city, prompting many to quit the town and seek a new start on small holdings in New Jersey and Long Island. By the time of Robert Hunter's arrival in 1710, most of the residents of New York's earliest free black community from "negro land" along the road to Fresh Water had sold up and moved away.[29]

For white residents of New York City, blackness was increasingly becoming synonymous with slavery and the miserable condition of people who were entirely dependent upon their masters for the necessities of life. The determination of slaves to resist this degradation and secure the means to live more independent lives prompted the city's first recorded crime wave in the 1690s. When the mayor, William Merrit, ordered home a group of slaves he found "making a disturbance" near his house, one of their number "assaulted the mayor upon the face." In 1695, the Quarter Sessions indicted a group of four black and Indian slaves for stealing a sloop; two years later, a gang of twelve slaves belonging to eight different masters from across the city were convicted of stealing a brass kettle, a petticoat, and bread belonging to "sundry persons." In response to these incidents, increasing white antipathies, and growing concerns for urban security, the Common Council introduced a raft of measures designed to restrict the activities of slaves within the city. Laws introduced in 1702 and 1708 increased the restrictions on slaves, giving masters the discretion to punish their bond people, forbidding slaves from gathering in groups of more than three, and ordering them to refrain from "making any hooting or disorderly noise" on the Lord's day. The Common Council also established the new municipal office of Common Whipper.[30] Finally, the new laws prohibited slaves from trading without their master's permission, thereby excluding them from the growing urban economy. Slaves needing or desiring anything more than what their masters deigned to provide had to resort to subterfuge and criminal exchanges, and tavern keepers and middling residents were regularly indicted for illegal commerce with bond people.

On the morning of 2 April 1712, New Yorkers awoke to news of a conspiracy by a group of slaves who had fired buildings in the town and left eight whites dead and a dozen more injured.[31] White New York responded with an orgy of violence, extracting confessions from those implicated in the plot by burning, hanging in chains, and "breaking on the wheel" and executing eighteen men. The violence vented on black bodies was quickly followed by a legislative catharsis in the form of an act "for punishing negroes" that included new restrictions on manumissions. Henceforth, any master freeing a slave first had to post a bond of two hundred pounds surety and provide twenty pounds annually toward the freed person's maintenance. This ensured a de facto end to deathbed manumissions unaccompanied by the requisite provisions. For the handful of blacks who might still find their way to freedom, the Assembly decreed that "no Negro, Indian, Mullatto, that hereafter be made free, shall enjoy, hold or possess any Houses, Lands, Tenements, or Hereditaments in this colony."[32]

The impact of the new restrictions was made clear the year after the conspiracy by the fate of Sam, a slave manumitted by the will of the butcher George Norton. In addition to his freedom, Norton bequeathed Sam thirty pounds and Robin, another slave. However, Norton's executor, Ebeneezer Willson, refused to provide the two hundred pounds surety or to honor the other provisions of the will, forcing Sam to remain in servitude. In 1717 Sam petitioned the Quarter Sessions, complaining that "Willson . . . will neither pay your poor petitioner the Thirty Pounds nor let him have said Negro Robin" and "in the winter when said Negro [Robin] want Cloaths he is forced to come to your poor petitioner for a supply. And so also when he is sick." However, "so soon as he is well and able to work, Mr. Willson takes him away and imploys him at his own service." The injustice of Sam's plight prompted Governor Hunter to act against the restrictions on manumissions. Hunter disapproved of the legislation, recognizing that it set slavery on a new and darker course by "cutting off all hopes from those slaves who by a faithful and dilligent discharge of their duty, may at last look for the reward of a manumission." As such the manumission restrictions threatened to turn city slaves into "not only careless servants, but excite 'em to insurrections more bloody than any they have yet attempted." When the Board of Trade threatened to disallow the act upon Hunter's recommendation, the Assembly revised the restrictions, allowing for manumissions where surety was provided that the manumittee would not become a public charge. Under these terms, Sam was able to secure his freedom after securing the backing of the joiner John Ellison and victualler Thomas Slow, allowing him to enter the trading economy, as a debtor, in November 1717.[33]

Despite the Assembly's legislative retreat, the city's attitude toward black workers and its slave labor force was changed for all time. Lacking Sam's assets and guarantees of annual maintenance, it is likely that Cresee would have lost his case and been considered chattel in satisfaction of Maria Levy's debt with Frederick Philipse. Considering these crucial early eighteenth-century decades and the drift toward a clear and determined commitment to racial slavery, it seems that the more comfortable white residents felt regarding the security of their individual and community rights and liberties the more at ease they were regarding the introduction of laws that denied these rights to others—laws that would have been unacceptable to the more insecure and watchful New Amsterdammers who first settled the town. In this respect, the incremental degradation of black workers served as an index of the rapprochement negotiated between the English imperial authorities and their multicultural colonial subjects in the early eighteenth century. As the city's pluralistic community embraced their membership in the British empire, following the 1707 Act of Union, they condemned black workers to unrelenting toil and the denial of fundamental political rights. The restrictions on manumissions ensured that the few who managed to attain their freedom were unable to participate in the trading economy without the support of creditors and a sizable debt, thereby condemning them to the lowest ranks of the debt-dependent laboring sort.[34]

The recategorization of black workers as slavish attests to the social power of the law and carries considerable import for our understanding of the changing status of early eighteenth-century city tradesmen. There was nothing inevitable about the final sequence in establishing racial slavery in New York, which was marked by incremental shifts in attitudes toward black labor as expressed in laws and orders restricting manumissions and prohibiting individual freedoms to assemble, own property, or trade. The impact of these and other measures attests to the power of law in defining the limits of freedom and slavery either by assertive and racially prejudicial legislation or by silence and a refusal to counter discriminatory practices. In a similar fashion, the diminishing purchase of claims for particularistic artisanal rights and privileges ensured the demise of earlier distinctions between freemen and stranger and for the undifferentiated treatment of free white labor, whether resident or nonresident, before the law. As administrative and legal attitudes toward black and white laborers shifted, so did the status

and perception of their work, the former becoming identified with dependence and servility and the latter with independence and liberty. However,
the creation of a servile black labor force to enhance commercial opportunities introduced new problems in a community whose members believed
themselves to share in the much-vaunted English imperial liberties. For
while slave labor created the possibilities for white unity by mitigating the
contests over surplus value between rich and poor, this unity was predicated
on the introduction of a new category of stigmatized, bound labor and the
risk of disaffection among the free white working population, should they
ever find themselves having to make do with menial work and slavish circumstances in the future.

*   *   *

The rising tide of Atlantic commerce and local prosperity that encouraged
New Yorkers to invest in slave workers also persuaded the municipal government to focus less on ensuring protectionist, occupational, and residential
privileges and more on encouraging and managing local trade. The common councilmen pump primed city business with investment incentives
ranging from protected public contracts to the distribution of franchises
encompassing everything from the operation of ferries to fishing rights. As
the city and its business interests grew, so did the number of offices within
the municipal administration.[35] However, whereas the earliest urban oligarchs had distributed offices as sinecures among a limited circle of associates, by the early eighteenth century such municipal preferments and the
benefits of enhanced credit and purchasing power were not so easily controlled. In some cases the award of city offices and contracts depended on
ethno-religious loyalties, in others they were auctioned off to the highest
bidder, and occasionally they were the subject of unseemly competition.[36] In
1718, for example, the contest for the ferrymaster's position prompted the
incumbent, James Harding, to seek the aid of governor Robert Hunter. Hunter
wrote to the Common Council, pointing out that Harding had offered "as
much for the ferry as any other and that his competitors have bragged that
they are resolved to overbid whatever he thinks fitt to offer." In the governor's view these boasts reflected poorly on Harding's competitors, who had
nothing to recommend them "except an earnest desire to be possest of the
ferry at any rate which indeed . . . renders them suspicious."[37]

The competition for the ferry franchise is one example of the willingness
of city residents to manipulate the provisions of municipal privileges and

ordinances in their own advantage, all the while claiming to act in the interests of the common good. In some cases, as is indicated by Hunter's concerns regarding the ferry, such jockeying for position doubtless reflected selfishness and individual ambition. In others, however, there appears to have been genuine confusion as the emerging English seaport town strained against the restrictive procedures introduced fifty years previously in accordance with Dutch practice. During this transition period, city artisans found themselves having to accommodate long-established arrangements and regulations while facing new conditions and challenges. Sometimes the older forms won out; at other times new forces and priorities proved too great to withstand. In all cases, however, the rights and privileges of resident artisans and their relationship to the city were subjected to scrutiny and sometimes contest and change. This was evident in two early eighteenth-century disputes concerning long-standing regulatory practice within the city.

The first, in 1710, involved the butcher Jeremiah Calcutt and the clerk of the market Jacobus van Cortlandt. Late that autumn, Calcutt began holding back the slaughter excise payable to Van Cortlandt, who waited for over a year before engaging the services of an attorney, Thomas George, to present the case in the Mayor's Court. George began by reminding the court of the fees payable to the clerk of the market for slaughtered cattle, declaring that "he the said [Jeremiah] for the time aforesaid . . . exercising the art and mystery of a butcher" owed Van Cortlandt thirteen pounds, eight shillings, and tenpence. To support his case, the attorney presented a copy of the city's 1686 charter, Van Cortlandt's commission as clerk of the market, a copy of the ordinance relating to slaughter fees, and evidence that Calcutt had "in the Occupation of his trade of a Butcher . . . killed cattle great and small within the said City of New York from the fourteenth day of October 1710." Finally, and one suspects, with a triumphant air, George presented the jury with a copy of the freeman's oath wherein Calcutt swore to obey the laws and ordinances passed by the Common Council and to do his duty as required of all citizens.[38]

The second dispute, in 1721, involved Cadwallader Colden—recently arrived in New York and in his third year as the weigh-house master—and the city's four licensed porters, who could trace their occupational privileges to the establishment of the burgher right in the 1650s. In a report submitted to the governor, Colden complained of declining excise revenues owing to inadequate enforcement of the order requiring the traders to weigh their flour and bread prior to shipping. The situation had gotten so bad, Colden recounted, that local boatmen and exporters "look upon it [the order] as repealed and think themselves at liberty to bring their Bread and Flower and other merchandize . . . to the weigh house or not as they please."[39] In addition to calling for a tightening up of regulations, Colden endeavored to increase weigh-house revenues by cutting the allowance granted to the porters. The allowance was assessed on the value of the goods weighed, and the regulations stipulated that each man receive a quarter share. However, when there were only three men in attendance, the custom had been for each porter to receive a third. Colden wanted to enforce the stipulation regardless of the number of men on hand, and, when the porters protested, he insisted that he was free to "employ whom he thinks fit and on such terms as he can agree with them." When Colden denied the porters their customary dues a second time, the men went "immediately to the weigh house where they made a great noise with threatenings what they would doe"—at which Colden "discharged them and hired others," it is worth noting, "by days wages in their stead."

In both of these disputes one discerns a clash between older regulatory and occupational conventions and newer circumstances and ambitions. Both Calcutt's refusal to pay duties and Colden's attempt to ignore customary practices in the interests of managerial efficiencies, indicate resistance to long-established procedures. In earlier times, an appeal to the municipal government or a stern word from the magisterial bench concerning the force of customary practices and the duties of burghers might have been sufficient to resolve these disputes. It is an indication of the changing character of municipal government that in both cases the disputants sought alternative forms of resolution. Colden and the porters appealed directly to the governor and his council, the former insisting on his freedom to manage the weigh-house as he saw fit, arguing that it would surely be improper for "your honours to determine what one shall give to such persons as he employs [and] what insolent servants they would be if thus employed." The governor's council convened a subcommittee that investigated the weigh-house's accounts and uncovered years of indebtedness and delays in paying the porters overseen by Colden's predecessor, John Graham.[40] In his suit against Calcutt, Van Cortlandt resorted to a common law action framed in the adversarial terms of formal writs and pleadings. Although Van Cortlandt won his case, the victory was far from clear cut, not least to the jury impaneled for the hearing. Faced with the legalese of common law pleading, the jury declared that they were unable to reach a verdict because "if the law is with Jacobus then Jeremiah is guilty and if not then Jeremiah is free."[41]

By the early eighteenth century, the older civic order and its provision for commercial regulations and the privileges and duties of freemen was under strain. In part, this reflected the impact of population growth and the difficulty of tracking the comings and goings of more and more traders. In 1702, for example, the dockmaster James Spencer complained to the Common Council concerning the boatmen who used the municipal wharves and docks but avoided paying their fees as "before he can gett the Mayor's officer to summon them . . . [the offenders] weight anchor and are gone." A decade or so later, Robert Hunter offered a different perspective on the same problem when he wrote to the Board of Trade concerning the unreliability of provincial registers that were supposed to record the names of militiamen, freemen, servants, and slaves. Such was the confusion of these records that Hunter despaired of ever "be[ing] able to obtain a compleat list of the numbers of Inhabitants of this Province."[42] Without a certain knowledge of who did and did not live in the city (let alone the province) and of their activities it was increasingly difficult for the authorities to enforce the civil and commerical regulations with the effectiveness of an earlier time. Consequently, for the free citizens at least, Robert Hunter's New York had an all together more liberated feel about it, than the era of Edmund Andros's brooding administration. The piecemeal decay of the older regulatory order also reflected the priorities of tradesmen who were as ready as any to invoke the provisions of long-established regulations when it suited them, and to ignore these same regulations when it did not. New York artisans were as much agents as victims of the decline of the earlier civic order, as was clear in the fates of the freemanship and city apprenticeships.

*   *   *

Historians have differing opinions regarding the fortunes of the freemanship in the decades after Leisler's Rebellion. For many years, the prevailing view considered the civic privilege a relic of English municipal practice that rapidly passed into disuse in New York. Scholars maintained that labor scarcities and an increasingly mobile workforce made the privileged status of city freemen largely obsolete and encouraged the municipal government to turn a blind eye to unregistered tradesmen working in the city. Residents only continued to register for the freemanship, these historians argued, to secure the suffrage right, and only then in times of controversy such as the close-run city elections of the 1730s and 1760s. More recently, however, the freemanship has been re-evaluated, as a "legal bond of attachment" that united residents with the municipal government in ways that indicated the transplantation of English corporate values that endured into the early nineteenth century. In this reading, the freemanship provided for social cohesion and a unity of purpose in an expanding and culturally diverse urban community and also for the political participation of working men in eighteenth-century politics. Both views offer insights. But taken together, they leave us with a contradictory impression of the freemanship that both declined and thrived in the eighteenth-century city.[43]

To resolve this contradiction, we can begin by noting the anglocentrism of the two views, which leads them to identify the civic status with archaic English municipal practice, slighting the freemanship's origins in the Dutch burgher right. This concern for English rather than Dutch practice derives from the focus on the long-term significance of the freemanship as the basis for urban adult male suffrage and the electoral participation of ordinary working men in the later eighteenth century. However, the franchise provision did not figure in the original burgher right, which accorded with the oligarchic and expressly nondemocratic mores of urban Dutch republican government. Moreover, given the lack of familiarity of Dutch and batavianized native-born and immigrant residents with recently imported English-style electoral contests, it is likely that the suffrage was of limited concern to many in the 1690s. With this in mind, we can more usefully reconsider the fortunes of the freemanship in the decades after Leisler's Rebellion less in terms of the waning of a medieval English municipal tradition—of which most residents would have had little if any knowledge—and more as part of the demise of an earlier Dutch civic culture.

The notion that the city and its residents possessed a unity of purpose had been foundational to the campaign for municipal government in New Amsterdam, culminating with the introduction of the burgher right in 1657. Thereafter, claims concerning the city's distinctive corporate identity and the priorities of its idealized prescriptive hierarchy, within which each enjoyed the privileges of their respective occupation and place, were reiterated in a variety of contexts: when the burgomasters proclaimed the city's staple right, when newcomers swore the burgher oath, and when freemen complained of encroachments or asserted their privileges as litigants in court and traders in local markets. In the 1650s and 1660s the burgher right was a vigorous civic institution that mattered in daily work and life. From the outset its vitality derived from the balance of privileges and duties that were widely credited with the maintenance of social order. And, inasmuch as the city prospered while the majority of male city residents registered with the city and adhered to municipal regulations, the burgher right had delivered: As the Nine Men had claimed, people and privileges did provide for prosperity.

Following the conquest, the English demonstrated their approval for the well-organized civic community by leaving its major institutions intact: the court, trade regulations, municipal officialdom, and the burgher right were all untouched in the first decade. Circumstances changed following the arrival of Edmund Andros in 1674, and the reforms that aimed to impress English ways upon the polyglot city. It is also noteworthy that, as emigration from the Netherlands slowed in the 1670s, so did the numbers registering for the anglicized freemanship. Worse followed in the 1680s, as residents faced demands for public works and new taxes for projects that many suspected were administered in the interests of the oligarchic commercial elite. In this way a civic privilege that had once symbolized New Amsterdammers' independence and liberty was transformed into a tool in the hands of a manipulative and increasingly unpopular English administration. Following the granting of Dongan's Charter in 1686, the Common Council issued repeated calls for residents and newcomers to register, but only a handful came forward. By the 1690s, then, the residency privilege had a long and somewhat checkered career—first as the burgher right and then as the freemanship. It was this recent and local history that best explains the diminishing interest in the freemanship.

In the aftermath of Leisler's Rebellion, the restored English authorities once again deployed the freemanship to monitor the townspeople's comings and goings as part of the drive to reestablish royal rule. In 1692, the Assembly and the Common Council reinstituted orders regulating provincial and urban trade and requiring tradesmen to declare their presence in the city or face a fine greater than the freemanship registration fee. When this failed to produce the necessary registrations, the authorities opted for a more lenient approach, signaling their desire to secure as comprehensive a census of resident traders as possible. In 1695 the council lowered the fee for those who had resided in the city in 1686 from five pounds for merchants and twenty-four shillings for tradesmen to a paltry ninepence. One of the city aldermen was instructed to make themselves available every Wednesday morning from nine to eleven to "administer an oath to all such as shall be made free or are already free according to the usage and practices of the corporations of England." The lowering of the fee was also an election ploy that enabled Fletcher (and subsequently Bellomont) to pack the register with electoral supporters. Between 1695 and 1698, some 369 men registered, including many who had long lived and traded in the city. The reregistration of these long-term residents suggests that they had been drawn in by the spate of contested city elections. Yet viewed in the context of the decline of the earlier burgher right ideal, for many, the manipulation of the freemanship in the service of an antagonistic electoral contest must have signaled the final sundering of any lingering connection between residential privileges and unity of purpose.[44]

In the ensuing decades, the Common Council manifestly failed to enforce the freemanship's registration requirement and trade monopoly, even among its own serving officers. In 1704, the "Petition of Sundry Principal Inhabitants of this Citty" seeking an order from the Assembly prohibiting the holding of retail sales by nonfreemen, was one of three similar pleas indicating that outsiders were trading in the city with impunity. The petitions—which further emphasized the diminishing authority of the municipal government in relation to its provincial superior—beseeched the Assembly to act against the holding of retail auctions by outsiders, "the Allowance whereof is much to the prejudice of this city's ancient and sworn freemen."[45]

The partial survival of municipal freemanship records means it is impossible to say for sure how many registered for the right. It is likely that some who came to the town shirked registration in order to avoid being added to city tax lists or called upon to contribute to public work when needed. However, the fact that the gaps in the register owe as much to inadequate contemporary record keeping as they do to the loss of historical sources over the passage of time, is a further indication of haphazard enforcement: an audit of debts owed to the city in January 1710 noted that David Provoost and Isaac de Reimer "hath not by any of the City Books Accounted for the Freedoms and Lycenses" issued during their mayoralties totalling fifty-two and fifty-five registrants respectively. Even the records that have survived contain bewildering irregularities including the aforementioned registration by long-term city residents who were already registered, but more often the failure of others to register although they lived and traded in the city for years and others still who held municipal office, but never joined the roster of city freemen.[46]

Disregard for the freemanship regulations was not limited to municipal officers and those responsible for enforcement. Tradesmen also demonstrated scant respect for the privilege and worked in the city without registering with the authorities; registered workers—who were supposed to be the beneficiaries of freemanship protections—displayed few qualms about engaging unregistered subcontractors. The shipwright Robert Bennet worked in the city for at least nine years, building a new sloop valued at 115 pounds for Abraham Wendell in 1717, before establishing his own shipyard and registering for his freemanship. Freemen such as the merchant William Smith and the tanner John Hunter provided credit and bail for the brickmaker Richard Moore and the currier John Gibson, neither of whom were registered with the city.[47] Similarly, the builder Dirck van der Burgh hired Enoch Aymes for a few weeks' bricklaying, and the carpenters Joseph Latham and Samuel Pell hired the shipwright William Ladd for almost a year. Yet, of the five men involved in these agreements, only Latham was a registered free-man at the time; despite his extensive business interests and distinguished municipal service, Dirck van der Burgh never appears to have registered for the freemanship of the city.[48] Bearing in mind that the magistrates who heard the civil cases from which these impressions are drawn were the same indi-viduals who were charged with enforcing the city's regulations, it is clear that the routine exclusion of unregistered workers from city employment had ceased by the early eighteenth century. New York's second generation of city artisans, it seems, were better connected and more confident than the first and the opportunities available in the trading economy displaced earlier desires for closed corporate markets, making formal restrictions such as the freemanship obsolete.

But if the freemanship was such a dead letter, then why did so many people continue to invoke its provisions? Notwithstanding their lack of en-forcement, the Common Council never repudiated the freemanship and, in 1707, revised the oath in line with the declaration sworn by freemen of Lon-don since the fourteenth century. The revised oath required that freemen continue to alert the mayor whenever they heard of "Forreigners" trading within the city and prescribed the terms under which apprentices were to serve.[49] Between 1695 and 1735 the municipal government registered and col-lected the excise from some seventeen hundred men. Moreover, as Jeremiah Calcutt discovered in 1712, municipal inspectors (and their attorneys) con-tinued to insist on the perquisites that trickled from municipal offices and inspectorates. Ordinary New Yorkers also invoked the provisions of the free-manship, when it served their purposes. For example, in 1702, William Wal-dron—a cooper and veteran of coopers' combination of 1679 and Leisler's Rebellion—petitioned the Common Council as "an ancient citizen of this corporation." Waldron beseeched the magistrates to take account of his "de-plorable condition" and that of his wife and "many small children . . . [with] nothing to support him but his own dayly labor" and "order him to be one of the publick corne measurers of this city."[50] In 1711, when the governor's council called for the impressment of city carpenters to construct three hundred flat-bottomed landing craft to assist the mobilization of troops up the Hudson River during the latter stages of Queen Anne's War, the Com-mon Council ordered city carpenters to work and contribute to "all other Charges, bearing your part as a Free-man ought to do." Most interestingly of all, the freemanship assumed particular significance for that erstwhile lowliest of trades, the city's carters. By tying the issue of carting licenses to freemanship registration, the carters managed to keep down the numbers in their trade and enjoy considerable influence over their conditions of service until the turn of the nineteenth century.[51]

What, then, are we to make of the conundrum presented by the freemanship's contradictory endurance and demise? The answer is to conceive of the civic privilege less as a component within a static and decaying English corporate "tradition" and more as a status claim that originated in the Dutch era and continued to serve a purpose in some eighteenth-century contexts while losing its resonance in others. The freemanship endured where it justified or expedited individual, group, and institutional objectives. Thus the ideal of the freemanship—of notions of civic duty and privilege—lived on in pleas for welfare relief, in municipal orders pertaining to tax assessments and public works, and as a cherished indicator of status and protectionist tool by the rudest and canniest of city tradesmen. Given that black residents—whether slave or free—were excluded from the roster, the freemanship also played a vital role in demarcating emerging racial boundaries while simultaneously enabling the municipal government to justify the requisitioning of forced public labor: when residents were forced to labor, they did so gladly and as a contribution to the greater good, or that, at least, was the theory. Finally, and as the petitions relating to strangers holding retail sales and similar protests indicate, when collective interests were threatened the whole community could rediscover its commitment to "ancient" principles and petition for the exclusion of "strangers." It is in these terms—as a claim which only partially retained its purchase on the public's attention— that the freemanship endured in the eighteenth century and, in this respect, it mirrored the fate of city apprenticeships.

* * *

The apprenticeship system in New York and elsewhere in the colonies had its roots in the medieval practice whereby adolescent boys, and occasionally girls, temporarily relinquished their liberty in order to learn a trade from a master craftsmen who secured their labor for the term of the indenture. Thus apprentices in New York promised to "serve the commandments of his Master," to "Gladly doe no hurte to his Said Master . . . or Suffer to be done," and not to "purloyne, waste, or Destroy" his master's goods, play a dice "or "any other unlawful Game," or frequent taverns and to seek his master's permission before absenting himself at day or night or before entering into a marriage contract. For their part, masters agreed to teach their apprentices a trade and to provide "meate drinke & bedding & all other Necessaries" in addition to any supplementary benefits agreed at registering of the indenture. Apprenticeship rested on the claims that each had in the other; these claims were given figurative form by the jagged edge of the torn indenture of which each party retained one half. By the early eighteenth century, however, fewer and fewer tradesmen and apprentices registered their indentures with the city and those who did were motivated more by the demands of the labor-hungry economy than out of respect for craft tradition.[52]

New York City's apprenticeship system developed in the 1650s as an adjunct to the establishment of a Dutch civic order in New Amsterdam. New Netherland's earliest indentures involving minors emphasized servitude rather than craft training and reciprocal arrangement of rights and obligations. Following the establishment of a burgher government and the Board of Orphanmasters in 1655, however, more clearly defined apprenticeship agreements calling for occupational training and in, many cases education in literacy and numeracy, became common.[53] After the conquest, the English authorities maintained this system of apprenticeship as the most effective way in which to regulate the young: the Duke's Laws instructed parents and masters to "in some honest Lawful calling Labour or Employment" and not to abuse their charges; apprentices were to serve their masters and mistresses faithfully and to abstain from fornication, marriage, gambling, running away, trading, or stealing from their masters; the 1684 "Act against Servants and Apprentices Frequenting Taverns" was the first of several measures that aimed to cut the ties between thirsty servants and unprincipled tavern keepers. Following the return royal rule in 1691, the Common Council affirmed the regulations relating to apprenticeship in the instruction that required city tradesmen to register for their freemanship: masters were instructed to register their indentures with the authorities and, upon completion of their term, apprentices were required to pay three shillings to become freemen in the city. The common councilmen followed this order with a regulation instructing masters not to "take an apprentice nor teach him a trade or calling without indentures bound before the Mayor or Recorder . . . [and] not for a less terme than four years." In 1711, the Common Council decided that four years was insufficient time to master a trade and extended the indenture time to seven years.[54]

The city authorities seemed committed to maintaining the apprenticeship system, but the records suggest that their commitment was not matched by local tradesmen who failed to register their charges with the city. There are two extant registers of indentures for New York City, covering the years 1694–1708 and 1718–27, providing information on 277 indentures that have been mined for impressions of the apprenticeship system.[55] The records reveal that apprentices worked in every major occupation and that the number of different trades registering indentures rose from twenty to thirty-one in the first three decades of the eighteenth century. There is also some evidence that English and Dutch masters favored apprentices from within their ethnocultural group. However, the most telling insight gleaned from the registers concerns the disproportionate withdrawal of one large and influential group and the implied snub this delivered to a once vigorous area of artisanal and municipal life. Dutch masters, it seems, withdrew from the apprenticeship system in disproportionate numbers. For, as late as 1730, Englishmen comprised only 40 percent of taxpaying artisans, but the indentures filed between 1718 and 1727 indicate that 60 percent of apprentices were registered with English masters and only 20 percent with their more numerous Dutch peers.

The destabilizing effects of Dutch withdrawal on the coherence and regularity of the city's apprenticeship system was compounded by the variation within the terms and conditions of those who were registered. All apprentices were entitled to insist that their masters supplied the basics of clothing, diet, and instruction, but extras such as schooling during winter evenings or a new suit of clothes upon completion were negotiable and fixed on the day of indenture—one of the biggest days in an early eighteenth-century teenager's life. Thus, in November 1718, David Noble and Martin Crankheyt both began work for the well-to-do shoemaker, Johannes Harperdinck. The following month Harperdinck and his apprentices went to register their indentures, the master undertaking to provide "training and sufficient meate, drink, apparell lodging and washing" in return for seven years' service. However, Noble was also promised "Every Year three Months Schooling and Stockings and his Wearing Clothes" and "six shirts, four neck cloths a Good beaver hatt, two pairs of shoes, One Coat, Wast Coat and a pair of Breeches" at the end of his indenture. For Crankheyt, on the other hand, there was no schooling or extra clothing, only a "good suit of clothes when his time of servitude is compleat."

The variance in apprentices' terms was also related to an individual's condition and connections at the time they registered the indenture. Local youths relied on the support of parents and family members who accompanied them to the ceremony. These supporters might negotiated extras or introduce stipulations such as the termination of the indenture, if the master failed to offer a proper training or moved away from the city. Alternatively, in the case of girls apprenticed to masters and mistresses, the indenture might provide for termination if the mistress of the house passed away. But these terms also varied from indenture to indenture and, for the less fortunate, things could be tougher. Orphans and the children of poorer parents were in a weaker negotiating position. They were more likely to be apprenticed in lower level trades such as shoemaking and to secure fewer extras such as schooling, clothing, tools, or cash upon completion of the indenture; they could also expect to serve for longer terms and from younger ages. There were some who seemed to make a practice of indenturing children from difficult circumstances. In December 1723, James Brown (who appears in the records at various times as barber, wig maker, and vintner) apprenticed Vandercliffe Baratel, "son John Baratel late of the city of New York chyrurgeon deceased." The following year, Brown registered the indenture of an eight-year-old orphan, William Mahon, for thirteen years. On the same day he apprenticed Sarah Cracraft, also age eight, daughter of Sarah Wignal, widow of Robert Wignall, a mariner. The indenture was for ten years, and Brown undertook "to teach [Cracraft] the art or mystery of housewifeness." Finally, in March 1725, this latter-day Fagin added John Eccles, "son of Lawrence Eccles, blacksmith, deceased" to his burgeoning household of orphaned and indigent children.

Masters and apprentices also employed probationary periods and backdated indentures to keep their options open for as long as possible while remaining within the letter of the law. For some, the apprenticeship began from a few weeks to several months prior to the registering of the indenture. Frances Champion lived and worked with Anthony Farmer and his wife Elizabeth for seven months before the Farmers registered her indenture in December 1698, promising to instruct her "to Reade and . . . in Spining, Sewing, Knitting or any other manner of housewifery." A probationary period enabled both sides to ponder their future together and to decide whether or not they wanted to proceed with the formality and expense of the indenture and a term of servitude lasting many years. In other cases, backdated indentures suggest that a previously private agreement was being publicly affirmed by mutual agreement. Thus, Edward Attrell served the carpenter John Ellison for eight years before the latter registered the indenture, with four years still to run, in September 1700. Delaying the registration until after the apprentice was trained in the mysteries of a trade ensured that a master such as Ellison only placed himself under a legal obligation after the apprentice became valuable as a skilled worker. For apprentices, the lack of an indenture need not be cause for concern, so long as they were decently clothed and fed and instructed in the ways of their chosen occupation.

The variations in terms and conditions of servitude were matched by discrepancies in the fortunes of apprentices who completed their indenture. Some learned trades and set themselves up as independent practitioners, whereas others were employed as general laborers and failed to become established in their own right. In the 1690s, the Scottish cordwainer William Jackson came to New York City, married Anna Wessels, and established a thriving business. In October 1698, the Jacksons took on John Dunlap for five years, promising to teach him the cordwaining trade and to give him "meat Drinke Washing and lodging and Cloathing fit for an apprentice and likewise his winters schooling" and also "two Suits of Cloathing One Suite to worke in the Other for Sunday's" upon completion of the indenture. Three years into Dunlap's time, and most likely in anticipation of his departure, the Jacksons took on John Reade, who was described as "a poor fatherless and Motherless child aged Eight Years and a halfe, or thereabouts." However, Reade joined Jackson on very different terms from Dunlap. Isaac Kip and Garret Viele, churchwardens and overseers to the poor, indentured Reade to William Jackson for twelve years "until he shall be twenty years." Jackson undertook to provide the "Usual provisions" and to teach the lad to "read and write the English tongue," but there was no mention of schooling during the winters or a suit of clothes at the end of the agreed term.

It is impossible to say what became of John Reade. He never reappeared on the city's register of freemen as a cordwainer, or in any other capacity, after leaving William Jackson's service. However, in 1703, John Dunlap completed his indenture and set about his business as a cordwainer. Although it seems to have taken some time to become established, Dunlap reappears in 1709, when he was sued by Garret van Laer for nonpayment of three pounds borrowed the previous year. The shoemaker's circumstances must have improved, however, because when, in November 1712, Abraham Gouverneur sued William Galt for four pounds' rent on a house, he identified the building in question as "behind John Dunlap's shop." In the ensuing decade, Dunlap worked his way into local retail and credit networks: in 1716, he secured a contract worth seven pounds, one shilling and ninepence supplying shoes to the city for distribution to the poor; it may have been this move to the municipal payroll that persuaded him to register for his freemanship in February of that year. Three years later Dunlap supplied shoes to John Dunn for resale to John Deprees and borrowed ten pounds from Richard Higgins; shortly thereafter, he entered municipal service as a petty constable, and later high constable, in the city's North Ward. As Dunlap found his footing in the trading economy, he moved from debtor to creditor, serving as a bondsman and providing bail for debtors in court. However, notwithstanding his successful graduation from apprentice to master shoemaker, Dunlap found it difficult to prosper: in the 1730 tax assessment, after almost thirty years of shoemaking and trading in the city, Dunlap was assessed at the minimum rate of five pounds.[56]

By the early eighteenth century, then, apprenticeship had largely ceased to function as an city institution with widely acknowledged regulations to which local craftsmen and their junior charges routinely adhered. The diminishing purchase of the freemanship and the privileges associated with residency meant that, in effect, apprenticeship offered a period of bound labor with few of the advantages that had once made it attractive over the longer term. Moreover, the superficial similarity in apprentices' legal status obscured a myriad of differences in their actual conditions, and the slippage between formal entitlements and actual benefits most likely explains apprentices' restlessness as the century wore on. For local youths with contacts in the credit and exchange networks, an apprenticeship with a well-established master continued to provide an opportunity to gain a skill and set themselves up in trade while saving their parents the expense of provisioning teenage children. However, as early as the 1690s, only one-third of apprentices whose indentures were registered with the city provided information on a living father, almost one-half were orphans or the sons or daughters of widows, and only two-fifths were promised schooling of one form or another. In other cases, one finds examples where details of wages and terms indicate that the "indenture" had become little more than labor contract in which vulnerable workers tried to access some of the protections afforded by apprenticeship's fading legal title. Thus, in July 1696, Bastian Congo, a twenty-seven-year-old free black man, agreed to work for the merchants Abraham and Jesse Kip for one year at the rate of thirty shillings a month and "after the manner of an apprentice or servant to dwell." In this and similar cases, it is clear that apprenticeship had become little more than a facade for labor agreements and the putting out of orphans and paupers, in which the provision for induction into craft skills and mysteries figured scarcely if at all.[57]

* * *

In the first three decades of the eighteenth century, the New York City Common Council watched over an urban trading economy with open markets and a liberal trading environment that would have been the envy of the Dutch West India Company's Amsterdam Board in the 1650s. The growth of credit-backed commerce appeared to confirm the Amsterdam Board's intuition regarding the money-making opportunities in an expanded community of free traders. The West India Company's conceit had been to expect such expansion and prosperity in the underpopulated community of New Amsterdam, surrounded by antagonists and competitors. In order to increase the colony's population and to attract private investment, the West India Company had to yield on the question of local administrative rights and privileges. Indeed, it is likely that New Amsterdam would have failed had it not been for the campaign by private merchants and artisans for the establishment of an urban civic order in accordance with Dutch republican practice. Thereafter, and particularly by the turn of the eighteenth century, New York prospered not only because of the growth of population (both free and enslaved) and its productive and consumption capacities, but also because of its status as a protected port in the British imperial trade. However, the opportunity cost of this expanding commerce and rising properity was the enervation of the earlier civic order with its roots in assumptions about natural hiearchy and the rights and privileges that accorded with each in his place.

The protracted demise of the Dutch civic order, begun with the introduction of Andros's reforms in the 1670s, continued with the rise of the provincial assembly and the demise of local regulations and privileges and generated new kinds of anxieties and struggles in early eighteenth-century municipal government. This was evident in micro struggles (such as those between Calcutt and Van Cortlandt and the porters and Colden), the decline of institutions such as the freemanship and apprenticeship, and the redirection of public attention away from the city and toward the provincial authorities. As early as the 1690s, when city coopers sought restrictions on the importation of casks and builders they had looked to the Assembly rather than the municipal government. In 1702, the builder Dirck van der Burgh pandered to English prejudices by petitioning for a regulation requiring local brickmakers to produce bricks of a uniform size and quality according to "English standards," although no such standard existed.[58] The undermining of municipal authority was also evident in the forthright challenges to its corporate rights. For example, in 1708, a group styling themselves the "Freemen, Citizens, and Inhabitants called Boatmen within this City of New York" petitioned the Assembly, "praying that they may be released from paying Dockage when they only make use of those Docks, Wharfs, and Slips that belongs to her Majesty." Others were bolder still, and appealed to the governor and provincial leaders against what the city considered long-held rights and privileges.[59]

By the 1720s, the city's municipal faculties were the subject of "diverse Questions Doubts Opinions Ambiguities Controversies and Debates" and the Common Council fought tenaciously to preserve the city's "Several Rights Liberties Privileges Advantages Jurisdictions Emoluments and Immunities." Matters came to a head in the late 1720s and a contest over the ferry monopoly between municipal government and Cornelius van Horne.[60] When Van Horne applied to Governor Montgomerie for a grant of a waterlot beyond the low-water mark—the limit of the rights granted to the city under the Dongan Charter—to establish an alternative ferry, the Common Council leapt to the defense of the city's "ancient Rights and Privileges." Following the settling of an 840 pound "gift," Montgomerie obliged municipal leaders with a charter that settled the question of the city's status and rights. The Montgomerie Charter affirmed the city's status as a corporation possessed of an estate comprising city hall, the market buildings, docks, bridges, waterfront, and all "waste and common land" under the water surrounding the southern end of Manhattan for four hundred feet beyond the low-water mark—settling the ferry question in the city's favor. In contrast to the 1686 charter that it supplanted, the Montgomerie Charter was primarily a defensive document and claimed little that was new. Thus, the most astute modern commentator characterizes the Montgomerie Charter as an awkward, prolix, and repetitious document with a mystifying structure and archaic language that guaranteed a hodge podge of earlier grants dating back to the mid-seventeenth century.[61]

Although the Common Council fought hard to protect the city's corporate identity and its franchises, properties, and estates, there was no similar defense of the equally long-standing residential and occupational rights and privileges of New York artisans. The combination of the diminishing authority of the municipal government, Dutch disaffection with anglicized civic institutions, and rising prosperity and artisanal disregard for restrictive commercial regulations resulted in the atrophying of previously valued civic privileges and duties. Just as the legal treatment and public perception of African workers had operated to redefine black labor as servile, so the diminishing public affirmation of particularistic artisanal rights and privileges provided for a reduction in the purchase of their idiosyncratic claims upon the community's attention. Without frequent assertion and public confirmation, long-standing civic rights and privileges became vulnerable to various kinds of challenge and, falling into obsolescence, permitted the rise of new perceptions of city workers. In 1730, the Common Council re-issued the freeman's oath under the auspices of the Montgomerie Charter and expunged earlier references to the city as an organic economic unit.[62] Thereafter, public order regulations lumped together slaves, servants, and apprentices who comprised the lower orders of the urban workforce, leaving city artisans to compete as free and equal men of property in the increasingly uncertain urban trading economy.

"So much as he should reasonably deserve to have": Tradesmen and the English Common Law

In May 1692, John Demares, a planter from East New Jersey, made a bargain with the brickmaker Jacob Fairen. Demares agreed to provide Fairen with meat, drink, and washing and to pay him "so much as he should reasonably deserve for his labor and pains" for making and burning a kiln of bricks on his land. That summer, Jacob Fairen erected a kiln and fired some twenty thousand bricks. Seven years later, however, the two men fell out over the value of Fairen's work. In November 1699, the brickmaker filed a complaint with the New York City Mayor's Court and sued for his just deserts under the common law writ of *indebitatus assumpsit*. Fairen was represented in court by Barne Cosens—an ambitious young lawyer, recently arrived from England, who drummed up trade in smaller towns along the Hudson River by riding out on the circuit with the Supreme Court magistrates. The brickmaker's case rested on the declaration that some time after he completed his work seven summers earlier Demares had built himself a fine house with the bricks and, given the value of the house and the terms of their original agreement, Fairen claimed that he "Reasonably Deserves the Sume of twelve pounds." The court issued a writ (of *capias ad respondendum*) authorizing the sheriff to take Demares into custody and to secure a bond giving surety for his future appearance. When Demares failed to appear at a subsequent court date, Cosens successfully called for the assignment of the bond to his client. By securing the bond, Cosens not only secured his client's case but also saved Fairen further delay and, in the event that Demares had decided to contest the suit, the additional expense of a jury trial.[1]

Fairen's agreement with Demares and his subsequent legal case reflected the assumption that he retained a right of property in his labor that limited the planter's purchase of the brickmaker's skills to the terms set out in their agreement. Fairen's right of property in his labor differentiated his status and the terms under which he was employed from that of servants, slaves, and other dependents who worked under the authority of another. Whereas servants and slaves held no title to what they produced, and day laborers negotiated a wage for general work, Demares purchased Fairen's skills for a specific task and was bound to pay him a just reward or, in the language of the writ filed in 1699, "so much as he should reasonably deserve." Thus Fairen felt justified in suing Demares after the completion of the planter's house even though it was long after the casting of their original agreement.

The assumption of a right of property in labor was widespread in early modern Europe and America and drew upon long-standing religious and political justifications. The Christian idea of "calling" depicted skilled work as both a gift and a duty and connected industry and thrift to worldly respectability and the search for spiritual salvation. The godly artisan whose diligence provided for technical innovation and the enrichment of the state was a crucial figure in the Reformation propaganda war against idlers and popery at home and abroad.[2] The natural law tradition also provided for the idea that freeborn subjects possessed a right to self-preservation, including a right to preserve oneself through the exercise of labor. In a view set out by Hugo Grotius and subsequently developed by English thinkers such as Thomas Hobbes and John Locke, natural rights were presumed to have been vested in a sovereign power in return for the distribution of civil rights that regulated commerce and society in the interests of the common good. This modification of natural liberty provided for an orderly social life governed by customary and civil laws that encompassed positive law ranging from state legislation to guild and municipal privileges and the provisions for common rights.[3] In this respect, the security of an independent artisan's right of property in labor and all the civil and customary laws that sustained this right served as key indicators of an individual's status as a freeborn subject. It is hardly surprising, therefore, that concerns for vitality of rights such as these figured prominently in the constitutional contests and workplace struggles that marked the emergence of a modern, capitalist market economy. Indeed, as late as the end of the eighteenth and early nineteenth centuries, traces of claims derived from the right of property in labor can still be discerned in the demands of Anglo-American workers for their "competence" and in the developing struggle over wages between the forces of labor and capital.[4]

Of course this assessment represents a highly schematic treatment of a vast and complex body of early modern political and economic debate on the development of capitalist social relations of production in the sixteenth

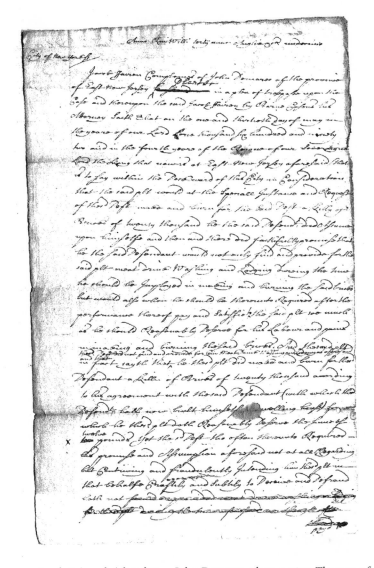

Figure 11. Jacob Fairen, brickmaker, v. John Demares, planter, 1699. The case of *Fairen v. Demares* reveals that local equity notions continued to be expressed within the newly imposed pleading forms of the English common law.

through the nineteenth centuries. Yet, in mitigation, one could argue that it was as schema—or a general outline of assumptions and principles that were subjected to closer interrogation by theorists and commentators—that ordinary men and women became aware of and subsequently asserted their rights in situations and struggles shaped by all manner of local idiosyncrasies. We have traced one variation on this theme in New Amsterdam, beginning in the 1640s with the resistance to Willem Kieft and in the subsequent campaign for municipal reform. Thereafter, the assertion of artisanal independence and a right to property in their labor was evident in the claims for residential and occupational privileges, the legal recognition of local equity values, and (in reverse) the denial of these same rights to African workers and slaves. In the four decades following the establishment of the Court of Burgomasters and Schepens in 1653, artisanal work acquired a public status that was based on a continuing negotiation concerning rights, obligations, privileges, and duties whose existence were both the basis and outcome of ongoing legal and political argument. The suspension of this negotiation during the Andros and Dongan administrations and the imposition of terms and conditions deemed arbitrary and tyrannical fostered the discontent that burst forth as Leisler's Rebellion in 1689–91.

When city artisans returned to court in the years following the reestablishment of royal rule they confronted a very different legal scene. On 6 May 1691, Henry Sloughter and the Assembly passed an Act for Establishing Courts of Judicature, revising the provincial and city court system.[5] The 1691 act eradicated all vestige of Roman-Dutch law and ended the period of Anglo-Dutch legal hybridity. Henceforth, the English common law supplied the terms under which tradesmen contracted for work in New York City. The case of *Fairen v. Demares* indicates that the assumption of a right of property in labor continued to inform work agreements, and for years to come, carpenters, masons, tailors, bricklayers, mariners, and all manner of tradesmen sued for rewards commensurate with their skills and sought their just deserts. However, now they did so through a punctilious system of forms of action such as *indebitatus assumpsit* that required litigants to recast their disputes in the language of the common law which governed the court's proceedings down to the final judgment. While the dependability of known and certain English law inspired confidence in provincial commerce and encouraged distant London financiers to invest in the city, the opportunity cost of investor confidence was the loss of the existing and accessible adjudication according to the Roman-Dutch law. In its place came a complex and arcane system of pleadings that mystified the legal process and provided for the rise of professional lawyers such as Barne Cosens who possessed the wherewithal to guide ordinary litigants through the procedural pitfalls of common law forms of action.

What changed, then, had less to do with how tradesmen thought about or conducted their business—still less the eagerness with which they sought out new opportunities and profits—and more the manner in which they litigated their disputes. In the new legal order, artisans could still pursue claims for their just deserts in accordance with local expectations regarding standards of workmanship and level of rewards, but they did so under new restrictions and, as the eighteenth century progressed, an increasing liability for costs. As the common law restrictions and expense of representation grew, the court considered fewer and fewer cases comprising claims derived from references to local practices and rights of property in labor. This change was not monolithic, nor could it have been because individual tradesmen and their customers occupied different positions in a system of social relations that was constantly in motion. However, considered in common with points made in the preceding two chapters, the trend in New York was manifestly moving away from public discussion of particularistic right and privileges and local idiosyncrasies and toward an equality of treatment before the law of all men, regardless of status, residence, or occupation.

*   *   *

Before considering some of the artisan litigants who brought their disagreements to the city's Mayor's Court, it is helpful to examine some of the complexities of the common law and to note what was distinctive about its establishment in New York. The earliest settlers who went to other English colonies such as Massachusetts and Virginia brought elements of English law with them in much the same way as they transported other social and culture models relating to practices ranging from marriage to agriculture and religion. Drawing on their Old World heritage, and innovating when required or so moved, over the course of the seventeenth century each colony developed its own distinctive legal system. In Massachusetts, this meant a combination of local, Mosaic, and English common law that favored arbitration in an effort to quell litigiousness within communal towns. In time, the New Englanders came to rely on the courts and the law to settle unavoidable commercial conflicts and thereby provide a safety valve for community harmony. In Virginia, on the other hand, the colonists combined English law and local regulations in a legal system that reflected the priorities of the tobacco economy and the need to attract and then regulate different forms of bound labor. Their differences notwithstanding, it is important to note that, in Massachusetts, Virginia, and elsewhere, English settlers were able to develop and adapt their legal systems over time and in response to local needs and demands.[6] However, there was little that was gradual about the introduction of English law in New York. Instead, it was imposed at the behest of a distant imperial authority and as a form of *deus ex machina*, perhaps intended to hasten the demise of Dutch institutions and practices and certainly to address a variety of civil and commercial needs.[7] Before we consider the effect of the common law on artisanal trade in New York City, we need to understand something of the law that New Yorkers were given.

The term "common law" referred to a set of rules applicable throughout England based on "the law of Nature or Reason, and the Principles and Maxims of the Law" that provided remedies for disputes that lay beyond the remit of statute law and local custom.[8] Common law rules and procedures governed the presentation of cases brought from every part of the realm and were set before the Westminster courts of King's Bench and Common Pleas by well-educated lawyers. Out in the provinces, subordinate municipal, county, and borough courts also heard common law suits presented by "pseudo-lawyers"—scriveners, manor stewards, town clerks, and vicars—who constituted a heterogeneous and active lower branch of the English legal profession.[9] Notwithstanding the boasts of eighteenth-century jurists regarding the immemorial pedigree of English precedents, the law introduced in New York had undergone extensive reform in the late fifteenth through the seventeenth centuries. In particular, common law lawyers established procedural reforms and legal fictions that resolved long-standing inadequacies relating to the adjudication of business disputes, which enhanced the ability of the common law to compete with other central courts, especially the equity court of Chancery, for lucrative commercial litigation.[10] These reforms provided for the ascendancy of the common law following a surge of litigation in the period 1560–1640 among merchants, yeomen, and middling artisans who participated in the increasingly dynamic market economy.[11]

One set of inadequacies related to jurisdictional and procedural strictures that limited common law courts to disputes originating in a narrowly defined geographic area. Lawyers overcame this with the adoption of legal fictions that enabled plaintiffs to bring cases originating in far-off places by simply asserting that the foreign place was situated within the jurisdiction of the court and providing for arrest and detention without binding litigants to a particular writ.[12] The second, and less tractable, problem concerned the inflexibility of the writ system that limited the common law to "real" actions, or formal agreements and executed contracts for specific services and sums.[13] In practice, this meant that the law lacked a writ that could deal with breaches of oral and otherwise informal or unexecuted agreements to perform a certain service or exchange wherein it was unreasonable to expect a written bond or deed. It was in response to these and other problems that common lawyers developed a family of writs or actions associated with nonforcible trespass under the generic title of "trespass on the case," or simply "case," which permitted plaintiffs to recover damages for breaches of oral or informal agreements.[14] The most significant of these writs for the future of contract law was the action of assumpsit.

The meaning of assumpsit is difficult to pin down, but, simply put, it assigned responsibility for a failed undertaking by asserting that a defendant had made himself strictly responsible for bringing something to pass and was therefore answerable if the event did not occur. This responsibility extended to defendants who had taken something into their control or use and (it was inferred) thereby assumed another's trust upon themselves. The extent of the defendant's obligation, it was further supposed, rested on the implied terms of their relationship with the plaintiff.[15] The foundations of these actions in the fictive failure of fictive undertakings meant that the language of the writ of assumpsit was filled with claims of attempted fraud and deception and implied attempts to evade payment. One important difference between assumpsit and other common law writs was that, because the former sought redress for trespass and involved uncertain sums and compensatory damages rather than a fixed amount (for example, as in a writ of debt), disputes that could not be compromised required a jury trial. In 1676, as a consequence of complaints by critics that assumpsit's fictive foundations undermined established forms and procedures, the Statute of Frauds restricted the kinds of agreements that could be brought by action of assumpsit, requiring demonstration of consideration for sales of goods over ten pounds and a written agreement for transfer of land.[16] As a consequence of these restrictions and the rising cost of legal representation, English litigation rates fell toward the end of the seventeenth and into the early eighteenth centuries.[17]

Recent scholarly debate concerning the implications of these and other changes of attitudes toward property and the commerce of ordinary men and women in early modern England centers on the themes of accommodation and restraint. For some, the law provided a amenable tool that was deployed by middling and laboring subjects to their own advantage.[18] For others, the era was characterized by a drive for social discipline led by an increasingly well-organized state that relied on the law to bolster old and impose new forms of restrictive arrangements that laid bare the ulterior rationality of capitalist definitions of property rights.[19] What is clear is that in the century or so leading up to their introduction in New York, procedural and technical reforms enabled common law courts to become the major forum for the settlement of civil cases relating to commerce and property in England. This ascendancy ensured that the common law figured prominently in not only seventeenth-century constitutional debates but also in the reification and ultimate alienation of rights and privileges previously associated with local and customary provision, craft preferences, civic protections, and all manner of incorporeal hereditaments such as common and usufruct rights.[20] This process, whereby the standardization of property definitions and relations chipped away at the finely graded privileges and preferments associated with the hierarchy of estates and degrees, contributed to the glossing of once more precise public distinctions and the emergence of a new "terminology of social simplification": a workaday language of sociability that characterized individuals and groups in broad terms as representatives of the better, middling, and lower or laboring "sorts," regardless of civic condition, trade skills, and other particularistic claims to what increasingly appeared as archaic forms of status.[21]

One final word before examining the impact of this much-revised common law on artisanal litigation in eighteenth-century New York City. Given that the developments sketched here occurred over the course of many decades, even centuries, one must resist the temptation to point to a particular period or era of transition. Whenever and wherever early modern struggles over privileges and property rights occurred, they reflected the substance of claims offered by opposing parties and the contemporary condition of the law as it was applied in various local contexts.[22] However, an inability to identify a single, critical period need not rule out comment on what constituted the manifest trend. For although the form of specific struggles and the tactics adopted by different parties varied across time and space, what was at stake remained broadly the same: the preservation or eradication (sometimes given the scholarly spin of "rationalization" or "modernization") of forms of property that had previously afforded their holders not only material benefits but also status and served as symbolic guarantees of the vitality and security of individual and community rights to liberty.[23] With this in mind, we can best consider the relationship between law and property less in terms of a linear progression to an increasingly individualized and alienable form and more as a sedimentary process in which successive layers of change over many generations gradually altered the legal and social landscape.[24] In this sense, then, the 1691 Act of Judicature in New York drew city tradesmen into a process of legal and social change that was already a century or more old in the provincial towns and villages of early modern England.

*   *   *

The establishment of the English common law in New York supplanted a well-worn legal system that had evolved to meet the colonists' need for public resolution of commercial and other civil disputes. As we have seen, beginning in the early 1650s, New Amsterdam's Court of Burgomasters and Schepens assumed a central role in community life and provided for the adjudication of disagreements in accordance with the formalities of the Roman-Dutch law and local practices and expectations. The town's growing and increasingly valuable commerce provided the foundation for a trading economy sustained by promises to pay at a future date. The Court of Burgomasters and Schepens relied upon litigants' oral testimony and evidence presented by "good men" who served as arbitrators and assessed the costs of materials, time spent, and standards of work completed before issuing a judgment. This process invited townspeople and tradesmen to appear on their own behalf and claim what they and their peers considered a reasonable sum for work undertaken and goods supplied. In this fashion, the court provided city workers a forum within which they sought acknowledgment for their status and occupational privileges and, in the process, recovered sufficient value in cash or commodities to meet creditor obligations and remain active in the urban trading economy.

The efficacy of this legal process in meeting New Amsterdammers' needs was evident from the vote of confidence it received following the English conquest in 1664. When faced with an English expeditionary force, the burgomasters and residents of New Amsterdam drew up Articles of Capitulation and surrendered to the conquerors, thereby preserving not only their lives and property but also their civic and legal order. Recourse to the law remained accessible and inexpensive, and the inquisitorial approach did not impose artificial procedural constraints upon litigants who were invited (where appropriate) to set their disputes within the broader context of their commercial dealings. The first two English governors were content to sustain the city as a privileged center of provincial trade and to merely anglicize court titles and insist on a right to trial by jury, which few appeared to take up. It was not until the Treaty of Westminster, following the end of the Third Anglo-Dutch War (1672–74), and the arrival of Edmund Andros that New York's legal system became the target of more thoroughgoing reform. Andros imposed English as the language of the law and introduced new fees and, although the court continued to combine Roman-Dutch and common law procedures, there is evidence of growing English technicalities within local law.[25] These reforms, I argued earlier, fueled the discontent that burst forth in Leisler's Rebellion in the spring of 1689.

Leisler's Rebellion divided New York along religious, ethnic, and class lines, leaving a legacy of suspicion and resentment toward the anti-Leislerian merchants, who had remained loyal to the Stuart appointees. Henry Sloughter and the returning royal authorities, who sided with this English, French, and anglicized Dutch anti-Leislerian minority, faced the difficult task of restoring order in what remained a predominantly non-English town. Sloughter and his counselors recognized the importance of legal reform when they introduced the 1691 Act of Judicature within weeks of the first meeting of the newly established provincial assembly. The Act confirmed the common law as the colony's civil code and set up a provincial supreme court, which sat as a court of original jurisdiction over criminal cases and civil pleas valued at more than twenty pounds and exercised appellate jurisdiction over cases for lesser amounts that had been decided in the lower courts; judgments of the Supreme Court worth one hundred pounds or more could be appealed to the governor and his council. Supreme court justices were authorized to introduce whatever supplementary procedural rules were deemed appropriate, subject to the one requirement that litigants be offered jury trials. The statute also outlined the form and function of the provincial lower courts, including the New York City Mayor's Court, which sat as a court of common pleas.[26]

Following the 1691 act, artisanal plaintiffs wishing to initiate a suit in the Mayor's Court informed the magistrates, who dispatched the sheriff with a summons requiring the person named to appear or face being taken into custody. The Mayor's Court continued to observe the exemption established by the burgher right in 1657 and only arrested resident defendants who had previously failed to appear when summoned or those who were suspected of planning to skip town. In March 1710, John Finch, a mariner, deposed that the saddler John Guest "has sent his wife and family away to Philadelphia . . . [and has] designs to follow them very speedily . . . the said John Guest having told the depont last night that he was looking for a boat."

Finch's deposition was accompanied by suits for debts of five and three pounds from William Provoost and William Thibaux.[27] When local residents were arrested, they usually put up bail and were not detained further. Once the parties to the case were established, the plaintiff filed and served a declaration, or complaint, and posted security for the costs; if he did not, the defendant could move to have him nonsuited. Once the complaint was served, the defendant had to enter a plea within a set time or lose the case; in practice, this usually meant three court days, or the time it took to enter three defaults. The court could enter a final judgment immediately following the third default, but only in cases involving a certain amount owed or if the damages were fixed—for example, in a debt claimed upon a penal bond where the liability was clear and agreed to in the original obligation. Otherwise the bench issued a writ of inquiry to convene a jury to determine the level of damages.[28]

If the defendant chose to contest the action, he would file a plea in defense selected from prescribed alternatives. A defendant could admit the facts but deny that they were sufficient to maintain the cause; this *demurer* raised a legal issue to be decided by the magistrates. If the magistrates found for the defendant, they entered judgment against the plaintiff and the case was closed. If they found for the plaintiff, then the case continued on to trial and resolution. Alternatively, the defendant could deny the validity of the general plea or plead specially, admitting certain facts asserted by the plaintiff but denying others or alleging different facts to which the plaintiff responded. The defendant could then offer a further rejoinder, and the process continued until the dispute was narrowed down to the point at which the legal issue was identified and then filed with the clerk of the court. It was only then that a case proceeded to trial before a jury that decided the dispute on the basis of whatever facts appeared on the issue roll. If the defendant was successful, the court usually ordered the plaintiff to pay his costs. If the plaintiff won, and the defendant failed to meet the judgment of the court, the plaintiff drew up a writ ordering the sheriff to seize the defendant's property to satisfy a financial claim or to seize the defendant himself and place him in custody until the judgment was met.

The authorities demonstrated their determination to make ordinary litigants pursue actions within the terms set by the common law by tightening up procedures and establishing new restrictions on jury qualification. In 1699, Governor Bellomont introduced new property restrictions on jurors to eliminate "the great hurt and damage [which] does arise to the inhabitants of this province by reason of the great abuses in the returning of jurors

not sufficiently qualified to discern the Causes in question upon Tryalls between party and party." Henceforth, to be a qualified juror, a man had to be
at least twenty-one and hold a ten-acre freehold or, in New York City and
Albany, a dwelling house free of all encumbrances or a personal estate valued at fifty pounds; the measure disqualified approximately two-thirds of the
city's adult white males from jury service. Although tradesmen continued to
constitute the majority of jurors, they were clearly drawn from the ranks of
the better off and employers rather than their less successful subcontractors.[29]
In 1702, the Mayor's Court introduced new rules governing the serving of
writs and court procedures, established regular hours and duties for court
officials, and required sheriffs and other officers to perform their duties effi-
ciently. This was one of nine such revisions that brought the procedures in
New York's courts in line with English practice in the first three decades of
the eighteenth century.[30] Indeed, as early as 1700, when asked to give an
account "of the method of proceeding in the several courts upon tryalls of
all sorts of causes within this province," Chief Justice William Smith reported
that the "rules and methods we are govern'd by in all tryalls is the common
law of England and . . . as near as may be according to the manner and
methods of His Majtys Courts at Westminster Hall."[31]

Clearly, the introduction of the common law, tightening of procedures,
and imposition of new constraints had recast the terms within which townsfolk presented disputes arising from work and daily life in court. However, one
has to be careful not to reify the 1691 act into too great a rupture in the city's
legal practice. Roman-Dutch law differed from English practice, and following the 1664, conquest local law had assumed a heterodox form; but the city's
legal culture had always been formal, and magistrates and litigants were
accustomed to working with written contracts, accounts, credit agreements,
financial instruments, and obligations drawn up under seal. The Mayor's Court
continued to meet once a week as it had since the issuing of the Dongan Charter in 1686, and even before the 1691 act, the minute books record cases with
pleadings that relied on common law fictions relating to venue and actions
commenced with a plea of "case" or "trespass upon the case," indicating an
understanding of the key terms and foundations for writ of assumpsit.[32]
Given these indications, it is likely that knowledgeable litigators and the
coterie of English-educated lawyers who lived and worked in the city greeted
the Act as a welcome clarification of legal procedure and practice.

Those most affected by the reforms introduced in 1691 were the more
numerous and less sophisticated artisanal litigators who had previously relied
on assembling witnesses and business records in order to present their own

cases, but who were now increasingly likely to require advice concerning the arcane vocabulary of an unfamiliar legal tradition. In some cases, the disorientating effects of novel common law proprieties were mitigated by the proximate character of English and Dutch legal ways and common conventions or "merchant customs" concerning trade. Where a plaintiff could produce a written agreement under seal showing that the defendant had promised to perform a certain action, he sued for breach of covenant much as before under the Roman-Dutch law. Thus, in 1713, Abraham Wendal sued Frans Wenne, "being a common carrier of goods wares and merchandize by water from the city of Albany to the city of New York," for nonfulfillment of an agreement to "buy tar at Albany and deliver it to New York City." Actions of covenant could also be brought for breaches of a lease, mortgage agreement, or apprenticeship or servitude indentures. In 1729, the joiner Thomas Griggs sued his apprentice Edward Griffeths for the cost of thirteen weeks' food and lodging when Griffeths married Anne Osburn without his master's permission and contrary to the indenture.[33] The action of account, which compelled a defendant to render a true and fair statement of the commercial relations between himself and the plaintiff, was also familiar to long-standing city residents. Thus, in February 1719, Henry de Tregrer sued John and Joseph Read, executors of the will of Thomas George de Tregrer, and demanded that the two "provide a reasonable account of the time that Thomas was Bayliffe for Henry and received monies for him" and provide details concerning the whereabouts of "three hundred pounds in various sumes and wares which he never tendered while alive."[34]

The most significant change of practice came in relation to suits for debts owed following oral and otherwise informal agreements and the employment of skilled labor. A common law suit for debt arose where a plaintiff claimed a specific amount for an agreement under seal or an executed contract for exchange of goods or services. Plaintiffs could not sue for uncertain sums, and if the debt was made up of different amounts, they had to specify the parts. Thus when Andries Barhyt sued his fellow shoemaker, Joost Sooy, he broke down the debt into money owed on an unpaid note for shoemaking work and for other, unspecified work and merchandise.[35] Once he had claimed a specific amount, the plaintiff had to hold to this figure throughout the pleading of the case. If he vacillated on the amount or presented it in uncertain terms, he risked being nonsuited. If the defendant successfully defended part of the suit, the plaintiff only succeeded in recovering part of the debt. And if the debtor could show that he owed *more* than the plaintiff claimed, the plaintiff stood to lose the whole case—the amount being deemed uncertain and unrecoverable under an action for debt. There was nothing to prevent a defeated plaintiff from returning to the court at a later date with a better-organized suit to try and recover a debt lost on a previous occasion. However, this required a repeat of the summons and pleading process and incurred the costs associated with a new suit.

In this fashion, the writs of covenant, account, and debt and the associated pleadings composed the facts of a case in a legally decidable form while simultaneously constraining litigants' freedom to present mitigating or historic conditions and limiting the options available to defenders. Debtors responding to a suit could only assert that whatever was claimed as owed had already been paid or deny the liability in the common law "manner and form" in which it was presented. The former was difficult to sustain in the face of a written instrument, a bond, or a promissory note giving details of the original agreement and repayment terms. The latter relied as much on one's legal knowledge, or that of one's representative, as it did on the dealings between the parties to the dispute. If the case proceeded to trial, those foolhardy enough to have an ill-planned or weak defense risked increasing their costs. Data on litigation rates gleaned from minutes of the Mayor's Court suggest that ordinary New Yorkers were mindful of these dangers, and although suits for debt were a common enough feature of the court's case load, most were settled without the need of a trial.[36] In the Dutch era, city magistrates had encouraged disputants to compromise their disagreements with privately or court-appointed arbitrators, who heard testimony concerning local practices and commercial dealings stretching back over many years. By the early eighteenth century, however, such imprecise assessments were no longer tolerated (let alone solicited) in suits presented within the forms of action at common law.

There remained one avenue of legal recourse through which city tradesmen could recover monies owed for goods supplied and services rendered on the basis of oral or otherwise informal agreements: the action of assumpsit. In addition to disputes resulting from broken promises and commercial letdowns, assumpsit could also accommodate claims concerning local norms and expectations and what tradesmen working their respective occupations could claim they reasonably deserved to have for their labor. It was not surprising, therefore, that variations on the writ of assumpsit quickly became the most popular form of action at common law, constituting two-thirds of all suits commenced in the first half of the eighteenth century.[37]

The action of assumpsit had various applications, but whatever the form in which it appeared, one can discern the presence of English legal fictions that provided the grounds for a complaint of a breach of contract and trespass. In cases of *indebitatus assumpsit,* plaintiffs claimed a specific sum in payment for services performed or goods provided where no formal agreement could be presented in support of the case. Thus, on 2 May 1724, Daniel Bonnet sued Richard Herring for nonpayment of six pounds, nineteen shillings, and tenpence halfpenny owed "for the work and labour of him the said Daniel as a shoemaker" in the preceding month. The grounds for Bonnet's suit rested on the assertion that Herring "assumed upon himself and to the said Daniel [did] then and there faithfully promise to pay" what was owed "when he should be thereunto afterwards required." However, Bonnet's writ continued, "the said Richard his promise & asumpcon aforesaid . . . not regarding but Imagining and fraudulently Intending him the said Daniel in this behalf craftilly and subtilly to deceive and defraud" had failed to pay.[38] The routine accusation of fictive fraudulent designs on the part of the plaintiffs reveals more about the enduring language of medieval legal fictions than they do about an individual defendant's integrity or lack thereof.

By employing a piece of summary shorthand—the phrase "diverse goods and merchandizes work found and provided"—they were able to recover multiple debts incurred over lengthy periods of time. In these cases, the writ could be phrased as an *assumpsit quantum valebant* or *quantum meriut* bearing claims for the estimated value of goods delivered or whatever an individual's labor should be reasonably worth. The first form was crucial for those involved in small-time trading of supplies and manufactured goods where closely calculated and unstable margins depended on realizing the maximum market price when goods were delivered rather than ordered. Thus, in May 1710, Phillip Travis sued Cornelius Dirckse, a cooper, for four pounds and two shillings for 370 oak bolts. Travis's complaint asserted that Dirckse had promised to pay "so much money as the said three hundred and seventy oak bolts should be reasonably worth to the said Philip" and that the "bolts at the said time of the sale and delivery thereof were then and there reasonably worth four pounds and two shillings current money."[39] The *quantum meriut* form of assumpsit was equally important for those who hired out their labor to others because it enabled artisans to recoup rewards that were commensurable with their skills and experience. In November 1718 Jeremiah Marshall sued John Hickford and Adolph Degrove for four pounds and ten shillings "for work done and performed before that time as a mariner at the special request of the said John and Adolph." Marshall's writ described how he had worked for thirty days "as a marriner on Board the sloop Rose . . . in the Rigging and fitting out of the said sloop" and how

Hickford and Degrove had promised to pay "all such sumes of money as the said Jeremiah reasonably deserve to have for his service." And "for his service aforesaid," the writ averred, Jeremiah "reasonably deserved to have of the said John and Adolph aforesaid the rate of three shillings a day." Despite this understanding and "their severall promises and assumptions aforesaid . . . not regarding," the writ charged Hickford and Degrove with "designing and fraudulently intending the said Jeremiah in this behalf craftily and subtily to deceive and defraud."[40]

Although the action of assumpsit enabled tradesmen to claim payment in accordance with locally established rates, it also required that they—or, as was increasingly likely, their attorneys—recast their disputes within the narrow compass of the writ. Consequently, what the court considered was less an explanation of the actual details and more the presentation of a particular litigant's position in its most favorable light, which left his opponent to challenge or contradict the facts as they were claimed. For example, in September 1728, William Jones sued the carpenter Charles Jandine, declaring that he was "indebted to the said William in the sum of eighteen pounds sixteen shillings and seven pence half penny Currant money of New York for the work and labour of him the said William as a carpenter and joyner . . . for the space and time of one hundred and thirty seven days." Thereafter, the complaint followed the usual form, casting Jones as an aggrieved carpenter denied his just deserts by Jandine who "imagining & fraudulently intending him the said William in this part Craftily and Subtily to deceive and defraud the aforesaid several sums of money or any part thereunto the said William hath not paid." The broader context of this dispute only becomes clear several weeks later, when Jandine launched a countersuit accusing Jones of defrauding him of 176 days work after first agreeing to serve as an apprentice for "313 days @ 2/9d per day," but later reneging on his promise.[41]

The rise of assumpsit reflected the force of new regulations requiring ordinary litigants to present their suits in the form of a common law writ, the advice given to these litigants by an emerging legal profession, and the need of city artisans to fit their oral and informal trade agreements to the new legal code. And yet the scope afforded by assumpsit was still limited when compared to the relatively liberal procedural and pleading options of earlier practice. As the examples make evident, the writ reduced the connection between litigants to a single dispute drawn from the continuum of their actual dealings, and the specificity of the agreements discussed sits uneasily with what we know of the ongoing relationships and informality of terms that characterized artisanal trade. Within the pleading forms afforded by assumpsit, it was still possible for tradesmen to demand recognition of their right to property in labor and payment in accordance with established and local expectations. However, in making such claims, middling traders became increasingly dependent on expert legal advice and, in disputed cases, jury trials. Any restrictions upon the access of ordinary litigants to either of these components would undermine the effectiveness of the court as a venue for the legal and public affirmation of artisans' particularistic privileges and right to be paid according to their just deserts.

*   *   *

The 1691 Act of Judicature and the 1693 Ministry Act were the keystones around which successive English governors endeavored to construct the arch of imperial governance in post-Leislerian New York. Numerous contemporary observers and subsequent scholarly commentators have noted the centrality of law and religion in England's much-vaunted mixed constitution: the king, the Lords, and the Commons constituted an indivisible and irresistible sovereign power credited with the wisdom of the common law and dignified by the divine authority of the Church of England. The legal and religious establishment provided more than merely static institutional support for the burgeoning military and fiscal state: law and religion also served as modes of political discourse within which the legitimacy and authority of imperial government were reiterated in daily life and work.[42] In religious matters, the authorities could depend on the devotional loyalties of colonial Anglicans and the endeavors of the Society for Promoting Christian Knowledge and its subsidiary, the Society for the Propagation of the Gospel in Foreign Parts. Both these missionary ventures, set up in 1699 and 1701, respectively, fostered the establishment of the English Church by providing financial support for clerical salaries, publishing Anglican literature, and funding the construction of church buildings in the American wilderness.[43] The same cannot be said, however, for the English legal profession, which paid scant regard to colonial practice law and did little or nothing to encourage the migration of knowledgeable lawyers and the establishment of a provincial bar without which the government's determination to settle the common law in New York would have likely failed.

The development of the legal profession in colonial New York was thus a private and entrepreneurial affair born of the 1691 Act of Judicature, which rapidly created a market for lawyers whose talents had previously been in little demand. Paul Hamlin identified forty-seven men who served another as a lawyer at some point in the late seventeenth century—although many if not most of these men served as a friend or business acquaintance rather than in a full-time professional capacity. This diverse group included college graduates with liberal educations such as William Anderson, James Graham, and David Jamison and others—such as James Emott, John Tudor, Edward Anthill, Barne Cosens, and William Huddleston—who could boast an English legal education.[44] However, in the 1680s and early 1690s, the majority of litigants continued to draw up their own complaints to be submitted to the court; those who did employ legal counsel tended to favor the advocacy of John Tudor, James Emmot, and Isaac Swinton.[45] The slow take-up reflected a variety of causes: the unfamiliarity with the role of a lawyer among Dutch residents who were more accustomed to relying on the services of a notary public; the close connection between the English lawyers and the unpopular Stuart and, later, Fletcher administrations.[46] The diminutive stature of the city's legal profession in the mid-1690s was highlighted by Abraham de Peyster's tactic of engaging all available legal talent to prevent his opponents, Onzel van Zweiten and John Cruger from securing representation, a ruse that prompted a bill "against feeing all Attorneys at Law."[47]

In the late 1690s, the connections between city lawyers and the anti-Leislerian, or "English," Party prompted Bellomont to denounce them for demonstrating such a "scandalous character" that "it would grieve a man to see our noble English laws so miserably mangled and prophaned." Bellomont declared (at least partially erroneously, we now know) that not a "man of 'em ever arrived at being an Attorney in England" and that "one of them was a Dancing Master, another a Glover by trade, [and] a third . . . condemned to be hanged in Scotland for burning the Bible and for blasphemy." When the gouty Irish Whig peer was not exercising himself with indignant harrumphs aimed at lawyerly elements within the local opposition, he acknowledged the need for qualified legal talent in the colony. Writing to the Lords of Trade in 1698, Bellomont reckoned that "Now that there is a prospect of doubling the revenue I am humbly of opinion we ought to have good Judges sent from England and King's Councel to mind the interest of the Crown." The restoration of Sampson Broughton as attorney general, in the aftermath of Nicholas Bayard's trial for treason in 1701, and the arrival of John Bridges and Roger Mompesson as chief justices in New York and New Jersey (following the departure of the pugnacious William Atwood) went some way toward meeting the governor's proposal.[48]

In the first three decades of the eighteenth century, the growing number of professional lawyers produced what one scholar termed a thoroughgoing metamorphosis of legal practice in the city. As legal procedures became more complex, the number of complaints identifying an attorney at the moment of filing climbed steadily to three-fourths and more by the 1730s. Lawyers ensured their indispensability by adhering to the letter of the Act of Judicature and drawing their precedents from English common law—consigning local practices and precedents prior to 1691 to a legal prehistory with no bearing upon eighteenth-century cases. An inflexible legal code and native legal profession developed in symbiotic connection, guiding the city and province toward strict adherence to the common law and the formalities of presentation.[49] The commitment to legal formalities also provided the knowledgeable representative with new kinds of technical challenges that could be lodged on behalf of a plaintiff or a defendant.

In marked contrast to the arbitrators who resolved disputes according to the Roman-Dutch law and local practices, common law attorneys relied on *not* presenting all pertinent facts and inviting the defense to contradict the view given in their own time and at their own expense. Magistrates no longer pursued all relevant information pertaining to the issue in search of a compromise, but considered every dispute as a discrete event to be decided by adversarial litigants in a zero-sum contest. Moreover, and in common with other common law writs, the action of assumpsit was open to various technical challenges: any discrepancy in the drawing up of the complaint could provide grounds for default, and when plaintiffs registered their disputes they were careful to ensure that the details were uniform throughout.[50] In the early eighteenth century, then, the focus of the law relating to commerce shifted from a concern for formality and equity based on a variety of admissible pleas to a formal but arguably more arcane system that precluded references to dealings beyond the case in question and that decided the issue on the basis of arguments made increasingly by professional representatives within the language of the common law.

In England, the precision of common law presentations had long provided opportunities for legal savants to issue technical and obscurantist rejoinders in an effort to secure an advantage for their clients—a practice that prompted the notable late seventeenth-century chief justice, Mathew Hale, to decry the pleadings as little more than "a snare and trap and piece of skill."[51] As legal practice in New York increasingly set lawyer against lawyer, technical challenges that had been rarely in evidence before the 1690s became more common. When the widow Susanna Elliot fell out with the bricklayer Daniel Ebbits concerning uncompleted work on her house, both sides resorted to technicalities. In October 1700, Ebbits sued Elliot for nonpayment, but her attorney, Edward Anthill, succeeded in having the builder nonsuited for filing his complaint incorrectly with the clerk of the court. The following week Elliot appeared "in her own proper person" to sue Ebbits for damages of ten pounds under an action for breach of covenant. Declaring that the builder "did bargain, covenant and agree with the said plaintiff to finish both within and without what appertains to either bricklayer or plasterer," Elliot complained that Ebbits had quit before the work was finished. To support her case, Elliot brought in "a certain agreement . . . in which covenant the said def did bind himself to the plaintiff faithfully and justly to perform sd work as will plainly appear in the sd agreement in his own handwriting." However, doubtless still smarting from his defeat the previous week, Ebbits had engaged Barne Cosens to act as his attorney. In his successful defense Cosens maintained that the action of covenant brought by Elliot could not stand because "the plat in the said declaration hath set forth that the said defendant did bargain covenant and agree to do something for the said plt *but* what when and whereto be done for what consideration the said plt in the said declaration hath not set forth."[52] The imprecision of Elliot's action in covenant and the omission of details pertaining to consideration cost her the case, which, as any good attorney would have advised her, should have been presented as an action in assumpsit with a claim for damages.

There is no record of Daniel Ebbits ever receiving payment for the work he had already done or whether Susanna Elliot's renovations were ever finished. If their working relationship was not already soured by delays, their costly clashes in court surely made a reconciliation unlikely. What is noteworthy about this case is the manner in which the legal process obscured rather than addressed the contention that divided the parties. Ebbits was rebuffed before having the opportunity to make his case for payment. And Elliot's invocation of the implied duties of a bricklayer and plasterer were characterized not as reasonable customer expectations—as they might have been during the Dutch period by a court-appointed arbitrator—but as imprecise terms that were inadmissible under the common law action of covenant. When plaintiffs felt that such lawyerly evasions went beyond reasonable bounds, they challenged the tactic and appealed to the court. For example, when the widow Christina Beenvos sued Hendrick Gerrits for "twelve pounds and one half pound beaver (Dutch weight)" for diverse goods and merchandise, David Jamison (Gerrits's attorney) rejected the suit, invoking the rule that cases be presented according to English rather than Dutch weight, which, despite the defendant's demonstrable Dutch ethnicity and long history of dealings with the Beenvos family, he described as a "foreign and outlandish measure." Following a challenge, the court declared Jamison's objection "evasive and insufficient," and Christina Beenvos won her case and the costs. [53]

As the injustices thrown up by the rigidities of the common law multiplied, so did calls for equitable remedies. When Governor Robert Hunter arrived in 1710, he reported being fairly "pelted with petitions calling for a court of equity" or chancery in New York and New Jersey where he was "acquainted with some cases which very much require such a Court, there being noe relief at common Law." However, no sooner had Hunter convened a Court of Chancery than he was condemned by the assemblymen for overreaching his authority and acting "contrary to Law without precedent and of dangerous consequence to the liberty and property of the subject." In this fashion, the settling of English law in New York called forth new sources of contention even as it imposed the will of the colonizers and endeavored to meet the demands of the colonized.[54]

The arrival of ambitious and well-educated English attorneys in the late seventeenth and early eighteenth centuries increased the time and costs involved in going to court, leading to periodic attempts at regulation. As early as 1693, the provincial assembly endeavored to regulate legal fees, publishing a schedule of costs chargeable by local attorneys. However, the recommendations never received the assent of Governor Fletcher and his council and were disregarded with impunity by the lawyers.[55] Although Bellomont had his own reasons to dislike sections of the local legal profession, his criticisms anticipated subsequent complaints regarding delays and costs: "The Lawyers here do so prey on the people that it is a melancholy thing to heare how unequally justice is and has been distributed in this Province; in so much as I am told a suit at Common law is more expensive and dilatory here than in England." In 1709, the Assembly again tried to enforce a ceiling of fifty shillings for cases taken to the Supreme Court and twenty shillings for cases in the Mayor's Court. However, local lawyers fought the regulation, arguing that such measures "reduces most of the Fees so low that . . . tis very difficult if possible for the Officers to live upon the profits of their places." Thereafter, the lawyers succeeded in having twenty-nine steps accepted as billable services.[56]

The adversarial nature of the legal process and the increasing amounts of time and money involved also prompted amendments in litigation practice, such as threatened suits and plea bargaining, to avoid lengthy and costly proceedings. Plaintiffs drew up complaints that suggested an imminent suit, but left the details concerning the principal sum and damages blank, to be filled in at a later date. Similarly, defendants came to court offering a partial settlement for less than the full amount if the plaintiff would drop the suit. For example, in August 1719, Wynaut van Zandt sued Johannes Ten Eyck for eight pounds, five shillings, and sixpence and damages of ten pounds "for the work as a turner and blockmaker and at his special instance and request for diverse wares and merchandises provided." Ten Eyck's attorney, William Bickley, appeared and declared that his client had brought "six pounds and five shillings and sixpence" to the court and pleads "discount as to the residue."[57]

In the wake of Queen Anne's War rising litigation rates and legal expenses prompted further regulatory reforms that simplified debt litigation, arguably in a way that favored creditors, and lessened the likelihood of smaller suits from individual artisans making it to court. The credit system in New York—based on various forms of borrowing and the use of bills, bonds, promissory notes, and exchanges on account—encouraged piecemeal litigation, as parties to a string of transactions had little choice but to sue on each individual debt. However, in 1714, the Assembly introduced legislation that permitted defendants sued "upon Bonds, Bills, Bargains, Promises, Accounts or the like" to offer in response any offsetting instruments of debt upon which judgment might be entered by jury verdict or otherwise. The statute was designed to decrease the number of suits brought on individual transactions and to encourage parties to regularize their accounts and debtor portfolios by grouping related debts under a single judgment. Clearly, this facility served the interests of those who carried multiple debtor obligations that could be used as offsets without further discussions of the details of each individual transaction. In practice, the legislation prompted a reduction in the total volume of debt litigation and an increase in the rate of default judgment. By the 1730s, attorneys used offsets with increasing frequency to manage their clients' accounts, contributing to the decline in the numbers of merchant creditors who appeared as defendants in suits presented to the court.[58]

The Assembly's revision of local laws relating to debt litigation and rising legal costs also encouraged the increasing use of a conditional bond intended to protect lenders from the effects of anticipated antagonistic suits. The bond was offered with a view to creating a debtor who could be used as an offset in the event that the issuer of the bond lost a forthcoming suit. Under the terms of the bond, the lender provided credit for the borrower on the condition that the borrower bound himself to repay the debt in the event that the lender was successfully sued by a third party and did not secure the judgment of costs. However, if the anticipated plaintiff did not bring forward his suit or defaulted—and through this default the lender/defendant was awarded costs and damages—then the obligation lapsed. In this way, lenders insured themselves against the threat of antagonistic suits, borrowers secured access to credit by speculating on the chances of their backers, and the effects of legal formalization were felt in the city's credit economy.[59]

In the late 1720s, the spiraling costs of legal fees prompted renewed complaints and calls for the regulation of provincial attorneys. But it was not until 1728 that Governor William Burnet appointed a "Committee to Hear Grievances in the Practice of the Law." Shortly thereafter, and most likely as a direct result of this committee's deliberations, several prominent members of New York's emerging legal profession took steps to regulate themselves and establish a provincial bar. In 1729, six leading attorneys formed an association to supervise legal education and to regulate the practice of the law. As a first step, the six agreed to refuse assistance to lawyers who obtained their license to practice after June 1725 and to clients who employed these representatives, declaring their intention to thereby expose "the ignorance and Inabilities of such practitioners."[60] Shortly thereafter, this attempt to monopolize local legal practice secured the support of the common councilmen, who petitioned the Assembly for legislation to the effect "that no attorney be Admitted to practice in the Mayor's Court but such as shall be chosen Elected and sworn by the Mayor Recorder and Aldermen and Approved of by the Governer." The following year, the Montgomerie Charter acceded to the city's demands and fixed a monopoly of the Mayor's Court business on Joseph Murray, John Chambers, William Smith, George Lurting, William Jamison, Richard Nicolls, and Abraham Lodge. Based on the evidence of complaints filed to initiate suits in the Mayor's Court thereafter, it appears that the monopoly was assiduously enforced until protests by those who served in the Supreme Court (but were excluded from the Mayor's Court) forced a legislative repeal in 1746.[61]

In her study of the long-term impact of the professionalization of the legal practice in colonial New York, Deborah Rosen has pointed to increased time delays and costs as the century wore on.[62] Increasing amounts of the magistrates' time was taken up with procedural motions, orders to plead or appear, and directions to court officers that meant delays even in relatively straightforward cases. For example, between 1690 and 1750, the number of court appearances needed to bring a case to trial in the Mayor's Court increased from less than four to ten and the time required from three to nearly ten months. A similar trend was evident in suits appealed to the Supreme Court: in the late seventeenth century, only 12 percent of the minute entries in the Supreme Court were taken up with orders directing

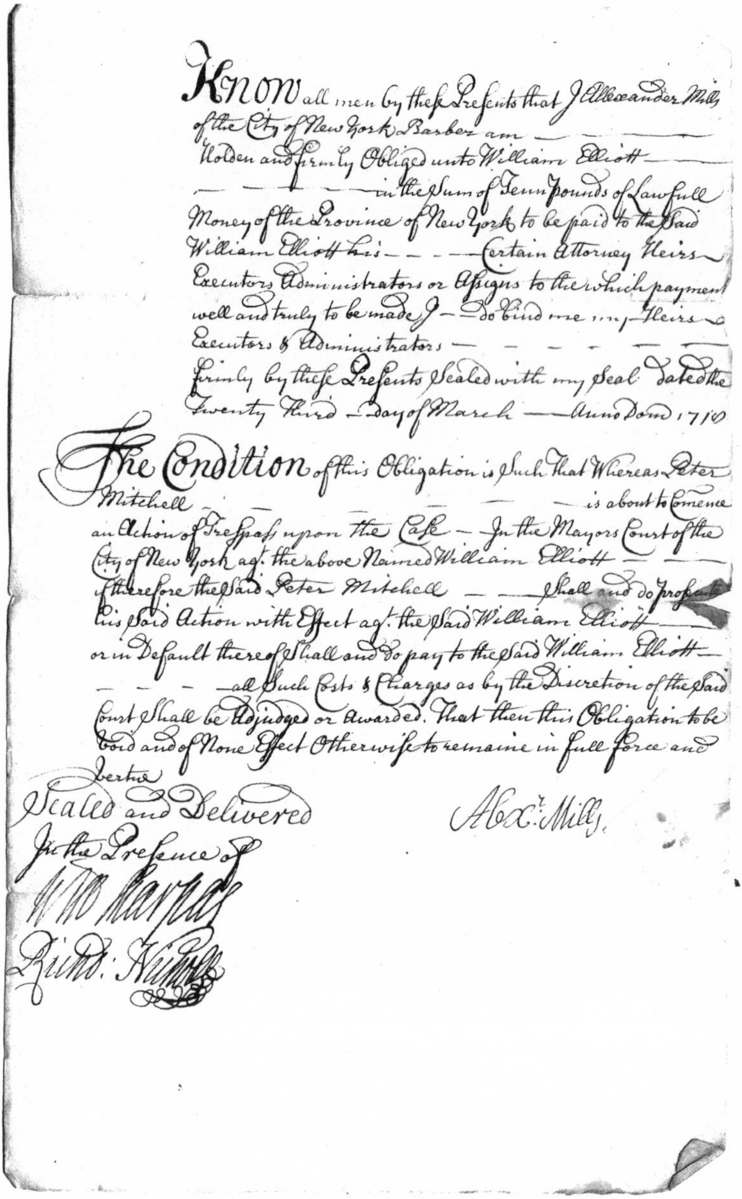

Know all men by these Presents that I Alexander Mills of the City of New York Barber am Holden and firmly Obliged unto William Elliott in the Sum of Tenn pounds of Lawfull Money of the Province of New York to be paid to the Said William Elliott his Certain Attorney Heirs Executors Administrators or Assigns to the which payment well and truly to be made I do bind me my Heirs Executors & Administrators firmly by these Presents Sealed with my Seal Dated the Twenty Third day of March Anno Domi 1718

The Condition of this Obligation is Such That Whereas Peter Mitchell is about to Comence an Action of Trespass upon the Case In the Mayors Court of the City of New York agt. the above Named William Elliott if therefore the Said Peter Mitchell Shall and do prosecute his Said Action with Effect agt. the Said William Elliott or in Default thereof Shall and do pay to the Said William Elliott all Such Costs & Charges as by the Discretion of the Said Court Shall be Adjudged or Awarded. That then this Obligation to be void and of None Effect Otherwise to remaine in full force and Vertue

Sealed and Delivered In the Presence of
Wm Sharpas
Richd: Nichols

Alexr: Mills

Figure 12. Conditional bond to defend a forthcoming suit. This bond was included in the papers submitted in the suit of Peter Mitchell v. William Elliot, 23 March 1718. The obligation bound the barber Alexander Mills to pay William Elliot if he failed to secure costs in Mitchell's anticipated suit.

litigants to plead, and less than 1 percent were orders terminating procedures for failure to do so; although the court only met for one week every six months, disputes were resolved quickly, and cases that proceeded to trial took an average of two to three court appearances over two months. In contrast, by the mid-eighteenth century approximately 26 percent of all minute book entries concerned orders to plead and 8 percent terminated proceedings for a failure to plead; cases proceeding to trial took an average of four to five court appearance over as many as twenty months to arrive at a judgment.

The increase in court appearances and delays added to the costs of going to court. In spite of attempts to place a ceiling on fees, New York's lawyers routinely operated outside the regulations and charged their clients for every appearance in court and every action taken in their behalf. For example, Abraham Lakeman's 1743 suit against Nathanial Stillwell identified sixteen chargeable items, including entering the action, filing a copy of the bond, and entering the return of the writ and pleas, in addition to payments for the recorder and bell ringer totaling two pounds and seventeenth shillings.[63] By the 1750s, plaintiffs who took a case to a jury trial required fifty billable services costing between fifteen and sixteen pounds, and this figure rose still higher if they lost the case and had to cover the defendant's costs as well. Defendants who hired attorneys to plead their case faced a bill of nine to ten pounds for a successful defense at jury trial. A defendant's costs would be significantly reduced, however, if they chose not to oppose the case and simply defaulted, incurring no attorney's fees at all. The evidence suggests that this was the option increasingly favored by middling residents, leading to veritable collapse in the rate of jury trials, especially for the small sums sought by city tradesmen.[64] Consequently, skilled workers' claims for rewards commensurate with their skills and local expectations were less and less likely to be pursued to the jury stage and heard in the city's Mayor's Court.

*   *   *

In 1691, the introduction of the English common law established a formal and, it must have seemed to many, arcane legal system in New York City. Prior to 1691, disputes concerning the values of commodities and services had been subject to considerations regarding the value of local commodities, the rightful reward for a given task, or the level of skill one might expect from a tradesmen that lay beyond the express terms of agreement. It was at these moments—in the meetings with arbitrators and presentations in court—that tradesmen articulated publicly acknowledged claims for consideration as skilled workers serving in recognized capacities and deserving of their just deserts. After 1691, and within actions of assumpsit, artisans continued to sue customers and partners for what they reasonably deserved to have and in accordance with local expectations and customs. However, the shift to assumpsit changed the nature of this claim in subtle ways: the court now considered each dispute as a specific and isolated debt or transgression, and defendants had to offer a formal defense and proceed to trial on that basis; presentations in court had shifted from consideration of the facts of the case, supplied by litigants, witnesses, and arbitrators to a consideration of the legal facts presented by professional attorneys in written pleadings. In this way, the introduction of a comprehensive and impersonal legal system served to squeeze out idiosyncratic references to individual circumstances and the endless variability of eighteenth-century commercial life.

What had changed, then, was less the eagerness with which tradesmen pursued their commercial interests and more the manner in which they resolved their disagreements. In the absence of major protestation, it is difficult to avoid concluding that the formulaic and increasingly expensive resolution offered by the English common law must have met at least some of the needs of local litigants. But as litigation rates increased, and the city traders sought their fortunes in the profitable but unpredictable Atlantic trade, it is also clear that the courts concerned themselves less and less with imprecise claims to custom and local expectations and more with the obligations of creditors and debtors under contracts adjudicated according to the formal procedures of the English common law. As public discussion of residential and occupational privileges yielded to claims made to the rights of men (and to a lesser extent, women) under contracts, city tradesmen were treated as equals before the law. In the process, and accompanied by regulatory amendments and the rise of an ambitious class of professional lawyers, the legal practice in the Mayor's Court assumed the guise of an impersonal and increasingly efficient system of cash collection. The commercial and political consequences of this drift would only become apparent during the severe economic recession and a falling out among the city's ruling elite in the 1730s.

Chapter 6
"C'mon brave boys let us be brave for liberty and law": Artisans and Politics, 1730–1763

Toward the end of September 1730, the surveyor James Lyne submitted his "Plan of the City of New-York" to William Bradford for inclusion in the *New York Gazette.*[1] The plan graphically confirmed the effects of more than three decades of urban expansion: in lower Manhattan, the well-to-do residents of Dock and Queen streets rubbed shoulders with mariners and waterfront workers, who made their way uptown via Broad Street, the city's central thoroughfare. Above the docks and commercial district, city blocks filled up with residences and independent businesses jostled for frontage along the narrow streets of the North and East Wards. In the West Ward, on the Hudson River side, the land owned by Trinity Church at Kings Farm had stalled the northward sprawl, prompting the construction of wharves named for leading traders and shipbuilders—the Waltons, Elsworths, and Frenches—along the East River as far north as Beekman's Swamp. Since the turn of the eighteenth century, the city's population had doubled to some 8,600 souls. New arrivals established homes beyond the pond at Fresh Water, once the marker that divided city residents from inhabitants of the rural Out Ward. The picture was one of growth and prosperity.

As the city expanded, its inhabitants paid less and less heed to the heterogeneous schedule of privileges and duties that had previously joined the municipal government to its townspeople and tradesmen by reciprocal ties of privileges and duties. In part, this reflected the diminishing proportion of residents who had grown up with the earlier civic and commercial strictures. By 1730, English residents, many of them recently arrived, comprised almost half of the city's population, and the proportion of those claiming Dutch ancestry had fallen to less than two-fifths; over the next two decades this latter figure would half again to less than one-fifth. Ambitious individuals also drove changes in attitudes toward municipal ordinances, evading

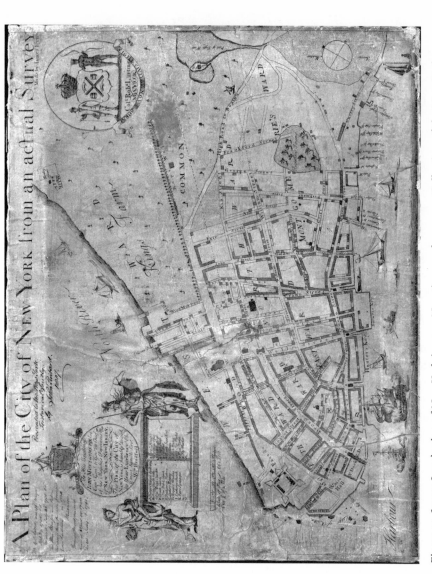

Figure 13. James Lyne's plan of New York in 1730. Negative number 15909, Collection of the New-York Historical Society.

the regulation of freemen and apprentices and measures relating to licensing and quality controls in the town. These same commercial ambitions nurtured the fragile dependencies and wretchedness that underpinned the city's prosperity: the ramified networks of credit and exchange within which "independent" traders risked their all in the Atlantic trade and the slave labor force—now fifteen hundred strong—whose miserable bondage provided city entrepreneurs with the brawn on which many of their ventures relied.[2]

Thus it was that the ideal of a closely controlled corporate community of free and independent burghers conceived in an earlier and less self-assured age yielded to a new, racialized, and increasingly libertarian laissez-faire urban society. The distinction between free and enslaved workers—and the apprentices and servants whose status marked the gradations in between—supplanted the earlier differentiation between residents and strangers. Prices and wages depended more and more on a market influenced by private and legal, rather than municipal, judgments. Given these incremental shifts in the city's civic and commercial life, changes in the status of artisanal work and the connections between tradesmen and the wider community were bound to follow, but what form would the new connections take? The anonymous social and economic processes that enervated the earlier prescriptive municipal order could not also decide the future form of any civic relationship. These processes reflected the aggregate impact of thousands of individual decisions and such a diffuse force could never have determined the character and particulars of future social relations.[3] Such changes required the articulation of an alternative vision of the proper relationship between the community and its skilled workforce, of the kind that had earlier provided for the establishment of a Dutch republican civic order in New Amsterdam. Just as in the mid-seventeenth century, this vision emerged out of the realm of politics—still oligarchic, but now electoral rather than aristocratic—in which a candidate's ability to secure popular support came to depend on their capacity to evince a reassuring sense of mastery over the changes wrought by the population expansion, rise of unregulated commerce, and spread of credit and slavery that were the source of so many opportunities and anxieties.

For almost four decades, New York City had fudged its response to the transformation of political and legal attitudes toward artisanal work since Leisler's Rebellion. In the mid-1730s, however, the combination of a crippling economic recession and a bitter dispute within the provincial elite over the division of patronage spoils once again brought the city to the brink of civil war. In a hitherto unprecedented appeal to the popular vote, those outside the governor's clique imported the rhetoric of radical English politics and championed the expression of consent by ordinary voters as the only foundation for legitimate government. It was in the course of this struggle that city tradesmen were cast as equal political subjects charged with the defense of the common good in the face of a corrupt and tyrannical administration. In subsequent decades, claims regarding this novel and elevated status—and declarations concerning the integrity, skills, and independence of city tradesmen—figured in electoral campaigns and public debates concerning the role and character of local artisans. In this way, the crisis of the 1730s ushered onto the political stage a new and idealized artisanal subject whose characteristics not only made sense of the transformation of urban working life in the preceding four decades but also provided a constituency for the establishment of a demotic, republican political culture in New York City.

*   *   *

In the same month that James Lyne submitted his "Plan of the City of New York" to the *Gazette,* he advertised his services as a teacher, perhaps intending to cash in on the celebrity afforded by his most recent commission: "At the custom-House in this City (where a convenient Room is fitted up)," the notice read, "James Lyne designs to Teach in the Evenings (during the Winter) Arithmetick in all its parts, Geometry, Trigonometry, Navigation, Surveying, Gauging, Algebra, and sundry other parts of Mathematical Learning."[4] Unfortunately, even as the enterprising draughtsman welcomed his first students into the makeshift classroom, New York City slipped into the most severe commercial recession in its history, from which it would not recover for some eight or nine years.

The city's core problems stemmed from the long-term decline of its maritime and West Indian trade. Merchants blamed the decline on the damage to the province's good name abroad following the end of the flour bolting and export monopoly. In this view, inadequate enforcement of quality controls allowed unregulated upriver traders to export unmerchantable product to the Chesapeake and Caribbean and the city's reputation suffered. However, the rise of Pennsylvanian suppliers who competed with New York for the trade in flour and foodstuffs was a more likely explanation.[5] In addition, to the Pennsylvanian rivalry the loosening of municipal controls and success of a city-merchant campaign against tonnage duties on imports in the late 1720s had encouraged Bermudian and other foreign exporters to use the port of New York, further increasing the competition in the Atlantic seaboard trade with city-based shippers. By the winter of 1730, all indices suggested that the maritime economy upon which the city's fortunes depended was in crisis: the locally owned merchant fleet had shrunk to fifty vessels, fewer than half the number at the turn of the eighteenth century; imports of slaves and commodities had fallen to their lowest level in more than a decade; shipyards languished for want of commissions and construction sites across Manhattan fell silent. News of the commercial downturn and the 150 fashionable homes available for rent in New York City circulated as far away as Boston and Philadelphia.[6]

In the ensuing three years, a series of body blows pummeled the remaining confidence out of the city and its trade. In 1730–31, a smallpox outbreak swept Manhattan, claiming seventy-six people in a single week and some six hundred souls in all. As wealthier residents arranged for inoculations and moved their families to Long Island's healthier climes, one city observer described how "many children dye . . . as well as grown Persons and the Country People are afraid to come to Town which makes Markets thin, Provisions dear, and deadens Trade, and it goes very hard with the Poor." While New York reeled from the effects of the epidemic, the Lords of Trade tightened imperial regulations in favor of English manufacturing and merchant interests. The Hat Act (1732) prohibited colonial manufactures and deprived New York of a trade that the governor, William Cosby, had earlier warned threatened to "make the greatest advances to the prejudice of Great Britain." Following the Hat Act, Cosby reported that the hat trade in New York "needs no more mention." The Molasses Act (1733) established duties on rum, sugar, and molasses shipped to New York from Dutch and French islands, granting English Caribbean planters a competitive advantage at the expense of city importers and consumers. New York merchants protested the hike in sugar prices and shipped more of their product with smugglers to mitigate the impact of the Act. But London's rejection of the New Yorkers' appeals further undermined the confidence of English financiers and discouraged investment in the struggling colonial town.[7]

New York City had suffered downturns before and might well have weathered this one but for one crucial factor that transformed a recession brought on by structural economic weaknesses and flagging investor confidence into a protracted slump: the collapse of the credit economy, which had underwritten the expansion of urban commerce in the preceding four decades. As we have seen, during the early eighteenth century, city tradesmen and their families relied on creditors, subcontracted employment, commercial partnerships, and on bondsmen and bondswomen to maintain themselves in trade. Unfortunately, the fragile financial clientage upon which the seaport had built its prosperity was highly sensitive to the ebb and flow of commerce and the movement of individuals into and out of the city. Whenever the city's commercial fortunes took a turn for the worse, nervous lenders called in debts, forcing periodic peaks in the number of cases initiated in the Mayor's Court. These peaks coincided with recessions following the end of Queen Anne's War and the collapse of the South Sea Bubble in the early 1720s. News of a debtor's likely departure also brought creditors to court seeking to recover what they could. In addition, the rise of professional lawyers meant that, by the early 1730s, lenders relied on an increasingly impersonal legal process and the court expended less and less time considering the idiosyncrasies of individual cases as it pushed on with the task of debt collection.

A tax assessment completed on the eve of the recession revealed that 50 percent of the fourteen hundred or so residents who qualified as New York taxables were assessed at the lowest rate of ten pounds or less. Assuming that the remaining seven thousand or so white and black residents who paid no taxes at all were no better off than these poorest taxables it is clear that the majority of working men and women possessed minimal assets and relied on credit, petty trading, and paid employment of one kind or another to survive.[8] When a sharp decline in the price of West Indian sugar prompted financial retrenchment among city financiers, the combined effect of previously noted structural weaknesses sent the city into recession; simultaneously, the smallpox epidemic, which claimed six hundred lives, mostly from the ranks of the poor and indebted, prompted an exodus of three hundred unemployed tradesmen, wreaking havoc with the delicately balanced credit arrangements.[9] The death or departure of a substantial section of the city's middling and, therefore, borrowing sort, sent shock waves through credit networks, prompting an all-time high in the number of cases for debt as lenders scrambled to recover what they could. The consequent credit crunch brought the econmy to a standstill, halving the value of city properties and reducing municipal tax revenues by some 5 or 6 percent.[10]

In response to the credit crisis and the rising tide of debt litigation, the Assembly introduced an act for the temporary relief of insolvent borrowers. Those arrested for debts of less than 100 pounds could regain their liberty by taking a pauper's oath and assigning their assets for the benefit of creditors—saving their household goods and trade tools up to a value of ten pounds.[11] Although debtors avoided jail, new lenders were difficult to find, prompting unprecedented numbers of appeals for relief. Between 1732 and

1735, the number of people seeking municipal assistance soared to almost four hundred, double the figure of a decade earlier. For the first time in the city's history, skilled workers joined the ranks of the elderly and infirm and abandoned mothers and children, seeking charity. However, although the number of claimants doubled, municipal spending on poor relief increased by only one-third as officials resorted to outmoded regulations and endeavored to separate the deserving from the undeserving poor. To restore urban trade, the common councilmen tightened up freemanship regulations, gesturing toward the protection of the local labor market and, following the 1734 city elections, they set some local men to work building a new poorhouse. The Common Council also directed the churchwardens to support "only such poor as have the badge on the right sleeve with the letters NY . . . and . . . to withdraw relief from the poor who refuse to wear the badge."[12]

The Common Council's determination to distinguish between "persons of good repute experiencing misfortune" and those who "had become poor through idleness or vice" emphasized the extent to which they misunderstood the nature of the crisis they faced.[13] The authorities resented using precious tax revenues for the support of able-bodied working men and women, and their misguided parsimony increased the distress among the middling and laboring poor. Municipal prudence also contributed to the crime wave that swept the city to which the courts responded with public whippings and increasingly draconian punishments.[14] Whatever the rights and wrongs of the common councilmen's approach, the suffering of working people was evident in parents' applications for assistance to pay for the funerals of children claimed by the smallpox and the decision taken by residents such as the victualler William Lane, who abandoned his home and three young sons and fled the city. Those who stayed organized lobbies in support of their trade interests and petitioned the provincial Assembly to take action to restore the city's trade. By 1734, the petitioning campaign had brought city artisans to center stage in a bitter dispute between provincial political leaders.

In September 1732, city shoemakers, tanners, and curriers petitioned the authorities to prevent the export of rawhides from the colony. The following month, "sundry Masters of Vessels, Shipwrights, Blockmakers, Smiths, and other Tradesmen of the City of New York" called for the reintroduction of tonnage duties on foreign vessels putting in at New York. Both appeals failed to secure protection for city trades and markets. Two years later, however, a second round of submissions successfully called for similar protections. On 2 May 1734, six city coopers petitioned "in behalf of themselves and the rest of the coopers" for duties on empty casks and barrels imported from New Jersey and elsewhere; on 28 May, a petition presented by merchants, tradesmen, and "upwards of one hundred hands" lamented the "great decay in trade and navigation of this city" caused by the "Bermudians who daily flock hither for freight" and warned that "if there be not some speedy and reasonable remedy applied," then "the greatest part of the workmen and laborer in the said city with their wives and families would shortly be obliged to leave." Three days later, a delegation of four master bakers "in behalf of themselves and the rest of the bakers" protested the "great quantities of bread [that] hath lately been imported into the city from neighbouring colonies." The rolling protest had the desired effect and the petitioners succeeded in securing duties on foreign vessels and upon bread, meat, and empty casks imported to the city.[15]

Both sets of petitions are lost, so we cannot know for sure who signed, but the Assembly minutes offer some insight into those who represented these trades by identifying a handful of coopers and bakers who served as delegates. The men who presented the petitions came from wards across the city and were mostly middling taxpayers. Some had previously held minor municipal posts, but there were also less well-off representatives who had not previously been prominent in civic life. The cooper Edward Man lived in the East Ward and had served as holder of the keys to the city armory; Daniel Dunscumb and Alexander Allair hailed from the South and Dock Wards; Gerardus Comfort had served as petty constable in the West Ward; Johannis de Graaf lived in the North Ward.[16] The bakers' petition identified a similarly mixed group, including Andries Marshalk and his brother Peter from the North Ward and Cornelius Cortreight and Everts Byvanck from the East Ward.[17]

There are several things to note regarding these trade representatives and other details gleaned from the presentation of the second and successful set of petitions to the Assembly. Bearing in mind the occupational clustering that marked artisanal residency patterns, the petitions' identification of representatives from different wards indicates a concerted, city-wide action among artisans to secure protectionist measures. For the first time since Leisler's Rebellion, the artisanal petitioning campaigns of the early 1730s provided local politicians with a politically engaged constituency of urban working men. However, while this earlier artisanal constituency had been rooted in civic and religious appeals made by freemen and defenders of the Protestant church, the protests in the 1730s focused more clearly on individual and collective economic interests. In 1690 the townspeople suspected

that executive corruption and papist conspiracies were the root of their problems; in the 1730s some still railed on about corruption, especially around
election time, but most recognized that their source of their problems lay
with the market and inadequate protection for local commerce. This is one
measure of the transformation that had taken place in the previous forty
years. What is equally striking is that the assemblymen charged with presenting the second and successful set of petitions were long-standing supporters
of the lobby that had both *opposed* similar duties (on freight tonnage) in the
1720s and rebuffed calls for the introduction of protective measures two
years earlier: Anthony Rutgers, the son of a family of wealthy brewers and
traders, and Stephen Delancey, the venerable patriarch of one of New York's
leading merchant families were not the sort of men who usually bothered
themselves with the concerns of local artisans. By the spring of 1734, however, these merchants and their associates were locked in a no-holds-barred
contest with their opponents for the support of urban workers. To understand how the vicissitudes of electoral politics had led to this volte face, it is
helpful to consider the broader political context of the Common Council
elections in 1734.

*   *   *

Lines of political allegiance in early eighteenth-century New York are notoriously difficult to pin down, but commentators have discerned two loosely
configured factions: a merchant lobby headed by Adolph Philipse—son of
New Amsterdam's Frederick Philipse—and the aforementioned Stephen
Delancey, and an upriver, landed faction whose principals were Lewis Morris Sr., Lewis Morris Jr., and fellow manorial landlord, Robert Livingston.
Beyond loyalty to these leaders and family ties, however, it is difficult to trace
any consistent interest or principle underlying provincial political divisions.
Both sides, if we can call them such, competed for control of the governor's
council and the Assembly in order to influence the raising of the "Revenue"—
the package of excise duties (particularly on liquor) and taxes on improved
land and personal property agreed upon periodically to provide official salaries and other government expenses.[18] Unsurprisingly, the Philipsites attacked
commercial levies that they argued served as a disincentive to mercantile
trade; the Morrisites were equally strident in their denunciations of land
taxes as a regressive burden on small farmers. However, once in office, both
lobbies favored a combination of commercial and property taxes.

Political principles do not offer a more reliable guide to factional loyalties.

Rather than adhering consistently to a particular ideology, both sides drew on radical and conservative themes within contemporary metropolitan political debate. What we know of the tenor of early eighteenth-century electoral contests indicates that, when the city's multiethnic and semiliterate electorate could be persuaded to turn out and vote, they favored the vociferous defenses of popular rights that characterized anti-incumbent campaigns.[19] Thus, depending on their fortunes in the preceding contest, the well-to-do representatives of either faction might prosecute a Whiggish campaign for Assembly seats in defense of popular rights against the governor's prerogative power. Alternatively, although all were mindful of the perils of being identified as cronies of the "court," both were equally prepared to collaborate with a pliant executive in return for the spoils of office. In this way, the the contenders' shared class characteristics and objectives mitigated the potential for instability provoked by factional divisions. For all the campaign acrimony and mutual deprecation, seasoned political observers knew well that "A Tory out of power adopts the principles ascribed to a Whigg and a Whigg in Power falls into the worst measures of those that are attributed to the Tories."[20]

The similarities which ensured that political disruption remained safely within cantish limits also presented provincial politicos with their greatest difficulty: how to differentiate between each other's positions in contests for legislative influence. Incumbents who enjoyed the governor's ear relied on conservative arguments in defense of royal and imperial authority. Those in opposition tended to drew their inspiration from critiques lifted from the metropolitan political scene. Thus, in the 1690s, the merchant campaign against Bellomont and his supporters capitalized on anti-Dutch sentiment in London, charging the governor with favoring ignorant Dutchmen over qualified English counselors. The protest against Lord Cornbury that culminated in ad hominem and defamatory attacks drew inspiration from the scurrilous scribblers of Grub Street. Robert Hunter endured innuendo regarding the state of his marriage and a provincial adaptation of the row between high and low churchmen that raged in England following the 1710 impeachment of Henry Sachevrell. In response, Hunter penned a scatological play ridiculing his critics and introducing New Yorkers to the art of political satire.[21] In the political crisis of the 1730s the opposition followed an established pattern, and drew upon the lastest rhetoric of political opposition from the English political scene.

The origins of the political falling out of the 1730s lay in the collapse of a legislative coalition forged by Lewis Morris Sr. to provide Hunter with an unprecedented five-year revenue in 1714–15. For fixing the problem of provincial expenses, Morris was appointed chief justice of the supreme court and held forth on the governor's council for the next thirteen years.[22] Unable to make headway on the council—particularly following the arrival of Hunter's successor, William Burnet (1720–28)—Philipse and his associates concentrated their opposition energies in the Assembly. When the Philipsites regained control of the province following the arrival of Governor John Montgomerie (1728–31), they repealed Burnet's trade laws (including those providing for tonnage duties), secured a new charter for the city, and hedged Morris's influence on the Supreme Court by appointing Frederick Philipse and James Delancey as junior justices. In the summer of 1731, Montgomerie's sudden death made a leadership contest between the two lobbies all but inevitable.

Following Montgomerie's demise, the provincial administration fell to Rip van Dam, as president of the governor's council, until the arrival of the new governor, William Cosby, in August 1732. Cosby was a well-connected and haughty man who regarded the governorship of New York as an opportunity to fill his pockets. Not long after his arrival, he commenced an action to recover half of the nineteen hundred or so pounds paid to Rip van Dam during his time as acting governor. When Cosby tried to avoid a jury trial, and possible local resistance, by having the case heard before the Supreme Court sitting as a chancery court, James Alexander and William Smith (Van Dam's lawyers) challenged the court's constitutionality. Chief Justice Morris agreed and threw out the case. Cosby was furious at the affront to his authority and replaced Morris with Adolph Philipse, who was supported by Delancey. Morris went on the offensive, protesting the threat to popular liberties represented by "Judges who must be entirely at the Disposal of the Governor."[23] By September 1733, it was clear that Cosby's heavy-handed attempt to recover a thousand pounds had gifted the Morrisite coalition a constitutional stick with which to beat his administration.

One cannot discount the self-interested motives that underlay the dispute that developed in the ensuing months. Both sides stood to lose valuable patronage and land deals if the other side secured the authority of the governor's favor, and, in many respects, the dispute was little more than the usual competition for spoils dressed up as a constitutional schism.[24] However, contemporary commentators and historians since have agreed that what differentiated the row that followed the Van Dam affair from previous spats was the manner in which the Morrisites used the crisis "as the chief handle laid hold of to incite the People against the administration." Never before had provincial politicians appealed in such vociferous and unrelenting terms to the popular vote and to the integrity and wisdom of the city's workingmen as the majority urban constituency. All who have studied the decade concur that the 1730s represented a turning point in the city's political history.[25]

The first clash came in October 1733, when Morris won the seat left vacant by the death of a Westchester assemblyman with a campaign marked by populist appeals and anti-Walpolian sloganeering imported from the contemporary English campaign against the introduction of a new excise.[26] The week after their victory, the Morrisites hired the printer John Peter Zenger and launched the *New York Weekly Journal* to challenge the official line put out by Bradford's *Gazette*. The following spring, both sides turned their attention to the disgruntled urban population and the Michaelmas Day (29 September) poll at which freeholders and freemen elected one alderman and an assistant in each of the city's six wards. Having ignored the *Journal's* first few issues, Bradford's *Gazette* went on the offensive, publishing extracts from celebrated English conservative texts.[27] It was in this context of a developing paper war that the Philipsite assemblymen, Anthony Rutgers and Stephen Delancey, championed the petitions drawn up by artisans seeking protections for city trade. Cosby also garnered support among city workers using his April address to declaim against the rise of Bermudian shippers "whereby building is discouraged, artificers are without employ their families reduced to want, and also vast sums of money are yearly carried out of the province by strangers who hardly spend anything here for their subsistence." The usually standoffish governor even "became more familiar with the people & invited many of low rank to dine with him."[28]

Sensing an attempt to steal their populist clothes, the Morrisites embraced a more radical program and called upon ordinary workingmen to stand forth and save the city from a corrupt and tyrannical administration. The opposition advocated the issuing of twelve thousand pounds' paper money to relieve debtors and the construction of a newpoor house to put idle hands to work; they also proposed measures to increase the Assembly's authority over the appointment of sheriffs and provincial agents.[29] The Morrisites distinguished themselves from the incumbents by denouncing the Philipsites' failed economic policies that, they claimed, had left the city at the mercy of the very shippers Cosby now decried. The charge that most inflamed electoral passions, however, was the opposition's denunciation of Philipsite pretensions to "Exalted Stations" and their condescension to those "they think below them . . . [whom] they call the Vulgar, the Mob, the herd of Mechanicks."[30] Elevating ordinary city artisans to a new status as equal political subjects, the Morrisites accused Cosby's supporters of assuming that "the Authority they are cloathed with intitle them to use all mankind as their inferiors"; but why, the Morrisites demanded to know, should freeborn residents defer to "greatness of Birth, Riches, and Honours" since "The Almighty Made us Equal all." In response, the Philipsites denounced the opposition's supporters as "the lowest Canaille of the People, of no Credit or Reputation, rak'd out of Bawdy-Houses and Kennels" and charged Zenger's *Journal* with endeavoring to "alienate the Affections" of "the common People" by spreading "seditious libels" and "lessen[ing] in the People's Minds the Regard which is due to a Person in his high Station."[31]

In the end, the mobilization of city tradesmen and anti-incumbent sentiment won the day for the Morrisite candidates; the Common Council that assembled later that month included a butcher, a bolter, and two of the bakers who had served as Assembly delegates that spring.[32] Shortly thereafter, Morris left for England to present the opposition's case for Cosby's withdrawal to the Lords of Trade. Back in New York, his supporters celebrated their victory with songs (and more anti-Walpolian slogans) that exhorted city tradesmen to "Come on brave boys let us be brave for liberty and law" and to "Boldly despise the haughty knave that would keep us in aw" and defend their "rights . . . like brave and honest men."[33] In the spring of 1735, the Philipsites finally moved against their detractors, gathering up copies of the "scandalous" songs and other inflammatory extracts from the *Journal* for public burning and consigning Zenger to jail and an eight-month wait for his trial on a charge of seditious libel.[34]

What we make of this populist turn in the campaigns of 1733–34 and its consequences is critical to the story, because it was in the midst of this contest that the figure of the politically equal and virtuous artisan was first glimpsed in eighteenth-century New York City. In the absence of any discernible commitment to democratic politics by members of either faction, scholars have tended to attribute Morrisite populism to an instinctive sense of the efficacy of appeals to the popular vote and to pressures exerted by city artisans, who insisted upon a radical platform as the price of their support.[35] It is certain that the Morrisites thought carefully about their tactics, and we have seen that the slump in trade had drawn a new and assertive artisanal lobby into electoral politics. However, there are reasons to qualify these assessments that would connect the machinations of the 1730s to the electoral campaigns and class agendas of the later eighteenth and early nineteenth centuries. First, there is the question of timing: New York's politicians had contested provincial elections for more than three decades without ever making the kind of dramatic appeals and adopting the rhetoric and platform that marked the campaigns of the 1730s. If the populist turn was so politically savvy, why did it take provincial politicians so long to take it? Second, one has to wonder at the return of voter disinterest (relative to the 1730s) and the reassertion of an elitist political style, albeit cast in the language of popular politics, in the ensuing two decades. Overall, it is hard to dissent from the view that it was only following the crisis decades of the 1760s and 1770s and the transformation inspired by the American Revolution that city politics acquired a truly democratic character.[36]

But if considerations of neither principle nor strategy can adequately account for the innovation that ushered the virtuous artisan onto the urban political stage, then what remains? One alternative is to concentrate less on what might have lain behind the opposition's claims and more on the claims themselves and the extent to which the language adopted by the Morrisites shaped their radical platform.[37] Morris and his associates knew all too well that in the world of imperial politics, style was often as important as substance in securing one's ends.[38] The question of convention and linguistic register was especially critical in New York City, where the opposition had to present a case that was vigorous enough to secure popular support while remaining within the bounds of loyalty and the law. The Philipsites routinely charged their opponents with inciting disaffection and, following the defeat in the Common Council elections, even drew up plans to indict Morris and his leading associates for treason. In the end, the incumbents satisfied themselves with the arrest and trial of the relatively minor figure, John Peter Zenger, but their determination to silence Cosby's critics meant that the opposition had to pick its words carefully.

It was for this reason that the Morrisites adhered to established opposition practices and looked to developments on the English political scene and, in particular, the ferocious critique of Walpole's "court" administration articulated by John Trenchard and Thomas Gordon and published as *Cato's Letters* in the *London Journal* (1720–23).[39] Although *Cato's Letters* had been prompted by the exposé of the corrupt practices precipitated by South Sea Company's collapse, the essays ran the gamut of radical Whig concerns. In Cato the Morrisites found celebrations of the English rights and the mixed constitution, analyses of the unceasing opposition between power and liberty, arguments on behalf of press freedom, and warnings of the deleterious effects of corruption in public life, all of which were tailor made for the campaign against the imperious Cosby and his merchant cronies.[40] At the core of Trenchard and Gordon's philosophy, however, lay a commitment to the natural equality of men who secured their rights and interests through the establishment of government, which was validated thereafter through the expression of the electoral will. Once committed to the language of the English "country opposition" the Morrisites could not avoid raising the question of consent and the political equality it implied. It was in the pamphlets, songs, and newspaper articles and letters that fired this aspect of the campaign that the figure of the politically equal artisan first emerged. The same body of election propaganda that more than two centuries later comprises the evidence of a populist turn in New York City politics.[41]

Catonic arguments appealed to the Morrisites because they desacralized executive authority, reconciled self-interest with virtue, and provided the foundations for arguments in favor of self-determination. In Cato's view, government was "nothing else, but the attendance of the trustees of the people upon the interest and affairs of the people." The preservation of liberty was preeminent among these interests and was celebrated as the "parent of virtue, pleasure, plenty and security" and "the Power which every Man has over his Actions and his Right to Enjoy the Fruits of his Labor." Liberty was crucial to the individual pursuit of wealth that Cato considered an indispensable element for a free and prosperous society. For "When there is Liberty, there are Encouragements to Labour, because People labour for themselves; and no one can take from them the Acquisitions which they make by their Labour." Unfortunately, and as the opposition lobbies in New York never tired of pointing out, corruption and vice led to abuses of power and arbitrary government that threatened to "extinguish liberty." To counter these destructive tendencies, Cato appealed to the public spiritedness or virtue of freemen protected by the checks and balances of well-structured institutions such as England's mixed constitution.[42]

Trenchard and Gordon's willingness to move beyond the conditions and limits imposed by earlier rhetorical adherence to precedent and custom and to advocate more abstract notions of subjective rights and consent as the basis of legitimate government had a manifest appeal in a colony whose history was littered with conquests, capitulations, and ambiguous territorial settlements. Moreover, in addition to reducing the imperial administration to little more than a convenience for the protection of the colonists' liberty and property, Cato's synthesis of Renaissance, Protestant, and natural rights arguments foregrounded universal human qualities of personhood and championed the rights of reasonable and self-interested men in a manner that was, in essence, egalitarian. And therein lies the significance of the importation of Catonic arguments into New York City's political crisis in the 1730s. Throughout the essays, Cato honored ordinary men who "have natural qualifications equal to those of their superiors" and among whom "there is oftener found a genius carrying a pitch-fork than carrying a white staff." Thus, the defense of liberty and property was not the preserve of a particular class or institution but of all free men because "Every cobbler can judge, as well as a statesman . . . whether he is paid for his work . . . and whether when a dragoon or a parish officer come to him for taxes, if he pay any." It bears emphasis that this new republicanism was not of necessity politically democratic. In common with other writers, Trenchard and Gordon would have restricted political participation to independent men of property. However, in their celebration of the natural equality of reasonable and self-interested men and of the consent expressed by wider political participation among freeborn subjects, the Whig writers pushed in a more egalitarian direction and, in so doing, inspired liberal political rhetoric and strategies within the Morrisite opposition.[43]

The rhetorical elevation of the status of artisans and ordinary freemen of the city as voters to the level of political equality enjoyed by their social and economic superiors sat well with local trends in civic and legal practice and culture. The egalitarian themes of Catonic republicanism dovetailed with the diminishing force of earlier municipal strictures—which had once posited the natural *inequality* of men arrayed in their various ranks—and with status-blind pleading and adjudication that accompanied the professionalization of the common law. It also sounded with the stark division between free and enslaved workers that now characterized the urban labor market. In place of the older ideal of an organic prescriptive hierarchy, Cato posited a community of freeborn white and male property owners who shared equal rights to life, liberty, and property and the obligations to protect these rights from the corruption and tyranny that led to slavery via free and fair elections. In this respect, Trenchard and Gordon's message was ideally suited to a colonial political contest that pit populist leaders of a culturally diverse electorate against a provincial government made vulnerable by the actions of an overbearing governor and an economic crisis. However, by choosing to frame their protest against Cosby's administration in Catonic terms, the Morrisites also committed themselves to a populist campaign that elevated the status of ordinary city voters as electors whose virtue and consent underpinned the justice and legitimacy of provincial political institutions.

*   *   *

Claims concerning the popular mind and appeals to "the people" had long figured in English electoral contests and played their part in provincial debates, most recently in the 1720s in an exchange of pamphlets tackling the duties levied on land and trade. However, the unprecedented emphasis on the popular vote in the 1730s raised thorny questions regarding the practice of politics and communication between would-be representatives and the voters whose favor they sought. How could candidates be assured that voters understood their rights and the structure and operation of political institutions? Could they rely on the ability of ordinary workingmen to distinguish between virtuous leaders and corrupt office seekers? In the atmosphere of crisis and contest that pervaded the middle years of the 1730s, the question of "public opinion" assumed new significance, prompting the launch of Zenger's *Journal* as an educational device and calling forth novel rhetorical strategies and subjective categories including that of the craft-proud and virtuous city artisan.[44]

The banner emblazoned across the top of the first page of each edition of the *Journal* promised readers "the freshest Advices, Foreign and Domestick"—a boast made good by the coverage of provincial and international affairs. However, in addition to current affairs and exposés of the administration's venality, Morrisite polemicists dedicated themselves to educating readers in current affairs and the arts of government. Each issue offered edifying articles, frequently extracted from Cato, or essays in the style of Trenchard and Gordon penned under Greek and Roman pseudonyms on topics ranging from the distinction between absolute and limited monarchy and the role of a free press in the preservation of liberty to the extent of the obligation subjects bore to obey a supreme ruler and the value of juries in the protection of property rights. Alternatively, comments were offered by a "patriot" who was presented as free of individual prejudice and only concerned to "promote the Welfare . . . [of the] Common Wealth."[45]

To supplement these abstract and frequently bombastic offerings, the editors included (and almost certainly penned) less didactic readers' "letters" and "reports." Readers' letters reiterated arguments previously offered as high-blown theoretical disquisitions in a more accessible, vernacular form. Thus, in an issue following a discussion of the importance of voters maintaining their independence and relying on their reason and virtue in the selection of candidates, the *Journal* published letters reporting the proffering of dinner invitations in return for promises of support. One contribution, from a reader identified only as "a poor Man and . . . tenant to several landlords," described how he had been treated well by all his landlords except the

"Last who has given me several affronts . . . But now of late he grows extremely Civil [and] I am invited and . . . entertain'd after the elegantest Manner." This exposé of attempted electoral corruption—cleverly set up as an exchange between a landlord and tenant familiar to middling readers— drew upon the republican trope that valorized independence and voting decisions that were free of compulsion and inducements. In other offerings, the editors presented a gendered and comedic variation on the same theme: a group of female readers identified only as "widows and she merchants" lamented that lacking the vote meant they received no corrupting dinner invitations "although *they* trade and pay duties and would defend the city as eagerly as any other"; still more pleas came from the city's "maids," who feared "never getting to widows since the young Gentlemen are so taken up with Politics that we hardly get one pretty thing said to us in a Month."[46]

The letters published in the *Journal* provide just one example among many of the two-handed utility of printed public discourse that offered would-be representatives a medium for authoritative instruction to the electorate while simultaneously casting ordinary voters in the role of political subjects possessed of the wherewithal for meaningful intervention in the political process. The *Journal* peopled its pages with "countrymen," "patriots," improbably named classical expositors, and a host of "tenants," "maids," and fictive characters who offered plain-spoken responses to what might otherwise have struck city tradesmen as abstruse philosophical debates.[47] The use of fictive and frequently thinly disguised personas also permitted authors to protect themselves from libel suits and to adopt highly principled stands in debates where their position may have been compromised by real-life practice.[48] Writing as an unaligned and frequently ordinary resident, well-known provincial figures pushed their partisan line in the name of the common good.

As both sides jockeyed for the support of the city's workingmen in the run-up to the city elections in 1734, an exchange of letters (most likely penned by James Alexander) called forth a new cast of fictive characters to present the Morrisites' case to artisanal readers. The letters presented an exchange between a carpenter, John Chisel (nicknamed "Chip"), who had written to Timothy Wheelwright on behalf of his "Brother Trades-Men" to seek his advice regarding the candidates in the upcoming Common Council elections.[49] Chisel's fictive brotherhood included representatives from the major trades in the city, all of whom were identified by an appropriate sobriquet, including Shuttle the Weaver, Steep the Tanner, Vulcan the Smith, Drive the Carter, Beaver the Hatter, and Snip the Tailor. In his letter, Chisel complained that he and his brother tradesmen "are very Poor and daily grow poorer," and that their difficulties had prompted him to send Squeeze the Shopkeeper to seek the advice of Gripe the Lawyer—and his brother Quibble—"whether we can mend ourselves or not and if we can which is the best way to do it." However, the lawyers were unable to help, and this left the tradesmen with the equally unsatisfactory counsel of Spintext the Parson, who urged that if they "would follow his Advice and pray heartily, all would be well in Time."

The letter began by presenting the complaints of different tradesmen who were united in common cause against the corruption and maladministration, which they blamed for the recession and feared as threats to popular liberty. Washball the Barber protested that while "there was but a few Trimmers of us" they made a good living but "now there are *so many* set up, that I have nothing to live by but the NightCaps I sell"; Dub the Shipwright complained that provincial timber that should have come into local shipyards was used to raise "nets to catch Pyrates Goods" and for warehouses needed in the Indian trade. When Knife the Butcher and Oven the Baker appeared, one of the assembled interjected that they are "the only thriving men among us" because they benefited from the demand for roast beef and bread to make sops for the well-to-do and corrupt. However, when Chisel gathered together the individual complaints into a denunciation of the political corruption, Knife and Oven redeemed themselves: responding to the criticism, the two tradesmen acknowledged that business had picked up, but only for a short time, because their "Guests eat so greedily of the SOPPS, that they spotted all their Cloaths . . . and [now] they are ashamed to appear here" anymore.

Thereafter the united brotherhood of tradesmen added others to their ranks and focused their charges on perceived corruption and abuse of power by the executive and municipal incumbents: Mournful the Widow regrets the loss of a small piece of ground in front of her house from where she had hoped to sell "Pike and Gudgeons for the Court and Country," but which has been "given away from me . . . for we are no Aldermen." The letter concluded with a general protest against an order to dig a ditch through Fresh Water Hill, whose sole purpose was to save the "Governor's Coach or some other great Men . . . going about a Hundred Foot further," but which "when done will cost more to keep it in Repair than it did to dig." In the view of Tar the Boatman, "this Digging has no Law to support it: And if by Summoning us poor Dogs, they can make us work as they please in this case, they'll do so in more."

The letter to the *Journal* is fascinating because of the way it speaks both to and beyond the experience of city artisans. The author clearly has a keen eye for detail and alludes to trends and incidents that were likely to strike a chord with local artisans: the complaint by Washball the Barber and Dub the Shipwright of the damage done by incomers and the resources diverted from the city tapped into grievances with a venerable history among residents; the references to improvements around Fresh Water reminded readers of the unpopular (among city tanners) draining of the swamp a few years previously at the behest of none other than the Philipsite assemblyman, Anthony Rutgers; the worthless counsel offered by Gripe, Quibble, and Spintext evokes negative attitudes toward equivocating lawyers and sanctimonious clerics.[50]

In other respects, however, the letters offer a picture of urban artisanal trade and life that is curiously at odds with what we know from other sources. Municipal records and court papers indicate that occupational titles frequently contained references to skills and materials—such as felters for hatters and turners for woodworkers—yet taken to extreme, as it is in Chisel's letter, this identification misrepresents the diversification that characterized urban trade and assumes, to the modern eye at least, a comical form. The only female figure granted a public persona is Mournful the Widow; the labor of wives and daughters in and outside the early eighteenth-century household economy does not figure in this depiction of masculine trade identities. The representation of a brotherhood of tradesmen also offers no sense of the divisions within trades, the sometimes fraught relations between artisanal employers and less successful subcontractors, the cultural pluralism and enduring Dutch presence in the urban workforce, or the work of slaves who we know labored alongside city artisans in the docks, workshops, and construction sites throughout the city. Finally, although lawyers and clerics are presented as the butts of popular chagrin, there is no mention of merchant and landed financiers and the collapse of the credit economy or of the spiraling legal costs and competition for skilled work that warranted petitions for relief from tradesmen in the 1730s. In short, the idealized brotherhood of the letter contains little of the day-to-day experience and concerns of city artisans in the early eighteenth-century city.

Although the stories of Chisel and Wheelwright sit uneasily with what we know of the realities of artisanal daily life and work, they provide consummate foils for the expression of Catonic ideals concerning the importance of popular consent in securing liberty and property. The references to corruption within city government, abuse of public funds, and the illegality of the forced work around Fresh Water, which, it was feared, presaged further arbitrary orders, cast the global and unceasing contest between power and liberty and the dangers of slavery in simple and local terms. Considering their options in the face of this threat, the brotherhood of tradesmen first thought of calling upon the assistance of the "Representatives of the County." However, they quickly agreed that the current administration was unlikely to heed their complaints. Pondering their situation, Tar the Boatman urged "Let's out with them and chuse others in their Room," to which Spintext offered a "sneering" retort: "Out with them! can you do it? Or if you can; are you assured you will not chuse as bad in their Room?" Faced with the minister's cynicism, the boatman offered a rejoinder worthy of any Catonic cobbler: "Ay, Ay, says Tar, we know that; but for all that, out with them . . . We know pretty well who has taken SOPPS and who not: Their Coats are too spotted to scape being seen if they appear."

In this way, the letters to the *Journal* championed the participation of an idealized artisanal political subject who bears an uncanny resemblance to both the Catonic ideal and the character who figured so prominently in later eighteenth-century popular politics: an independent and virtuous tradesmen (white and male) whose dedication to craft work and identification with his fellow tradesmen is abstracted from the vicissitudes of the trading economy within which some secured lives of wealth and comfort, while most struggled to maintain themselves and their families. Far from drawing upon the experiences and material conditions of ordinary working men and women, this new republican artisan was constructed largely in defiance of those conditions. Its coherence derives from the attribution of personal and moral qualities—integrity, skill, craft pride, and virtue—that artisans were presumed to share with each other and that provided for their sense of collectivity and clarity of purpose. Moreover, whereas late seventeenth-century city artisans had invoked metropolitan and local customs and practices to justify claims concerning their privileges and duties within the prescriptive hierarchy, these new republican and politically equal tradesmen eschewed the guidance of history and custom and relied instead upon self-assessment of their interests and of the characters of those who stood as their would-be representatives. Or, as John Chisel had it, "We are not so rich as others, but I dare say as honest, and scorn to sell our Liberties for a Sopp of Bread."

However, if the 1734 Common Council campaign marked the entry of an new artisanal republican figure to the urban political stage, it was a debut whose radical possibilities were limited by the continuing commitment to elite rule by "good men." This much was clear in Wheelwright's reply to Chisel, which ended with an account of the arrival of his friend, Colonel Quondam of Queens County, as he was reading the carpenter's letter.

Wheelwright and Quondam—who the former described as "a timorous Man, but sincere in the Interest of his Country"—discussed Chisel's request for advice, and through the medium of Wheelwright's reply, Quondam counseled Chisel and his brother tradesmen to use their "great and valuable Privilege" of voting in the next election. The city's tradesmen "have Numbers sufficient," the timorous colonel declares, "And if you dare to chuse Good Men, these Good Men will dare to stand by you." Driving home his point, Quondam emphasizes the influence enjoyed by ordinary voters: for "If you Dare assert the Rights and Liberties of your Country, those that are willing to overthrow or sell them, Dare Not attempt the doing of it; and you'll make the most haughty of them tremble." However, he cautions city tradesmen that if they fail to turn out and vote, they will encourage the administrations tyrannical designs and leave themselves no grounds for complaint in the future.

In the municipal elections of 1734 city artisans turned out in unprecedented numbers and awarded Morrisite candidates a comfortable majority of the 879 votes cast. But victory in the Common Council elections did nothing to improve the opposition's standing in the provincial assembly or council, and by the following spring, their prospects looked bleak: Morris's mission to London failed to secure Cosby's recall, Zenger awaited trial in jail, and the opposition lobby in the city was cowed.[51] All changed, however, following Cosby's unexpected death from tuberculosis in November 1735. George Clarke assumed the governor's office and—following Morrisite victories in the 1737 Assembly elections—restored James Alexander and William Smith to the New York Bar, approved elements of the opposition's radical platform, and installed Lewis Morris Jr. (who had previously railed against corruption and patronage appointments) as Speaker of the Assembly.[52] Ousted from their Assembly seats, Philipse and Delancey denounced their erstwhile radical foes as "plumb Courtiers" and launched their own opposition campaign in defense of popular rights and liberties.[53] The stage was set for a decisive electoral contest between the two factions, in which divisions within the ranks of city artisans, momentarily obscured by the 1734 campaign, had a crucial impact on the vote.

*   *   *

In September 1738, the death of the Morrisite city assemblyman Gerrit van Horne prompted a by-election contested by Adolph Philipse and Cornelius van Horne, the deceased man's son. Following weeks of vigorous campaigning by both sides more than eight hundred city voters turned out. On election day, Cadwallader Colden wrote, "the sick, the lame, and the blind were all carried to vote . . . out of Prison and out of the poor house" in a poll that was marred by tumults and fistfights and which "lasted from half an hour after nine in the morning till past nine at night." When the count was in, Philipse had defeated Van Horne by fourteen votes—wiping out the Morrisite's majority of four years previously. Refusing to accept defeat by such a slender margin, the Morrisites marched to Fort George and presented a petition signed by hundreds of supporters denouncing the result as a sham. Following an investigation and recount, however, Philipse was declared the winner.[54]

The shift in urban loyalties that provided for Philipse's victory reflected a noteworthy division within artisanal ranks. Just as in previous contests, the city's principal merchants and landowners backed Philipse, but the majority that sealed his victory depended on the support of better-off artisans. Abandoning the popular party and throwing their support behind candidates who had been condemned for corruption and elitist condescension in the Common Council elections three years earlier, successful and aspirant city artisans returned to the city merchant faction. The Morrisites retained the backing of prominent opposition families—such as the Van Dams, Beekmans, and Waltons—and a cross-section of voters from Dutch backgrounds. However, the bulk of Van Horne's votes came from poorer tradesmen who had suffered the worst effects of the commercial recession.[55] The story of the by-election was the split in the artisan vote, and although the evidence is sketchy, there are indications that this division was informed by disagreements regarding the employment of slaves in skilled occupations—particularly coopering.

The Van Horne by-election coincided with a revival in the city's commercial fortunes following the settling of contracts for the construction of a handful of new vessels. As shipwrights and those in related trades drifted back to work commercial prospects improved, and some merchants and master artisans employed their own or hired slaves from others to work at skilled occupations.[56] Whether the shortage of local labor following the exodus of working families in the preceding five years or an effort to minimize financial outlays in a still-recovering urban economy prompted this decision is unclear. However, the employment of slaves so soon after the slump fostered discontent among jobless artisans. In his April address to the Assembly, Clarke noted, "The artificers complain and with too much good reason of the pernicious custom of breeding slaves to trades whereby the honest and industrious tradesmen are reduced to poverty for want of employ." In September, two days prior to the Van Horne poll, "sundry coopers" petitioned the Assembly complaining of "several considerable merchants . . . [who] employ great Numbers of Negroes in that Occupation not only to supply their own Occasions of Casks but sell and dispose thereof to other[s]." A second petition submitted by "a great Number of the Inhabitants of the City of New York" insisted that "Negroes may be supprest of having the Benefit of poor Laborers and Tradesmen."[57] Given that we know of the distribution of slaveholding favored the prosperous over the poorer artisans, the protests most likely reflected the dissatisfactions of less-successful, non-slave holding artisans. This division between well-to-do and unfortunate tradesmen was mirrored in the support of the candidate in the by-election: if Van Horne had secured the votes of the better-off coopers in addition to their struggling peers, he would have beaten Philipse to the Assembly seat.[58]

The popular party never recovered from its defeat in the Van Horne by-election. However, the fallout from the Van Dam and Zenger affairs and the regularizing of elections thereafter convinced provincial leaders that the surest path to sustained influence lay in establishing their position independent of the governor's favor. The ease with which the Philipsites repositioned themselves as defenders of popular rights demonstrated the adaptability of the rhetorical innovations ushered in during the 1730s, which became a regular feature of provincial and city elections thereafter.[59] In the ensuing two decades, competing provincial lobbies, city tradesmen, and their representatives fleshed out the practical implications of radical English political ideas, and the divisions within artisanal ranks evident in the Van Horne by-election vote grew in response to far-reaching social and economic changes. The declarations on behalf of the rights and liberties of free and equal men that resonated through election campaigns did not mask the fact that New York City's vigor and prosperity rested on the labor of a burgeoning population of slaves and growing numbers of impoverished day laborers and wage workers.

In the 1740s and 1750s New York City boomed once again as city merchants and tradesmen agreed on contracts for the construction of new ships and provisioning of the imperial armies engaged in King George's War with Spain (1739–45) and the French and Indian War (1757–63). Leading merchant families—the Delanceys, Bayards, Livingstons, Beekmans, and Wattses—presided over a threefold increase in the city-owned and -operated fleet (from 157 to more than 450 vessels) and realized handsome returns supplying the English, and frequently French, forces.[60] They also invested in the growing sugar trade, supplying Europe's insatiable sweet tooth and privateering ventures, which scoured the Caribbean for French ships and booty. The profits from these and other ventures provided for the participation of wealthy New Yorkers in the pursuit of a genteel lifestyle and a provincial adaptation of metropolitan society. Well-to-do urbanites ordered the latest London fashions, furnished their houses according to new, refined styles, and joined their peers at turtle feasts, balls, and concerts featuring popular composers such as Handel and Bach. The return of prosperity also stimulated an urban renaissance: some built fine houses in the latest Georgian fashion in the city's East Ward; others contributed to public institutions of higher learning such as King's College (now Columbia University) and the New York Society Library, both established in 1754. Visitors to the city admired its fine residences and public buildings so "elegantly built of brick . . . and the streets paved and spacious" and found it "extremely pleasant to walk in the town, for it seemed like a garden."[61]

It was not only the upper classes who developed a fascination for consumer goods and genteel pursuits in the middle decades of the eighteenth century. As the city's population increased to eighteen thousand, the rising economic tide also improved fortunes among the ranks of artisans, shopkeepers, and petty traders.[62] Successful city tradesmen joined the elite in elevating ordinary activities—such as dressing, eating, and drinking (particularly tea)—to new levels of refinement. They also became avid readers of local newspapers and magazines, and attended scientific lectures, took lessons in dance and deportment, and socialized at card parties or on walks through the city's "pleasure gardens." Although gentility posited a clear demarcation between the refined and the rough, it was a distinction that depended more on purchasing power and manners than inherited rank or estate. As such, at least as far as the middling sort were concerned, gentility could be acquired and cultivated, and its pursuit placed respectability within reach of aspirant artisans who identified their interests with other consumers in the burgeoning "empire of goods."[63] Unfortunately, New Yorkers' affection for English imports and luxury commodities also produced staggering trade imbalances and chronic indebtedness with metropolitan suppliers. But while some railed against the fascination for luxuries and the pretensions of the city's middling residents as evidence of public vice, most forgot the unfortunate side effects amid a rising tide of commercial fortunes and busy social calendars. As one mid-century correspondent to the *New York Mercury* had it, "one might as well be out of the world as out of the mode."[64]

Beneath the elite and aspirant middling sort gathered a class of men and women whose survival depended on day laboring and waged work and who were more likely to be found dining on oysters and mussels harvested from the shore of the East River than they were on turtle soup and pastries bought from local retailers. The combined effects of dwindling supplies of desirable land and stiffening Indian resistance to white settlement in the rural hinterland drove hundreds into the city where they encountered hundreds more recently arrived from Europe who were unable to move inland from their Manhattan landfall. In the thirty years following the arrival of Governor George Clinton in 1743, ten thousand immigrants established homes in New York City, double the number of newcomers in the preceding four decades.[65] This rapid increase in population—the highest rate of growth of any community in North America—and the availability of free labor (in addition to slaves and servants) for hire mitigated the perennial problem of the labor shortage and allowed employers to rely on taking on hands when needed. This rapid increase in urban population could not be serviced by existing patron-client credit arrangements, and given the still-minimal provision for municipal poor relief, this left a substantial section of the city dependent on seasonal and waged work. For generations, New York's employers had griped about the dearth of local labor for hire; now they grumbled about the fecklessness and character of the laborers they had. Thus one correspondent to the *New York Post Boy* bemoaned the "Carpenters, Masons, Shoemakers, Tanners, Smiths, Taylors . . . who are Jobbers and Cobblers [rather] than Workmen," noting that "It is almost incredible to think what Number of such Insects infest this Country." Others decried the city's "want of workmen and the Villainy of those we generally have . . . [who] are usually low, profligate, drunken, and faithless." It was from the ranks of this impoverished and motley proletariat, which mingled with slaves and mariners on the city's waterfront, that a conspiracy to fire the town emanated in the spring of 1741.[66]

The conditions of the urban underclass inspired new survival strategies among those who settled the city's margins. During the good times, underwritten by wartime contracts for military supplies, laboring men and women found work on the wharves, on construction sites, in workshops and retailers, on nearby farms, or on the sloops and barques engaged in the coastal and Hudson River trade. When commerce took a downturn, the desperate appealed to religious and ethnic charities or the city for relief, others turned to crime or prostitution, and some sought better fortunes in military service; most clung on as best they could.[67] Whatever the season or state of the local economy, however, laboring men and women supplemented their earnings by participating in the informal economy that developed as a seamy underside to the trade in luxury commodities and manufactured goods. In dockside taverns, grog shops, and the alleys that criss-crossed the North and West Wards working men and women exchanged, fenced, and pawned clothing, scraps of silk and lace, buckles and candlesticks, parcels of sugar and tobacco, and innumerable other items acquired via fair means or foul. Provincial leaders railed against the covert economy, which provided "ready . . . [and] . . . large" credit for those unable to secure the backing of respectable lenders and thereby promoted "a habit of idleness" among the lower orders "that may in time prove ruinous to the whole Province." However, the authorities could do little to prevent the trade.[68]

The character of mid-century urban life and politics was also influenced by the emergence of new forms of public association and crowd activities. In the seventeenth and early eighteenth centuries, collective action involving ordinary New Yorkers had remained within the bounds set by civic and religious principles—for example, in Leisler's Rebellion—and by the emerging racial animus, in reaction to the 1712 slave conspiracy. Beginning in the 1740s, however, ethnic, fraternal, and trade associations provided city artisans with new vehicles for public activism ranging from charitable giving to the celebration of craft solidarities; herein lay the origins of the fire companies and occupational lobbies that served as the forerunners of nineteenth-century trades unions.[69] At the same time, the emergence of crowd activities fused defenses of custom and the common good with belligerent assertions of Protestant and English rights and liberties. In the late 1740s, for example, middling and laboring New Yorkers transformed the city's Pope's Day celebrations—formerly a muted, official commemoration of the failure of Guy Fawkes's 1605 plot to blow up the Houses of Parliament—into a sometimes violent celebration of liberty. In 1754, a merchant plan to devalue pennies in relation to shillings to redress an exchange imbalance in the city's trade with England filled the streets with working men and women, "armed with Clubs and Staves," who protested what they considered a scheme to drive down local wages. Four years later, and again in 1760, middling and laboring townspeople campaigned against impressment, refusing to provision English vessels in the harbor and fighting running battles with the press-gangs that ventured ashore.[70]

The emergence of novel social distinctions and public collectivities filled the vacuum created by the waning of an earlier, more closely controlled civic order and provided new avenues for the affirmation of popular rights and political agency. The conditions of the mid-eighteenth-century city also presented elite politicians with new challenges and opportunities. The lack of poll returns for the middle decades means that we cannot know for sure how many voted and for whom, but the limited evidence suggests that voter interest diminished relative to the rambunctious campaigns of the 1730s. Enduring familial and religious loyalties and constitutional differences—coupled with control of the nomination of candidates—ensured that landed and urban lobbies retained their coherence. However, would-be aldermen, assistants, and Assembly representatives associated with provincial factions still needed to secure their places at election, and in the city their task was made more difficult by not only voter disinterest but also divisions within the ranks of city artisans, who comprised the single largest urban constituency. In the absence of the coherent artisanal lobby that provided for the success of the Morrisites and their radical platform in the 1730s, candidates had to construct majorities from a smaller pool of electors who were subdivided by economic, religious, and ethnic concerns. Provincial leaders had to balance tickets, build coalitions, and run well-organized party machines to hammer home their campaigns on behalf of popular rights and liberties and secure the required votes on election day.[71]

*   *   *

For two decades following the collapse of the Morrisite popular party, provincial politics was dominated by Chief Justice James Delancey, who managed the interests of powerful lobbies while championing popular rights and liberties. Delancey's background and metropolitan contacts made him the logical choice for lead counselor following George Clinton's arrival as governor in 1743.[72] When the two fell out regarding plans for an expedition against the French in Canada, however, Delancey and his associates organized the most vociferous opposition party ever faced by a New York governor. In four fiercely contested Assembly elections held between 1745 and 1751 the Delanceyites competed with Clinton and his supporters for the popular vote.[73] The chief justice, who had once decried the Morrisites' attempts to "stir up the people to tumults and seditions," was himself denounced for "election jobbing," "treating," inciting a "spirit of levelling," and endeavoring "to instigate the passions of the lowest ranks." Frustrated by Delancey's relentless opposition and "pretended Endeavors for the Liberties and Properties of the People," Clinton was finally recalled to London in 1753. Delancey took charge of the colony in his capacity as lieutenant governor, presiding over provincial affairs until his death in 1760.[74]

Figure 14. Fire company meeting notification. Courtesy of the New York Public Library. The notification, which includes an image of a contemporary street scene, alerts the recipient to a meeting of the Hand-in-Hand Fire Company in March 1762. It is an example of the kind of printed material associated with artisanal trade and public life that was common by the later eighteenth century.

It was not only the governor and his supporters who despaired of Delancey's inflammatory rhetoric and divisive electoral tactics. William Livingston—scion of a leading provincial family, rising provincial politico, and avid student of English radical politics—was also perturbed by the chief justice's "thirst after popularity." Livingston contributed to the anti-Clinton campaign in the late 1740s, but broke with Delancey over the King's College controversy in 1753 and emerged thereafter as his leading political adversary.[75] Livingston's opposition to Delancey reflected not only familial and religious differences but also political sensibilities that led him to suspect and even fear Delancey's penchant for popular politics.[76] Livingston's political philosophy rested on two assumptions: that reason could allow virtuous administrators to ascertain the public good, and that unfortunately man's natural predisposition was to follow his appetites and passion leading to corruption and disorder in public life. Because the end of a just and moral administration was to "preserve and promote the true Interest and Happiness" of rulers and the ruled, it followed that the sphere of government was the proper preserve of the sort of men who possessed reason and virtue enough to temper their passions and, distinguishing between private and public concerns, administer provincial affairs in the interests of the common good. In Livingston's view, appeals to the popular will and the pursuit of party politics, were only justifiable in moments of crisis, when fundamental civil and religious liberties were threatened. However, if routinely resorted to, as Livingston believed was the case with Delancey, such appeals perverted unprepared minds, fostered degenerate passions, and undermined the beneficent rule of wise and virtuous men: "For the Moment that Men give themselves wholly up to Party . . . the calm Deliberations of Reason are imperceptibly fermented into Passion; and their Zeal for the common Good, gradually extinguished by the predominating Fervor of Faction."[77]

James Delancey and William Livingston were representatives of not only competing provincial lobbies but also the varieties of the Whig political thought that provided the backdrop for the development of a rights-based political culture of revolutionary America.[78] The two men shared an admiration for England's libertarian heritage and mixed constitution, which, in their view, provided the surest guarantee for the security of liberty and property. As relentless competitors for provincial influence and imperial spoils, however, they also deployed Whig political arguments against each other and the royal prerogative. In so doing, scholars have argued, Delancey, Livingston, their many peers and associates gave vent to the radical ideas and principles that ultimately provided for a flourishing republican political culture during the era of the American Revolution. However, even granting the importance of two decades of radical exchanges and the rise of "interest" politics, the predisposition of elite politicians to explore the egalitarianism that comprised the radical kernel of Real Whig ideology was clearly limited by the social conservatism that gave their declarations on behalf of popular rights a facile and empty air.[79] For all their claims concerning "reason," the provincial gentry were committed to a prejudicial view of man that made it impossible for them to ever conceive of popular politics as anything other than representative of baser human impulses. Thus even as Delancey, Livingston, and men of their ilk conceded that "the people" possessed a basic moral sense and skills that were essential for provincial prosperity, they remained wary of working men and women, whom they considered docile (until acted upon), easily charmed (and, ergo, misled), and inclined toward disorderly behavior and (if roused) assaults on liberty and property.[80]

The justification for the participation of ordinary citizens in the founding and ongoing scrutiny of their own government was the most important legacy of the Revolution and, in time, served as the "essence of American democracy."[81] However, the earliest articulation of this justification for popular participation had less to do with the radical musings of a socially conservative elite and more to do with the actions of middling artisans in defense of their own political rights and interests, frequently in opposition to their provincial betters. As the rapid increase in urban population and continued reduction in the efficacy of municipal regulation loosened controls of expanding city markets, new arrivals increased competition and threatened delicately balanced middling fortunes. The poorer and laboring sort who lacked local organization and influence made their way in the city's formal and informal economies as best they could. However, for aspirant city artisans who coveted consumer goods and the status they conferred, the unpredictable market for local skills represented an unacceptable threat to individual and collective ambitions. In response, they acted to protect their trade interests, invoking long-standing justifications and resorting to novel claims and forms of communication. In these campaigns urban artisans contradicted the gentry's condescending assessment of their limited political abilities and explored the practical implications of the idealized Catonic subject called forth in the 1730s. In so doing, New York City artisans demonstrated a willingness to innovate in political exchanges and a determination to protect their interests that laid the foundations for the flourishing of artisanal republicanism and the challenge to gentry political hegemony in the late eighteenth century and early nineteenth centuries.

Artisans' collective action in defense of their trade interests combined appeals for protection with challenges to the municipal and provincial government and, in some cases, the withdrawal of labor. In the 1740s, city bakers twice suspended baking in protest at the published weights and prices resulting in complaints from the townsfolk. In 1747, ninety-five building workers petitioned the governor seeking protection of their rights and privileges as "ancient freemen" in the face of competition from companies of itinerants who came to the city "after the laying of our taxes . . . to exercise their several handicraft trades . . . [and] carrying away Such Moneys so Surreptiously got here . . . [and] not so much as buying a pair of Shoes . . . but frequently bringing Nails and other materials for Building with them"; three years later, builders and tilers appealed against regulations requiring the use of slate rather than wooden shingles on roofs, urging the Common Council to reconsider on the grounds that the order would drive up building costs and thus prices. In 1752, a delegation of city butchers protested the maladministration of the public slaughterhouse and sought permission to establish a new, cooperative facility at their own expense beyond Fresh Pond. In the mid-1750s the shipwrights abandoned public work on the construction of bateaux for an expedition against the French in favor of more remunerative private employment, refusing to return to work until the introduction of legislation requiring their presence.[82]

The provenance of aspects of these justifications for collective action can be traced back a century or more to the 1650s and the founding of the city and its municipal government. By the mid-eighteenth century, however, the anachronistic nature of these claims and the brittleness of the relationship between local artisans and city and provincial authorities was evident in the responses such actions garnered. The city rejected the bakers' complaints and levied heavy fines upon those who failed to bake according to the regulations; although in 1755 the bakers took advantage of wartime exigencies to increase prices, once more prompting residential complaints. The builders' appeal secured a mordant rebuff from Clinton, who noted that "the Bulk of the persons . . . are obscure people altogether unknown to us" and chided the petitioners for failing to register for the privileges whose protections they now invoked. The butchers' application to establish a new slaughterhouse fell foul of the Common Council's determination to preserve a long-established source of revenue. And although the shipwrights managed to embarrass the governor by requiring the introduction of legislation before they returned to work, they could do nothing to prevent a subsequent merchant combination to fix wages at eight shillings per day for skilled men and half that for their laborers.[83] At every turn it seemed as if the previous limits set on such disputes by deference to respected civic hierarchies and the common good were being challenged by the more narrowly conceived individual and trade interests and concerns for institutional interests and profitability.

If city artisans turned to claims concerning ancient rights and privileges and the withdrawal of labor to defend their collective interests, they relied on the emerging medium of print and advertising to distinguish themselves from competitors in an increasingly cut-throat marketplace.[84] The growing demand for high quality services and products and middle class status anxiety increased public scrutiny of artisanal work and afforded it a new, symbolic cultural value. Thus early artisanal advertisements aimed to do more than publicize the presence of reliable workmen who labored for competitive rates. In notices addressed to not only "customers" and "ladies and gentlemen" but also to "friends" and "the Public," artisanal advertisers pandered to residents' desires and insecurities, enticing prospective purchasers with allusions to arcane technologies (or "arts" and "mysteries") that had previously figured little, if at all, in legal and political debate. In addition to stressing their particular skills and talents, city artisans gauged their offerings against the all-important benchmark of metropolitan standards. Thus James Lyne—the engraver whose plan of the city opened this chapter —bragged that his design was "engraved on a Copper Plate and printed on a sheet of demy Royal Paper"; Willoughby Loftus, an architect, declared that "he has, by a Number of Years Practice Acquired the Art of forming Designs for Buildings"; Jonathon Brown, a coachmaker, undertook to provide chariots and chairs made with "Trimmings of the newest and genteelest Sorts." William Williams, a glazier, offered "Painting upon Glass (commonly call'd burning upon Glass) . . . [and] Views neatly colored for the Camera Obscura" and John Brinner boasted of the "six artificers well skilled" in his employ who could supply locals with any of the furniture "in gothic or Chinese styles" found in Thomas Chippendale's *Gentleman's Cabinet-Maker's Directory*.[85]

By contrast with the seventeenth-century connections drawn between local residence and occupational status and privilege, later eighteenth-century artisans used print to trumpet skills and reputations acquired elsewhere in order to distinguish their superior talents and products from merely local practitioners and offerings. The combmaker Thomas Dunn claimed to have "had the honour to serve most of Dublin's nobility" before coming to America; Joseph Simon promoted himself as a "seal cutter and engraver from Berlin." James Hutchwaite and Stephen Callow were "upholsterers from London" and promised customers "the newest fashions"; George Riley and Joseph Cox offered chairs and couches "according to the latest style as practices in London," and the buttonmaker Henry Whiteman, who "served my Apprenticeship with Casper Wister . . . in Philadelphia," offered buttons and buckles "as cheap and as good as can be purchased in Philadelphia"; John Julius Sorge, a self-proclaimed "Jack of all trades," was "Very much noted among the Nobility in Germany."[86] As the associations uniting occupation, status, and local community waned, New York City artisans increasingly looked outward and identified themselves more as men of skill and probity who hailed from diverse backgrounds and regions and shared a commitment to serve the customer and get ahead in the expanding city.

The actions of mid-eighteenth-century city bakers, butchers, and builders in defense of their trade interests, so evocative of the struggles of New Amsterdam artisans a century or so earlier, addressed a very different set of circumstances. Whereas earlier struggles figured in the construction of a hierarchical civic order organized in relation to objective rights and privileges, obligations, and duties modelled on Dutch practice, by the 1750s, city workers were coming to terms with the diminishing purchase of these claims and seeking new grounds for the defense of their individual and collective trade interests and their liberty as freeborn and equal men. Separated by a century or more, the superficial similarity of artisanal struggles of the mid-seventeenth and eighteenth centuries largely depend on the claims concerning municipal practices and principles that groups of urban artisans hoped might retain some of the force of previous times.[87] However, as they grappled with exigencies of contemporary conditions, skilled workers drew upon not only long-standing justifications but also the lessons of recent political contests and employed innovative arguments and technologies in defense of their interests and liberty. In the process, city artisans articulated a powerful new sense of self that implicitly rejected the condescension of their betters and simultaneously differentiated their status as middling male property owners and political agents from the status of women, slaves, and impoverished workers, who were deemed dependent, subordinate, and inferior. In time, these claims would feed into discourses of "respectability" aimed at foreign-born or intemperate workers and of masculine ideals centered around generosity, sexual prowess, rowdiness, and self-indulgence.[88]

For now, the proliferation of public debate concerning virtuous and skilled city workers provided the beginnings for the articulation of a new and powerful ideology of small-producer and egalitarian artisanal republicanism.[89]

*   *   *

Viewed from the perspective of 1760, the political crisis that threatened to tear the city apart almost thirty years previously constituted the most critical period of innovation in political rhetoric and tactics since the conflicts following the establishment of a provincial assembly in the wake of Leisler's Rebellion. The commercial slump brought on by structural weaknesses in the city's trading economy and the consequent contraction of credit fostered discontent among hundreds of city tradesmen whose protests became embroiled in a factional contest for influence and provincial spoils. In the process, the Morrisite opposition, and those who followed, adapted the rhetoric and tactics of English political radicalism to colonial conditions—proclaiming the equality of male electors, championing the consent of ordinary voters, and connecting these novel claims regarding political subjectivity to the idealized figure of the honest and virtuous artisan. In the middle decades of the eighteenth century, and for their own and sometimes very different reasons, elite politicians and artisans fleshed out the implications of the radical and idealized figure, so that by the early 1760s the skilled and virtuous and politically equal workingman, whose consent provided the foundation for legitimate government, was central to urban artisans' self-image.

In August 1760, Pierre de Rigaud de Vaudreuil de Cavagnial, the governor-general of New France, surrendered to Jeffrey Amherst's combined force of Indians, English regulars, and provincial troops, ending French dominion in New France and, to all intents and purposes, the French and Indian War.[90] The conquest of Canada, and the shift of military operations to the Caribbean, meant the end of lucrative war contracts in New York City. The slump in the European sugar market, the rising prices of British wholesale goods, and a naval crackdown on smuggling between the city and the French Caribbean exacerbated the business downturn and heralded a new imperial determination to regulate colonial trade. By 1763, food shortages required the introduction of stringent price controls, prompting city butchers to boycott local markets and assert their rights as "born free Englishmen" to sell "our own effects at our own liberty." The introduction of the Sugar and Currency acts the following year signaled the beginnings of an intrusive revenue-raising policy that dashed residents' hopes of relief from London. When news of Parliament's intention to impose a direct tax in the form of a stamp duty levied on all printed materials reached the colonies, the city experienced a wave of riots and tumults. Thus it was that in the autumn of 1764 the streets were once again filled with impoverished and radicalized working men and women, and a divided provincial elite competed for the support of New York City artisans.[91] On that occasion, however, the genie of democratic assent proved rather more difficult to get back into the bottle.

Chapter 7
Conclusion

This book began by observing that the view of a general and fundamental shift from independent and amenable craft work to alienated and penurious wage work, and the implied causal relationship between this shift and the formation of a new kind of working-class politics in the late eighteenth and early nineteenth centuries, rested on a mischaracterization of the conditions of earlier American artisanal work. This mischaracterization reflected the influence of two assumptions regarding the transformative effects of changes in later eighteenth-century urban artisanal working conditions: first, that the emergence of capitalism and the rise of a dynamic market economy driven by self-interested pursuits, which most agreed were increasingly in evidence after 1750, displaced earlier household and communitarian forms of production; second, that in the course of this change and the struggles it engendered preindustrial artisans and the laboring sort were transformed into a politically conscious working class distinguished by its members' sense of their shared structural position and their articulation of an alternative social vision. In the last forty years or so, scholarly fascination with the beginnings of the market economy and the "making" of this American working class has inculcated a view of this "transition to capitalism" as the chronological endpoint of early modernity. In the process, earlier American artisans have been marooned in a rose-tinted "precapitalist" world where they await (without ever fully comprehending) the impact of anonymous material forces that will one day deliver them into modernity.[1]

In the last two decades or so the debate concerning the transition to capitalism has waned, and the concept of class that figured in so many influential interpretive narratives has been the focus of considerable critical scrutiny.[2] In addition, early Americanists have begun to investigate assumptions concerning individual motives, business acumen, and the operation of markets, and to subject colonial commerce to the kind of "thick description" that has long been applied in other early modern contexts.[3] The study of popular politics has been slower to follow. In part this has been because of a tendency to employ categories derived from the nineteenth century in analyses of earlier American conditions, for example in the equating of political activity with voting and the distinction drawn between the radicalism of nineteenth-century class conflicts and the localized, conservative, and essentially deferential character of colonial American popular struggles.[4] Consequently, the more sophisticated our understanding of late eighteenth- and early nineteenth-century popular political culture has become, the more keenly one has felt the absence of earlier, colonial roots—especially in politically precocious urban communities such as New York City. Left unchallenged, this gap in our knowledge encourages the depiction of the middling city artisans—who arguably engineered the civil strife that precipitated the crisis of the 1760s and 1770s—as johnny-come-latelies who underwent a crash course in republican education following the Stamp Act Crisis, only realizing the meaning and implications of claims on behalf of equality, rights, and the importance of consent at the moment at which these faculties were most imperiled.[5]

By adopting a longer-term view of work and politics in colonial New York, this book has aimed to free seventeenth- and early eighteenth-century New York City artisans from this unenviable historiographical fate. Artisans were present in the city from its earliest days and pursued their interests as petty dealers, boat owners, farmers, creditors, and practitioners of various skilled occupations. There is little evidence of claims concerning occupational status and rights and the social and political salience of skills outside the specific municipal and legal contexts considered in the previous chapters; there is a similar dearth of documentary sources detailing workshop traditions and craft "mysteries" prior to the development of artisan associations and advertising in the mid-eighteenth century. Instead, earlier artisanal trade was characterized by fleeting connections and multiple dependencies, and the effects of commercial ambition—evident in the success and social mobility of some and failure of others—were clear as early as the third quarter of the seventeenth century. The most significant changes in artisanal working conditions in the city's first hundred years had less to do with the emergence of a market economy, which was always present, and more to do with the changing priorities of imperial governance and the increasing reliance on slave workers. Slaves supplied the hard labor that underpinned the rise of New York City as a prosperous seaport town. This prosperity and the opportunities it afforded middling New Yorkers provided for social and political stability in the decades after Leisler's Rebellion. However, the enslavement of black workers also stigmatized menial and dependent toil and offered a daily reminder of the misery of servility that stood in marked contrast to the city's Dutch republican roots and its celebrated membership in an English empire dedicated to liberty and property.

While the working conditions and practices of resident artisans changed little in New York City's first century, their status and relationship to the wider community altered a good deal. Tradesmen in New Amsterdam occupied a preferential position in the civic order, sustained by a bundle of identifications that marked them as freeborn subjects, burghers, and craft practitioners who claimed privileges and bore reciprocal duties to work at their occupations in the interests of the common good. Questions regarding artisanal status, privileges, and duties figured in public debates and controversies ranging from the campaign for municipal government in the 1650s to the revolt against the maladministration and perceived tyrannical intent of the Stuart-appointed provincial government in Leisler's Rebellion. In the early eighteenth century, however, changes in the city's administrative and legal practice diminished earlier distinctions drawn between residents and strangers and eroded the grounds on which city artisans claimed special occupational consideration and protection. The shift of political influence from city to province, the rise of English-style elections, the introduction of the English common law, and the professionalization of legal recourse all undermined claims regarding local practices and privileges by either reconfiguring or denying access to the public fora within which such claims had previously been asserted, debated, and validated.

When structural weaknesses in the local and regional economy and the contraction of urban credit precipitated an economic collapse, provincial politicians and their constituencies collaborated in the articulation of a new conception of the relationship between the city and its tradesmen. Artisans and other ordinary male property holders were now cast as plainspeaking and virtuous political subjects whose consent legitimated provincial and imperial government. In this fashion, the crisis of the 1730s ushered onto the political stage a new and politically equal artisanal subject whose characteristics not only made sense of the transformation of urban working life in the preceding four decades but also provided a constituency for the development of a populist republican political culture in New York City. In the 1740s and 1750s claims regarding the integrity, skills, independence, and rights of city tradesmen figured in electoral campaigns and public debates on topics ranging from the bread supply to the qualities of high-status artisanal goods and services. By the end of the French and Indian War, city artisans had developed a sense of themselves as men of virtue and integrity and possessed of equal rights and individual and collective interests that they were determined to defend against imperial and provincial tyrants alike.

These findings question the causal force attributed to a common artisanal experience of worsening working conditions and suggest the need to consider the importance of earlier colonial influences on the processes of innovation and conceptual change that provided for the development of artisanal republicanism and its contribution to a rights-based political culture in eighteenth-century America. New York City's tradesmen may have been unfamiliar with the texts and subtle arguments of well-educated constitutional thinkers, but they nevertheless lived in a world that was shaped by the political languages of natural rights and republicanism within which these texts and arguments figured. Moreover, rather than a single set of meanings discerned by prominent theorists and political leaders, the liberal and republican philosophies that animated the American Revolution and the early national era were worked out over generations in conversations carried on in families, workplaces, and communities and were informed by a multiplicity of struggles among racial, gendered, and class interests, in addition to the final contest between imperial rulers and colonists. Far from an unalloyed political consciousness arising from a common experience of immiserization, then, artisanal republicanism in New York City emerged in response to conditions left over from the earlier Dutch civic order, to the rise of slavery, and to the importation of radical English political ideas and their adaptation to colonial circumstances. Rather than a monolithic, "popular" ideology, artisanal republicanism gave voice to the hopes and fears (and gendered and racial chauvinism) of its white, male, middling, and aspirational artisan proponents. Although constrained by the limits of time, place, and prejudice in its imagined social and political possibilities, artisanal republicanism was democratic in its implications. Herein lay the radicalism of the American Revolution. For in time artisanal republicanism gave voice to the hopes and fears of ordinary, working Americans who pushed the elitist and socially conservative gentry in directions that they were otherwise loath to pursue.

Notes

Introduction

1. Influential studies include Edward P. Thompson, *The Making of the English Working Class* (1963; reprint, London, 1980); Eric Foner, *Tom Paine and Revolutionary America* (New York, 1976), chs. 2, 5; Gary B. Nash, *The Urban Crucible: Social Change, Political Consciousness, and the Origins of the American Revolution* (Cambridge, Mass., 1979). For New York City, see Jesse Lemisch, "Jack Tar in the Streets: Merchant Seamen in the Politics of the Revolutionary America," *William and Mary Quarterly* (hereafter *WMQ*), 3d ser., 25 (1968): 381–95; Howard B. Rock, *Artisans of the New Republic: The Tradesmen of New York City in the Age of Jefferson* (New York, 1979); Sean Wilentz, *Chants Democratic: New York City and the Rise of the American Working Class, 1788–1850* (New York, 1984).

2. The dearth of studies of earlier colonial labor has been noted by Richard S. Dunn, "Servants and Slaves: The Recruitment and Employment of Labor," in Jack P. Greene and J. R. Pole, eds., *Colonial British America: Essays in the New History of the Early Modern Era* (Baltimore, 1984), 158, and John J. McCusker and Russell R. Menard, *The Economy of British America, 1607–1789* (Chapel Hill, N.C., 1985), 245–47. The only published study dealing with tradesmen in early New York City is Graham Russell Hodges, *New York City Carters* (New York, 1986).

3. For analysis of tax lists and other civic registers see Bruce Martin Wilkenfeld, *The Social and Economic Structure of the City of New York, 1695–1796* (New York, 1975), 17–136; Nash, *Urban Crucible*, 395; Nan Rothschild, *New York City Neighborhoods: The Eighteenth Century* (San Diego, 1990), 109–20; Joyce D. Goodfriend, *Before the Melting Pot: Society and Culture in New York City, 1664–1730* (Princeton, N.J., 1992), 65, 71.

4. The reference that led to the Mayor's Court Papers came from Evarts B. Greene and Richard B. Morris, *A Guide to the Principal Sources for Early American History in the City of New York* (New York, 1953), 209–11. The full collection of papers is scattered through various New York City archives. There are a handful of documents in the Rare Books and Manuscripts section of the New York Public Library and a few more in the New York Historical Society. However, most are held in the Division of Old Records, County Court, 31 Chambers St., and in a second large collection at the Rare Books and Manuscripts Division of Columbia University.

5. My thinking here and elsewhere is informed by Michael Sonenscher's *The Hatters of Eighteenth Century France* (Berkeley, Calif., 1987), and his *Work and Wages: Natural Law, Politics, and the Eighteenth-Century French Trades* (Cambridge, 1989). On the economy of the bazaar, see Clifford Geertz, *Peddlers and Princes* (Chicago, 1963), 33–47, and "Suq: The Bazaar Economy in Sefrou," in Clifford Geertz, Hildred Geertz,

and Lawrence Rosen, eds., *Meaning and Order in Moroccan Society* (New York, 1979), 124–25, 219.

6. Stephen Innes has also stressed the significance of continuity rather than change—with the exception of the rise of human chattel slavery—in seventeenth- and early eighteenth-century work relations; see his "John Smith's Vision," in *Work and Labor in Early America* (Chapel Hill, N.C., 1988), 43–44.

7. For a discussion of this artisanal republican politics and examples of its iconography, see Paul A. Gilje and Howard B. Rock, *Keepers of the Revolution: New Yorkers at Work in the Early Republic* (Ithaca, N.Y., 1983), introduction, 66–120.

8. This is one of the mechanisms that Pierre Bourdieu identifies as central to the social experience of *doxa*, in which the naturalization of the arbitrary assignment social meanings and signs serves the production and reproduction of power relations by obscuring the arbitrariness of the sign that assumes the authority of a component within the taken-for-granted or natural world. See his *Outline of a Theory of Practice*, trans. Richard Nice (New York, 1977), 164–67, 176–78. Also see Alf Lüdtke, ed., *The History of Everyday Life: Reconstructing Historical Experience and Ways of Life* (Princeton, N.J., 1995), introduction; Harald Dehne, "Have We Come Any Closer to *Alltag*? Everyday Reality and Workers' Lives as an Object of Historical Research in the German Democratic Republic," 116–49; Patrick Joyce, ed., *The Historical Meanings of Work* (New York, 1987), introduction.

9. Alice Kenny, *Stubborn for Liberty: The Dutch in New York* (Syracuse, N.Y., 1975). For overviews of the flourishing of studies on Dutch New York, see Eric Nooter and Patricia U. Bonomi, eds., *Colonial Dutch Studies: An Interdisciplinary Approach* (New York, 1988); Nancy Anne McClure Zeller, ed., *A Beautiful and Fruitful Place: Selected Rensselaerswijck Seminar Papers* (Albany, N.Y., 1991); Wayne Bodle, "Themes and Directions in Middle Colonies Historiography, 1980–1994," *WMQ* 51 (July 1994): 357–58; Joyce D. Goodfriend, "Writing/Righting Dutch Colonial History," *New York History* 80 (January 1998): 5–28.

10. Oliver Rink, *Holland on the Hudson: An Economic and Social History of Dutch New York* (Ithaca, N.Y., 1986), 172–213; Dennis J. Maika, "Commerce and Community: Manhattan Merchants in the Seventeenth Century" (Ph.D. diss., New York University, 1995), 80–162; Cathy Matson, *Merchants and Empire: Trading in Colonial New York* (Baltimore, 1998), part 1.

11. Jacob Price, *Holland and the Dutch Republic in the Seventeenth Century: The Politics of Particularism* (Oxford, 1994), 11–19; Willem Frijhoff and Marijke Spies, *Dutch Culture in a European Perspective* Vol. 1: *1650: Hard-Won Unity* (Basingstoke, 2004), 174–77, 184–90.

12. Richard Dagger, "Rights," in Terence Ball et al., eds., *Political Innovation and Conceptual Change* (Cambridge, 1989), 292–303. Also see Richard Tuck, *Natural Rights Theories* (London, 1979), 143–56; Knud Haakonssen, *Natural Law and Moral Philosophy: From Grotius to the Scottish Enlightenment* (New York, 1996), 15–31, 310–21; Michael Zuckert, *Natural Rights and the New Republicanism* (Princeton, N.J., 1994), 3–18.

13. Thomas Condon, *New York Beginnings: The Commercial Origins of New Netherland* (New York, 1968), 144–72; Rink, *Holland on the Hudson*, 19.

Chapter 1

1. James Franklin Jameson, *Narratives of New Netherland, 1609–1664* (New York, 1909), 6–28; Rink, *Holland on the Hudson*, 24–29.

2. Jameson, *Narratives*, 7–8.

3. G. M. Asher, ed., *Henry Hudson the Navigator: The Original Documents in Which His Career is Recorded, Collected, Partly Translated, and Annotated* (London, 1860), 98–130.

4. For a discussion of the notion of negotiated authority in an early modern English context, see Paul Griffiths, Adam Fox, and Steve Hindle, eds., *The Experience of Authority in Early Modern England* (Basingstoke, 1996); Tim Harris, ed., *The Politics of the Excluded, c. 1500–1850* (Basingstoke, 2001); Michael J. Braddick and John Walter, eds., *Negotiating Power in Early Modern Society: Order, Hierarchy, and Subordination in Britain and Ireland* (Cambridge, 2001), introduction.

5. Hugh Brodhead, *History of the State of New York*, 2 vols. (New York, 1853), 1: 21–23, 134; J. Franklin Jameson, "Willem Usselinx," American Historical Association, *Papers*, 2, no. 3 (1887); C. R. Boxer, *The Dutch Seaborne Empire, 1600–1800* (London, 1990), 27, 53–56; Jonathan I. Israel, *Dutch Primacy in World Trade, 1585–1740* (Oxford, 1989), 156–71.

6. I. N. P. Stokes, *The Iconography of Manhattan Island 1498–1909*, 6 vols. (1915–25; reprint, Union, N.J., 1998), 1: 10–11; Jameson, *Narratives*, 75; E. B. O'Callaghan, ed., *Documentary History of the State of New York* (hereafter *DHSNY*), 4 vols. (Albany, N.Y., 1849–51), 3: 49. For the most comprehensive single volume history of New Netherland, see Jaap Jacobs, *New Netherland: A Dutch Colony in Seventeenth-Century America* (1999; Leiden, 2005).

7. A. J. F. van Laer, trans. and ed., *Documents Relating to New Netherland, 1624–1626* (San Marino, Calif., 1926), 2–17, 39, 113–14, 117; J. H. Wessels, *History of Roman Dutch Law* (Grahamstown, Cape Colony, 1908); R. W. Lee, *An Introduction to Roman Dutch Law* (Oxford, 1953); Brodhead, *History*, 134–36; Martha Shattuck, "A Civil Society: Court and Community in Beverwijck, New Netherland, 1652–1664" (Ph.D. diss., Boston University, 1993), 26–29; Condon, *New York Beginnings*, ch. 2.

8. Edgar J. McManus, *A History of Negro Slavery in New York* (Syracuse, N.Y., 1966), ch. 1; Graham Hodges, *Root and Branch: African Americans in New York and East Jersey, 1613–1863* (Chapel Hill, N.C., 1999), 8–12; Ira Berlin, *Many Thousands Gone: The First Two Centuries of Slavery in North America* (Cambridge, Mass., 1998), 51–55.

9. Jameson, *Narratives*, 89, 130; Condon, *New York Beginnings*, 102–3.

10. Contemporary estimates put the costs of importing food and supplies at ten times the expense of producing them in New Netherland; see Condon, *New York Beginnings*, 77; Van Cleaf Bachman, *Peltries or Plantations: The Economic Policies of the Dutch West India Company in New Netherland, 1623–1639* (Baltimore, 1969), 74–154.

11. Jameson, *Narratives*, 197.

12. "The Assembly to the States General, 23 October 1629," in E. B. O'Callaghan and Berthold Fernow, eds., *Documents Relative to the Colonial History of New York* (hereafter *DRCNY*), 15 vols. (Albany, N.Y., 1856–87), 1: 39; Bachman, *Peltries or Plantations*, 79.

13. For example, in 1635, Styntgen Huygen—wife of the smith Cornelius Thomassen who sailed for New Netherland three years previously—petitioned the Amsterdam Chamber for two months' wages. The same year, Tryntgen Jones, New Netherland's midwife, petitioned for "an increase in wages and some necessaries." The petition of Vrouwtgen Michiels, wife of the carpenter Jan Hillebrantsen, who sailed more than two and half years previously, put his wages at twenty guilders a month, roughly equivalent to earnings in Amsterdam. See "Minutes of the Amsterdam Chamber of the Dutch West India Company, 1635–1636," in *New York Genealogical and Biographical Record* (hereafter *NYGBR*) (July 1918): 217–28; Jonathan Israel, *The Dutch Republic: Its Rise, Greatness, and Fall, 1477–1806* (Oxford, 1995), 352; Stokes, *Iconography*, 4: 85.

14. *NYGBR* (July 1925): 260; E. B. O'Callaghan, ed., *Calendar of State Papers in the Office of the Secretary of State* (hereafter *Calendar*), 2 vols. (Albany, N.Y., 1866), 1: 3. For the careers of some of New Netherland's other early residents, see Morton Wagman, "Struggle for Democracy in New Netherland" (Ph.D. diss., Columbia University, 1969), 268–69, 299–302, 316–24.

15. For calculations regarding skins and dietary needs, see Donna Merwick, *Possessing Albany, 1630–1710: An Archaeology of Interpretations* (Cambridge, 1989), 96–97, 205. For informal trading, see Margriet de Roever, "Merchandises for New Netherland: A Look at Dutch Articles for Barter with the Native American Population," in Alexandra van Dongen et al., eds., *"One Man's Trash Is Another Man's Treasure": The Metamorphosis of the European Utensil in the New World* (Rotterdam, 1995), 71–93.

16. Maria van Rennselaer, *History of the City of New York in the Seventeenth Century*, 2 vols. (New York, 1909), 1: 141; E. B. O'Callaghan, ed., *Laws and Ordinances of New Netherland, 1638–1674* (hereafter *Laws and Ordinances*), (Albany, N.Y., 1868), 10, 148–50. For a discussion of the significance of the staple right in early modern European ports and New Amsterdam, which secured the right of sole entrepôt in 1633, see Maika, "Commerce and Community," 179.

17. The carpenter Jacob Janse van Amsterdam and Frederick Lubbertse, a wagonmaker, also quit their skilled trades in favor of trading furs and muskets with the Indians. "Patent to Kiliaen van Rensselaer for a Tract of Land on Hudson's River," *DRCNY*, 1: 44. On the patroonship experiment and the problems of populating New Netherland, see Bachman, *Peltries or Plantations*, 95–140; Merwick, *Possessing Albany*, 6–67; Rink, *Holland on the Hudson*, 102–16, 197–202; Richard Schermerhorn Jr., *Schermerhorn Genealogy and Family Chronicles* (New York, 1914), 47–50.

18. Darret Rutman, *Winthrop's Boston: A Portrait of a Puritan Town, 1630–1649* (New York, 1965), 179; Faren R. Siminoff, *Crossing the Sound: The Rise of Atlantic American Communities in Seventeenth-Century Eastern Long Island* (New York, 2004), 87–132. The West India Company's accounts for 1634 and 1635 show New Netherland as a net loss, see Stokes, *Iconography*, 4: 79.

19. "Resolution of the States General urging the colonization of New Netherland, 26 April 1638," *DRCNY*, 1: 106–7; "Proposed articles for the colonization and trade of New Netherland," *DRCNY*, 1: 110–15; E. B. O'Callaghan, *The History of New Netherland*, 2 vols. (New York, 1845–48), 1: 392–93; Philip L. White, "Municipal Government Comes to Manhattan," *New York Historical Society Quarterly* 37 (1953): 146–57; Albert E. McKinley, "The English and Dutch Towns of New Netherland," *American Historical Review* 6 (October 1900): 1–18.

20. Donna Merwick has described the seasonal trading cycle in *Possessing Albany*, 68–133.

21. "Kiliaen van Rensselaer to Worter van Twiller, 23 April 1634," in A. J. F. van Laer, ed., *Van Rensselaer Bowier Manuscripts* (Albany, N.Y., 1908), 266–88; Stokes, *Iconography*, 4: 112, 113, 183; *DHSNY*, 4: 21–22; *Calendar*, 1: 15, 18–22, 36, 44, 62, 76. The apprenticeship of Cornelius Janszen Jonker to Evert Duycking is cited in *NYGBR* (October 1928): 309. Population figures are in Rink, *Holland on the Hudson*, 158–59, 164–65, 210.

22. In 1645, the West India Company's board estimated that, with the discharge of key workers, the colony could be administered by nine officials and sixty soldiers at a cost of twenty-thousand guilders annually. "Report on the Proceeding of the Assembly of the XIX, 1645," *DRCNY*, 1: 155–56; Condon, *New York Beginnings*, 147.

23. Kieft has generally been regarded as something of a bigoted blunderer. For example, Van Rensselaer, *History of the City of New York* 1: 220–40 and, more recently, Edwin Burrows and Michael Wallace, *Gotham: A History of New York City to 1898* (New York, 1999), 36–37. Willem Frijhoff has recently offered a more generous assessment of Kieft and his administration in "Neglected Networks: New Netherlanders and Their Old Fatherland: The Kieft Case" (unpublished paper presented at New Netherland at the Millennium: The State of New World Dutch Studies, New York City, 19–21 October 2001).

24. Kieft introduced severe punishment for public order offences, established livestock fairs in October and November and a ferry service between New Amsterdam and Breuckelen, set quality controls on tobacco and flour traded in New Amsterdam and exchange rates for local seawan, and capped profits on necessaries bought from the Company store at 50 percent. *Laws and Ordinances*, 26. E. B. O'Callaghan provided a list of the prices of some of the goods available at the Company store in 1640, which included "hard bread" at fifteen stivers, rye bread at five stivers, wheaten bread at seven stivers, and corn bread at four stivers per loaf. Without knowing the loaf sizes, we cannot know whether the bread was fairly priced, but the Company's tendency to mark up supplies by as much as fifty routinely provoked complaints from the colonists. O'Callaghan, *History of New Netherland*, 1: 227; Stokes, *Iconography*, 4: 87, 95, 97–98; David Valentine, ed., *Manual of the City and Corporation of New York*, 27 vols. (1842–69) (New York, 1855), 557.

25. The representatives formed committees of "Twelve" and Eight Men" comprising local male property holders and including Hendrick Jansen, tailor and disaffected fur trader, sailor Maryn Andriesen, Jacob Walingen van Winkle, an illiterate adventurer, and David Pietersen de Vries, who was a well-travelled and learned man and had invested heavily in New Netherland. Wagman, "Struggle for Democracy," 268–324; "Journal of New Netherland," *DRCNY*, 1: 185–86, 190–91, 206, 304; Jameson, *Narratives*, 213; "The Eight Men to the Assembly of the XIX" and "Extracts from the Papers of Director Kieft," *DRCNY*, 1: 202, 415–16.

26. "Remonstrance of New Netherland," *DRCNY*, 1: 313; John H. Innes, *New Amsterdam and Its People. Studies, Social and Topographical, of the Town under Dutch and Early English Rule* (New York, 1902), 104; Arnold J. F. van Laer, trans., *New York Historical Manuscripts: Dutch*, 4 vols. (Baltimore, 1974), 1: 230–31.

27. *Laws and Ordinances*, 38; "Excise Law of 1644," *DRCNY*, 1: 189. The manumitted slaves' tribute was set at one fat hog, valued at twenty guilders, or thirty

skepels of maize, wheat, peas, or beans. "Remonstrance of New Netherland," *DRCNY,* 1: 302. For the predisposition to manumit long-serving slaves, see Peter R. Christoph, "The Freedmen of New Amsterdam," in Zeller, ed., *A Beautiful and Fruitful Place,* 159.

28. Jameson, *Narratives,* 270–84. For the miserable condition of the colony following Kieft's War, see "Memorial of Eight Men at the Manhattans to the States General" and the "Report of the Board of Accounts on New Netherland, 1644," *DRCNY,* 1: 139, 149–56, 190–91; *DHSNY,* 4: 1–19; Rink, *Holland on the Hudson,* 117–18.

29. Rink, *Holland on the Hudson,* 134–38.

30. Matson, *Merchants and Empire,* 31–32; Kenny, *Stubborn for Liberty,* 91–93; Thomas O'Donnel, ed., *A Description of New Netherlands: Adriaen van der Donck* (Syracuse, N.Y., 1968), 12; Condon, *New York Beginnings,* 144–72.

31. "Remonstrance of New Netherland," *DRCNY,* 1: 202; A. J. F. Van Laer, ed., *New York Historical Manuscripts, Dutch: Council Minutes, 1638–1649* (Baltimore, 1974), 389.

32. "West India Company to the States General, 13 July 1646," *DRCNY,* 1: 175–79. For Stuyvesant's early career in New Amsterdam see Jameson, *Narratives,* 458; *DHSNY,* 1: 689; *DRCNY,* 14: 44; Innes, *New Amsterdam and Its People,* 27, 113; Berthold Fernow, ed., *The Records of New Amsterdam from 1653 to 1674 Anno Domini* (hereafter *RNA*), 7 vols. (1897; reprint, Baltimore, 1976), 1: 3–17; Rink, *Holland on the Hudson,* 223–25; Drake de Kay, "The Administration of Petrus Stuyvesant," parts 1–6, *De Halve Maen* 53, no. 1 (1978): 1–2, 12; 53, no. 2 (1978): 1–2, 12–13; 53, no. 3 (1978): 7–8, 15–18; 53, no. 4 (1978): 1–2, 15; 54, no. 1 (1979): 6–7, 11; 54, no 2. (1979): 7–9.

33. As an alternative, the Amsterdam Chamber recommended that itinerant traders should keep an open store, thereby qualifying for tax payments, in the town. New-York Historical Society, Collections (hereafter NYHS, Collections), (1885), 1–4. *Laws and Ordinances,* 148–50; Harold C. Syrett, "Private Enterprise in New Amsterdam," *WMQ,* 3d ser., 11 (October 1954): 536–50.

34. For early modern diet and carbohydrate requirements and the importance of bread, see A. Th. van Deursen, *Plain Lives in a Golden Age: Popular Culture, Religion, and Society in Seventeenth-Century Holland* (1978; reprint, Cambridge, 1991), 6–8, 23–24; Merwick, *Possessing Albany,* 96; Betty Hobbes Pruitt, "Self-Sufficiency and the Agricultural Economy of Eighteenth-Century Massachusetts," *WMQ,* 3d ser., 41 (July 1984): 333–64. For the Dutch preference for bought rather than home-baked bread see Simon Schama, *The Embarrassment of Riches: An Interpretation of Dutch Culture in the Golden Age* (New York, 1987), 158–60, 188.

35. In August 1628 the Reverend Jonas Michaelius wrote to the Reverend Adrianus Smoutius in Holland describing the colony and reporting that "they are making a windmill to saw wood and we also have a gristmill"; see *DRCNY,* 2: 769. Various men served as millers from 1638 onward: Abraham Pietersen (1638), Philip Gerritsen (1640), Petrus Cornelissen (1650), Abraham Martins Clock (1655), Jan De Witt (1661). John A. Bogart, "New Amsterdam Windmills Made History: 1," *De Halve Maen* 35, no. 2 (1960): 5–6; E. B. O'Callaghan, *The Register of New Netherland, 1626–1674* (Albany, N.Y., 1865), 117.

36. Rink, *Holland on the Hudson,* 102–16, 151; Stokes, *Iconography,* 2: 269; "Remonstrance of New Netherland" and the "Petition of Joost Teunissen," *DRCNY,* 1: 312, 326–29, 342.

37. On the early modern preference of white over brown bread and the tendency of bakers to bake the latter, see E. P. Thompson, "The Moral Economy of the English Crowd in the Eighteenth Century," *Past and Present* 50 (February 1971): 76–136; Steven Laurence Kaplan, *The Bakers of Paris and the Bread Question, 1700–1775* (Durham, N.C., 1996), 33–40, 442–45; Schama, *Embarrassment of Riches*, 150–88. In sixteenth-century England, there were even different guilds of bakers for white and brown bread. John Ashton, *The History of Bread from Pre-Historic to Modern Times* (London, 1904), 83–88.

38. *RNA*, 1: 14.

39. *Laws and Ordinances*, 111, 115.

40. For example, in 1497, a local English law itemized the bakers' expenses and included moneys laid out for the furnace and wood, salt, yeast, candles, and sack bands; the fees paid to the miller and the costs of provisions for two journeymen, one apprentice, the baker, his wife, and even his cat and dog. Strict observation of the regulated price of bread began to break down in the early seventeenth century, when millers ceased to serve only the bakers and increasingly sold grain and flour on their own account. S. and B. Webb, "The Assize of Bread," *Economic Journal* 14 (1904): 190–218; Sylvia Thrupp, *A Short History of the Worshipful Company of Bakers of London* (Croydon, 1933), 12–39; Steven L. Kaplan, *Bread, Politics, and Political Economy in the Reign of Louis XV*, 2 vols. (The Hague, 1976), 1: 52–97. For cookie baking in New Amsterdam, see J. J. Schilstra, "Dutch 'Koekplanken' of the 17th and 18th Centuries," *De Halve Maen* 42, no. 3 (1967): 17–18, 22; Kenny, *Stubborn for Liberty*, 87–88.

41. There is some evidence that Stuyvesant may have been partially responsible for the 1650 shortage: following the introduction of regulations in 1649, the director-general allegedly attempted to corner the market in flour and grain by buying on "credit at a high price payable in the spring, all the provisions which were on hand" and promptly shipping them for resale in Barbados. Locals complained that Stuyvesant's actions left "the poor people much reduced to extremity and great scarcity" and that "no supplies of bread, butter, beef, and pork can now be had except for beaver or silver coin." In "Remonstrance of New Netherland," *DRCNY*, 1: 385–86.

42. *RNA*, 1: 15–16; *Laws and Ordinances*, 115 -17, 119.

43. The activities of part-time bakers accounts for the tendency for complaints of bread shortages to occur during and just after the trading season in September and November. Between 1649 and 1661, the inhabitants complained about the bread supply on six different occasions, in 1649, 1650, 1656, 1657, 1659, and 1661. Unusual circumstances provoked the bakers' suspensions in April 1650 and January 1657. However, on the other four occasions, the inhabitants complained in the months between September and November. *RNA*, 1: 14, 26, 31, 43, 46–48. For the importance of these autumn months in England's baking and grain trade, see Thompson, "Moral Economy," 207.

44. In 1641, there were five unpolished beads and four polished beads per stiver and four strung and six loose beads to a stiver; in 1650, there were six white or three black beads per stiver for high-quality "merchantable" seawan and eight white or four black beads per stiver for "bad strung" seawan. In 1656, these rates were held, but in November 1657, there was a general devaluation of all seawan to the 1650 rate for poor quality beads. In 1662, the West India Company devalued the seawan it paid

to its employees so that it took sixteen to twenty-four white and twelve black beads to make a stiver. John J. McCusker estimates that between 1641 and 1658 seawan depreciated by about 60 percent and fared much worse thereafter. McCusker also argues that beaver and seawan were equally inflationary; however, the bakers' petitions suggest that beaver held its value better. See John J. McCusker, *Money and Exchange in Europe and America, 1600–1775* (Chapel Hill, N.C., 1987), 42–45, 156–57; Matson, *Merchants and Empire*, 32–34, 341–42 n. 54; *DRCNY*, 1: 425; *RNA*,1: 16; "Secretary van Tienhoven's Answer to the Remonstrance from New Netherland," *DRCNY*, 1: 425; *RNA*,1: 16. For seawan production, see Daniel Richter, *Ordeal of the Longhouse: The Peoples of the Iroquois League in the Era of European Colonization* (Chapel Hill, N.C., 1992), 84–96.

45. The calculation of the city bakers' customer base rests on estimates of the number of working bakers and population size between 1648 and 1664. Counting the seven master bakers who registered with the city in 1661 and who appeared in other contexts as full-time bakers (Jacob Teunissen De Key, Hendrick Jansen, Reynier Willemsen, Jan Gerretsen, Andries de Haas, Antony de Milt, and Hendrick Willemsen) and adding six of the fourteen others who likely worked at some time at the trade (Cornelius Barentsen van der Cuyl, Joost Teunissen, Jan Harmensz, Jan Hendricksen, Jacob Hendricksen, Willem Jacobsen, Thomas Laurens, Nicholas Backer, Joghim Wessels, Hugo Barentsen, Evert Luykese, Hans Sodurat, Souverain Ten Houte, and Johan Verpronck) suggests a baking trade comprising a dozen or so key producers. For estimates of New Amsterdam's population and other occasional bakers, see O'Callaghan, *History of New Netherland*, 1: 386; Goodfriend, *Before the Melting Pot*, 19; *RNA*, 1: 46–48; Rosalie Fellows Bailey, "Emigrants to New Netherland: Account Book, 1654–1664," *NYGBR* (October 1963): 193–200; *DHSNY*, 3: 52–63; NYHS, Collections, 18 (New York, 1885), 19, 20, 23, 25. If we overestimate the city's population in the 1650s, by using the figure of fifteen hundred identified in 1664, this gives an approximate ratio of 110–50 inhabitants per baker. This provided New Amsterdam's bakers with a much smaller core market than their European contemporaries. In Antwerp, in 1650, 169 bakers catered for a population of approximately eighty thousand, roughly one baker to every 450 inhabitants; the eighteen bakers who worked in the village of Graft in the Netherlands in the mid-seventeenth century served a population of three thousand. Steven Kaplan has calculated a similar ratio of one baker to roughly four hundred inhabitants in Paris. Geoffrey Parker, *The Dutch Revolt* (London, 1990), 23, 26; Kaplan, *Bakers of Paris*, 84; Shattuck, "A Civil Society," 9, 20, 94.

46. Quotes from Amsterdam Board in this paragraph are taken from "Letter from the Directors to Stuyvesant, March 1654," *DRCNY*, 14: 251–53; for the ordinance prohibiting retailing by brewers issued 12 July 1648, see Charles T. Gehring, trans. and ed., *Laws and Writs of Appeal, 1647–1663* (Syracuse, N.Y., 1991), 12; on city porters, see *RNA*, 7: 145–47, and *Calendar*, 1: 185.

47. For a sample of the Company's arguments against restrictions on independent fur traders, see "Patroons of New Netherlands to the States General, 1 June 1634," "The Assembly of the XIX to the States General, 25 October 1634," and "Remonstrance of New Netherland," *DRCNY*, 14: 84, 194, 208; *Laws and Ordinances*, 149–50.

48. "Council Minutes . . . , 12 February 1652" and "Letter from the Directors to Stuyvesant, 12 March 1654," *DRCNY*, 14: 155, 252.

49. For grain shortages, see *RNA*, 1: 91–92; Matson, *Merchants and Empire*, 30–31. For Litschoe v. De Haas and other cases involving bakers suing or being sued for debt, see *RNA*, 1: 100, 108, 114, 120, 123, 125, 322, 377; *RNA*, 2: 39, 90, 93, 159. For Litschoe as tavern keeper, see Kenneth Scott, "New Amsterdam's Taverns and Tavern Keepers," *De Halve Maen* 39, no. 3 (1964): 14. Charles T. Gehring, trans. and ed., *Council Minutes, 1655–1656* (Syracuse, N.Y., 1995), 4–5.

50. Historians agree that the fur trade peaked in 1656–57 when forty thousand beaver and otter skins were shipped to New Amsterdam from upriver. Donna Merwick has calculated that if only half of the beaver pelts traded in 1657 were purchased with seawan then more than thirty-nine million black and white shells, strung in the customary lengths, would have been exchanged in trade. Merwick, *Possessing Albany*, 77; Thomas E. Burke Jr., "The New Netherland Fur Trade, 1657–1661: Response to Crisis," in Zeller, ed., *A Beautiful and Fruitful Place*, 283–95. For the early history of Beverwijck and the bakers' complaints, see Shattuck, "A Civil Society," 20–72, 208–15; *Calendar*, 1: 175–76.

51. *Laws and Ordinances*, 261–63; *RNA*, 1: 25–27; O'Callaghan, *Register of New Netherland*, 135.

52. The prices set on 26 October 1656 were 14 stivers for a double coarse loaf of 8 lbs., 7 stivers for a single loaf of 4 lbs., and 3.5 stivers for a half-loaf of 2 lbs. White bread sold for 8 stivers for a double loaf of 2 lbs., 4 stivers for a single loaf of 1 lb., and 2 stivers for a halfloaf of .5 lb. *RNA*, 1: 26; 2: 204. Beginning in 1650, the baking regulations set prices by the pound of baked bread. Thus Stuyvesant set the prices at 1.75 stivers per pound for wheat bread and 1.5 stivers per pound for rye. White bread weighing a .25, .5, or 1 lb. was supposed to sell for no more than 3 stivers a pound. As competition for local grain intensified and the value of grain and its products increased, the regulated price was maintained even as the value of seawan declined. In 1656, the bakers were only offered a better margin on the white bread which they could sell for 4 stivers per pound in loaves weighing up to 2 lbs.

53. *Laws and Ordinances*, 75–76; "Remonstrance of New Netherland," *DRCNY*, 1: 307, 315; "Letter from the Directors to Stuyvesant, 4 November 1653," *DRCNY*, 14: 218–19.

54. "Petition of the Commonalty of New Netherland to the States General, 13 October 1649," "Additional Observations on the Preceding Petition," the "Remonstrance of New Netherland," and the "Short Digest of the Excesses and Highly Injurious Neglect," in *DRCNY*, 1: 259–63, 271–318, 332–37.

55. Aside from the lawyer Adriaen van der Donck, the petitioners were wealthy merchants or men who had made good since arriving in New Netherland. Govert Loockermans and August Herman had both started out as colonial agents for Amsterdam merchant houses before establishing successful businesses of their own. Oloff Stevens, whom we encountered earlier, came to New Netherland as a soldier; Thomas Hall, the only Englishman in the Nine, arrived as an indentured servant; both men had risen to prominence as traders and landowners. Cornelius Melyn boasted some of the trappings of rank as a Company shareholder and patroon of Staten Island; he had been a thorn in the provincial government's side since Kieft's

failure to defend his patroonship from Indian attacks in the winter of 1643–44. But even Melyn had started out as a humble leather dresser in Amsterdam before making his fortune and investing in overseas ventures. Jacob van Couwenhoven inherited his business contacts—and a head start in fur dealing, land speculation, and brewing—from his father, Wolphert Gerritsen van Couwenhoven, who came to the colony in 1625. Some of the Nine were also business partners and had previously campaigned for reform: Jan Evertse Bout came to New Netherland in 1632 and had worked for the Company and the patroon of Pavonia before serving as a member of the Twelve and then Eight Men. Following Kieft's War, Bout settled on a farm in Breucklen where he served as a schepen and went into partnership with Jan Jansen Damenm, who was also one of the Nine. The remaining petitioners were Arnoldus van Hardenbergh, Machuyel Janssen, Elbert Elbertsen, and Hendrick Hendricksen Kip. Wagman, "Struggle for Democracy," 330; Innes, *New Amsterdam and Its People,* ch. 11; Van Rensselaer, *History of The City of New York,* 1: 277–308.

56. Before coming to New Netherland, Van der Donck attended Leiden University and worked as an advocate in Holland's Supreme Court. Soon after arriving, the twenty-two-year-old Van der Donck demonstrated an independent streak when he settled on a farm away from the location specified by Van Rensselaer and was less than assiduous at enforcing his employers' orders relating to the control of the fur trade and local laborers. His work extolling the virtues of New Netherland was published as *Description of New Netherland (such as it now is) Comprehending the Nature, Character, Situation, and Fruitfulness of That Country; together with the profitable and desirable opportunities which it offers for the support of people (whether natives or foreigners). Also the manners and peculiar characteristics of the Indians or aborigines of the country. And a particular account of the wonderful nature and habits of the beaver; to which is also added a Discourse on the situation of New Netherland between a New Netherlands Patriot and a New Netherlander,* General Jeremiah Johnson translated in 1656; *NYGBR* (July 1936): 234–36. For a recent reappraisal of Van der Donck's role in the campaign for municipal rights, see Russell Shorto, *The Island at the Center of the World: The Epic Story of Dutch Manhattan, the Forgotten Dutch Colony That Shaped America* (New York, 2004), part II.

57. The term "true republican" is taken from Richard Tuck, *Philosophy and Government, 1572–1651* (Cambridge, 1993), 154–58. Also see Haitsma Mulier, *The Myth of Venice and Dutch Republican Thought in the Seventeenth Century,* G. T. Moran, trans. (Assen, 1988), 26–77; Herbert H. Rowen, "The Dutch Republic and the Idea of Freedom," in David Wooten, ed., *Republicanism, Liberty, and Commercial Society, 1649–1776* (Stanford, Calif., 1994), 310–41.

58. Piet van der Cun was acquainted with Grotius and had been a student and teacher at the University of Leiden, where he lectured on Latin and politics. There were at least seven editions of his *De Republica Ebraeorum* published between 1617 and 1700, including an English translation in 1653, at the height of republican revival. In his work, Van der Cun warned of the dangers to Dutch liberty posed by the military and a commercial aristocracy and stressed the importance of preserving the rights and privileges of all freeborn Dutch citizens. Tuck, *Philosophy and Government,* 154–58. In the early 1660s, and following the reforms effected by the Nine Men and their supporters, radical Dutch thinkers and activists even dreamt of

transforming New Netherland into a democratic republic of yeomen farmers and small landowners to counterbalance the centralizing forces that threatened republican liberties in the Old World. See Jonathon Israel, *Radical Enlightenment: Philosophy and the Making of Modernity, 1650–1750* (Oxford, 2001), 175–83.

59. "Petition of the Delegates from New Netherland, 2 February 1650," *DRCNY*, 1: 346–47.

60. Israel, *Dutch Republic*, 600–609; Peter Geyl, *The Netherlands in the Seventeenth Century*, 2 vols. (New York, 1964), 1: 13–25. Dennis Maika discusses the connections between the campaigns in New Amsterdam and in the Dutch Republic in "Commerce and Community," 1: 95–118.

61. Van Deursen, *Plain Lives*, 142–43; Schama, *Embarrassment of Riches*, 41.

62. Quentin Skinner, *The Foundations of Modern Political Thought*, 2 vols. (Cambridge, 1978), 1: 3–48, 153–54. Also see his essay on positive liberty, *Liberty before Liberalism* (Cambridge, 1998), 59–101. For the Dutch context, see Martin van Gelderen, *The Political Thought of the Dutch Revolt, 1555–1590* (Cambridge, 1992), 260–88; Tuck, *Philosophy and Government*, 154–58.

63. E. H. Kossman, "Popular Sovereignty at the Beginning of the Dutch Ancien Régime," *The Low Countries History Yearbook* 14 (1981): 4, and "The Development of Dutch Political Theory in the Seventeenth Century," in J. S. Bromley and E. H. Kossman, eds., *Britain and the Netherlands*, vol. 1 (London, 1960); Eco Haitsma Mulier, "The Language of Seventeenth-Century Republicanism in the United Provinces: Dutch or European?" in Anthony Pagden, ed., *The Languages of Political Theory in Early Modern Europe* (Cambridge, 1987), 179–95.

64. "Petition of Joost Teunissen, baker, burgher in New Netherland, to their High Mightinesses, the Lords States General of the United Netherlands, 13 December 1649" and the "Petition of Sibout Claessen, house carpenter and burgher of New Netherland to their High Mightinesses, the Lords States General of the United Netherlands, 13 December, 1649," both submitted with the "Remonstrance of New Netherland," *DRCNY*, 1: 312, 326–30.

65. Ibid., 266, 346.

66. "Report of the Committee of the States General on the Affairs of New Netherland" and "Plan for the Colonization of New Netherland," *DRCNY*, 1: 359–76, 388–95.

67. *DHSNY*, 1: 598–602. For discussions of the municipal government's broadening administrative remit, see Elva Kathy Lyon, "The New Amsterdam Weighhouse," *De Halve Maen* 69, no. 2 (1996): 1–10; Valentine, *Manual* (1848), 385–86; John E. O'Connor, "The Rattle Watch of New Amsterdam," parts I and II, *De Halve Maen* 43, no. 1 (1968): 11–12, and 43, no. 2 (1968): 9–12; Scott, "New Amsterdam's Taverns," part I, 39, no. 1 (1964): 9, 10, 15; Adriana van Zweiten, "The Orphan Chamber of New Amsterdam," *WMQ*, 3d ser., 53 (April 1996): 319–40.

68. Merwick, *Possessing Albany*, introduction, 103–27; Valentine, *Manual* (1862), 513; *RNA*, 4: 57.

69. *Calendar*, 1: 177, 180.

70. The ordinance of 1657 was reissued by Stuyvesant and his council in 1660 and by the burgomasters and schepens in 1660 and 1661. See NYHS, Collections (1885), 12–36; *RNA*, 2: 262.

71. "Resolution of the Council of Amsterdam on the Conditions for the Encouragement of Emigration to New Netherland" and "Draft of Conditions Offered by the City of Amsterdam to Emigrants to New Netherland" in *DRCNY*, 1: 618–25.

72. *Calendar*, 1: 181. For orders relating to the regulation of trade and civic life, see *RNA*, 6: 67; 7: 191, 201, 206, 220, 228; *RNA*, 7: 155, 195, 227; *DRCNY*, 14: 433, 442, 450. The expanding role of local government in New Amsterdam and Beverwijck is discussed in Maika, "Commerce and Community," 68–80, and Shattuck, "A Civil Society," 20–72.

73. NYHS, Collections (1885), 19.

74. *RNA*, 1: 122; Maika, "Commerce and Community," 210–15.

75. *RNA*, 2: 410.

76. *RNA*, 1: 40–43, 46–48; Syrett, "Private Enterprise in New Amsterdam," 540–41.

77. Michael Kammen has argued that Stuyvesant introduced the burgher right to "keep control in the tight grasp of an elite." *Colonial New York: A History* (New York, 1974), 55. A. G. Roeber considers the director-general's support for the burgher right as part of an effort to create "a self-conscious governing cadre," in "'The Origin of Whatever Is Not English among Us': The Dutch-Speaking and the German-Speaking Peoples of Colonial British America," in Bernard Bailyn and Philip D. Morgan, eds., *Strangers within the Realm: The Cultural Margins of the First British Empire* (Chapel Hill, N.C., 1991), 224. In a similar vein, see Lyon, "New Amsterdam Weighhouse," 2; Maika, "Commerce and Community," 162–94; Matson, *Merchants and Empire*, 30–31.

78. Between 1657 and 1661, some 210 tradesmen registered for the lessor burgher right. NYHS, Collections, 18 (1885), 16–32. Joyce Goodfriend's analysis posits an able-bodied male population of approximately 315 in 1664, excluding those living in the Bouwerie village and Harlem village or what would eventually become the city's Out Ward. Goodfriend, *Before the Melting Pot*, 14–15.

79. "Letter from Director Stuyvesant and the Council to the Directors in Holland, 23 July 1659," *DRCNY*, 14: 438–39.

80. Arenzen had come to New Amsterdam from Swartensluys in 1654, under contract for three years to Lourens Andriessen, a master turner from Boskerk; he later fled Andriessen's service to marry Grietje Pieters of Breda, with whom he established a home as a registered burgher in the city. Berthold Fernow, trans. and ed., *Minutes of the Orphanmasters of New Amsterdam, 1655–1663*, 2 vols. (New York, 1902–7), 2: 132–33; Stokes, *Iconography*, 2: 219, 247; NYHS, Collections, (1885), 21.

81. Hendrick Willemsen was one who benefited from municipal contracts in addition to securing the office of baking inspector; other bakers were also appointed to municipal positions as Stamper (certifier) of Cans and Weights and Measurer of Grain and Lime. *Calendar*, 1: 191; *RNA*, 3: 16, 27, 259; O'Callaghan, *Register of New Netherland*, 135; Valentine, *Manual* (1862), 504. I have offered a fuller discussion of the bakers' various protests in "How It Came That the Bakers Bake No Bread: A Struggle for Trade Privileges in Seventeenth-Century New Amsterdam," *WMQ*, 3d ser., 58 (April 2001), 347–72.

82. *Laws and Ordinances*, 361; RNA, 7: 219.

83. Scott, "New Amsterdam's Taverns," part I, 39, no. 1 (1964): 9, 10, 15; *RNA*, 1: 263–64; 7: 145–47, 258–59; *Calendar*, 1: 203.

84. For the formality of law and reliance on written evidence and formal instruments, see Julius Goebel Jr., "The Courts and the Law in Colonial New York," in A. C. Flick, ed., *History of the State of New York*, 10 vols. (New York, 1933), 3: 4–43; Shattuck, "A Civil Society," 116–39, 293–95; Maika, "Commerce and Community," 239–41. See also Linda Briggs Biemer, "Criminal Law and Women in New Amsterdam and Early New York," in Zeller, ed., *A Beautiful and Fruitful Place*, 73; Jacob A. Schiltkamp, "On Common Ground: Legislation, Government, Jurisprudence, and Law in the Dutch West Indian Colonies: The Order of Government of 1629," *De Halve Maen* 70, no. 4 (1997): 73–80. For arbitration, see John R. Aiken, "New Netherlands Arbitration in the Seventeenth Century," *The Arbitration Journal* 29 (September 1974): 145–60.

85. For magistrates' decisions that referred to the "by-laws and customs of Old Amsterdam" in the judgment, see *RNA*, 1: 101–2, 273.

86. My emphasis. Willem Albersten v. Claes Terhaer, *RNA*, 1: 55–56. For similar disputes and arbitration involving tailors, shipwrights, house carpenters, and masons, see *RNA*, 1: 50, 62, 206, 418; 4: 137, 311; 5: 25, 36, 83; *Calendar*, 1: 176.

87. Stokes, *Iconography* 4: 158. On the militia in the United Provinces, see Price, *Holland and the Dutch Republic*, 11–18; Paul Knevel, *Burgers in het geweer: De Schutterijen in Holland* (Hilversum, 1994).

88. The dispute over the costs of repairing the town's defenses arose when Stuyvesant insisted that the burgomasters supply additional funds to pay for side arms supplied by the Company and for ironwork, nails, and grain. The burgomasters countered with evidence of their own trouble and expense in contributing to the repair of the city's defenses. Challenging Stuyvesant to leave the city defenseless—and fail in his duty as the head of the provincial government and representative of the West India Company—the burgomasters declared that they were unable to pay for the side arms, but offered to return them "should the Director General so require." The dispute rolled on until the end of the year, when the threat to suspend militia patrols forced a compromise in which the burgomasters increased their contributions to the costs of repairs in return for securing control of the liquor excise. *RNA*, 1: 65–68, 72–74, 90–92, 103–4, 126, 128, 130; *Calendar*, 1: 131–32, 135.

89. Gehring, *Laws and Writs*, 50; *RNA*, 3: 17–18; "Directors of the West India Company to Stuyvesant, 13 February 1659," *DRCNY*, 14: 432; "Director Stuyvesant to the Directors in Holland on the Militia Question, 15 July 1662," *DRCNY*, 13: 223–24. The militia's petition for the exclusion of Jews appears to have succeeded, at least until 1657. In April, the Jewish trader Asser Levy applied for his burgher right and asserted that "he ought not to be refused as he keeps watch and ward like other Burghers; shewing a Burgher certificate from the city of Amsterdam, that the Jew is a burgher there." The Court of Burgomasters refused Levy's request, but their ruling was later rescinded by Stuyvesant, who granted Levy permission to trade. *RNA*, 2: 265; *NYGBR* (July 1971): 130–32.

90. For the brede middenstand and Dutch civic culture, see Schama, *Embarrassment of Riches*, preface; Gabrielle Dorren, *Eenheid en verscheidenheid: De Burgers van Haarlem in de Gouden Eeuw* (Amsterdam, 2001). Details on Van der Wel and Pos are in *RNA*, 1: 149–50; 2: 99; *Laws and Ordinances*, 237. The sense of city as a community of commercially ambitious and civic-minded individuals is captured best in Stokes's breakdown of city households based on the 1660 (Castello) Plan of New Amsterdam in *Iconography*, 2: 215–341.

91. "Letter from the Directors to Stuyvesant, 25 April 1659," *DRCNY,* 14: 435–38.

92. Slaves also retained the right to marry, own movable property, sue in court, and the rights of the criminally accused to a trial and testify in their own defense. In 1635 five slaves petitioned the West Indian Company's office in Amsterdam for unpaid wages. See Innes, *New Amsterdam and Its People,* 15, 31; Hodges, *Root and Branch,* ch. 1; Christoph, "The Freedmen of New Amsterdam," 159.

93. For a discussion of half-freedom and its benefits, see McManus, *Negro Slavery in New York,* 13–16, and the more skeptical assessment by Leslie M. Harris, *In the Shadow of Slavery: African Americans in New York City, 1623–1863* (Chicago, 2003), 23–26.

94. Stuyvesant recognized the continuing usefulness of free and enslaved black defenders in 1660: while away from New Amsterdam during the fighting of the Second Esopus War, Stuyvesant wrote to his council requesting that they ensure that "the free and the Company's Negroes keep good watch on my Bouwery." Christoph, "The Freedmen of New Amsterdam," 162.

95. "The Directors to Suyvesant, 7 April 1657," *DRCNY,* 14: 387; Stokes, *Iconography,* 4: 181; Joyce Goodfriend, "Burghers and Blacks: The Evolution of Slave Society in New Amsterdam," *New York History* (April 1978): 131. Peter Christoph argues that Stuyvesant's report constituted a "dubious generalization" in his "The Freedmen of New Amsterdam," 160; Berlin, *Many Thousands Gone,* 51.

96. For women working as bakers and at other trades in New Netherland, see Shattuck, "A Civil Society," 140–92; *NYGBR* (April 1973): 71; Linda B. Biemer, *Women and Property in Colonial New York: The Transition from Dutch to English Law, 1643–1727* (Ann Arbor, Mich., 1983), introduction, and her "Criminal Law," 73–83.

97. The following draws on Firth Haring Fabend, "Sex and the City: Relations between Men and Women in New Netherland" (unpublished paper presented at New Netherland at the Millennium: The State of New World Dutch Studies, New York City, 19–21 October 2001); Shattuck, "A Civil Society," ch. 3; David E. Narrett, "Dutch Customs of Inheritance, Women, and the Law in Colonial New York City," in William Pencak and Conrad Edick Wright, eds., *Authority and Resistance in Early New York* (New York, 1988), 34, 35. Also see Peter R. Christoph, "The Colonial Family: Kinship and Power," in Zeller, ed., *A Beautiful and Fruitful Place;* Firth Haring Fabend, *A Dutch Family in the Middle Colonies, 1660–1800* (1991, reprint; New Brunswick, N.J., 1999); Cynthia Kierner, *Traders and Gentlefolk: The Livingstons of New York, 1675–1790* (Ithaca, N.Y., 1992).

98. Firth Fabend has argued that there was little evidence of disputes between husbands and wives following the settlement of families in the 1640s and that married partners pursued all manner of commercial enterprises together. In the Council minutes for the eleven years 1638–49, for instance, men and women appear in court in an adversarial position about one hundred times, or an average of 1.3 times per month, yet very few of these cases involved husbands and wives; see "Sex and the City."

99. The term "gendered protection" is taken from Shattuck, "A Civil Society," 167. Firth Fabend found that men slandered women three times more than women slandered men and women had to sue men for payment or satisfaction of a contract almost four times more than men sued women, see "Sex and the City." This situation

in New Netherland contrasted sharply with the female-centered slander in Virginia in the same period, see Kathleen Brown, *Good Wives, Nasty Wenches, and Anxious Patriarchs: Gender, Race, and Power in Colonial Virginia* (Chapel Hill, N.C., 1996), 146.

100. Susan Dwyer Amussen, "'The Part of a Christian Man': The Cultural Politics of Manhood in Early Modern England," in Susan Dywer Amussen and Mark Kishlansky, eds., *Political Culture and Cultural Politics in Early Modern England* (Manchester, 1995); Philip Carter, *Men and the Emergence of Polite Society: Britain, 1660–1800* (Harlow, 2001). On patriarchy and seventeenth-century order and governance, see Susan Dwyer Amussen, *An Ordered Society: Gender and Class in Early Modern England* (Oxford, 1988), and Mary Beth Norton, *Founding Mothers and Fathers: Gendered Power and the Forming of American Society* (New York, 1997).

101. In 1664, the magistrates estimated the population of New York City at fifteen hundred male residents, excluding women and slaves, almost 60 percent of whom had arrived in the colony within the previous decade. O'Callaghan, *History of New Netherland*, 1: 540; *RNA*, 6: 110; Goodfriend, *Beyond the Melting Pot*, 15; Evarts B. Greene and Virginia D. Harrington, *American Population before the Federal Census of 1790* (1932, reprint; New York, 1966), 93; McCusker and Menard, *Economy of British America*, 188–200.

102. Fernow, *Minutes of Orphanmasters*, 2: 185–90.

103. Israel, *Dutch Primacy*, 196–291.

Chapter 2

1. "Private Instructions to Coll. R. Nicolls," *DRCNY*, 3: 57–61. For contemporary accounts of the conquest, see "Rev. Samuel Drisius to the Classis of Amsterdam, 15 September 1664" and Peter Stuyvesant's "Report on the Surrender of New Netherland" and "Extract from the Register of the Principal Events . . . and Reduction of New Netherland," *DRCNY*, 2: 364–70, 411–13; Jameson, *Narratives*, 414–17, 458–66. The handbills were copies of a proclamation made by Nicolls on board the *Guinea* prior to the invasion. Brodhead, *History of New York*, 2: 24.

2. "Chamber at Amsterdam, to the Director and Council of New Netherland, 21 April 1664," *DRCNY*, 2: 235; "Report of the Honble Peter Stuyvesant, Late Director-General of New Netherland, on the Causes Which Led to the Surrender of That Country to the English," *DRCNY*, 2: 369; "Remonstrance of the People of New Netherland, 5 September 1664," *DRCNY*, 2: 248–49; *RNA*, 5: 115–16.

3. The export of furs fell from about approximately forty thousand pelts in 1664 to fewer than ten thousand in 1690, Matson, *Merchants and Empire*, 36–121.

4. "Articles of Capitulation on the Reduction of New Netherland," *DRCNY*, 2: 250–53; for Stuyvesant's report on the surrender, see *DRCNY*, 2: 365–70; Jameson, *Narratives*, 465–66; Brodhead, *History of New York*, 2: 49–51.

5. "An Order Requiring Shipsmasters to Report on Arrival, 13 September 1664," in Peter and Florence Christoph, eds., *New York Historical Manuscripts: English—Books of General Entries of the Colony of New York, 1664–1673, 1673–1682. Orders, Warrants, Issues, Letters, Commissions, Passes and Licenses Issued by the Governor Richard Nicolls and Francis Lovelace* (hereafter *General Entries*) (Baltimore, 1982), 52;

Maika, "Commerce and Community," 228; Robert C. Ritchie, *The Duke's Province: A Study of New York Politics and Society, 1664–1691* (Chapel Hill, N.C., 1977), 48–49, 56.

6. *The Colonial Laws of New York from the Year 1664 to the Revolution* (hereafter *Colonial Laws*), 5 vols. (Albany, N.Y., 1894), 1: 6–71; Ritchie, *Duke's Province*, 34–37, 52.

7. *DHSNY*, 1: 602–4; *RNA*, 5: 248–52; Maika, "Commerce and Community," 340–67; Kammen, *Colonial New York*, 74.

8. "Colonel Nicolls to the Duke of York," *DRCNY*, 3: 106.

9. Maika, "Commerce and Community," 138–42, 144–46, 229; Cathy Matson, "Commerce after the Conquest: Dutch Traders and Goods in New York City, 1664–1764," *De Halve Maen* 59, no. 1 (1987): 8–12; Ritchie, *Duke's Province*, 57–58; Victor H. Paltsits, ed., *Minutes of the Executive Council of the Province of New York: Administration of Franics Lovelace, 1668–1673* (hereafter *Executive Council Minutes*) (Albany, N.Y., 1910), 2: 522–23. For petition of Frederick Philipse, 9 March 1668, requesting that Albany's trade be restricted, see *RNA*, 6:138–41; *General Entries*, 357.

10. For example, in June 1665, Timothy Gabry was given responsiblity for the slaughter and burgher right excise. *RNA*, 5: 153, 255, 302. The branders' excise was set at three guilders for a horse and two for a cow, out of which Langestraat and Cornelissen took twenty-five and fifteen stivers per beast. *RNA*, 215, 222. For Teunis Cray's career, see Goodfriend, *Before the Melting Pot*, 28; *RNA*, 6: 90; Innes, *New Amsterdam and Its People*, 81–90. For Jan Jansen van Brestede, see *RNA*, 2: 357; 5: 31, 224; 6: 75, 113, 304. For other entries relating to municipal inspectors and commercial regulations, see *RNA*, 6: 26, 27, 75, 83, 84, 139, 141, 170, 177, 184, 189, 214–15, 222, 225, 231, 232, 273, 291, 393; 7: 35, 176; Maika, "Commerce and Community," 293. Generally, see Arthur Everett Peterson and George Edwards, *New York as an Eighteenth-Century Municipality*, 2 vols. (New York, 1917), 1: 40–125; Carl Bridenbaugh, *Cities in the Wilderness: The First Century of Urban Life in America, 1625–1742* (New York, 1938), 207, 213, 218, 232, 239.

11. The list of those registering for the burgher right and the records of New Amsterdam for 1657–74 identify approximately 130 or so men working at twenty or more trades. This figure tallies with the number identified by Joyce Goodfriend in her conquest cohort and equates to, again approximately, 50 percent of male city residents. See Goodfriend, *Before the Melting Pot*, 19. David Cohen's analysis of passenger lists between 1654 and 1664 finds that more than half of male immigrants for whom an occupation was given were either craftsmen or soldiers. David Cohen, "How Dutch Were the Dutch of New Netherland," *New York History* 62 (January 1981): 47. By contrast, in 1696, Gregory King estimated that in England "freeholders" and "farmers" outnumbered "artizans and handicrafts" by a factor of seven to one, and similar ratios prevailed in the the the Dutch Republic. See J. Thirsk and J. P. Cooper, eds., *Seventeenth-Century Economic Documents* (Oxford, 1972); Israel, *Dutch Republic*, 620–33.

12. In June 1666 fifteen tavern keepers renewed their licenses: Werner Wessells; Bartholdus Maan; Freryck Gysbersen; Mighiel Tades; the former West India Company soldier Lucas Dircksen; the baker Anthony de Milt; the butcher Eghbert Meyndertsen; Dirck Storm; Barent Cours; Anneke Litschoe, who was the widow of Daniel Litschoe; Jestntje Verhagen; Patrix Hay; Grietje Provoost; Geertje Corssen; and

Andrees Rees. See *RNA*, 5: 263, 330. For license renewals in 1672 and 1673, see *RNA*, 6: 356, 403. There were likely other, more opportunistic tappers who avoided paying the license excise. Kenneth Scott identifed more than a hundred innkeepers and tapsters operating in New York between 1645 and 1675 in "New Amsterdam's Taverns," parts 1–3, no. 1 (April 1964): 9–10, 15; no. 2 (July 1964): 9–10, 15; no. 3 (October 1964): 13–15.

13. The sworn butchers included Eghbert Meyndertsen, Assur Levy, Roelof Jans van Meppel, Gerrit Vulevever, Cornelius Jorissen, Richard Nicolls, Richard Dodomit, and Jan Hendricksen van Gunst. *RNA*, 5: 312–13; Richard B. Morris, *Government and Labor in Early America* (1946; reprint, Boston, 1981), 160; Fernow, *Minutes of the Orphanmasters*, 2: 163–65. The regulation of the butchers in 1672 is in *RNA*, 6: 359; Maika, "Commerce and Community," 292–93, 360–66; Stokes, *Iconography*, 4: 222.

14. In December 1665, Meyndertsen accused Abraham de la Noy, whom he employed to keep a tally of slaughtered beasts, of issuing permits without collecting the excise. *RNA*, 5: 329.

15. Barent Jansen Cool the Elder acted as overseer and recorded the issue of permits to ensure that only the recognized porters carried wine and beer on city streets. In 1665, the sworn porters and beer carriers were Barent Jansen Cool, Tousein Briel, Crein Jacobs, Jacob Swart, and Nicolaas du Puys. *RNA*, 5: 256, 266. In March 1666, Joost Goderis and Geerit Hendricx van Amsterdam were sworn in as laborers at the public scales following the death of Cryn Jacobs. *RNA*, 5: 346; in July 1666, the magistrates reissued the weigh-house laborers' oath. *RNA*, 6: 27. Porters and weigh-house laborers also worked at other trades. For example, Jacob Swart worked as a carpenter, and Andries Andriessen worked as a mason in the 1650s and 1660s. *RNA*, 6: 7; 7: 146.

16. The cases of Van Rys and Aarsen are noted in *RNA*, 5: 166, 169. Also see Peter Steenhuysen's petition "to be a burgher of this Citty." *RNA*, 6: 190. For Katherine Evans's petition "humbly Cravinge of this Honn^ble Court Permission for to Inhabit in this Citty of New Yorke. And alsoo a License for to Retaile or draw drink, in wch employment she engageth to demeane hurselfe Civilly to all Persons." *RNA*, 6: 26. For charges against Hanna Ackleton and Elizabeth Juwel, 19 November 1667, that "they without Licence of the Govern^r & this Court, Contrary to the Lawes of this Governmt Are come to dwele within this Towne," and the order that they "depart out of this place in 8 days time uppon penalty of 5 lb Sterlg," see *RNA*, 6: 101. For burgher privileges exercised in court, see *RNA*, 6: 75, 116.

17. Samuel McKee, *Labor in Colonial New York, 1664–1776* (New York, 1935), 17, 76; Peterson and Edwards, *New York as a Municipality*, 70; Bridenbaugh, *Cities in the Wilderness*, 47.

18. For example, in June 1666 Jacob Wolfersen van Couwenhoven sued Jacob Stoffels for the balance of fifteen skepels of wheat in payment for a boat that Couwenhoven declared he had delivered to Stoffels twenty-three years previously. *RNA*, 6: 11, 16, 20, 22.

19. See, for example, the cases of Johannes de Witt v. Jacob Couwenhoven, 1666; Henry Breser v. Egbert Myndersen, January 1668; Dirck Claesen Pottebacker (brickmaker) v. Teunis Tomissen (a mason), March 1670; and Captain Richard Martin v. John Cooley, 24 September 1667, in *RNA*, 6: 96, 170, 225, 259, 264.

20. For a case in which a Dutch defendant called for a jury trial having first lost the suit according to Roman-Dutch law procedure, see Hendrick Obe v. Frederick Philipse, July 1666. *RNA,* 6: 6, 12, 15. Legal recourse remained accessible and inexpensive after the conquest, and the English administration maintained the regulation of court officers' fees commenced under the Dutch. On 11 June 1667, the court fixed the fees charged by the "Sheriff, Secretary, Messenger, and Attornies of this City." In 1672, "Uppon Complaints Made to this Court that some of the Officers do exact their fees much more as by the Law is allowed," the magistrates required that in future the fees and charges be signed off by the Mayor or his deputy. This provision ran until 1687, when a committee formed to investigate legal fees recommended limits adopted in the 1690s. *RNA,* 1: 220; 3: 46, 168, 199, 205; 6: 77, 106, 107, 178, 363–64; *Colonial Laws,* 1: 136; Herbert Osgood, ed., *Minutes of the Common Council, 1675–1784* (hereafter *MCC*) (New York, 1905), 1: 63; Paul M. Hamlin and Charles E. Baker, eds., *Supreme Court of Judicature of the Province of New York, 1691–1704,* in *Collections of the New-York Historical Society for the Years 1945–47,* 3 vols. (New York, 1952–59), 1: 260–61.

21. For Goert Olphertsen v. Annatie Gerrits Olpherstsen, see *RNA,* 6: 313, 317; for Mistress Anthonie v. Jan Harmensen, 1671 see *RNA,* 6: 304. For similar compromises and other cases involving tradesmen as arbitrators, see Fredrick Arentsen v. John Cooley, 1665, *RNA,* 5: 326; John Cooley v. Captain Hatshwell, 1667, *RNA,* 6: 96; Andries Claasen, a tailor, v. Cornelius Clopper, blacksmith, *RNA,* 5: 150; and Jan Aarianson as arbitrator, *RNA,* 3: 330; 4: 133, 137, 144, 238, 257, 260, 267, 272, 311, 317; 5: 25, 36, 65, 82.

22. For Adam Onckelbach v. Frederick Philipse, see *RNA* 5: 176; Howard S. F. Randolph, "Teuntje Teunis and her Descendants," *NYGBR* (January 1928): 14–15. For other references to accepted or customary practices and values, see Rabba Cooty v. John Coely, 11 June 1667, *RNA,* 6: 74–75; Peter Stuyvesant v. Jan Vigne and Pieter Stoutenburgh execs of estate left by Rachel Tienhoven, *RNA,* 5: 199.

23. *Executive Council Minutes,* 1: 28, 40, 63, 68, 80, 82, 109. Also see reports by Governors Nicholls, Andros, and Dongan on their adminstrations in *DHSNY,* 1: 85–93, 147–89, and an account describing a brawl and the manhandling of a tavern keeper's wife following a row over billeting. *RNA,* 5: 211. Cases of Dutch traders dealing with soldiers and taking blankets and bedding in exchange for drink suggests that fraternization was as much a problem for the military authorities as ethnic tensions. *RNA,* 6: 64, 113. Donna Merwick has argued that anti-English sentiment in outlying provincial towns grew out of disagreements following close personal contact and commercial transactions rather than simple ethnic antipathy "Becoming English: Anglo-Dutch Conflict in the 1670s in Albany and New York," *New York History* 62 (October 1981): 391–93, 403.

24. J. R. Pole, *Political Representation in England and the Origins of the American Republic* (Berkeley, Calif., 1966), 51; J. G. A. Pocock, "The Classical Theory of Deference," *American Historical Review* 81 (June 1976): 516–23; Haakonssen, *Natural Law and Moral Philosophy,* 316–17.

25. *RNA,* 6: 30–31.

26. Ibid., 6: 66–68; for Morisen v. Pluvier, see *RNA,* 6: 95. Barentsen and Van Gelder subsequently fell out in a competition over the collection of fees. See *RNA,* 6: 111, 214, 225.

27. My emphasis. The council reissued the order prohibiting exports in June 1672 and July 1673 and reassessed the value of wampum following a petition by the bakers submitted to the "surveyor or cure master of bread and flour." The export embargo was reaffirmed in 1675 and 1676, when the council denied Jonathan Selleck's petition to ship grain to Barbados. Berthold Fernow, compiler, *Calendar of Council Minutes 1668–1783* (hereafter *Calendar of Council Minutes*) (1902; reprint, New York, 1987), 13, 16, 18, 19, 21, 25, 24; Maika, "Commerce and Community," 293–94.

28. The bakers who made the list of wealthy inhabitants were Hendrick Willemsen, Reynier Willemsen, Lourens van der Spiegel, and Jacob Teunissen, see "Valuation of the Best and Most Affluent Inhabitants of This City," *DRCNY*, 2: 699–700; *RNA*, 1: 367–75; 5: 30–33, 221–25; "Answers of Govenor Andros to Enquiries about New-York, 16 April 1678," *DRCNY*, 3: 261. Also noteworthy is the 1668 rental agreement between Francis Lovelace and Hendrick Willemsen for the latter's house on the west side of Winckel Street. Stokes, *Iconography*, 2: 257.

29. Rosevelt Waldron v. Romein Servein and Thomas Verdon, December 1659, *RNA*, 3: 91, 93, 156, 159, 211; Allard Anthony v. Jan Smede, March 1665, *RNA*, 5: 189–90; Allard Anthony v. William Kock, June 1666, *RNA*, 6: 18. Anthony and Kock were old adversaries and had fallen out the previous October when the sheriff "repeatedly warned" Kock "not to stand on his cart but walk beside it," but Kock refused saying "Mayor Willet allowed him to do so because he was so weak in the bones." *RNA*, 5: 316. For other cases demonstrating the prickly relationship between the carters and their customers and associates, see Hendrick Suyringh v. Tomas Fransen, September 1661, *RNA*, 3: 365; Jan Arriansen v. Thomas Fransen, *RNA*, 5: 139, 140, 306.

30. When Sigismundus Lucas died in 1681, his estate comprised two houses with grounds and thirty-three pounds in cash. *RNA*, 5: 5, 6; John Coursen, alias John Cherry, was identified as a shoemaker by Ann Watkins in her suit charging him with slandering her as "a whore, a damned whore, and horse faced bitch." See *RNA*, 6: 18, and Minutes of the New York City Mayor's Court (hereafter MCM), 1675–77, Division of Old Records, County Court, 31 Chambers Street, New York City, 133. For Thomas Verdon and his appointment as weigh-house porter, see *RNA*, 2: 84. Thomas Fransen married Elsie Jans in May 1656 and registered as a lessor burgher and "carman" in the city the following spring. He and Elsie made their home in a house purchased from Samual Edsal in September 1658, but moved to Pearl Street in 1661. NYHS, Collections (1885), 21; *NYGBR* (July 1915): 220.

31. For Wolphert Webber and his life as a farmer, see *RNA*, 1: 162, 168, 247, 326, 334, 339, 355, 390; 2: 10,127; for Webber and innkeeping, see Martha J. Lamb, *History of the City of New York* (New York, 1877), 182; for Sarah Webber and Laurens van der Spiegel, see *NYGBR* (April 1932): 118.

32. Stokes, *Iconography*, 2: 234–35. Jan Smedes purchased his house and farm from the estate of Rachel Tienhoven in April 1673. See NYHS, Collections (1913), 9, 10. Details of the 1677 tax on "houses and Vacant Lands . . . for the Defraying and discharging of the Citty debts," is in *MCC*, 1: 50–62. In an earlier levy the previous year, four carters were assessed at fifty pounds and two at one hundred pounds in *MCC*, 1: 29–33.

33. Complaints by carters that "boys" were riding carts and taking from their employment emphasizes how open their work was *RNA*, 7: 122.

34. *RNA*, 5: 345, 346. Langestraat had served as a member of the city's watch since 1658 and was assessed at fifty pounds in 1676. *MCC*, 1: 36; *RNA*, 6: 68–71; 7: 195. In January 1670, he secured the position of overseer branding of horses and cattle feeding in the city, and subsequently worked as a carter and was favored with city contracts *MCC*, 1: 205, 206. There is evidence of occasional tension between the residents of Fresh Water and the city's carters. In May 1666, the tavern keeper and Fresh Water resident Ariaen Cornelissen sued Wolphert Webber for slandering him as a "corn and cattle thief" and, the following court day, Jan Langestraat sued Lysbeth Smedes, Jan Smede's wife, whom he charged had "grossly caluminated him with abusive words." *RNA*, 6: 3.

35. The carters' petition is mentioned in *RNA*, 6: 70. There were eight carters bound that day: Thomas Fransen, Willem Kock, Jan Meyndersen, Ambrosius de Weerham, Jan Smedes, Pieter Wessels, Pieter Roelofs, and Joris Jansen.

36. *RNA*, 5: 147, 340, 303, 321; 6: 69, 74, 99, 105.

37. Captain John Manning v. Thomas Fransen, April 1668, *RNA*, 6: 123, 217–18; order relating to garbage collection is in *RNA*, 6: 273. Thomas Fransen, Willem Kock, Ambrosius de Weerham, Jan Smedes, and Jan Mynderse remained from the original company of carters. Aernout Webber, son of Wolphert, applied for and was given a position in August 1670, and three new Englishmen—John Watkins, Thomas Griffin, and Charles Floyd—were confirmed as city carters. *RNA*, 6: 251, 360–61.

38. Daniel Denton, *A Brief Description of New York: Formerly Called New Netherland* (1670; reprint, New York, 1845), 12.

39. For a sample of the extensive reorganization of the government of New Orange and other provincial towns, see "Proclamation Altering the Form of Government in the City of New Orange," *DRCNY*, 2: 575, 578–79, 583–84, and the "Provisional Instruction for the Schout, Burgomasters and Schepens of the City of New Orange," *DRCNY*, 678–81; *RNA*, 7: 36–43; "Petition to the Valiant Commanders and Honble Council of War . . . " *DRCNY*, 2: 598–600; the negotiations to return the colony to the English are broached in "Letter of the States-General to King Charles II, 19 December 1673," *DRCNY*, 2: 531; "Nathaniel Gould's Account of the Recapture of New York," *DRCNY*, 3: 200–202; the settlers' reaction is quoted in Brodhead, *History of New York*, 2: 252.

40. Andros's commission and instructions are in *DRCNY*, 3: 215–19; *DHSNY*, 3: 66–79; RNA, 7: 138; *MCC*, 1: 26; Ritchie, *Duke's Province*, 85–107. For the appointment of new magistrates, see *MCC*, 1: 1–2; *Calendar*, 2: 72–84, 186, 196.

41. For the petition of leading citizens, including Nicholas Bayard, who refused to swear a new oath of allegiance and were arrested, see "Petition of Dutch Burghers, 16 March 1675," *DRCNY*, 2: 740–43; Ritchie, *Duke's Province*, 140–42. The bondsmen who provided bail for Bayard's release included the bakers Jacob Teunis de Kay and Reynier Williams *Calendar*, 1: 243.

42. On anglicization, articulation of Dutch ethnicity, and batavianization, see Goodfriend, *Before the Melting Pot*, 219–21; John Murrin, "English Rights as Ethnic Agression," in Pencak and Wright, eds., *Authority and Resistance in Early New York*, 56–94. For women and inheritance, Biemer, *Women and Property*, introduction; David D. Narrett, *Inheritance and Family Life in Colonial New York City* (Ithaca, N.Y., 1992). It is noteworthy that one of the earliest orders of the short-lived administration of New Orange concerned the enforcement of weights according to the "real Amsterdam

measure and weight." See "A Council in Fort Willem Hendrick, 15 February 1674," *DRCNY*, 2: 687–88. For the persistence of Dutch weights long after Andros's attempt to enforce English measures. See *Colonial Laws*, 1: 64, 95, 98, 554. Also see John Lewin's finding that locals continued to calculate beaver weights at the Dutch eighteen, rather than the English sixteen, ounces to evade customs duties levied by the pound in "Mr. Lewin's Report on the Government of New-York," *DRCNY*, 3: 305; the question of weights and measures is raised again in the early eighteenth century in "Lord Cornbury to the Lords of the Treasury, 12 July 1703," *DRCNY*, 4: 1064–65.

43. William Churcher was an English stonemason who had come to the colony as part of the English force in 1674 . He remained in the city, married a local Dutch woman (Susanna Brasier), and served as a court arbitrator. The batavianized group included more prominent members who would play leading roles in the 1689 rebellion, for example, Jacob Milbourne, Samuel Edsall, and Jacob Leisler. See David William Voorhees, "'In Behalf of the true Protestants' Religion': The Glorious Revolution in New York" (Ph.D. diss., New York University, 1988), appendix two.

44. Hamlin and Baker, *Supreme Court*, 1: 260.

45. Robert Ritchie has argued that cases involving two Dutch litigants became less common, except among leading merchants, and that ordinary Dutch settlers withdrew from the anglicized court in *Duke's Province*, 143; Eben Moglen has also posited a decline in Dutch participations as litigants and jurors in "Settling the Law: Legal Development in New York, 1664–1776" (Ph.D. diss., Yale University, 1993), 39. Drawing on these and other studies, William Offut Jr. has traced a continued decline from the mid-1670s to the end of the seventeenth century in "The Limits of Authority: Courts, Ethnicity, and Gender in the Middle Colonies," in Christopher L. Tomlins and Bruce H. Mann, eds., *The Many Legalities of Early America* (Chapel Hill, N.C., 2001), 371–74. In contrast, Dennis Maika has argued that the per capita litigation rate was steady in the mid to late 1670s and that the total number of cases heard per court session remained constant or increased. Moreover, Maika argues, the similarities between Dutch and English procedures relating to commercial law made for an easy transition, and Dutch merchants continued to bring their cases before the court in which their bilingual peers served as magistrates. Although the juries were dominated by Englishmen, Maika points out that they actually heard a fraction of the cases, "Commerce and Community," 442–43.

46. Linda Briggs Biemer found that the number of female fur traders in Albany fell from 46 to 10 and in New York City from 134 to 43. In the decade before the conquest, Biemer identifies at least fifty female tavern keepers, but in the decade after the conquest only seventeen. The number of civil cases involving women as litigants also fell—from 176 in 1662–63 to 55 in 1673–74—whereas the number of criminal cases involving women defendants rose: between 1654 and 1674 women counted for less than 1 percent of criminal defendants and were mostly charged with offences relating to illegal tapping and, in a handful of cases, theft; by the early eighteenth century, women accounted for almost 10 percent of criminal convictions, and female larceny and prostitution was increasingly common. Biemer, *Women and Property*, 1–11, and "Women in New Amsterdam and Early New York," 73–83. For crime rates in the early eighteenth century, see Douglas Greenberg, *Crime and Law Enforcement in the Colony of New York, 1691–1776* (Ithaca, N.Y., 1974), 49–53, 76.

47. Van Rensselaer was the younger son of the upriver patroon Kiliaen van

Rensselaer and had endeared himself to the Stuarts during the interregnum when he prophesied the restoration of Charles II in a sermon preached during the latter's exile in Brussels. Randall Balmer, *A Perfect Babel of Confusion: Dutch Religion and English Culture in the Middle Colonies* (New York, 1989), 16–21; Lawrence H. Leder, "The Unorthodox Domine: Nicholas van Rensselaer," *New York History* 35 (April 1954), 166–76; Gerald Francis De Jong, "Dominie Johannes Megapolensis: Minister to New Netherland," New-York Historical Society, *Quarterly* 52 (1968): 7–47; Lamb, *History of New York*, 285; Ritchie, *Duke's Province*, 146–47.

48. Collaborators such as Nicholas de Meyer, William Beekman, Nicholas Bayard, and Johannes de Peyster all found places in the new English administration. Ritchie, *Duke's Province*, 99–101.

49. The revised freemanship law is in *MCC*, 1: 10; on Nicholas Blake registering as freeman in 10 May 1677, see Ritchie, *Duke's Province*, 262.

50. Merwick, "Becoming English," 411–12; Richter, *Ordeal of the Longhouse*, 135–37.

51. Andros enlisted the services of local Indians to enforce his orders relating to the upriver trade, promising to grant the whole value of cargoes to Indians who reported traders shipping goods without the necessary permit. "Council Minute, 12 March 1676–77" and "Council Minute, 20 August 1678," *DRCNY*, 13: 502–3, 531–32; *Colonial Laws*, 1: 93. The sale of the city's graveyard is mentioned in *MCC*, 1: 47. Also see Ritchie, *Duke's Province*, 112–13.

52. *RNA*, 5: 220–25; *MCC*, 1: 29–37; Nash, *Urban Crucible*, 395; Goodfriend, *Before the Melting Pot*, 71.

53. Stephen van Cortlandt, son of Oloff Stevense van Cortlandt, followed in his father's mercantile footsteps and served on the provincial council from 1675 to 1685. In 1677 he also became the city's first native-born mayor, a post to which he secured reappointment in 1686 and 1687. Frederick Philipse served as city surveyor (1666), alderman (1674), and member of the provincial council (1675–88). See Voorhees, "'In Behalf of the true Protestants' Religion,'" appendices.

54. For the deal with Griffeth, see MCM (1674–75), 35; his role in the reconquest is discussed in Brodhead, *History of New York*, 2: 270. One hundred weight was equivalent to approximately 112 lbs. For tax and property assessments, see note 52 and *MCC*, 1: 50–62. In 1677, Laurens van der Spiegel and Anthony de Milt both listed properties and city lots in addition to their residences. Dennis Maika discovered a daybook belonging to Teunis de Kay, baker, containing details of his business with local exporters in the Special Collections New York State Library. See "Commerce and Community," 420.

55. Anthony de Milt was an unsuccessful candidate for schepen in 1661, but he was appointed schout during the brief return of Dutch rule in 1673. Laurens van der Spiegel served as a constable in 1680, and in 1683 Anthony de Milt and Jacob de Kay were appointed as assessors in New Amsterdam. By 1688, De Milt held the keys to the city's meat market and sat on the Common Council as an aldermen with Hendrick Willemsen, who first entered the municipal service as a bread inspector thirty years earlier. See *RNA*, 6: 265; *DRCNY*, 2: 575; *MCC*, 1: 115, 193; O'Callaghan, *New Netherland Register*, 113; Hamlin and Baker, *Supreme Court*, 2: 323; Goodfriend, *Before the Melting Pot*, 36, 52.

56. Complaints of bread shortages and response is in MCM (1677–82), 312; *Executive Council Minutes*, 1: 176–77. Grain production and export is discussed in Cathy Matson, "Damned Scoundrels and Libertisme of Trade: Freedom and Regulation in Colonial New York's Fur and Grain Trades," *WMQ*, 3d ser., 51 (July 1994): 389–418; Matson, *Merchants and Empire*, 100.

57. The presence of female bakers on this schedule suggests that, despite public invisibility, women worked regularly at the trade. The official schedule listed the following practitioners. Mondays: Hendrick Willemsen, Thomas Lawrence, Huyg Barentson, Gersie Lewis. Tuesdays: Hendrick Johnsen van Veurden, Antony Demilt, Catrina Hooghlant. Wednesdays: Jacob de Kay, Marretie the widow of Nicles the baker, Gerret Cornelissen, David Provoost. Thursdays: Brymer Willemsen, Luycas Kierstede, Peter Jansen de Paap. Fridays: Jasper Nessipat, Anna Van Vleck widow, Lendert Huygen de Kleyn, Johannes Van der Spregel. Saturdays: Teunis de Kay, Jan Van Slensburgh, Nicholas Demeyer, Isaac Forrest, Jacobus Virhulst, Anna Popelaers widow. *MCC*, 1: 172–74, 176. For the debate concerning flour-bolting monopoly and baking regulations, see *MCC*, 1: 102–5, 113–15, 149–53; *Colonial Laws*, 1: 326; *Calendar of Council Minutes*, 37–39.

58. The 1676 tax lists revealed a dramatic increase in the English merchant class who now constituted twenty-two of the forty-eight men judged to be of considerable estate. Ritchie, *Duke's Province*, 139, 156–67; Maika, "Commerce and Community," 400–401. For expansion of English merchant endeavors, see Robert Brenner, *Merchants and Revolution: Commercial Change, Political Conflicts and London's Overseas Traders, 1550–1653* (Princeton, N.J., 1993), conclusion.

59. Richard Ashcraft, *Revolutionary Politics and Locke's Two Treatises of Government* (Princeton, N.J., 1986), 181–227; Zuckert, *Natural Rights and the New Republicanism*, 100–120. The charter is in *Colonial Laws*, 1: 111–16; David S. Lovejoy, *The Glorious Revolution in America* (New York, 1972), 98–121.

60. In May 1683, the city seized 142 barrels and 16 half-barrels of flour, "being made bolted and imported into this city contrry to the libertys and privileges thereof, condemend and forfeited," from John Schouten's vessel, the *Hopewell* See MCM (1682–95), 50–55. "Petition of the Mayor and Common Council of New-York for a New Charter," *DRCNY*, 3: 337–39; *MCC*, 1: 102–5, 113–15; *Colonial Laws*, 2: 575, 577; Ritchie, *Duke's Province*, 164–78; the gift given to Dongan is mentioned in *MCC*, 1: 178.

61. "A List of all Barkques Sloopes and open boates Blonging to this Porte, 23 February 1684," in *MCC*, 1: 128–29. On the growth of trade, see "Answers of Governor Andros to Enquiries about New York, April 1678," *DRCNY*, 3:260–62; "Governor Andros's Answer to Mr. Lewin's Report, 31 December 1681," *DRCNY*, 3: 308–13; "Dongan to the Lords of Trade, 22 February 1687," in *DRCNY*, 3: 398; "Instructions from Governor Dongan to Captain Palmer, 23 July 1689," in *DRCNY*, 3: 475–77; Ritchie, *Duke's Province*, 59–68, 108–11; the increase in land values is discussed in Lamb, *History of New York*, 278.

62. Bernard Mason found that a hard core of some twenty-five to thirty-five city merchants enjoyed a controlling influence on the governor's council and the city's common council between 1664 and 1688. While some supported the rebellion, most formed the backbone of the anti-Leislerian opposition, which included Cornelius Steenwyck, Frederick Philipse, Nicholas Bayard, Stephen van Cortlandt,

Gabriel Minvielle, John Robinson, George Heathcote, William Pinhorne, James Graham, John West, and John Winder. See Bernard Mason, "Aspects of New York's Revolt of 1689," *New York History* 30 (April 1949): 166–68.

63. Joyce Goodfriend estimates that the population of New York grew from 1,500 in 1664—including approximately 250 men—to roughly 3,500 in 1685. However, fewer than half (104) of the men identified in Goodfriend's 1664 conquest cohort were members of the Dutch Reformed Church. *Before the Melting Pot*, 15, 61. The proportion of local men who were members of the Dutch Church declined in the ensuing twenty years: in 1686, Domine Henricus Selyn identified 556 communicants comprised of 344 female and 212 male members. See "Domine Selyn's Records," in Holland Society of New York, *Year Book* (1916), 21–35. For Byrd's observations, see Burrows and Wallace, *Gotham*, 94; "Governor Dongan's Report on the State of the Province," *DRCNY*, 3: 415. The indifference observed by Bullivant could have reflected popular disaffection with the Dutch Reformed ministers who opposed Leisler's administration during the rebellion.

64. Studies focusing on economic, familial, and ethnic discontents include Bernard Mason, "Aspects of the New York Revolt of 1689," *New York History* 30 (January 1949), 165–80; Jerome K. Reich, *Leisler's Rebellion: A Study of Democracy in New York, 1664–1720* (Chicago, 1953), preface and 172–73; Lawrence Leder in Michael G. Hall, Lawrence H. Leder, and Michael Kammen eds., *The Glorious Revolution in America: Documents on the Colonial Crisis of 1689* (Chapel Hill, N.C., 1964), 84–85; Thomas J. Archdeacon, "The Age of Leisler—New York City, 1689–1710: A Social and Demographic Intepretation," in Jacob Judd and Irwin Polishook, eds., *Aspects of Early New York Society and Politics* (Tarrytown, N.Y., 1974), 73, 79. Charles Howard McCormick considers the popular revolt as an example of paranoid reaction following years of tension in his otherwise excellent account, *Leisler's Rebellion* (New York, 1989).

65. For Salem, see Chadwick Hansen, *Witchcraft in Salem* (New York, 1969), and John Demos, *Entertaining Satan: Witchcraft and the Culture of Early New England* (New York, 1982), ch. 2.

66. The following draws upon Peter Lake, "Anti-popery: the structure of a prejudice," in Richard Cust and Ann Hughes, eds., *Conflict in Early Stuart England: Studies in Religion and Politics, 1603–1642* (New York, 1989), 72–107. Also see John Walter, *Understanding Popular Violence in the English Revolution: The Colchester Plunderers* (Cambridge, 1999); Peter Burke, *Popular Culture in Early Modern Europe* (New York, 1978), 185–204; Derek Hirst, *Authority and Conflict: England, 1603–1658* (London, 1986), 84–87, and Stuart Clark, *Thinking with Demons: The Idea of Witchcraft in Early Modern Europe* (Oxford, 1997), part I.

67. Deposition of Peter Godfrey and Henry Carmer Colonial Records Series 5/1081, Public Record Office, Kew, London (hereafter PRO, CO5), 82; deposition of Daniel Clarke, 26 September 1689, in PRO, CO5/1081, 63, 64.

68. "Address of the Militia of New York to William and Mary, 1 June 1689," *DRCNY*, 3: 583.

69. For the classic argument considering the social stresses associated with leadership by a recently risen elite, see Bernard Bailyn, "Politics and Social Structure in Virginia," in James Morton Smith, ed., *Seventeenth-Century America: Essays in Colonial History* (Chapel Hill, N.C., 1955), 90–115.

70. *MCC,* 1: 61. For Pinhorne, see *DRCNY,* 3: 716 n. 2; Dongan's land sales are noted in Thomas J. Archdeacon, *New York City, 1664–1710: Conquest and Change* (Ithaca, N.Y., 1979), 83. Details concerning Rombouts, Steenwyck, and Dongan's gardens are taken from Valentine, *Manual* (1853), 382; (1855), 543; (1858), 513; (1860), 543; (1861), 527.

71. The free black community settled along the road to Stuyvesant's Bouwery following the director-general's grant of multiple house and garden plots adjacent to well-watered and fertile land to a group of freedmen in 1659–60. See Christoph, "Freedmen of New Amsterdam," in Zeller, ed., *A Beautiful and Fruitful Place,* 164.

72. James Bartlett Burleigh and James Franklin Jameson, eds., *The Journal of Jasper Danckaerts* (New York, 1941), 165–70.

73. Swarts had migrated from Vlissingen to New Netherland some forty-five years previously and lived at Gravesend on Long Island in the late 1650s before moving back to the city. In 1663, he was appointed as a public porter, and in 1676 the tax assessment estimated Swarts's estate at one hundred pounds. By the time of Danckearts's arrival in 1679, Swarts and his wife, Teuntje Jacobs, were living with other middling and laboring residents in the area around Smith's Valley. *MCC,* 1: 32; "Tuentje Teunis and Her Descendants," *NYGBR* (January 1928): 4–7.

74. Burleigh and Jameson, *Journal of Jasper Danckaerts,* 239–40.

75. Ibid., 244. On the prohibition on distilling grain unless it is unfit for bolting and export, see *MCC,* 1: 25.

76. In 1680, the year following Danckearts's visit, John Lewin's investigation unearthed similar concerns and suspicions to those reported by Danckearts, in particular that the townspeople "say a considerable sum of money was raised upon their stocks both Inhabitants and Merchant Strangers for making the Docke att first, but never any accot made to them of it, though they conceive there may be considerable surplusage." See "Mr. Lewin's Report on the Government of New-York," and "Governor Andros's Answer to Mr. Lewin's Report"; on the idea that these monies were managed by the city authorities, see *DRCNY,* 3: 303, 309; Reich, *Leisler's Rebellion,* 43.

77. Burleigh and Jameson, *Journal of Jasper Danckaerts,* 238.

78. The Common Council's order is in MCM (1677–82), 187. On the precision involved in seventeenth-century coopering, see John Beilby, *Several Useful and Necessary Tables for the Gauging of Casks* (London, 1694).

79. The rates established were five shillings for a hogshead, two shillings and sixpence for every barrel, one shilling and sixpence for a half-barrel, and three shillings for a "tite" barrel for beef and pork. Coopers subscribing to the 1679 combination included Deirck Jansen de Groet, Richard Elliot, Luickes Gersen, Pijeter Brestee, Willem Hoppen, Claes Burger, Evert Wessells, Willem Waldr[on], Jan Vinsent, Pieter Stevensz, Andris Brest, Clement Sebrock, Marten Clock, Guyles Provoste, John Petterson, John Crooke, Jon Makernes, Pieter Abrahamse, Wouter Brestee, and Cornelius Wynhart. Peter Christoph and Florence Christoph, eds., *The Andros Papers: Files of the Provincial Secretary of New York during the Administration of Governor Sir Edmund Andros,* 3 vols. (Syracuse, N.Y., 1989–91), 3: 185–86; Van Rensselaer, *History of the City of New York,* 2: 219–20.

80. Christoph and Christoph, *Andros Papers,* 3: 187.

81. The Kermers were long-standing members of the Dutch community, and Marten Clock and Derick Jansen de Groet had served in the same militia company since the brief return to Dutch rule in 1673. Other details pertaining to individuals cited are taken from *MCC*, 1: 29, 31, 63, 71, 75, 78; Valentine, *Manual* (1858), 125, 327–28; Stokes, *Iconography*, 2: 323; *NYGBR* (October 1930): 357.

82. The butchers relocated to a "Generall or Publique slaughter howse" constructed by Asser Levy and Garret Jansen Rose to the north "att Smith's fly." Levy and Rose had secured a monopoly of public slaughtering in return for their investment in the construction *MCC*, 1: 20, 46, 67, 68, 217.

83. The shoemakers' purchase was most likely prompted by the decision of the long-term city tanners, Stoffel and Arian van Laer, to quit the trade and sell their premises to merchant David Provoost. For details on the land purchases, see "New York Deeds, 1673–74," in NYHS, Collections (1913), 9–10, 22, 77. Coenraet Ten Eyck had started out as a small-time tobacco trader in the early 1650s *RNA*, 1: 71, 76; also see Henry Waterman George, "The Ten Eyck Family," *NYGBR* (1932): 152–61.

84. *MCC*, 1: 22–24.

85. Frederick Philipse's shipping accounts with English partners for the late 1670s and 1680s show an increase in the number of hides. See Patricia U. Bonomi, *Factious People: Politics and Society in Colonial New York* (New York, 1971), 61; Lamb, *History of New York*, 277. For tanners' and shoemakers' discontent see NYHS Collections (1893), 430–31; on the movement of tanneries after 1676, see *Calendar*, 2: 84; for Andros's increase of export duties on hides, see *Colonial Laws*, 1: 111–21; Burleigh and Jameson, *Journal of Jasper Danckaerts*, 248.

86. The estimate of stone required is in Bridenbaugh, *Cities in the Wilderness*, 24.

87. There were eight carters in 1667 and ten by 1672. *RNA*, 6: 70, 360. In April 1674, the government of New Orange denied Ambrosius de Weerham's petition to rejoin the registered carters after an absence, maintaining that "the number of cartmen is full." *RNA*, 7: 79. Weerham had to wait until Wolphert Webber retired that summer before being readmitted as a carter. In September, the carters complained of "certain boys" who rode in carts "above the number [of carters] fixed." The authorities prohibited all except the official carters from the trade, and adding Jan Langestraat and Jan Pietersen the elder to the roster brought their number up to thirteen. *RNA*, 7: 122.

88. Of the twelve carters dismissed, Jan Langestraat, Peter Wessels, Symon Lucas, and Ambross Warren are recognizable from earlier rosters; John Maynarde could be an anglicized version of Jan Mynderse and Hensbord Elbertyes was related to Geerite Elbertyes, an official carter. Thomas Griffin worked as a carter in 1670, disappeared from the roster following the Dutch reconquest in 1673, but reappeared as one of those dismissed in 1677. William Cooke, Claus Johnson, John Coursen, Hendrick the Spaniard, and Daniel Waldren all appear as carters for the first time. Thus, whether or not all the carters were suspended in 1677 must remain an open question, and it is clear that they were not all suspended in 1684. This puts my interpretation at odds with Hodges, *New York City Carters*, 1–56; *MCC*, 1: 65.

89. In April 1678, the Mayor's Court allowed John Pound to cart provided he obey the laws and customs and "carry for the use of the city thirty loads." MCM (1677–82), 83. In 1680, the Common Council admitted Henry Garnsey to "ye office

of Carmen" and required the usual duties *and* a sponsor, Francis Hendricks: the two men were "jointly bound in the summe of Tenn Pounds" to ensure that Garnsey "performe the Said Office faithfully according to the Lawes and Customes here Established." In August, Coneradus Vanderbeake and Egburt Vanderson were admitted as carters, and Hendrick Johnsen provided ten pounds surety for Vanderbeake, and Timothy Vanbursom for Vanderson. On the same day, however, the council admitted Tunis Hercks, Garret Cozyn, and Egbery Ffopen without bonds. See *MCC*, 1: 84–86.

90. In February 1677, the Common Council noted the "Complaint beinge made of the great abuse Practized by diuers [persons] who Expose Firewood to Sale in the Government and Particularly in this Citty by reason the inequality of the sticks for length and bigness" and decreed that after the first of May "noe firewood bee exposed to sale in the Gouerment or Brought to this city but by the Cord The Length of Each stick to bee foure foote The cord fure foot in height and Eight foote in Length and fitt Corders to be appointed." *MCC*, 1: 41; *Calendar of Council Minutes*, 29. On porters also dimissed on 14 September 1685 for refusing to cord wood in line with the order. See *MCC*, 1: 169 and *NYGBR* (January 1943): 2.

91. *MCC*, 1: 145.

92. After considering the petition of the porters and appointing a committee to consider "their number, and the rates and prizes by them taken," the suspended fifteen carters were Jan Langestraat, Jan Myndersen, Clas Jansen, Hendrick Jansen, Egbert Forken, Conradus Verbeck, Jurain Hagle, William Pearce, Thomas Griffin, Gisbert Egbert, Jan Carlissen, Paulus Verbeck, Garrit Cousine, William Morse, and Joris Jansen. *MCC*, 1: 47; The Common Council Papers, 2 vols. (hereafter CCP), Municipal Archive, Chambers Street, New York City, 1: 5. "Petition of the owners and masters of sloops and boats, March 1684" CCP, 1: 4. Under these terms three of the striking carters—Joris Jansen, Garrit Cousine, and John Carlissen—were readmitted.

93. For example, in 1684, the fee payable upon registering as a freeman was changed from two beavers to one pound and four shillings, and those who left their property unattended in the city risked losing it to a compulsory public purchase. *MCC*, 1: 3, 7, 10, 11, 14, 17, 19–20, 21, 24, 26, 75, 78. In the same year, the Court of Assizes was abolished by the short-lived General Assembly and replaced with a Court of Chancery, which served as the province's supreme court. Four years later, the Superior Court of the Dominion of New England superceded the Court of Chancery, adding further to the confusion regarding the colony's judicial system. *Colonial Laws*, 1: 228; Hamlin and Baker, *Supreme Court*, 1: 13–22.

94. MCM (1674–75), 52; *MCC*, 1: 13, 15, 25, 76, 81; Lamb, *History of New York*, 277, 309; Reich, *Leisler's Rebellion*, 36; Maika, "Commerce and Community," 228–29.

95. Bridenbaugh, *Cities in the Wilderness*, 27, 65, 76–77, 218. Also see *MCC*, 1: 27–28, 90, 134–36, 147, 160, 266, 390; *RNA*, 1: 255; Lamb, *History of New York*, 309.

96. *MCC*, 1: 178–79; Bernard Mason, "Aspects of the New York Revolt," 174–75; Voorhees, "'In Behalf of the true Protestants' Religion,'" 112–14; *MCC*, 1: 123–26, 132, 153–56.

97. In 1676, seventy-six merchants were assessed at £500, but by 1695 that number had dwindled to six. See Ritchie, *Duke's Province*, 194. The price of wheat fell from four shillings a bushel in 1684 to three shillings and sixpence a bushel in 1691.

Matson, *Merchants and Empire*, 106. The assessed value of New Yorkers' real and personal property fell from £103,457 in 1676 to £78,231 in 1688. Voorhees, "'In Behalf of the true Protestants' Religion,'" 60.

98. In the aftermath of King Philip's War (1675–76), Andros estimated New York's provincial force at two thousand men divided into companies of one hundred, with "about 140 horse in three troops," whom the governor believed were "indifferently armed with fire-armes of all sizes." "Answers of Governor Andros to Enquiries about New-York" and "Governor Andros's Answer to Enquiries of the Council of Trade," *DRCNY*, 3: 260, 263. Ritchie, *Duke's Province*, 190, 195. The expedition is described in Brodhead, *History of New York*, 2: 481–90.

99. "Dongan to Lord President of the Privy Council, 19 February 1688," *DRCNY*, 3: 511. "Dongan's Report to the Committee of Trade on the Province of New York, 22 February 1687," *DHSNY*, 1: 150, 161; "Governor Dongan to the Lord President, 12 September 1687," *DRCNY*, 3: 477–78.

100. NYHS, Collections (1868), 241–43; Voorhees, "'In Behalf of the true Protestants' Religion,'" 89, 118, 122.

101. "Sir John, Werden to Governor Andros, 28 January 1676," *DRCNY*, 3: 237; "Instructions to Col. Nicolls, 23 April 1664," "Private Instructions to Coll. R. Nicolls, 23 April 1664," and "Instructions for Governor Dongan, 27 January 1683," *DRCNY*, 3: 54, 60, 333. On the militia in the United Provinces, see Price, *Holland and the Dutch Republic*, 91. Although professional soldiers such as Andros and Dongan took a dim view of provincial irregulars, they could not dispense with them and paid close attention to the arming and training of the militia. In 1685, for example, when faced with a renewed French threat, Dongan dispatched Major Patrick Magregoire on a tour of the provincial militias, ordering him to ensure that "all men be fitted with a sword musket and Bandoliers" and to give "trayning and disciplining [of the] Souldiers and in particular how to handle their arms." For military plans and actions involving the militia, see "Colonel Nicolls to Secretary Arlington, 12 September 1667" and "Governor Lovelace to Governor Winthrop," *DRCNY*, 3: 167, 198. Magregoire's tour is discussed in *DRCNY*, 3: 395, and his disciplining of a group of Quakers who failed to muster when ordered in Brodhead, *History of New York*, 2: 459. Also see *Second Annual Report of the State Historian of New York* (Albany, N.Y., 1897), 391–92.

102. There was also a noteworthy continuity in the militia command with individuals such as Steenwyck, Van Cortlandt, Minvielle, Bayard, and others holding senior positions under the briefly restored Dutch regime in 1672–74 and following the return of English rule. "Anthony Colve, Governor-General of New Netherland," *DRCNY*, 2: 670, 676; militia parades are mentioned in *RNA*, 6: 144; *Calendar*, 2: 136. Charles McCormick has suggested that the militiamen looked upon their officers as quasi-representatives in *Leisler's Rebellion*, 176.

103. Hendrick Cuyler, who spoke little English and had moved to the city from Albany in the late 1680s, served as lieutenant in De Peyster's company; Joachim Staats served as lieutenant in Leisler's company with ensign Joost Stol, a drayman and committed Calvinist; William Churcher served as a sergeant in Lodwick's company. On election of officers under the Dutch, see *DRCNY*, 2: 592, 626–27; Valentine, *Manual* (1850), 424–25.

104. NYHS, Collections (1864), 244–45; "Stephen van Cortlandt to Governor

Andros, 9 July 1689," *DRCNY,* 3: 592–94. Although the city's residents could not have known it, Louis XIV and his generals had devised a plan that aimed to capture the city, send any French Protestants home, and set the tradesmen and laborers to work fortifying the city. Brodhead, *History of New York,* 2: 547; "Project of the Chevalier de Callieres, January 1689," *DHSNY,* 1: 285–91, 295; "Nicholson and Council to the Board of Trade, 15 May 1689" and "Declaration of the Freeholders of Suffolk County, Long Island," *DRCNY,* 3: 575–77, 591; NYHS, Collections (1864), 260–62, 352.

105. The committee of workmen, which included future Leislerians such as Suert Olferts and anti-Leislerians such as Dirck van der Burgh, recommended extensive repairs to the dilapidated fortifications. NYHS, Collections (1864), 253, 277; "Stephen van Cortlandt to Governor Andros, 9 July 1689," *DRCNY,* 3: 593.

106. NYHS, Collections (1868), 267; McCormick, *Leisler's Rebellion,* 175–78.

107. "Van Cortlandt to Andros, 9 July 1689," *DRCNY,* 3: 594; NYHS, Collections (1868), 292–93; on deposition of Hendrick Jacobsen, see *DHSNY,* 2: 11–12; on soldiers as papists, see "Declaration of the Inhabitants Soudjers Belonging Under the Severall Companies of Train Band of New Yorke," *DHSNY,* 2: 10–11.

108. Voorhees, "'In Behalf of the true Protestants' Religion,'" 224. As recently as May 9, Leisler joined the other militia captains, Common Council, and Nicholson's council in condemning the "malitious and most wiked persons . . . even in the hart of this our Citty" who spread "allarm and disquiet the Common peace and tranquility of the inhabitants thereof . . . by raising of jealousies against the cheefe members of the Government . . . by words and libels in writing, suspecting them to be Popish affected," PRO, CO5/1081, 9. Leisler continued to attend meetings of the provincial government until May 22, and affidavits presented at his trial confirmed that he did not enter the fort until it had been taken by the rank and file militiamen.

109. NYHS, Collections (1868), 281, 283; Knevel, *Burgers in het geweer,* 411–15.

110. Donna Merwick, "Being Dutch: An Interpretation of Why Jacob Leisler Died," *New York History* (October 1989): 373–404.

111. On Bacon's Rebellion, see Charles Andrews, ed., *Narratives of the Insurrections, 1675–1690* (1915; reprint, New York, 1943), 22–23, 114–15; Kathleen Brown, *Good Wives,* 161–162. For Boston, see Nash, *Urban Crucible,* 38–44.

112. The militia company comprised fifteen New Yorkers of Dutch ancestry, fifteen Englishmen, eight Dutchmen, one German, one Welshman, two Scots, one Dane, two Frenchmen, two Swiss, one Bostonian and a Barbadian. "A list of the Souldjers appointed by the Comity," in PRO CO5/1081, 7; McCormick, *Leisler's Rebellion,* 12. Studies by David Cohen and A. G. Roeber highlight the numerical significance of non-Dutch immigration to New Netherland, undermining arguments concerning the city's Dutch culture and monolithic Anglo-Dutch ethnic tensions in the later seventeenth century. See Cohen, "How Dutch Were the Dutch of New Netherland," 43–60, and Roeber, "Origins of Whatever Is Not English," 221–29. Leisler and his supporters consistently rejected any attempt to characterize the rebellion as an ethnic Dutch affair. See *DRCNY,* 2: 55–58; *DHSNY,* 2: 9, 10; on militia regulations, see NYHS, Collections (1868), 294, and Leisler's response to the charge by some Long Island townspeople that Englishmen were excluded from the militia is in PRO CO5/1081, 116.

113. "Representation of Committee of Safety, 9 November 1689," *DRCNY,* 3:

630–34. McCormick describes the rebellion as a Calvinist coup d'etat in *Leisler's Rebellion*, 198.

114. The captains of both companies of regular soldiers, Anthony Brockholes and Jervais Baxter, were Catholics, as was the customs collector Mathew Plowman. There were also a handful of Jesuits who had established a school to which William Pinhore, John Tudor, John Palmer, and James Graham sent their children. McCormick, *Leisler's Rebellion*, 160.

115. "Representation of Committee of Safety, 9 November 1689," *DRCNY*, 3; 630–34; *DHSNY*, 2: 320–30.

116. Sloughter's council included Stephen van Cortlandt, Frederick Philipse, Gabriel Minvielle, Wiliam Smith, Thomas Willet, William Pinhorne, Childey Brooke and Jospeh Dudley, but not yet William Nichols and Nicholas Bayard, whom Leisler still held in jail. For Sloughter's commission, see *DRCNY*, 3: 624; for an account of the surrender, see Reich, *Leisler's Rebellion*, 106–26.

Chapter 3

1. H. T. Dickinson, "How Revolutionary Was the 'Glorious Revolution' of 1688?" *British Journal of Eighteenth Century Studies* 11 (1988): 125–42; Zuckert, *Natural Rights and the New Republicanism*, 117; Ashcraft, *Revolutionary Politics*, 598.

2. For the significance of Blackstone's conception of sovereignty and of law in eighteenth-century Anglo-American politics, see Bernard Bailyn, *Ideological Origins of the American Revolution* (Cambridge, Mass., 1969), 70–73, 198–229; Gordon Wood, *The Creation of the American Republic 1776–1787* (Chapel Hill, N.C., 1969), 34–354; Howard Nenner, *By Colour of Law: Legal Culture and Constitutional Politics in England, 1660–1689* (Chicago, 1977); Haakonssen, *Natural Law and Moral Philosophy*, 321; Steve Hindle, *The State and Social Change in Early Modern England* (Basingstoke, 2000), 29–33.

3. Carl Lotus Becker, *The History of Political Parties in the Province of New York, 1760–1776* (1909; reprint, Madison, Wisc., 1960), 5–23; Alan Tully, *Forming American Politics: Ideals, Interests, and Institutions in Colonial New York and Pennsylvania* (Baltimore, 1994), 51, 213–49.

4. "Letter from Peter De La Noy Relative to Governor Fletcher's Conduct," *DRCNY*, 4: 221; *Colonial Laws*, 1: 392–93, 462–65; Henry B. Hoff, "Manors in New York," *New York Genealogical and Biographical Newsletter* (fall 1999) and (winter 2000).

5. For the campaign for the flour trade, see "Petition of the City to the King of England" requesting the "sole bolting of flower and baking of biskett for transportation" and the "Report of the Committee for Addressing his Majesty for Repealing the Bolting Act," and "Report of Committee for examining the Ancient Rights and Privileges," in CCP, 1: 8; *MCC*, 2: 6, 30–36; Cathy Matson, "Damned Scoundrels," 389–418.

6. It was this lobby that was widely suspected of furnishing Fletcher with a four-hundred-pound bribe to oppose the city's case when it reached the provincial assembly. *DRCNY*, 4: 223; Matson, *Merchants and Empire*, 115.

7. Tully, *Forming American Politics*, 452.

8. Haakonssen, *Natural Law and Moral Philosophy*, 15–61, 310–36; Peter Birks and Grant McLeod, "The Implied Contract Theory of Quasi Contract: Civilian Opinion in the Century Before Blackstone," *Oxford Journal of Legal Studies* 6 (1986): 46–85; J. G. A. Pocock, *The Ancient Constitution and the Feudal Law: A Study of English Historical Thought in the Seventeenth Century* (Cambridge, 1957), 1–56, 255–389, and his "Post-Puritan England and the Problem of Enlightenment," in P. Zagorin, ed., *Culture and Politics from Puritanism to the Enlightenment* (Berkeley, Calif., 1980), 91–111.

9. J. C. D. Clark, *The Language of Liberty, 1660–1832: Politics, Discourse, and Social Dynamics in the Anglo-America World* (New York, 1994), part III.

10. *MCC*, 1: 254, 264, 329, 339, 373, 375, 407, 418, 426; Kenneth Scott, *New York Court Records, 1684–1760: Genealogical Data from the Court of Quarter Sessions* (Washington, D.C., 1982), 11,13; Matson, *Merchants and Empire*, 108.

11. "Letter from Lord Cornbury to Mr Secretary Hedges in London,15 July 1705," *DRCNY*, 4: 1150–56; Samuel McKee Jr., "The Economic Pattern of Colonial New York," in Alexander C. Flick, ed., *History of the State of New York*, 10 vols. (New York, 1933–37), 2: 249–82; Burrows and Wallace, *Gotham*, 118–38.

12. One indication of the growth of New York's trade in imported English manufactured goods, and its relation to neighboring ports, is offered by figures detailed in Sir Charles Whitworth, *State of the Trade of Great Britain in Its Imports and Exports* (London, 1776), 63–66, cited in Herbert A. Johnson, *The Law Merchant and Negotiable Instruments in Colonial New York, 1664–1730* (Chicago, 1963), 59–60.

Period	New York	New England	Pennsylvania
1667–1698	£14,929	£80,992	£ 6,851
1699–1708	£31,021	£86,006	£12,387
1709–1718	£44,535	£128,397	£14,755

13. Elizabeth Bancker's inventory is listed in Valentine, *Manual* (1855), 517; "An Inventory of the goods and chatells rights and credits of Robert Benson late of the Citty of New York mercht decsd taken and made by and at the request of Cornelia Bensing widdow relict and Administratix of all and singular the goods chattells rights creditts of the said deceased 24 August 1716," New York Public Library, Rare Books and Manuscripts.

14. Population figures are taken from *DHSNY*, 1: 689–94; Gary Nash, "The New York Census of 1737: A Critical Note on the Integration of Literary and Statistical Sources," *WMQ*, 3d ser., 36 (July 1979): 428–35. For estimates on the size of the urban artisanal population, see Wilkenfeld, *Social and Economic Structure*, 28, 31, 87; Deborah A. Rosen, "Courts and Commerce: The Formative Period of Legal Practice in New York, 1690–1760" (Ph.D. diss., Columbia University, 1990), 216–17. For a breakdown of taxpayers and tradesmen by occupation and ethnicity, see Goodfriend, *Before the Melting Pot*, 65–70, 156; also see the useful and oft-studied "Burghers of New Amsterdam and the Freemen of New York," in NYHS, Collections (1885), passim.

15. Figures on slave population and ownership are in Hodges, *Root and Branch*, 41; Goodfriend, *Before the Melting Pot*, 76, 113; Benjamin Guterman, "The 'Ancient' Freemen of New York City: Artisans and the Development of Urban Society, 1664–1776" (Ph.D. diss., University of Maryland, 1994), 137.

16. Bridenbaugh, *Cities in the Wilderness*, 188–89; "Robert Livingston to the Lords of Trade, 13 May 1701," *DRCNY*, 4: 871–73.

17. "Gabriel Ludlow (1663–1736) and his Descendants," *NYGBR* (January 1919): 34–36; for Walter Thong, see *NYGBR* (October 1952): 200–203; Jacob de Kay is discussed in Goodfriend, *Before the Melting Pot*, 98, 179. Thomas Archdeacon considers the inroads made by English and French merchants into the upper fifth band of city taxpayers in *Conquest and Change*, 41, 58–77; Cathy Matson provides a comprehensive account of the activities of New York's middling merchants in *Merchants and Empire*, 89, 121–215, 134–39. Also see Wilkenfeld, *Social and Economic Structure*, 54–55; Kammen, *Colonial New York*, 161–73.

18. Lawrence A. Harper, *The English Navigation Laws* (1939; reprint, New York, 1964); John J. McCusker, "The Current Value of English Exports, 1697–1800," *WMQ*, 3d ser., 28 (October 1971): 607–28. For the shortage of currency and pressure to pay debtors in England, see Virginia D. Harrington, *The New York Merchant on the Eve of the Revolution* (New York, 1935), 164–206; Lawrence Leder and Vincent P. Carusso, "Robert Livingston (1654–1728): Businessman of Colonial New York," *Business History Review* 30 (March 1956): 26.

19. *MCC*, 2: 261; "Robert Hunter, to the Board of Trade 12 November 1715," *DRCNY*, 5: 461–62; Bridenbaugh, *Cities in the Wilderness*, 192. For merchant resistance to paper money and a table of provincial issues, 1709–71, see Matson, *Merchants and Empire*, 240–248, 325.

20. *RNA*, 6: 11, 16, 20–23, 46, 91, 96, 304; John Anderson v. Edward Royle, mariner, 1725, Mayor's Court Papers, (hereafter MCP) Division of Old Records, County Court, 31 Chambers Street, New York. Daniel Cavore and Francis Lee v. Mathew Force, 1685, MCP; Stephen Van Cortlandt Ledger, 1695–1700, in the New-York Historical Society; Jonathon Gleaves v. Jacob Hayes, 1723, MCP. For examples of the variety of currencies circulating locally, see the 1681 report of a committee reporting on the contents of a chest once owned by a Mr. Kirk Hall, in CCP, 1: 1; Christian Van Rijk v. Garrett Wendell, 1721, MCP; Hodges, *New York City Carters*, 28–61; Curtis P. Nettels, *The Money Supply of the American Colonies Before 1720* (Madison, Wisc., 1934), 203–28.

21. Andries Barhyt v. Joost Sooy, 1724, MCP.

22. For amendment to local law in 1684, "A Bill Concerning the Assignment of Specialtyes," *Colonial Laws*, 1: 17, 153. John de Bruyn v. John Marsh, 1690, Mayor's Court Papers (hereafter, MCPCU), Columbia University Rare Books and Manuscripts Division.

23. On financial instruments and the rise of penal bonds see Johnson, *Law Merchant*, passim; J. Sperling, "The International Payments Mechanism in the Seventeenth and Eighteenth Centuries," *The Economic History Review*, 2nd ser., 15 (1962): 446–68.

24. Thus, in 1709, the merchant Nicholas Bayard sued John Staples for payment of twenty-seven pounds on a bill of exchange originally drawn up by George Lane of Maryland on the London merchant Samuel Grumo which Lane made payable to Thomas Lee and thence to Staples, who signed it over to Bayard. Also see Joseph Bueno, merchant, v. George Lockhart, surgeon, 1686, MCP; Zachariah Angerin v. Jeremiah King, vintner, 1701, MCP; David Bonefoy and wife Catherine v. Daniel Pelltroe,

leatherseller, 1701, MCP; George Norton, butcher, v. Isaac De Riemer, merchant, 1706, MCP; John Cholwell v. Adolph DeGrove, mariner, 1713, MCP; Thomas Staples v. Daniel Ponton, 1720, MCP; Thomas Clarke v. John Kelly, 1723, MCP.

25. "Governor Burnet to the Lords of Trade, 21 November 1724," *DRCNY*, 5: 738.

26. For Benson's accounts see note 13 and for similar patterns in an earlier set of city accounts, see Harriet Styker-Rodda, "Asser Levy's Estate," *NYGBR* (July 1971): 133–35 and (October 1971), 240–47; Merwick, "Becoming English," 401. For credit in other Anglo-American early modern contexts, see Bruce H. Mann, *Neighbors and Strangers: Law and Community in Early Connecticut* (Chapel Hill, 1987); Daniel Vickers, *Farmers and Fishermen: Two Centuries of Work in Essex County, Massachusetts* (Chapel Hill, N.C., 1994); Craig Muldrew, *The Economy of Obligation* (Basingstoke, 1998), 95–103. The advertisement appeared in the *New-York Gazette*, 23 and 31 August and 11 November 1728.

27. Dunn's registration as a freeman appears in New-York Historical Society, Collections (1885), 92. The cases discussed are James Wyatt v. John Dunn, 1716, MCP; Joseph Latham Jr. and Samuel Pell v. John Dunn, MCM (1723–28), 221; Scott, *New York Court Records*, 32, 34. In May 1720, John Dunn and Thomas Lyell, a gentleman, provided security for Mary Horton's good behavior after she was sued for assault, see Elizabeth Bawler v. Mary Horton, 1720, MCP; John Dunn, tailor and owner of sailing boat, *Mary* v. John Yeats, 1722, MCP; Peter Marschalck v. John Stephens, mariner and master of the *Swallow* with John Dunn as bondsman, 1725, MCP.

28. John Dunn v. John Deprees, November 1721, MCP. A bailbond liberated a debtor from jail following arrest for debt and provided surety for their future appearance in court. A bailpiece freed a debtor after losing the case against them and provided surety that they would pay the debt in accordance with the judgment of the court. In both cases, nonperformance of the obligation made the debtor and his or her bondsmen liable for a penalty, see Rosen, "Courts and Commerce," 44.

29. Stephen Mileman v. Daniel Ponton, 1721, MCP; Frances Holfmaier v. John Dunn, 1723, MCP; MCM (1723–28), 454; Francis Harrison and Gilbert Livingston v. John Dunn, 1720, MCP; Elias Brevoort v. John Dunn, 1724, MCP; John Palmer v. John Dunn, 1724, MCP; MCC, 3: 264; Scott, *New York Court Records*, 39; promissory note of John Salnave, John Dunn, and Roger Groves for £108 to Samuel Weaver, 20 May 1727, MCP; John Hybon v. John Dunn, 1727, MCP. NYHS, Collections (1894), 82; Dr. John W. Francis, *Old New York Reminiscences*, vol. 13 (New York, 1895), no. 90.

30. Abraham de Peyster's Account Book; Mrs. Elizabeth Schuyler's Ledger, 1737–51; and Thomas Sander's Account Book, 1699–1703, in Sanders Papers, Box 19; Peter Jay's Account, 1724–48, all in New-York Historical Society.

31. Shaloon was a closely woven woolen material chiefly used for linings. For similar dealings, see the entries in Elizabeth Schuyler's ledger relating to Samuel Goodness, blacksmith, 46; John Pieters, baker, 76; Henry Breasted, hatter, 78, 165; Andries Breasted, joiner, 89; John Heyer, cooper, 100; Mathias Wolf, mariner, 107; Ann Brown, midwife, 122; John Wulph, tailor, 139; Francis Basset, pewterer, 178; Jacob Kip, cordwainer, 178; John Bogaert, baker, 222, 234; and Jacobus Johnson, tailor, 232.

32. Drugget was a fabric made of wool and silk or linen mix, and bengal probably refers to a printed or painted calico, sometimes used for internal décor. Lancaster

Simms v. Jeremiah King, 1699, MCP; Moses Levy, merchant, v. Edward Cole, vintner, 1701, MCP; Garret van Horne v. Ralph Potter, 1720, MCP; Thomas Noxon v. Ralph Potter, 1725, MCP; Samuel Benson v. Nicholas Evertsen, 1710, MCPCU; John Tiebout v. John Marshall, 1710–11, MCPCU; Nicholas Matthieson v. Thomas Day, 1730, MCP; Peter Jay's Account, July 1724, in New-York Historical Society; Goodfriend, *Before the Melting Pot,* 15. Also see Francis Wessells, bolter, v. Johannes Pluvier, victualler, 1701, nonpayment for rum, MCP; John Searle, mariner and ropemaker, v. James Alexander, merchant, 1725, nonpayment for 272 yards of striped satin, MCP; Peter Marschalk v. Roger Groves, glover, 1729, nonpayment of ten pounds, fourteen shillings, and fourpence for one ton of fine bread, MCP.

33. For De Witt and Smith and a similar case involving confusion concerning attached goods, see MCM (1695–1704), 164, 165, 173, 177. When the mariner Richard Robinson was offered a cape by John Harvey and William Laden, he suspected that it might have been stolen but, as he later told the court, he took it home to keep "in his house until he could find its owner." Richard Robinson's deposition, 1719, MCP.

34. Herman M. Stoker, *Wholesale Prices for 213 Years, 1720–1932.* Part II: *Wholesale Prices at New York City, 1720–1800* (Ithaca, N.Y., 1932), 213–14; Benjamin D'harriette v. Jeremiah Chardavine, tailor, 1719; also see Arthur Green v. Robert Duncan, 1720, MCP.

35. Thomas Willis v. Peter Adolph, 1700, MCP. For examples of payment substitution and legal obfuscation, see Gabriel Minvielle v. Jan Hendrick Van Gunst, MCM (1677–82), 332; Susanna Elliot v. Daniel Ebbits, a bricklayer, 1701, and John Leisley, mariner, v. Thomas Roberts, cooper, 1706, both in MCP.

36. For Robert Crannel's accounts, see CCP, 2: 3; Jacob Mayle, merchant v. Gersie Vanderclife, widow, 1698, MCP; Paulus Turke v. Gersie Vanderclife, 1699, MCP; Jospeh Bueno, merchant v. Judith DeMerse, widow, 1700, MCP; Mathew Ling, merchant and bolter, v. Engeltie Garret, widow, 1700, MCP; Sarah Sanford v. Adolph Dyrck, 1702, for nonpayment for cedar timber, MCP; William Cullen v. Elsie Leisler, widow, 1708, MCP; William Sharpas v. Elizabeth White, widow, 1700, MCP; John Leisley v. Katherine Apple, widow, 1709, MCP; Mary Payne v. Joseph Meeker Jr., 1709, MCP; Miriam Napthaly v. Anthony Young, tallow chandler, 1709, MCP; Dorothy Wright, widow v. Joseph Berry, tailor, 1710, MCP; Joanna De Bruyn, widow v. Thomas Parmiter, pipemaker, 1710, MCP; Joanna Markham v. Thomas Whitehead, 1712, MCP; Elsye Vandewater, seamstress v. Daniel Mesnard, 1720, MCP; Miles Foy v. Elizabeth Jourdan, 1722, MCP; Andries Hardenbrook v. Margaret Rottery, 1723, MCP; Catherine Brett, widow, v. John Baker, 1723, MCP; Rachel Levy v. Victor Bicker, joiner, 1728, MCP.

37. Peter Willemse Roome in *NYGBR* (January 1944): 17; John Deforeest, by order of his mother Sara Deforeest v. Obe Kendrick, 1684, MCP; John Barberie v. Ann Culyer, widow, 1693, MCM (1682–95), 358; Gertruyd Van Cortlandt v. Servis Marriset, armourer, 1704, for nonpayment of rent for a house in Cannon St., MCP; Hellogond Selightenhorst v. Jacob Swan, 1707, MCM (1704–10), 283; Ann Van der Spiegel v. Gerret De Grauw, carpenter, for nonfulfilment of conditions of a lease, MCP; Jane Tothill v. James Wright, 1710, MCP; Anne Graveraedt, widow, v. John Garner, 1712, for nonpayment of rent on a house, MCP; Agnis Janeway v. Jacob Swan, hatter, 1718, for nonpayment for one year's rent on a house and an unpaid bond,

MCP; Mary Bloodgood v. Francis Garrabrant, 1722, MCP. Also see Jean P. Jordan, "Women Merchants in Colonial New York," *New York History* 58 (October 1977): 412–39.

38. Capt. John Manning v. Mary Gosens, *RNA*, 6: 176; "The Humble Petition of Elizabeth Jourdain," in the De Peyster Papers, vol. 1695–1710, New-York Historical Society. For attendees, see Lamb, *History of New York*, 427; Elizabeth Jourdain v. Henry Campbell, 1721, MCP. Also see Katherine Evans v. John Thomas, "indebted to her 82 florins wampum as appears by a bill under his hand for fictualls and drinck," *RNA*, 6: 197; Anne Elderton v. Marmaduke Freeman, "for food lodging and washing for him and his three slaves," 1725, MCP; Rachel Hunt v. Lewis Taliten, mariner, 1700, MCP; also see "Gabriel Ludlow's Memorandum Book," 1693–1745, and "William De Witt's Barber and Wigmaker's Day Book, 1739–1752," both in New-York Historical Society. For men suing for the provision of food and drink and washing, see Warner Wessels, hatmaker, v. Daniel Toy, gentleman, 1701, MCP; John Enrique, mariner v. John Drummy, 1713, MCP; John Williamson, yeoman, v. Joseph Harwood, merchant, 1701, MCP; John Gara v. John Purnell, 1722, MCP.

39. John Ackerson v. Edmund Heynes, 1702, MCP.

40. Simeon Soumaine, silversmith, goldsmith, and victualler, 1701, MCP, and NYHS, Collections (1909), 161; Jacob Swan, a hatter, felter, and vintner, in cases in 1718, 1719, and 1722, MCP; Theophilus Elsworth, carpenter, ferryman, merchant, and vintner, CCP, 2: 13; *MCC*, 3: 362; NYHS, Collections (1885), 193; 1723, MCP; Abraham van Laer, mariner and vintner, 1703, 1706, MCP; Daniel Ebbits, bricklayer and vintner, 1703, MCP; MCM (1704–1710), 98; Joost Sooy, shoemaker, cooper, and innkeeper, NYHS, Collections (1885), 103 and (1909), 179, 180; Robert Crannel, soldier, municipal officer, and innkeeper, CCP, 2: 12; 1716 and 1722, MCP; MCM (1723–28), 15; *MCC*, 3: 364. William Wieblin, butcher, ferryman, and innkeeper, 1718 and 1720, MCP; CCP 2: 5; Lawrence Eckles, gentleman, victualler, and innkeeper, 1702 and 1704, MCP.

41. Nicholas Stengthen v. Jospeh Barker, mariner, 1698, MCP; Cornelius Quick, mariner v. Thomas Clark, merchant, 1700, MCP; William Symonds mariner v. James Beard, mariner, 1701, MCP; Ralph Row, mariner, v. Jacobus Davis, mariner, 1701, MCP; Joshua David v. Andrew Depue, mariner, 1704, MCP; John Davis, mariner v. John Macklening, 1704, MCP; John Leisly, mariner, v. Thomas Roberts, cooper, 1706, MCP; John Perow, mariner, v. Jacob Swan, feltmaker, 1708, MCP; Harman Rutgers v. Dirck Adolph, mariner, 1709, MCP; John Leisly, mariner v. John Ellison, joiner, 1709, MCP; William Kippin v. Barent Rynders, 1722, MCP. For activities of Gerrit van Horne, see Scott, *New York Court Records*, 12; *MCC*, 2: 250; John Corbet v. Gerrit Van Horne, 1702, for nonpayment of charges relating to a voyage to Surinam, MCP. Peter Willemse Roome v. Mary Thompson, 1701, MCP; *MCC*, 2: 4, 22, 99; and 3: 147; Isaac Neptheli v. John Meyer, 1725, MCP.

42. This draws upon Michael Sonenscher's characterization of artisanal trade in eighteenth-century France in *Work and Wages*, 130–74, and his adaptation of studies by Clifford Geertz, *Peddlers and Princes*, 33–47, and "Suq," 124–25, 219. For a similar assessment of the diversity of artisanal labor in the medieval era, see Gervase Rosser, "Crafts, Guilds and the Negotiation of Work in the Medieval Town," *Past and Present* 154 (1997): 3–31. For an excellent synthesis of much recent work on early

modern European artisans, see James Farr, *Artisans in Europe, 1300–1914* (Cambridge, 2000).

43. Rothschild, *New York City Neighborhoods,* 118–19; Nash, *Urban Crucible,* 71; Wilkenfeld, *Social and Economic Structure,* 23; James Henretta, "Economic Development and Social Structure in Colonial Boston," *WMQ,* 3d ser., 22 (January 1965): 75–92.

44. Jeremiah Callcutt's monopoly privilege is mentioned in Thomas F. DeVoe, *The Market Book, containing a Historical Account of the Public Markets in the Cities of New York, Boston, and Brooklyn* (New York, 1862), 68–69; Norton's petition is in *MCC,* 2: 352.

45. For example, in July 1700, Jacob Adams, a butcher, sued Robert Smith, a New Jersey farmer, for failure to deliver two oxen for which Adams had paid fourteen pounds and ten shillings the previous September. When the ferryman James Harding delayed the transport of William Wieblin's cattle from Long Island in 1719, Wieblin soon ran short at the market and had to borrow some meat from a fellow butcher. Jacob Adams, butcher, v. Robert Smith, New Jersey farmer, 1700, MCP; William Wieblin's petition in CCP, 2: 1; John Knowles, butcher, v. William Hill, boatman, 1712, MCM (1710–15), 242–45; John Clapp v. George Norton, butcher, 1706, for nonpayment for pasturing cattle, MCP. For regulation of butchers and innkeepers, see RNA, 1: 20, 32; *MCC,* 1: 215–16, 313; De Voe, *Market Book*; Morris, *Government and Labor,* 160–61; Scott, "New Amsterdam's Taverns," no. 1 (April 1964): 9–10, 15; no. 2 (July 1964): 9–10, 15; no. 3 (October 1964): 13–15.

46. Goodfriend, *Before The Melting Pot,* 71, 79.

47. "Earl of Bellomont to the Lords of Trade, 2 January 1701," *DRCNY,* 4: 826; "Garret Abeel's Records," *Holland Society Yearbook* (New York, 1916), 70.

48. For Trinity Church and building records, see "First Recorded Minutes Regarding the Building of Trinity Church in the City of New York, 1696–1697," in the Trinity Church Archives, New York City; Hodges, *New York City Carters,* 28, 31, 43–49, 60–61, and his "Legal Bonds of Attachment: The Freemanship Law of New York City, 1648–1801," in Pencak and Wright, eds., *Authority and Resistance,* 227–44. Bullivant is discussed in Goodfriend, *Before the Melting Pot,* 66.

49. For example, see the carpenter John Ellison's 1699 lease on the market house by the bridge, *MCC,* 2: 90.

50. On occasion, the Assembly also established monopolies to protect new initiatives. Thus, in 1694, the assembly approved Isaac Lansen's petition that he "shall have the benefit and privilege of grinding and making of Rape and Linseed oil for the space and terme of seven years . . . and that no other person . . . do presume to counterfeit, imitate or in any other way grind or make any rape of linseed oil." *Journal of the Votes and Proceedings of the General Assembly of the Colony of New York: Began the 9th Day of April, 1691 and ended the 27th of September 1743,* 2 vols. (New York, 1764), 1: 43; also see the 1712 act granting John Pameter a monopoly of the production of lampblack—a fine black powder used in paints and inks—which passed to his wife, Susannah, upon his death, in "Robert Hunter to Lords of Trade, 23 June 1712," *DRCNY,* 5: 344.

51. Nessepot and Marsh, *MCC,* 2: 98–99. Dugdale and Searle and Josiah Quincy, CCP, 1: 14; 2: 5; *MCC,* 3: 193–94. Also see Mathias Dubois's plan to erect a blacksmith

shop, Susanna Dally's petition that the council "grant her a licence to sit in the said [Fly] Market and sell coffee, chocolate, cakes, and pies," the baker Abraham Delanoy's petition for "liberty to build an oven under the ground fronting his house," and Roger Baker for a slip of ground in Smith's Street, *MCC*, 3: 46; CCP, 1:10.

52. In 1717, John Searle was sued by members of his crew for nonpayment of wages. Given Searle's prospective partnership with Dugdale, it is possible that he was trying to shortchange the crew and maximize his investment in the ropewalk. Samuel Browne v. John Searle, 1717, MCP; John Morton v. John Searle, 1717, MCP; Roger Thomas v. John Searle, 1717, MCP. In 1719, Dugdale and Searle purchased John Galloway's remaining time of eleven years and three months as an apprentice from Peter Colvell, promising to teach Galloway "to be a reaper." NYHS, Collections (1911), 120–21. For their involvement in the grain and flour trade, see William Dugdale and John Searle v. Thomas Kearney, 1721, MCP; MCM (1720–23), 292. William Dugdale was subsequently elected high sherrif of New York and both men served as church wardens for Trinity Church. See Scott, *New York Court Records*, 40, 88; "Succession of Rectors, Churchwardens, and Vestrymen of the Corporation of Trinity Church from 1697," in New-York Historical Society. When Dugdale quit the partnership, John Pintard, a wealthy merchant, bought his share, and Searle continued to operate the walk until his death in 1734. For more on artisanal partnerships in trade, see Matson, *Merchants and Empire*, 121–69.

53. Harding's accounts are in CCP, 1: 21; also see Robert Crannel's claim for three pounds and ten shillings for his salary and as marshall and for "horse Hire, fire and Candles for the Watch, & paid A Bricklayer for Mending Chimneys." CCP 1: 19.

54. For example, in 1712, alderman Walter Thong hired out his slave to the city for seventeen days at one pound and eighteen shillings, or just over two shillings a day, see *NYGBR* (October 1952): 203.

55. On the connections between Albany's Lutheran community and the English authorities, see Merwick, "Becoming English," 406–7. Van der Burgh was arrested and subjected to rough treatment during Leisler's Rebellion. See "Capt. McKenzie to Captain Nicholson, 15 August 1689," *DRCNY*, 3: 612, 614. For Cornelius van der Burgh and examples of his silverwork, see Roderic H. Blackburn and Ruth Piwonka, *Remembrance of Patria: Dutch Arts and Culture in Colonial America, 1609–1776* (Albany, N.Y., 1988), 279–80.

56. Howard Thomas, *Lucas Dircksen Vanderburgh of New Amsterdam and his son Dirck: Progenitors of the Vanderburgh Family of Dutchess County, New York* (New York, 1951). For the fate of Dirck van der Burgh's cruel stephfather, Jacob Fabritius, see Miecislaus Haiman, *Poles in New York in the Seventeenth and Eighteenth Centuries* (Chicago, 1938), 44–50. For Van der Burgh's municipal service see *MCC*, 1: 428; Bridenbaugh, *Cities in the Wilderness*, 207. Bay Crosevelt registered as freeman and feltmaker, NYHS, Collections (1885), 73. The land in Dutchess County would be the Van der Burgh family home for the remainder of the eighteenth century.

57. See Van der Burgh's account for nine hundred pounds for work on Kings Chapel in *DHSNY*, 3: 406–7; Dirck's bills for work ordered by the city in NYHS, Collections, (1909), 13, 22, 32, 47, 55, 60, 66, 70, 74, 82, 97; *Calendar of Council Minutes*, 98, 103, 104, 108, 109, 112, 113, 114, 119, 121, 125, 128, 147, 152, 164, 177, 187. Dirck van der Burgh v. Claus Gysbertson, 1695, MCM (1695–1704), 16–18; Enoch Aymes, bricklayer,

v. Dirck van der Burgh, bricklayer, 1701, MCP; *MCC*, 1: 428; Dirck van der Burgh v. John Tudor, 1701, MCP. In October 1698, Dirck successfully won the reprieve of the death sentence passed on one of his slaves convicted of burgling a neighbor's house. In November 1698, he received a silver tankard valued at twelve pounds for his part in the building of Trinity Church. Dirck continued to buy and sell land. In February 1706 he sold a lot on the south side of Queen Street to Ebeneezer Wilson. In February 1707, he sold a lot on Smith's Fly to Rosevelt Waldron. In Thomas, *Lucas Dircksen Vanderburgh of New Amsterdam*, 27–35. Details on Van der Burgh's estate is in NYHS, Collections (1892), 279–80.

58. "A list of the Souldjers appointed by the Comity," PRO CO5/1081, 8; NYHS, Collections (1885), 72; Scott, *New York Court Records*, 9; *MCC*, 2: 88, 92, 94, 101, 109, 113, 239, 362, 383, 386, 403, 408–9, 413, 415, 419; Joahnnes Tiebout v. John Marshall, 1 May 1711, MCM (1710–15), 91.

59. *MCC*, 3: 4, 149, 191, 218, 239, 262, 280, 327, 340, 361, 427; CCP, 2: 1, 3, 5, 6, 7, 8.

60. Christine Daniels has found that craft dynasties were also more likely in trades that required high capital investment in tools or property. See "From Father to Son: Economic Roots of Craft Dynasties in Eighteenth Century Maryland," in Howard B. Rock, Paul A. Gilje, and Robert Asher, eds., *American Artisans: Crafting Social Identity, 1750–1850* (Baltimore, 1995), 3–17.

61. "Earl of Bellomont to the Lords of Admiralty, 15 October 1700," "Earl of Bellomont to the Lords of Trade, 17 October 1700," and "Earl of Bellomont to the Lords of Trade, 20 November 1700," *DRCNY*, 4: 711, 722, 784–85. Bellomont subsequently placed Latham in charge of the cutting of selected timber to be sent back to England. The governor's correspondence with Abraham de Peyster suggests that Latham disappointed his employer, who suspected the shipwright of overcharging him. See the De Peyster Papers, 1695–1710.

62. Bridenbaugh, *Cities in the* Wilderness, 37, 184. For cases involving shipbuilding, see Samuel Bayard v. Beverly Latham, 1711, for thirty-eight pounds, MCP; William Smith v. Samuel Pell, 1728, for twenty-one pounds, MCPCU; William Robinson v. Samuel Pell, 1728, for twenty pounds and nine shillings for "sundry parcels of oak plank," MCP.

63. Riche hired out his slave Chattam to the baker Samuel Roux for ten months at nine pounds seventeen shillings (or just under five shillings a week), traded substantial amounts of plantation products—300 lbs. of brown sugar, 300 lbs. muscovado sugar, 300 lbs. powdered sugar, and 5,000 pieces of logwood. Dennis Riche v. Samuel Roux, 1728, and Dennis Riche v. Benjamin Conyard, 1728, MCP. For the Lathams and property deals see Valentine, *Manual* (1855), 593; "Deed to Joseph Latham for Land in Orange Street, 7 August 1716," in New York City Deeds, New-York Historical Society.

64. Joseph Latham, Accounts for building the Dolphin, 20 November 1729, in the New-York Historical Society. Carl Bridenbaugh, *The Colonial Craftsman* (New York, 1950), 94–95; John Parlie's Petition, CCP, 2: 3.

65. John Foster, carpenter, v. John King, 1714, MCP, for fifty-five shillings per month for a voyage from England; Samuel Belknap, carpenter v. Cornelius van Horne, 1723, MCP, for six shillings per day for Belknap and three shillings for his servant; Victor Bicker, carpenter, v. Andries Coeysman, 1727, MCP, for six shillings per

day for Bicker, five shillings for journeyman James Davie, and four shillings sixpence for journeymen Isaac Filkin; William Ladd, carpenter, v. Joseph Latham, 1727, MCP, for five shillings and ninepence per day for work as a carpenter. Also see the estimates for repairing the dock and bridge in July 1723, which figured three hundred pounds for eighteen laborers paid at the rate of two shillings sixpence per diem. In *MCC*, 3: 325–26, and the carpenter John Roome's accounts for the 1733 repair of the ferry house at Brooklyn in which Roome charged six shillings per day for himself, five shillings for a journeyman, two shillings for an apprentice, and two shillings threepence for a free black laborer. CCP, 3: 7. Finally, see Isaac Dawson master of the *Success*, anchored in London, who hired William Stratton to serve as master at twenty-three shillings per month. In Rosen, "Courts and Commerce," 134.

66. The residential concentration of trades around the city struck Bruce Martin Wilkenfeld as "remarkable" *Social and Economic Structure*, 39, 95. Joyce Goodfriend discusses the importance of the ethno-religious dimension of artisanal communities in *Beyond the Melting Pot*, 61–81, 155–86. For tax assessments and residences in 1701, see Rothschild, *New York City Neighborhoods*, 185–204.

67. The importance of associations and contacts was noted by the most famous of early eighteenth-century American artisans, Benjamin Franklin, who feared that David Harry (his competitor in the printing trade) would better him because "his friends were very able and had a good deal of interest." Benjamin Franklin, *Autobiography*, ed. Louis P. Masur (New York, 1993), 81–92.

68. Steven Ross estimates that 661 people sought first-time relief between 1712 and 1740. "Objects of Charity: Poor Relief, Poverty, and the Rise of the Almshouse in Early Eighteenth century New York City," in Pencak and Wright, eds., *Authority and Resistance*, 138–72; Raymond Mohl, "Poverty in Early America, a Reappraisal: The Case of Eighteenth-Century New York City" *New York History* 50 (1969), 5–27. Irma Carra found that very few people received any form of poor relief between 1691 and 1711, and those who did fell within the traditional definition of the deserving poor. In "Who Cares: Poor Relief in Colonial New York City" (Ph.D. diss., New York University, 2002), 58–59, 115. For the more favorable assessment, see Wilkenfeld, *Social and Economic Structure*, 29, 91.

69. "Instructions to Benjamin Fletcher Esquire, Governor of New York, March 1692," *DRCNY*, 3: 823–24; "Instructions for the Earl of Bellomont, April 1699," *DRCNY*, 4: 290.

70. For the comparatively poorer conditions of working people after 1740, see Gary Nash, "Urban Wealth and Poverty in Pre-Revolutionary America," *Journal of Interdisciplinary History* 6 (spring 1976): 545–84, his "Up from the Bottom in Franklin's Philadelphia," *Past and Present* 77 (1977): 57–83, and *Urban Crucible*, part I. For conditions in New York, see Burrows and Wallace, *Gotham*, 130.

71. Bruce Wilkenfeld, "New York City Neighborhoods, 1730," *New York History* 57 (April 1976), 164–82; *DHSNY*, 1: 694; Burrows and Wallace, *Gotham*, 144.

72. [38] Deborah Rosen's analysis of the inventories of estates in wills and probate records shows that the number of better-off city residents who died as creditors with outstanding debtors almost doubled (from 36 to 65 percent) between 1690 and 1740. Deborah A. Rosen, *Courts and Commerce. Gender, Law and the Market Economy in Colonial New York* (Columbus, Ohio., 1997), 43; for the increasing rate of tenancies

among middling residents, see Adrian Howe, "Accommodation and Retreat: Politics in Anglo-Dutch New York City, 1700–1760," (Ph.D. diss., University of Melbourne, 1984), ch. 1.

73. Kenneth Scott, "The Church Wardens and the Poor in New York City, 1693–1747," *NYGBR* (March 1968): 158–62. Also see MCM (1680–83), 12, 26; *Colonial Laws,* 1: 132, 237–38; Maria Obia's Petition to Benjamin Fletcher, June 1695, *NYGBR* (July 1971): 155–56.

74. "Mr. Robert Livingston to the Lords of Trade, 13 May 1702," *DRCNY,* 4: 875.

75. Quarry traced the problem to the advantage enjoyed by colonies such as Virginia and Maryland which could settle London accounts with tobacco and retain valuable specie that flooded out of New York, and proposed the "reducing all the Coyn of America to one standard." "Colonel Robert Quarry to the Lords of Trade, 1703," *DRCNY,* 4: 1,047; "Governor Hunter to the Lords of Trade, 12 November 1715," *DRCNY,* 5: 461.

76. Benjamin Kiersted v. Moses Hart, 1725, MCP.

77. Hugh Mosier v. William Golding and Daniel Sexton, 1728, MCP; Richard Tinker v. John de Forest, 1685, MCP; John Marsh v. John Mulliner, 1693, MCPCU.

78. For discussions of the trust between creditors and long-term debtors in colonial America and early modern England see Mann, *Neighbors and Strangers,* 11–47; T. H. Breen, *Tobacco Culture: The Mentality of the Great Tidewater Planters on the Eve of Revolution* (Princeton, N.J., 1985), 90–96; Muldrew, *Economy of Obligation.*

79. Cure sued and won after Captain Ropinkthman's ship had come and gone and Elsworth had still failed to repay the sailors' debts. John Cure v. John Elsworth, 16 June 1712, MCM (1710–15), 279, 280. On John Elsworth's success as a carpenter, see *NYGBR* 64 (April 1933): 154–67, 255–67.

80. Elizabeth Jordain, widow, v. Evert Garner, mariner, 1706, MCP.

81. Thomas Pope v. William Davenport, yeoman of Westchester, 1717, MCP; Vincient Marine v. Peter Ponyade, 1719, MCP; Patrick MacKnight v. Alexander Mills, 1719, MCP; Joseph Wright v. William Lyford, 1721, MCP; Thomas Slowe v. William Lyford, 1721, MCP; Benjamin Rushin v. John Sommerfield, 1720, MCP.

82. David Bonefoy and wife Catherine v. Daniel Peltrow, 1702, and the plea that when the bill was drawn up, Catherine was under *feme couvert* being the wife of one Merciere, MCP; Isaac Bedlow v. Samuel and Catherine Staats, 1709, for a debt before she was married, MCP; John Ellison v. Thomas Hooke Jr., and his wife Mary, executor of the will of John Gurney, barber, 1712, MCP; Crispin Hooper and wife Susan v. Jacob Francisco, 1721, MCP; John Gale v. William Simon and Alice his wife, late Alice Ketcham widow, 1723, nonpayment of fifteen pounds for sheep and lambs bought when she was *feme sole,* MCP; Tirwhyt Cayley and wife Elizabeth, late Elizabeth Glencross, widow, v. Abraham Wendell, merchant, for bond debt made when she was *feme sole,* 1724, MCP, and MCM (1723–28), 239. For suits following death and departure, see Joanna De Bruyn v. Thomas Parmiter, pipemaker, 1710, MCP; Victor Bicker, carpenter, v. John Hyer and Peter, post executors of the estate of John Hybon Jr., 1728, MCP; Joseph Bahr, mariner and executor of the will of William Bahr, mariner, deceased, v. Janet Boyle, executor of will of William Boyle, shoemaker, deceased, 1710, MCP.

83. For multiple and sequential suits by merchants, see Benjamin Faneuil v.

Edward Cole, vintner, and Bartholomew Feurt, mariner, 1701, MCP; William Glencross v. Benjamin Bill, mariner, Roger Brett, merchant, and Edward Taylor, mariner, 1709, MCP; Giles Shelley, merchant, v. William Huddleston, Hans Kiersted, and Johannes Ten Eyck, 1710, MCP; William Anderson, merchant v. Lawrence Eckles, Johannes Ten Eyck, and Peter Van Dyke, 1710, MCP; Francis Harrison v. John Johnson, Thomas Noxon, George Parker, and Richard Torr, 1717, MCP; Francis Harrison and Gilbert Livingston v. Thomas Banks, Edward Blagg, John Dunn, James Bussey, Edmond Hawkins, and Jacob Swan, 1721, MCP. For innkeepers, butchers, and shopkeepers see Thomas Weyman, innkeeper, v. Thomas Taylor, and Valentine Jones, 1685, MCP; Edward Buckmaster, innkeeper, v. Fredrick Arentsen, John Peterson Slott, and Henrick Bemicke, 1691, MCP; George Norton, butcher, v. Richard Lloyd, Robert Crannel, John Corbett, John Stevens, Mary Parker, Joseph Prosser, and Richard Lloyd, MCM (1704–10), 498, 514, 519, 522, 538, 557; George Norton v. John Corbett, Joseph Prosser, John Stevens, and Henry Swift, 1710, MCPCU.

84. George Sydenham v. Vincient Delamontagne, 1700, MCP; MCM (1695–1704), 146, 153, 160, 162, 164, 179, 182. The two ended up in the Supreme Court, where Sydenham called the brickmaker John Ackerson as a witness against Delamontagne. Hamlin and Baker, *Supreme Court*, 2: 233. This was not the first time Sydenham had been to court to seek compensation following damages caused to his property by roving livestock. See George and Elizabeth Sydenham v. John Clapp, November 1698, and Clapp's rejoinder, both in New York City Mayor's Court, Box 42, Miscellaneous Manuscripts, New-York Historical Society.

85. John Finch v. John Guest, 1710, and Finch's affidavit that Guest was planning to leave for Philadelphia, MCP; William Glencross v. Benjamin Bill, mariner, 1711, MCP; Garret van Horne v. Jonathon Hunter, 1721, MCP; John Cruger v. George Nicholls, 1729, MCP.

86. Thomas Dobson v. John Munro, and William and Joseph Haynes v. John Munro, and John Scot v. John Munro, 1727, MCP.

87. When the city invited Ebbits to undertake subsequent repairs, the builder declined "unless the money his Work Shall amount to be paid him Weekly." Stokes, *Iconography*, 4: 448, 451.

88. *Colonial Laws*, 1: 7, 14, 159–60; Peter J. Coleman, *Debtors and Creditors in America: Insolvency, Imprisonment for Debt, and Bankruptcy, 1607–1900* (Madison, Wisc., 1974), 105–30; Rosen, *Courts and Commerce*, 52–53.

89. Gabriel Minvielle v. John Righton, 1700, MCP; MCM (1695–1704), 146, 153, 155.

90. For the difficult circumstances of a debtor assigned to work off her debt see the Petition of Mary Vanderige, CCP, 2: 2, also cited in Morris, *Government and Labor*, 359.

91. Rosen, "Courts and Commerce," 179.

92. Elizabeth Jarrat v. William Norman, 1700, MCP; Elizabeth Jarrat v. Rip Van Dam, MCM (1695–1704), 176, 177, 179, 182.

93. Wynaut van Zandt v. Johannes Ten Eyck, 1719, MCP; Richard Dyer v. Kenneth Cowan, 1720, and John Dunn v. Kenneth Cowan, 1720, MCP; Claude Boudewin, merchant, v. Bartholomew Feurt, mariner and formerly part owner of sloop *Katherine*, 1701, MCP.

94. Philip Cockrem v. John Jardin, 1720, with Charles and Katherine Jardine providing bail, MCP; Jacob Phoenix and his wife, Elizabeth, v. Mary Schamp, spinster, 1720, with John Stave and Jane Schamp, widow, providing bail, MCP; John Kramer v. Henry Vandewater, shoemaker, 1723, with William Beek, cordwainer, as bondsman, MCP; Dirk Benson v. Victor Bicker, bricklayer, 1722, with John Burger, bricklayer, providing bail, MCP.

95. The Mayor's Court Papers contain 177 bail agreements drawn up between 1710 and 1730, 136 of which include details on the occupations of bondsmen. Merchants provided bail in fifty-nine cases, tradesmen in fifty-two cases, and merchants and tradesmen in partnership in twenty-five cases. For examples, see Thomas Rawlings v. Samuel Gordon, bondmen Patrick Macknight, merchant, and Alexander Mills, barber, 1718, MCP; Peter Breasted v. Thomas Odell, bondsmen, Theophilus Elsworth, merchant, and Thomas Evans, bricklayer, 1719, MCP; David Wyatt, infant represented by Stephen Boux v. Richard Horwood, bondsmen, Henry DeWilde, mariner, and William Gilbert, baker, 1719, MCP.

96. On reputation, business, and gender in early America, see Mary Beth Norton, "Gender Defamation in Seventeenth-Century Maryland," *WMQ*, 3d ser., 44 (January 1987): 3–39, and for the later eighteenth century, see Toby Ditz, "Shipwrecked; or, Masculinity Imperilled: Mercantile Representations of Failure and the Gendered Self in Eighteenth-Century Philadelphia," *Journal of American History* 81 (June 1994): 51–80. For the notion of symbolic capital, see Bourdieu, *Outline of Theory and Practice*, 171–83.

Chapter 4

1. "Lord Cornbury to Secretary Hodges, 1705," *DHSNY*, 1: 711–12; "Lord Cornbury to the Board of Trade, 1 July 1708," *DRCNY*, 5: 59. For a recent rehabilitation of Cornbury's reputation as a governor and his dedication to the office, see Patricia U. Bonomi, *The Lord Cornbury Scandal: The Politics of Reputation in British America* (Chapel Hill, N.C., 1998), 58–99.

2. All the counties elected two representatives except New York, which elected four assemblymen. The three manors—Rensselaerswyck, Livingston, and Cortlandt—each sent one representative.

3. "Colonel Robert Quary to the Lords of Trade, 16 June 1703," *DRCNY*, 4: 1054; "Governor Hunter to Secretary St. John, 12 September 1711," *DRCNY*, 5: 255–56; Tully, *Forming American Politics*, 54–57; Bonomi, *Factious People*, 78–81.

4. Thus Nicholas Varga argues that the Assembly was little more than a quibbling "third wheel" at the turn of the eighteenth century and only really came into its own following the constitution crisis of the 1730s. See Nicholas Varga, "New York Government and Politics during the Mid Eighteenth Century" (Ph.D. diss., Fordham University, 1960), 51.

5. Kammen, *Colonial New York*, 162–67; Bridenbaugh, *Cities in the Wilderness*, 143, 303. Although convicted felons were often sent from the mother country as indentured servants, New York received only a tiny fraction of the total number. Most of the convicts wound up in the Chesapeake or the West Indies. Roger Ekirch,

Bound for America: The Transportation of English Convicts to the Colonies, 1718–1775 (Oxford, 1987), passim; Abbot Emerson Smith, *Colonists in Bondage: White Servitude and Convict Labor in America, 1607–1776* (Gloucester, Mass., 1965), 117; McKee, *Labor in Colonial New York*, 90–91.

6. "Instructions for the Earl of Bellomont, 31 August 1697," *DRCNY*, 4: 284–92. Also see John C. Rainbolt, "A 'great and usefull designe': Bellomont's Proposal for New York, 1698–1701," *New-York Historical Society Quarterly* 53 (October 1969): 335–37.

7. "Earl of Bellomont to the Lords of Trade, 17 April 1699," *DRCNY*, 4: 506.

8. Ibid., 504.

9. "Mr. Robert Livingston to the Lords of Trade, 13 May 1701," *DRCNY*, 4: 871–73.

10. "Governor Fletcher to the Lords of Trade, 10 June 1696," *DRCNY*, 4: 160; "Governor Fletcher to the Duke of Shrewsbury, 9 November 1696," *DRCNY*, 4: 233; "Governor Fletcher to Messrs. Brooke and Nicolls, 20 December 1696," *DRCNY*, 4: 247; "Governor Fletcher to the Lords of Trade, [no date, but c. 1696]," *DRCNY*, 4: 274; "Earl of Bellomont to the Lords of Trade, 22 June 1698," *DRCNY*, 4: 325; "Report of the Board of Trade on the Affairs of the Province of New York, 19 October 1698," *DRCNY*, 4: 394; "Letter from Peter De La Noy Relative to Governor Fletcher's Conduct, 13 June 1695," *DRCNY*, 4: 221.

11. "The Lords of Trade to the Earl of Bellomont, 23 February 1698," *DRCNY*, 4: 298; "Earl of Bellomont to the Lords of Trade, 25 May 1698," *DRCNY*, 4: 314.

12. "Lords of Trade to Bellomont, 19 September 1700," *DRCNY*, 4: 699–709; "Earl of Bellomont to the Lords of Trade, 14 December 1698," *DRCNY*, 4: 440; "Earl of Bellomont to the Lords of Trade, 17 April 1699," *DRCNY*, 4: 501–7; "Earl of Bellomont to the Lords of Trade, 15 May 1699," *DRCNY*, 4: 518; "Earl of Bellomont to the Lords of Trade, 22 July 1699," *DRCNY*, 4: 531–32; "Earl of Bellomont to the Lords of Trade, 20 October 1699," *DRCNY*, 4: 588–89; "Earl of Bellomont to the Lords of Trade, 22 June 1700," *DRCNY*, 4: 668–79.

13. "Earl of Bellomont to the Lords of Trade, 20 October 1699," *DRCNY*, 4: 588–89; "Earl of Bellomont to the Lords of Trade, 22 June 1700," *DRCNY*, 4: 668–79.

14. "Lords of Trade to Bellomont, 29 April 1701," *DRCNY*, 4: 852–53.

15. Fearing that he would be accused of acting beyond his authority by ever-watchful provincial opponents, the governor believed that he could only lay hold of the lands ceded by Fletcher once the Act was confirmed, which Parliament was slow to do. By 1700, Bellomont declared himself "amaz'd at the delay that's us'd in approving the [Vacating] Act of Assembly" that "raises the insolence of the faction here, and is a mortification to all those honest people that stood by me." See "Bellomont to Secretary Vernon, 6 December 1700," *DRCNY*, 4: 815–17.

16. "Mr. Robert Livingston to the Lords of Trade, 13 May 1701" *DRCNY*, 4: 871–75.

17. "Brigadier Hunter to the Board of Trade, 28 July 1720," and "The Conditions, Grievances, and Oppressions of the Germans, 1720," both in *DHSNY*, 2: 705–14. Also see A. G. Roeber, *Palatines, Liberty, and Property: German Lutherans in Colonial British America* (Baltimore, 1993), 9–12.

18. "Earl of Bellomont to the Lords of Trade, 28 November 1700," *DRCNY*, 4: 788.

19. "Bellomont to the Lords, 16 April 1699," *DRCNY*, 4: 505–6.

20. Harrison quoted in Hodges, *Root and Branch*, 79; "Mr. Colden's Account of the Trade of New York, 1723," *DRCNY*, 5: 688.

21. "Churchwardens and Vestry of Trinity Church, New-York, to Archbishop Tenison, 22 May 1699," *DRCNY*, 4: 526–28. The tiny Anglican congregation lacked its own place of worship until the opening of Trinity Church in 1698. Even then it was dwarfed by the 450 families who worshipped in the Dutch Reformed Church.

22. Brown, *Good Wives*, 110–12. Also see Thelma Wills Foote, *Black and White Manhattan: The History of Racial Formation in Colonial New York City* (New York, 2004), introduction. For a stimulating discussion of the manner in which law names, blames, and claims inside formal and informal settings as official orders and regulations and, critically for our purposes, as repetitive practices that gain local acceptance, see Tomlins and Mann, *Many Legalities of Early America*, introduction. Also see Lüdtke, *History of Everyday Life*, introduction, and Michel De Certeau, *The Practice of Everyday Life* (Berkeley, Calif., 1988), 1–3.

23. At least four hundred slaves were delivered to New Amsterdam between 1660 and 1664, and by the time of the English takeover slaves constituted approximately one-fifth of the city's population. Goodfriend, "Burghers and Blacks," 138.

24. Hodges, *Root and Branch*, 35–43.

25. In the 1690s, the term "black" was as easily applied as an epithet by the English Party to their opponents in the Leiserian or "Black Party" as it was to African American workers. "Lord Cornbury to the Lords of Trade, 9 September 1703," *DRCNY*, 4: 1071.

26. "Instructions for the Earl of Bellomont, 31 August 1697," *DRCNY*, 4: 290. For examples of free and enslaved black resistance to white commands and violence see MCM (1677–82), 207; on black families, see Joyce Goodfriend, "Black Families in New Netherland," in Zeller, ed., *A Beautiful and Fruitful Place*, 147–55; Henry B. Hoff, "Researching African-American Families in New Netherland and Colonial New York and New Jersey," *NYGBR* 136 (April 2005): 83–97.

27. For Cresee's case, see MCM (1682–95), 282, 287, 292, 295. His butcher supporters were Joachim Rowlandson, Claus Gysberg, and David Valentine. For a similar case from 1677, see the account of William Corwan's suit for his freedom against the mariner Thomas Thatcher in Hodges, *Root and Branch*, 37.

28. "Number of Negroes Imported from 1701–1726," *DHSNY*, 1: 707. For slave population percentages in proportion to whites and the surge in imports after Queen Anne's War, see Goodfriend, *Before the Melting Pot*, 76, 113; Hodges, *Root and Branch*, 41; Matson, *Merchants and Empire*, 202.

29. William Bradford v. George Elsworth Jr., 1722, MCP; Elizabeth Berton v. Mattyse Nicholas, blacksmith, 1724, MCP; Dennis Riche v. Samuel Rout, baker, 1728, MCP. For the slowing of manumissions after 1700, see Hodges, *Root and Branch*, 36. Peter Christoph found that the parcel of land that remained in one black family's hands the longest was that patented to Pieter Santomee in 1644, which was ultimately sold by his daughter-in-law and grandchildren in 1716 and which now forms part of Gramercy Park. See Christoph, "Freedmen of New Amsterdam," 165.

30. Scott, *New York Court Records*, 1–19; Peter Charles Hoffer, *The Great New York Conspiracy of 1741: Slavery, Crime, and Colonial Law* (Lawrence, Kans., 2003), 30–31.

31. As the details leaked out, New Yorkers learned that a group of Coroman-tine, Yoruba, and Angolan slaves had plotted to raise an alarm and murder all those who attended. The conspiracy reflected the influence of African beliefs and cosmol-ogy: the plotters had used sorcery to protect themselves, rubbing a magic powder on their clothes and sucking blood from each other's hands to seal the plot. There was also evidence of the unifying force of Christian despair, as many of the conspirators had been denied access to catechism classes run by Elias Neau, a Huguenot refugee who had established an Anglican mission for the instruction of local slaves nine years earlier. The Reverend John Sharp noted, "the Persons whose Negroes have been found guilty are such as declared opposers of Christianizing Negroes." See Hodges, *Root and Branch*, 60–62.

32. Kenneth Scott, "The Slave Insurrection in New York in 1712," *New-York Historical Society Quarterly* 45 (1961): 45–67.

33. "Hunter to Board of Trade, 15 November 1715," *DRCNY*, 5: 460–61; Sam's bond mentioned in Scott, *New York Records*, 32.

34. Thereafter the differential punishments accorded white and black crimi-nals was just one more indication of divisions within the city's racialized urban order. For example, the hatter Jacob Swan received a two shilling fine for his assault on Trintie Thurman; Andrew Andrewson, who stole a pair of spectacles and their case from John Mackenan, was sentenced to be whipped "until his body bleeds, [or] two or three times" at the judge's discretion. However, when two slave women, Betty and Franks, were convicted of stealing a brass kettle, valued at tenpence, from John Cooke, they were sentenced to be stripped from the waist upward and receive forty lashes at the tail of a cart: five at the city hall, five at the corner of Wall Street, five at Burgers Path, five at the corner of Vincent Street, five at the corner of Broadway, five at the corner of Beaver Street, five by the English Church, and five on their return to city hall. *MCC*, 1: 267, 389; 3: 153; Rex v. Betty and Rex v. Frank, 5 May 1719, in Min-utes of the Court of Quarter Sessions (3 May 1715–11 February 1721), in Columbia University Rare Books Library. Also see Hodges, *Root and Branch*, 47–52.

35. The best survey of the diverse functions of early eighteenth-century municipal government remains Peterson and Edwards, *New York as a Municipality*, 40–125.

36. For example the case of Teunis Tiebout in the preceding chapter; for the sale of digging privileges on public commons, see *MCC*, 2: 110, 113, 126–28; Johannes Edsall v. Hendryk Cordas, brickmaker, 1706, MCPCU.

37. The following week, James Harding secured another term as ferrymaster. Harding had started out as a cooper and was elected a petty constable before secur-ing the ferry franchise. See CCP, 1:13; NYHS, Collections (1885), 74; Scott, *New York Court Records*, 96. For a similar competition in 1729 for the office of keeper of the ammunition store and the presentations made by the three candidates—Edward Man, Robert Crannel, and Garret Viele—see CCP, 2: 11; 3: 1. Also see Bridenbaugh, *Cities in the Wilderness*, 207, 213, 218, 232, 239; Hendrick Hartog, *Public Property and Private Power: The Corporation of the City of New York in American Law, 1730–1870* (Chapel Hill, N.C., 1983), ch. 1.

38. Jacobus van Cortland v. Jeremiah Callcutt, 8 January 1712, MCM (1710–15), 168–70, 174; NYHS, Collections (1885), 82; *NYGBR* (July 1968), 158.

39. "Abstract of Colonial Commissions, 1677–1770" and "Cadwallader Colden to William Burnet, 19 January 1721," New York Colonial Manuscripts (hereafter NY Col Mss), 102 vols., 63: 16, 33. Both in the New York State Archives, Albany.

40. The committee noted a revenue of £1, 095 from duties collected in the two years prior to Colden's appointment in 1717. Of this, £803 had been paid to the provincial treasury, £22 charged for "reasonable . . . incidents," and the balance of £270 retained for the salaries and costs of the weighmaster. However, scrutiny of Graham's accounts revealed that all but £4 of the sum claimed by the weighmaster as his salary was owed to him by eighty-one city merchants ranging from substantial traders such as Stephen Delancey, and Abraham van Horne to smaller operators such as Patrick MacKnight and Walter Thong. See NY Col Mss, 60: 175; 61: 80, 88, 89; 62: 6, 7, 97; 63: 30–32.

41. MCM (1710–15), 174.

42. The court gave Spencer the authority to detain offenders, hold their property, and bring them before the mayor. *MCC*, 2: 198; Scott, *New York Court Records*, 12; "Hunter, to the Board of Trade, 12 November 1715," *DRCNY*, 5: 459.

43. Robert Seyboldt, *The Colonial Citizen of New York* (Madison, Wisc., 1917); Beverly MacAnear, "The Place of the Freeman in Colonial New York," *New York History* 21 (1940): 418–30; Milton Klein, *Politics of Diversity: Essays in the History of Colonial New York* (Port Washington, 1974), 21–23, 32; Graham Hodges, "Legal Bonds of Attachment," in *Slavery, Freedom, and Culture Among Early American Workers* (Armonk, N.J., 1988), 3–19.

44. "An Act for the Settling of Ffaires and Marquets in Each Respective Citty," in *Colonial Laws*, 1: 296–98; *MCC*, 1: 103, 222, 228, 248, 264, 373, 394; *MCC*, 2: 31; Scott, *New York Court Records*, 11, 13; MacAnear, "Place of the Freemen," 420–421.

45. MacAnear, "Place of the Freemen," 421.

46. *MCC*, 2: 431. In 1713, Elias Chardavine was disqualified as the elected constable of the West Ward because he was not a freeman, and he did not register himself as such for a further three years. A 1720 schedule of twenty-eight municipal officers includes the names of eight men who only became freemen following their election and seven others for whom there is no record of their ever registering with the city. A third or more of the seventy-five men elected to municipal office in the contested elections of 1734 were not freemen. See Guterman, "Ancient Freemen," 115, 235; MacAnear, "Place of the Freeman," 422.

47. NYHS, Collections (1885), 76, 97, 108; William Smith v. Richard Moore, 1709, MCP; George Ashton v. John Gibson, 1725, MCP.

48. Samuel Pell registered for his freemanship two years after hiring William Ladd, who resided in New Jersey and worked off and on in the city during the 1720s without ever securing permission from the municipal government. Other details are in Enoch Aymes v. Dirck van der Burgh, 1701 MCP; William Ladd v. Joseph Latham and Samuel Pell, 1721 MCP; Peter Barberie v. William Ladd, 1723, MCP; James Alexander v. William Ladd, 1723, MCP; NYHS, Collections (1885), 98, 103. Also see use of nonfreeman as subcontractors in Paulus De Scher v. John Hybon, 1729, MCP; Luke Peek v. Charles Jandine, 1729, MCP.

49. NYHS, Collections (1885), 460–61; Hartog, *Public Property*, 38.

50. Waldron petition is in CCP, 1: 7. Also see "Petition of William Bogard to Be

Treasurer of the City of New York," CCP, 1: 5; "Petition of Sarah Vanaernam, widow," for a piece of ground with her house and garden on, CCP, 1: 12; "Petition of Inhabitants of Burghers Path for a market," CCP, 1: 10; "Petition of the Inhabitants of Broad Street," CCP, 1: 9; Norton's petition is in *MCC*, 2: 352; John Marsh's petition for liberty to build a mill near Hell's Gate, *MCC*, 2: 112; "Petition of the inhabitants of South Ward for a market," and "of the inhabitants of the East Ward for a market at Clorhos Slip" and of "Capt DePeyster [and others] . . . on behalf of themselves and other inhabitants," requesting the city to fill in a certain pier, all in CCP, 1: 13, 14; Abraham Delanoy, a baker, for "liberty to build an oven under the ground fronting his house," *MCC*, 3: 46; "Petition of Roger Baker for a Slip of Ground in Smith's Street," CCP, 1:10.

51. Stokes, *Iconography*, 4: 472. Hodges, "Legal Bonds of Attachment," 226–42. Also see the claims concerning baking and grain shortages following the end of Queen Anne's War in 1714. *MCC*, 3: 87; Scott, *New York Court Records*, 34.

52. Historians have long noted the beginnings of a decline in the system of apprenticeship in the early eighteenth century, but they have struggled for an explanation beyond general claims regarding youthful restlessness and the ineluctable waning of early modern labor practices. For example, see McKee, *Labor in Colonial New York*, 62–63; Kammen, *Colonial New York*, 182.

53. Van Zweiten, "Orphan Chamber,", 319–40.

54. *Colonial Laws*, 1: 26, 158–59; *MCC*, 1: 373–74; NYHS, Collections (1885), 461, 464–65; McKee, *Labor in Colonial New York*, 62–65; Morris, *Government and Labor*, 363–89.

55. The 1695–1707 register details 108 indentures, and the 1718–27 an additional 169. The following draws upon the analysis in Ronald W. Howard, "Apprenticeship and Economic Education in New Netherland and Seventeenth-Century New York," in Zeller, ed., *A Beautiful and Fruitful Place*, 205–18 and Guterman, "Ancient Freemen," 183–86. The examples given are drawn from the "Indentures of Apprenticeships, 9 February 1694 to 24 January 1708," in NYHS, Collections (1885), 565–622, and "Indentures of Apprenticeships, 21 October 1718 to 7 August 1727," NYHS, Collections (1909), 113–99.

56. Garret van Laer v. John Dunlap 1709, MCP; Abraham Gouverneur v. William Galt, 1712, MCP; Kenneth Scott, "Church Wardens," 161. Also see "New York City Assessment Roll," *NYGBR* (October 1964): 199; NYHS, Collections (1885), 97. In February 1720, Dunlap joined Thomas Hodges, also a cordwainer, as a bondsman for John Deare to satisfy Richard Bishop in a suit for twenty pounds; the following year, Dunlap sued Michael Spragg for nonpayment of thirty pounds, and Spragg was forced to call upon John Dyer, a tallow chandler, and Thomas Mortimer, a cordwainer, to put up bond guaranteeing the debt. See John Dunlap v. Richard Higgins, 1719, MCP; John Dunn v. John Deprees, 1721, MCP; John Dunlap v. Michael Spragge, 1721, MCP; Scott, *New York Court Records*, 94, 107.

57. Also see the agreement between Brandt Schuyler, a merchant, and John Packer, in 1701, under which Packer agreed to "Serve in doing and performing all Such Bricklayers worke" in return for twenty-five pounds and "Meate Drinke Apparell washing and Lodging and all other things meet and Convenient for a Servant." NYHS, Collections (1885), 599. For apprentices and masters suing following the

breakdown of indentures specifying agreed wages, see Enoch Hill v. George Stanton, 1701, MCP; Ephraim Sylvester v. John Bailey, 1727, MCP; Charles Jandine, carpenter v. William Jones, 1728, MCP; James Wallace v. James Wiley, 1738, MCP.

58. In March 1694, the Assembly referred a petition by city coopers to the Common Council on the grounds that "the matter contained in the said petition does not lye before this House." Five years later, however, the assemblymen legislated in favor of the city coopers' cause. See *Journal of the Votes and Proceedings of the General Assembly* 1: 38–39, 98. For Dirck van der Burgh and the standard of local bricks, see "An Act to Ascertain the Size of Casks, Weights and Measures, and Bricks, within This Colony," *Colonial Laws*, 5: 554–57. The act was reported by Lord Cornbury at the time as evidence of the growing anglicization of the colony and has been described by historians in like manner. See "Lord Cornbury to the Lords of Trade, July 12, 1703," *DRCNY*, 4: 1064–65; Goodfriend, *Before the Melting Pot*, 187.

59. The revenue of the city declined from 731 pounds in 1722 to an average well below 300 pounds by 1730 David T. Valentine, "Financial History of the City of New York, from the Earliest Period," in *Manual* (1859), 506, cited in Hartog, *Public Property*, 33; *Colonial Laws* 2: 596–97.

60. *Journal of the Votes and Proceedings of the General Assembly*,1: 220–25, 228; "Petition for additional ferry between N.Y. and Long Island," *DHSNY*, 3: 422–27; *MCC*, 2: 221–22, 278, 341–45; Hartog, *Public Property*, 16, 26–27.

61. Hartog, *Public Property*, ch. 1.

62. *Colonial Laws*, 4: 121; Hartog, *Public Property*, 40; McKee, *Labor in Colonial New York*, 87–88

Chapter 5

1. Jacob Fairen v. John Demares, 1699, MCP; MCM (1695–1704), 136. For Barne Cosens's background and his activities in the Hudson River town courts, see Hamlin and Baker, *Supreme Court*, 1: 52–64.

2. See for example, Paul S. Seaver, *Wallington's World: A Puritan Artisan in Seventeenth Century London* (Stanford, Calif., 1985); Patrick Collinson and John Craig, eds., *The Reformation in English Towns, 1500–1640* (Basingstoke, 1998); Christopher Hill, *Society and Puritanism in Pre-Revolutionary England* (London, 1991), 129; Van Deursen, *Plain Lives*, ch. 15.

3. For the importance of Grotius in English political theory and the broader meaning of property in seventeenth-century debate, see Richard Tuck, *Natural Rights Theories: Their Origin and Development* (Cambridge, 1979); Haakonssen, *Natural Law and Moral Philosophy*, 15–61; James Tully, *An Approach to Political Philosophy: Locke in Contexts* (Cambridge, 1993), 118–36; John Brewer and Susan Staves, eds., *Early Modern Conceptions of Property* (London, 1996); Ashcraft, *Revolutionary Politics*, 119–46.

4. As late as 1751, Malachy Postlethwayt argued that "the ingenuity and dexterity of [England's] working artists and manufacturers . . . [was] owing to that freedom and liberty they enjoy to divert themselves in their own way . . . Were they obliged to toil the year round, the whole six days in a week, in repetition of the same

work, might it not blunt their ingenuity and render them stupid instead of alert and dexterous." Cited in Christopher Hill, "Pottage for Freeborn Englishmen: Attitudes Towards Wage-Labour," in *Change and Continuity in Seventeenth-Century England* (1974; reprint, New Haven, Conn., 1991), 234; Tully, *Locke in Contexts*, 71–96; John Rule, "The Property of Skill in the Period of Manufacture," in Joyce ed., *The Historical Meanings of Work*, 99–119; Daniel Vickers, "Competency and Competition: Economic Culture in Early America," *WMQ*, 3d ser., 47 (1990): 4.

5. *Colonial Laws*, 1: 226.

6. David Thomas Konig, *Law and Society in Puritan Massachusetts: Essex County, 1629–1692* (Chapel Hill, N.C., 1979), especially chs. 1, 4; John Rushton Pagan, *Anne Orthwood's Bastard: Sex and Law in Early Virginia* (New York, 2003), passim; Lawrence M. Friedman, *A History of American Law* (New York, 1973), chs. 1–3.

7. Goebel, "Courts and the Law in Colonial New York," 3: 1–43; Kammen, *Colonial New York*, 128–29; Herbert A. Johnson, "The Advent of Common Law in Colonial New York," in *Essays on Colonial New York Legal History* (Westport, Conn., 1981), 37–55.

8. Pagan, *Anne Orthwood's Bastard*, 69.

9. C.W. Brooks, *Pettyfoggers and Vipers of the Commonwealth: The "Lower" Branch of the Legal Profession in Early Modern England* (Cambridge, 1986), 30–47.

10. For the early modern English fascination with ancient pedigrees and immemoriality, see Pocock, *Ancient Constitution*, ch. 2.

11. For differing assessments of the causes for the decline in King's Bench litigation, compare F. W. Maitland, *English Law and the Renaissance* (Cambridge, 1901), and W. A. Holdsworth, *History of English Law*, 17 vols. (London, 1903–72), 4: 253–59, and Marjorie Blatcher, *The Court of King's Bench, 1450–1550: A Study in Self Help* (London, 1978), ch. 5, with Brooks, *Pettyfoggers and Vipers*, 75–93. Scholars who trace a decline in litigation before the courts of King's Bench and Common Pleas attribute it to the availability of more popular remedies offered in the Court of Chancery. For example, and ironically given the transformation of legal practice in late seventeenth-century New York, the Court of Chancery was preferred because of its inquisitorial approach, which offered a more amenable and speedy resolution than the common law's restrictive writ system and jury trial requirement. Indeed, Marjorie Blatcher characterizes the proceedings in Chancery as "Romanized" and closer to the Roman-Dutch law as practiced in the United Provinces. Blatcher, *King's Bench*, 24–33.

12. The fiction worked equally well for defendants who had never set foot in the county because, once the arrest warrant was issued, the sheriff would return to report that, unsurprisingly, the defendant was "not found" (*non est inventus*). The plaintiff would then return to court and assert that the defendant "lurks and runs about" (*latitat et discurrit*) in, let's say, Yorkshire, and the court would issue a writ to the appropriate local officer instructing them to detain the person named. By the early seventeenth century, the procedure was so common that the court regularly issued the *latitat et discurrit* at the outset, assuming that the trespass in Middlesex had already been declared, and the sherrif would retunr to court to declare *non est inventus*. See J. H. Baker, *Introduction to English Legal History* (London, 1979), 36–41; Blatcher, *King's Bench*, ch. 7.

13. In real actions the plaintiff complained of a wrong committed against him

or her, which the common law court aimed to rectify. Wrongs that could not be put right sounded in tort and trespass and were dealt with by a second family of writs concerned with the punishment and compensation for uncorrectable injustices. As J. H. Baker has it, whereas a common law writ ordered the defendant to do right or else explain himself, a trespass writ summoned the defendant to come and explain why he had committed a wrong that could not be put right. *Introduction*, 56.

14. Ibid., 90–92. On the ramifications of this struggle through the seventeenth century, see Mike McNair, "Common Law and Statutory Imitations of Equitable Relief under the Later Stuarts," in C. W. Brooks and Michael Lobban, eds., *Communities and the Courts in Britain, 1150–1900* (London, 1997), 115–31.

15. This supposition has been traced to two fifteenth-century fictions that provided the grounds for common lawyers to assert that a trespass had occurred and a wrong committed. A. W. B. Simpson, *History of the Common Law: The Rise of Assumpsit* (Oxford, 1975), 125–270. The first fiction asserted that officeholders or tradesmen had a duty to undertake their tasks with due care and attention and that failure to do so constituted an actionable wrong; the second contended that the defendant had purposefully set out to deceive or trick an individual into an agreement or purchase that they otherwise would not have made. By the sixteenth century, it was usual to allege an implied duty to perform a stated task, and the attempted deception or trickery, as a matter of course in order to establish a legal case to answer at common law.

16. By the late seventeenth century, and partly owing to the easing of venue rules, juries functioned less and less as bodies of locally knowledgeable men and more as panels charged with assessing the facts of a case as they were presented in the manner prescribed by the law. Simpson, *History of the Common Law*, 599–620; Baker, *Introduction*, 272–87; Holdsworth, *History of English Law*, 6: 388.

17. It has been argued that the reforms advanced the interests of creditors and the powerful over ordinary debtors. The rise of actions in assumpsit and jury adjudication in place of the older writ of debt prompted the demise of compurgation or wager law which had generally favored poorer defendants. Simpson, *History of the Common Law*, 139–42, 297–300; W. A. Champion, "Recourse to the Law and the Meaning of the Great Litigation Decline, 1650–1750: Some Clues from the Shrewsbury Local Courts," in Brooks and Lobban, eds., *Communities and the Courts in Britain*, 179–199; C. W. Brooks, "Interpersonal Conflict and Social Tension: Civil Litigation in England, 1640–1830," in A. L. Beier, David Cannadine, and James M. Rosenheim, eds., *The First Modern Society: Essays in English History in Honour of Lawrence Stone* (Cambridge, 1989), 357–99.

18. Michael Braddick, *State Formation and Early Modern England c. 1500–1700* (Cambridge, 2000), 159; Amy Louise Erickson, *Women and Property in Early Modern England* (London, 1993), 102–14, 174–17, 237–41; David E. Underdown, "The Taming of the Scold: The Enforcement of Patriarchal Authority in Early Modern England," in Anthony Fletcher and John Stevenson, eds., *Order and Disorder in Early Modern England* (Cambridge, 1985), 116–36.

19. Edward P. Thompson, *Customs in Common: Studies in Traditional Popular Culture* (New York, 1991), 128–29, 135; E. P. Thompson, *Whigs and Hunters: The Origin of the Black Act* (1975; reprint, London, 1990), 258–69; Christopher Hill, *Liberty Against the Law: Some Seventeenth-Century Controversies* (London, 1996), part v.

20. For example, see Alan Cromartie, "The Constitutionalist Revolution: The Transformation of Political Culture in Early Stuart England," *Past and Present*, no. 163 (May 1999), 76–120.

21. For terminology of social simplification, see Keith Wrightson, *English Society, 1580–1680* (1982; reprint, London, 1993), ch. 1, and his "Estates, Degrees, and Sorts: Changing Perceptions of Society in Tudor and Stuart England," in Penelope Corfield, ed., *Language, History, and Class* (Oxford, 1991), 32–44, which is revisited in "'Sorts of People' in Tudor and Stuart England," in Jonathon Barry and Christopher Brooks, eds., *The Middling Sort of People: Culture, Society, and Politics in England, 1550–1800* (Basingstoke, 1994), 28–51.

22. The problems inherent in the identification of a particular era of transition were evident in the debate concerning the individualistic and/or communitarian nature of eighteenth- and early nineteenth-century American law. See William Nelson, *The Americanization of the Common Law, 1760–1830* (1974; reprint, Athens, Ga., 1994); Morton Horowitz, *The Transformation of American Law 1780–1860* (Cambridge, Mass., 1977) and the critiques of these interpretations in Mann, *Neighbors and Strangers*, introduction, and Rosen, *Courts and Commerce*, 59–74; Stanley Katz, "Colonial American Legal History," in Greene and Pole, eds., *Colonial British America*, 457–91.

23. For studies that trace the contests over property rights, see Andy Wood, *Politics of Social Conflict* (Cambridge, 1999), and his *Riot and Rebellion and Popular Politics in Early Modern England* (Basingstoke, 2002), 82–112; Brian Manning, *The English People and the English Revolution*, (1976; reprint, London, 1991), ch. 6; J. M Neeson, *Commoners: Common Right, Enclosure, and Social Change in England, 1700–1820* (Cambridge, 1993), 191; John Rule, *The Experience of Labor in Eighteenth-Century Industry* (London, 1981), 194.

24. I have borrowed the metaphor of sedimentation from Steve Hindle, *State and Social Change*, introduction.

25. For example, see Jacob Melyns v. Stephen Cregoe, shipmaster, 7 August 1683, MCM (1682–95), 65. When Melyns sued Crego for failure to deliver twenty-two pounds of silver plate, Cregoe hired the English-trained lawyer John Tudor, who tried various approaches to impede the suit. First he requested more time to prepare the witnesses, but the court refused and went ahead with impaneling a jury. Then he argued that because the contract was made on the "high seas," Melyn's action could only be heard in a Court of Admiralty. Next he invoked a minor variance in the pleading, declaring that his client was "arrested to answer an action on the case and declared agt in *trespass* on the case." Having exhausted the procedural niceties, Tudor turned to the substance of the suit, which he declared invalid. Cregoe and Tudor lost the case but won on appeal following the discovery of compelling "new evidence." For John Tudor's legal training, see Paul Hamlin, *Legal Education in Colonial New York* (New York, 1970), 5. Also see James Graham acting for the plaintiff in William Moore v. Edward Read, 15 January 1683, MCM (1682–95), 89–90. On the distinction between actions of trespass and trespass on the case, see Baker, *Introduction*, 57–59.

26. "An Act for the Establishing Courts of Judicature for the Ease and Benefitt of Each Respective Citty Town and County within This Province," in *Colonial Laws* 1: 226. Hamlin and Baker, *Supreme Court*, 1: 3–78; Richard B. Morris, *Select Cases of the Mayor's Court of New York City, 1674–1784* (Washington, D.C., 1935), 40–48; Moglen, "Settling the Law," 53–57.

27. John Finch's affidavit, 1710, MCP; William Provoost v. John Guest, 1710, MCP; William Thibaux v. John Guest, 1710, MCP. For similar affidavits, see John Vreedenburgh, a carpenter, on George Booth's departure to England, 1709, MCP; Tucker Mansfred on Anthony Farmer's voyage to Newfoundland, 1716, MCP; Anthony Webb, a baker, on Thomas Bankes's departure to Providence, 1722, MCP; and the glover Thomas Dobson's declaration that the butcher Michael Hamlin was making plans to move to Shrewsbury, in New Jersey, 1724, MCP.

28. The discussion of legal process in this and the following paragraph relies on Rosen, "Courts and Commerce," 41–51.

29. Bellomont's revision of the jury law was undertaken at the behest of the king and the act was affirmed in 1710, 1726, and 1729. Hamlin and Baker, *Supreme Court*, 1: 178–79, 112–37; *Colonial Laws*, 1: 708, 1021; 2: 345; Morris, *Select Cases*, 31. In 1741, the proportion of adult white males excluded rose again, so that less than one fourth of men met the property qualifications to sit on a jury. Deborah Rosen found that 67 percent of jurors were drawn from the ranks of propertied tradesmen in the 1710s and that this figure fell to 51 percent by the 1730s.

30. "Colonel William Smith to the Earl of Bellomont, 26 November 1700," *DRCNY*, 4: 828. The revisions of the Mayor's Court rules are in MCM (1695–1704), 199–202. Also see Morris, *Select* Cases, 75–77. In Hamlin and Baker, *Supreme Court*, the appendix details the introduction of procedural rules in 1699, 1702, 1703, 1704, 1706, 1721, 1722, 1727, and 1730.

31. Chief Justice Smith's report is qualified, however, by Bellomont's assessment of him as "no sort of lawyer, having been bred a soldier" and someone who lived "four score mile off, and comes but twice a year to this town . . . just to earn his sallary." "Colonel William Smith to the Earl of Bellomont, 26 November 1700," *DRCNY*, 4: 828–29.

32. For the venue rule, see George Lockhart v. David Mudy, 1685, MCP; John Adams v. Elias Haskett, 1687, MCP. For the earliest examples of suits commenced as actions of trespass upon the case, see Joseph Benbrigg v. Thomas Hook, 1686, MCP; David Mudy v. James Wayes, 20 March 1684, MCM (1682–95), 143.

33. Abraham Wendal v. Frans Wenne, 1713, MCP; Thomas Griggs v. Edward Griffiths, 1729, MCP. Covenants were also used by ships masters and captains when engaging mariners. Thus in 1701 Robert Meers, master of the *Unity* sailing between Antigua, New York, and London, sued two of his mariners, James Bell and David Bird, for failing to adhere to their agreement to serve for forty shillings in "Current money of Carolina (p month)." Robert Meers v. James Bell and David Bird, 1701, MCP; also see Peter Jacobus Marius v. Johannes Groendyke, for breach of covenant relating to the lease of a house, 1698, MCP; John Ackerson v. Edmond Heynes, concerning the division of profits from a summer's brickmaking, 1702, MCP; Jacobus Kronkheyt and wife Elizabeth v. Johanes Van Norden, a baker, for nonpayment of a year's rent on a house, 1710, MCP; Samuel Chahane v. Mary Thompson, for nonpayment of four years' rent for half a house on Pearl St., 1712, MCP.

34. If there was any money found to be owing after the reckoning, the plaintiff could recover the amount under an action in debt. For example, see Henry De Meyer v. John Read and Joseph Read Executors of will of Thomas George, 1720, MCP; Jasper Bush v. Isaac Bellow, 1722, MCP. For actions of account in England, see Simpson, *History of the Common Law*, 177.

35. Andries Barhyt v. Joost Sooy, 1724, MCP.

36. Rosen, "Courts and Commerce," 143.

37. This approximation accords with the impression gained from Rosen's findings based on an analysis of the minute books that record a similar proportion of actions in assumpsit of all suits submitted to jury trial. Ibid., 122–23.

38. Daniel Bonnet v. Richard Herring, 1724, MCP.

39. Philip Travis v. Cornelius Dirckse, 1710, MCP.

40. Jeremiah Marshall v. John Hickford and Adolph Degrove, 1718, MCP. For other examples of concerns for wage differentials, see Samuel Browne v. John Searle, master of the *Content*, for work "as a mariner" at the rate of two pounds, two shillings per month, 1715, MCP; George Farrington v. John Searle, for service "as a Boat coxwaine" aboard the *Content* at the rate of three pounds, twelve shillings, and sixpence per month, 1720, MCP. Other examples include Jacob Swan, hatter v. Edmund Thomas, victualler, 1707, MCP; Luke Peek v. Charles Jandine, 1710, MCP; John Harris, mariner v. Jacob Booker, master of the *Phoenix*, 1720, MCP; Mathew Parry v. Henry Coerten, 1719, MCP; Daniel Riche v. John Stout, 1721, MCP; Patrick Jackson v. Cornelius de Peyster, 1726, MCP.

41. William Jones v. Charles Jandine, 1728, MCP; Charles Jandine v. William Jones, 1728, MCP.

42. J. C. D. Clark, *Language of Liberty, 1660–1800: Political Discourse and Social Dynamics in the Anglo-American* World (Cambridge, 1993), 5.

43. Patricia U. Bonomi, *Under the Cope of Heaven. Religion, Society, and Politics in Colonial America* (New York, 1984), 52–54, 56; Jon Butler, *Awash in a Sea of Faith: Christianizing the American People* (Cambridge, Mass., 1990), ch. 2.

44. Barristers-at-Law included George Farewell, Alexander Griffith, John Guest, Francis Hall, Thomas Johnson, Mathias Nicolls, Thomas Owen, John Palmer, John Spragge, and John Stevens. College attendees and graduates: William Anderson, John Holden, and John West. Those with a liberal education included Edward Anthill, Isaac Arnold, Nicholas Bayard, Barne Cosens, Samuel Edsall, James Emmot, James Graham, William Huddleton, David Jamison, John Rider, William Sharpas, Isaac Swinton, John Tudor, and Samuel Winder. For the full lists, see Hamlin, *Legal Education*, appendix 2.

45. Of the 127 extant complaints drawn up between 1680 and 1695, only 57 identify an attorney at the time of filing, and, of these, more than half (35) identified either John Tudor, James Emmot, or Isaac Swinton as the attorney.

46. For example, James Graham had served on Andros's provincial council and was imprisoned with the Dominion's governor in Boston before making his way back to New York, where he served as Benjamin Fletcher's attorney general. David Jamison served as clerk of the council during Fletcher's administration and on the first vestry of Trinity Church. "Earl of Bellomont to the Lords of Trade, 17 October 1700," *DRCNY*, 4: 719; "Governor Robert Hunter to Lords of Trade, 7 May 1711," *DRCNY*, 5: 208. For English Party support among English lawyers, see Howe, "Accommodation and Retreat," appendix A.

47. "Petition of Onzel van Zweiten and John Crugar to have councel assigned," NY Coll Mss, 41: 81. The bill was defeated, but a subsequent act limited litigants to two attorneys per case. Hamlin and Baker, *Supreme Court*, 1: 84; Hamlin, *Legal Education*, 135–50. The case of De Peyster v. Van Zweiten and Cruger rolled on (and on)

and its effects were felt in De Peyster's will, which provided for bequests to his brother and the English, Dutch, and French churches on the condition that he won the case. See Wills in New York State Archives, Liber 12: 156.

48. "Earl of Bellomont to the Lords of Trade, 15 December 1698," *DRCNY,* 4: 441–42.

49. Julius Goebel identified the critical period of legal change as beginning after 1700 and especially after 1714. Goebel, "Courts and the Law in Colonial New York," 3: 35–37.

50. In July 1719, John Marsh sued Clement Elsworth for wages of eleven pounds and one shilling for "the work of him the said John as a mason." Before the complaint was filed with the court, however, "mason" was crossed out, and Marsh was identified as a carpenter, see MCP. The first draft of Luke Peek's complaint against Charles Jandine, in 1710, declared his claim for wages following service as a "carpenter" and then, further down the page, as a "carpenter and joiner." Peek's lawyer, John Chambers, made sure to insert "joiner" in the first part of the declaration before matters progressed. Luke Peek v. Charles Jandine, 1710, MCP.

51. On common law writs and procedures, see F. W. Maitland, *The Forms of Action at the Common Law* (Cambridge, 1936), 1–13. Mathew Hale quoted in Baker, *Introduction,* 74. Defendants were also constrained in their presentation and in response to a writ of assumpsit could only assert that the debt was paid or deny its existence "in manner and form."

52. Daniel Ebbits v. Susanna Elliot, MCM (1695–1704), 212–16; Susanna Elliot v. Ebbits, 1702, MCP.

53. Christina Beenvos, widow v. Hendrik Gerrits, MCM (1710–15), 25–27, 271. Also see Garret van Laer v. John Dunlap, 1710, MCP; Thomas Willet v. Philip Battin, butcher, MCM (1710–15), 14; Rynmerick Vanderburgh and Henry Vandenburgh, executors of the estate of Dirck van der Burgh, v. Arian Clavar, MCM (1710–15), 15–17.

54. In fact, Hunter was well within his authority, as was confirmed by the Lords of Trade and his council, who declared that since "the trust of the Scales . . . constitute a Chancellor . . . there can be noe Chancellor but himself." Hunter later acknowledged that the assemblymen's denunciation was a purely political act designed to embolden their authority by insisting that he include them in the authorization for the court, something the governor refused to do because he recognized that it would have "Complimented the Assembly with the powers granted by Her Majesty to the Govr and Councill." "Governor Hunter to the Lords of Trade, 7 May 1711," *DRCNY,* 5: 208. For the beginnings of chancery courts in New York, see *Calendar of Council Minutes,* 157–60, 202; Stanley N. Katz, "Politics of Law in Colonial America: Controversies over Chancery Courts and Equity Law in the Eighteenth Century," in *Perspectives in American History,* vol. 5 (Cambridge, Mass., 1971), 273.

55. "Governor Hunter to the Lords of Trade, 7 May 1711," *DRCNY,* 5: 216.

56. "Earl of Bellomont to the Lords of Trade, 15 December 1698," *DRCNY,* 4: 441–42; NY Col Mss, 53: 88, 89; 54: 80.

57. Wynaut van Zandt v. Johannes Ten Eyck, 1719, MCP.

58. Act for Preventing the Multiplicity of Suits, 14 September 1714, *Colonial Laws,* 1: 827; Moglen, "Settling the law," 130; Rosen, "Courts and Commerce," 220.

59. There are several early examples of this type of bond among Dutch and

English litigants—for example, Stephen Cregoe v. Wouter Brestead, 1686, MCP, and Benjamin Fanueil v. Bartholomew Fuert, 1701, MCP—but its usage undoubtedly increased as the 1700s progressed. See Peter Mitchell and William Elliot, 1718, MCP; Richard Higgins and John Dunlap, 1719, MCP; Vincient Marine and Peter Ponyade, 1719, MCP; Patrick Macknight and Alexander Mills, wigmaker, 1719, MCP; Thomas Slowe, shopkeeper and William Lyford, mariner, 1721, MCP.

60. The Burnet inquiry resulted from the case of Philipse v. Codrington which highlighted the problem of greed and unethical behavior among some practicing attorneys. The six attorneys who joined the combination were George Clowes, William Smith, Joseph Murray, James Alexander, John Chambers, and Henry Wileman. See Kammen, *Colonial New York*, 210–11; Morris, *Select Cases*, 53.

61. For example, 97 of 108 extant complaints filed between 1735 and 1740 identify an attorney acting for the plaintiff, and in every case it is one of the attorneys sworn under the monopoly granted by the Montgomerie Charter. Also see Hamlin, *Legal Education*, 135–50; Milton Klein, "The Rise of the New York Bar: The Legal Career of William Livingston," *WMQ*, 3rd ser., (1958): 334–58; Anton-Hermann Chroust, *The Rise of the Legal Profession in America*, 2 vols. (Norman, Okla., 1965), 1: 161–74.

62. The figures in this paragraph are from Deborah Rosen, "Courts and Commerce," 160–210.

63. Abraham Lakeman v. Nathaniel Stillwell, 1743, MCP; also see William Jamison's bill in the case of John Johnston v. Samuel Cohen, 1743, MCP.

64. In the 1690s, only 13 percent of defendants defaulted or confessed judgment without challenging the case. By the 1750s, defendants defaulted in over 75 percent of the cases brought into court. Between 1694 and 1696, 17 percent of the cases handled by the Mayor's Court went to jury trial, but by 1754–55 this figure had fallen to 4 percent. Factoring in an increase in caseload of the court as the colony's population and the number of litigants increased, the rate of jury trial in the 1750s was less than one-fifteenth of what it had been at the start of the century. Rosen, "Courts and Commerce," 160–210. By 1765, Cadwallader Colden reported—admittedly in a harangue aimed at his political opponents which included leading city lawyers—"In general all the Lawyers unite in promoting contention, prolonging Suits & increasing the expense of obtaining Justice every artifice and chickanery in the Law has been so much connived at or rather encouraged, that honest men who are not of affluent Fortunes are deterred from defending their rights or seeking justice." See "Cadwallader Colden's Account of the State of the Province of New-York, 6 December 1765," *DRCNY*, 7: 796.

Chapter 6

1. Lyne based his plan on a survey conducted by Cadwallader Colden, the province's surveyor general, earlier that summer. Colden's survey was commissioned by the Common Council to confirm the corporate rights, lands, and jurisdiction secured under the recently granted Montgomerie charter. The Bradford Map or Lyne Survey, titled a "Plan of the City of New York from an Actual Survey Made by James Lyne," is reproduced in Stokes, *Iconography* 1: plate 27.

2. Goodfriend, *Before the Melting Pot*, 155; Bruce Martin Wilkenfeld, "Revolutionary New York," in Milton Klein, ed., *New York: The Centennial Years, 1676–1976* (Port Washington, N.Y., 1976), 44.

3. This draws upon Dror Wahrman's observations concerning the political processes that provided for the emergence of a "middle class" in late eighteenth-century Britain, see his *Imagining the Middle Class: The Political Representation of Class in Britain, 1780–1840* (Cambridge, 1995), introduction.

4. *New York Gazette*, 31 August 1730.

5. John J. McCusker and Russell R. Menard, *The Economy of British America, 1607–1789* (Chapel Hill, N.C., 1985), 191–95.

6. Nash, *Urban Crucible*, 123–24, 452 n. 107; Matson, *Merchants and Empire*, 183–214.

7. "Lords of Trade to the Lords of the Privy Council, 19 November 1729," *DRCNY*, 5: 897–99; "Governor Cosby to the Lords of Trade, 18 December 1732," *DRCNY*, 5: 937–38; Matson, *Merchants and Empire*, 122–28, 166, 254.

8. Wilkenfeld, "New York City Neighborhoods, 1730," 164–82; *DHSNY*, 1: 694; Burrows and Wallace, *Gotham*, 144.

9. The figure of three hundred was an estimate given in the *New York Weekly Journal* in April 1734. While the epidemic claimed an estimated 6 percent of the city's population, the number of taxpayers in 1730 and 1734 remained constant. This indicates that it was the poorer and borrowing sort who suffered the ravages of the epidemic. Howe, "Accommodation and Retreat," 264–66. Also see Bridenbaugh, *Cities in the Wilderness*, 400; Mohl, "Poverty in Early America," 5–27; Wilkenfeld, *Social and Economic Structure*, 29, 91; Ross, "Objects of Charity," 138–72.

10. Lewis Morris, "Reasons in Support of Triennial Elections, 1738," *DHSNY*, 4: 246; Deborah Rosen's analysis of the inventories of estates in wills and probate records shows that the number of better-off city residents who died as creditors increased from 36 to 65 percent between 1690 and 1740. Rosen, *Courts and Commerce*, 43. Adrian Howe estimates the shrinkage of the city's tax base of approximately £1,400 between 1730 and 1734. "Accommodation and Retreat," 268–69; Wilkenfeld, "New York City Neighborhoods," 171.

11. "An Act for the relief of Insolvent Debtors within the Colony of New York, 29 October 1730," *Colonial Laws*, 2: 669.

12. The budget for expenditure on the poor rate increased by almost half, from £456 in 1726 to £607 in 1735. "Minutes of the Church Wardens," *NYGBR* (July 1968): 158.

13. "Minutes of Church Wardens," *NYGBR* (July 1970): 164–66.

14. Greenberg, *Crime and Law Enforcement*, 136–37.

15. *Journal of the Votes and Proceedings of the General Assembly*, 1: 637, 661–62.

16. Dunscomb and Allair were assessed at five and twenty pounds, respectively; Gerardus Comfort was assessed at twenty-five pounds, and assuming the Johannis De Graaf mentioned in the assembly minutes was the John de Grave noted in the 1730 assessment, he was rated in the North Ward at forty pounds; Robert Richardson was not listed in the 1730 assessment. "New York City Tax Assessment," *NYGBR* (December 1964): 31, 171, 173, 197, 199; Scott, *New York Court Records*, 93, 107; NYHS, Collections (1885), 108.

17. Andries Marshalk was assessed at fifty pounds and Cornelius Cortreight at twenty five. "New York City Tax Assessment," *NYGBR* (December 1964): 30, 167–68; Everts Byvanck is identified as a baker and freeman in 1731, in NYHS, *Collections* (1885), 117; he was elected as an assistant in the East Ward in 1734. *MCC*, 4: 229.

18. Bonomi, *Factious People*, 60–97; Tully, *Forming American Politics*, 51–68.

19. Robert J. Dinkin, *Voting in Provincial America: A Study of Election in the Thirteen Colonies, 1689–1776* (Westport, Conn., 1977), 93–120; Tully, *Forming American Politics*, 322–23.

20. "Portius, 'O Liberty thou Goddess heavenly bright,' 1732," Livingston Family Papers, New York Public Library; Tully, *Forming American Politics*, 247; Linda Colley, *In Defence of Oligarchy: The Tory Party, 1714–1760* (Cambridge, 1982), 3–24.

21. For anti-Dutch sentiment in 1690s London, see Julian Hoppit, *England 1680–1727* (New York, 2000). For gossip and scurrility in Anglo-American politics, see Bonomi, *Lord Cornbury Scandal*, ch. 4. The Sachevrell controversy is discussed in J. R. Jones, *Country and Court: England, 1658–1714* (Cambridge, Mass., 1978), 334–36. The earliest satire on New York politics was a critique of Leislerian vices, "A Satyr upon the Times, 1702," cited in Lawrence H. Leder, *Robert Livingston, 1654–1728, and the Politics of Colonial New York* (Chapel Hill, N.C., 1961), 178–79; Robert Hunter, *Androboros*, edited and explicated by Lawrence H. Leder, "Robert Hunter's *Androboros*," *New York Public Library Bulletin* 68 (1964): 153–90.

22. Morris also secured a new issue of paper money and the Naturalization Act, confirming the status and rights of non-English residents. See Mary Lou Lustig, *Robert Hunter, 1660–1734* (Syracuse, N.Y., 1983), 122–25.

23. Stanley Nider Katz, *Newcastle's New York: Anglo-American Politics, 1732–1753* (Cambridge, Mass., 1968), 67.

24. Morris valued the position of chief justice and was peeved by his dismissal. He also served as interim governor of New Jersey following Montgomerie's death and received a salary that might have to be repaid if Cosby's suit against Van Dam succeeded. Alexander and Smith were uneasy about the implications of a governor-appointed exchequer court for their provincial legal practices. The three men in the opposition were also partners in a land deal, which, they had hoped, would secure Cosby's support. See Katz, *Newcastle's New York*, 80–81.

25. For example, Becker, *History of Political Parties*, 16–18. Milton Klein argued that John Peter Zenger's newspaper was "the prototype of a new aggressive from of popular journalism." Klein, *The American Whig. William Livingston of New York* (New York, 1993), 185. Patricia Bonomi maintained that populist themes and tactics of the 1730's "were to become common currency by the era of the Stamp Act Crisis." Bonomi, *Factious People*, 284. Michael Kammen argued that the Morris/Cosby dispute established "a new consciousness of constitutionalism and an awareness of administrative reform." Kammen, *Colonial New York*, 212. Gary Nash noted that "direct appeals for electoral support . . . first appeared in the 1730s." Nash, *Urban Crucible*, 143. And Cynthia Kierner considers the decade "a watershed in New York's political development." Kierner, "Traders and Gentlefolk: The Livingstons of Colonial New York, 1675–1790" (Ph.D. diss., University of Virginia, 1986), 408.

26. The account of the election appears in *Weekly Journal*, 5 November 1733. Also see Nicholas Varga, "Election Procedures and Practices in Colonial New York,"

New York History 61 (July 1960): 265–68; Katz, *Newcastle's New York*, 69; Paul Langford, *The Excise Crisis: Society and Politics in the Age of Walpole* (Oxford, 1975), 9–16.

27. For example, Thomas Hooker's *Laws of Ecclesiastical Polity*, and Edward, Earl of Clarendon, *History of the Rebellion*, discussed in Stanley N. Katz, ed., and James Alexander, *A Brief Narrative of the Case and Trial of John Peter Zenger, Printer of the New York Weekly Journal* (Cambridge, Mass., 1963), 10.

28. *Journal of the Votes and Proceedings of the General Assembly*, 1: 654; "History of Governor William Cosby's Administration," Colden Papers, vol. 9, in NYHS, Collections (New York, 1936), 298, cited in Nash, *Urban Crucible*, 147.

29. In subsequent years, the Morrisites sponsored bills seeking more frequent elections, clarification of court jurisdictions, and the reporting of the division of assemblymen on particular votes. Kammen, *Colonial New York*, 212.

30. *Weekly Journal*, 18 March, 8 April 1734; McAnear, "Politics in Provincial New York," 265–82, 326–60.

31. Nash, *Urban Crucible*, 147; Howe, "Accommodation and Retreat," 284, 375; Bonomi, *Factious People*, 115–16.

32. Everts Byvanck was elected as an assistant and Johannes Graaf a collector in the North Ward; Peter Marschalk secured the post of assessor in the South Ward; and Samuel Dunscomb, a likely relative of Daniel Dunscomb, was elected as an assessor in the West Ward. George W. Edwards, "New York City Politics before the American Revolution," *Political Science Quarterly* 36 (1921): 590; *MCC*, 4: 199, 229.

33. The song continued in the same vein, with stanzas emphasizing the wholesome virtues of ordinary voters and the importance of their role in defending popular liberty. Thus,

Our Country's Rights we will defend
Like brave and honest men
We voted right and there's an end
And so we'll do again
We vote all signers out of place
As men who did amiss
Who soil'd us by a false address
I'm sure we're right in this

The pettyfogging knaves deny
Us rights of Englishmen
We'll make the Scoundrel raskals fly
And ne'er return again
Our Judges they would chop and change
For those that Serve their turn
And will not surely think it strange
If they for this should mourn

34. Stephen Botein, ed., *Mr. Zenger's Malice and Falsehood: Six Isssues of the New York Weekly Journal, 1733–1734* (Worcester, Mass., 1985); Katz, ed., and Alexander, *Brief Narrative of the Case and Trial of John Peter Zenger*; Leonard Levy, *The Emergence of a Free Press* (New York, 1985), ch. 5; Michael Warner, *Letters of the Republic: Publication and the Public Sphere in Eighteenth-Century America* (Cambridge, Mass., 1990), 59–65.

35. Katz, *Newcastle's New York*, 74–75; Nash, *Urban Crucible*, 143.

36. Edwin Burrows and Michael Wallace follow others in asserting that ordinary voters appeared content to leave politics to the gentlemen in the middle decades of the eighteenth century. Burrows and Wallace, *Gotham*, 179. Also see Bruce Wilkenfeld, "The New York City Common Council, 1689–1800," *New York History* 52 (1971): 249–74; Tully, *Forming American Politics*, chs. 6 and 9, especially 365.

37. This draws upon points made by Quentin Skinner, "The Principles and Practice of Opposition: The Case of Bolingbroke versus Walpole," in N. McKendrick, ed., *Historical Perspectives: Essays in Honour of J. H. Plumb* (London, 1974), 93–128. For a fuller discussion of Skinner's approach, see James Tully, ed., *Meaning and Context: Quentin Skinner and His Critics* (Princeton, N.J., 1988), part II.

38. While cooling his heels waiting for an audience with the Lords of Trade in Westminster, Lewis Morris Sr. was reminded that the manner in which one framed a protest was as critical to its reception as its substance. Writing to supporters in New York, Morris reported that as far as the metropolitan authorities were concerned, "the most nefarious crime a governor can commit is not by some counted so bad as the crime of complaining of it." When he protested in behalf of individuals such as Rip van Dam, Morris worried that his case "look[ed] too much like the Effect of resentment." Yet when he remonstrated in the name of "the Assembly or Some such great body of the People," he feared being charged with "Ex[c]iting the people to clamour and weakening the hands of the government." Stanley Katz ed., "A New York Mission to England: The London Letters of Lewis Morris to James Alexander, 1735–1736," *WMQ*, 3rd ser. (July 1971): 446, 451–52, 460.

39. The influence of Cato on the Morrisite cause in particular and eighteenth-century American political culture in general is incontrovertible. James Alexander, who edited Zenger's paper, has been described as Cato's "principal disciple" in the colonies (Levy, *Free Press*, 124) and the *Journal* as "a veritable anthology of the writings of Trenchard and Gordon" (Bailyn, *Ideological Origins*, 33–36, 43). Also see Clinton Rossiter, *The Political Thought of the American Revolution* (New York, 1963); Bernard Bailyn, "The Central Themes of the American Revolution," in Stephen J. Kurtz and James H. Hutson, eds., *Essays on the American Revolution* (Chapel Hill, N.C., 1973), 3–25; Chad Reid, "'Widely Read by American Patriots': The *New York Weekly Journal* and the Influence of *Cato's Letters* on Colonial America" (unpublished paper), 4.

40. For a discussion of the collapse of the South Sea Company, see Geoffrey S. Holmes, *Making of a Great Power: Late Stuart and Early Georgian Britain, 1660–1722* (New York, 1993), 266–76. Only 12 of the 138 letters were devoted to the South Sea scandal. For examples of alternate themes, see John Trenchard and Thomas Gordon, *Cato's Letters: Or Essays on Liberty, Civil and Religious, and Other Important Subjects* (hereafter *Cato's Letters*), ed. Ronald Hamowy, 2 vols. (Indianapolis, Ind., 1995), 1: 48, 164–67, 185, 194–97, 214–21.

41. Until recently, *Cato's Letters* were usually understood within the terms set by a classical republican or civic humanist tradition and as an essential component in the "republican synthesis." See Bailyn, *Ideological Origins*, ch. 2; J. G. A. Pocock, *The Machiavellian Moment: Florentine Political Thought and the Atlantic Republican Tradition* (Princeton, N.J., 1975), 467–77; Robert E. Shallope, "Republicanism and Early American Historiography," *WMQ*, 3rd ser., 39 (1982): 334–56. There has been

no shortage of debate on this topic, but the studies that inform the view given in the following paragraphs are Zuckert, *Natural Rights and the New Republicanism,* especially chs. 6 and 10, and Ronald Hamowy, "*Cato's Letters,* John Locke and the Republican Paradigm," *History of Political Thought* 11 (summer 1990): 273–94.

42. Hamowy, "*Cato's Letters,*" 284; *Cato's Letters,* 1: 48, 185. Zuckert argues that the concept of virtue in *Cato's Letters* was very different from the classical, self-abnegating notion described by Pocock and more closely resembled Locke's thoughts on man's innate moral sense. In this view, virtue derives from the self-interested desire to be thought well of by others and, more importantly, from the faculty for moral choice that provides the highest expression of what it means to be free, self-determining, and human. Zuckert, *Natural Rights and the New Republicanism,* 315–17.

43. *Cato's Letters,* 1: 174; Hamowy, "*Cato's Letters,*" 284; Zuckert, *Natural Rights and the New Republicanism,* 318–19; Gordon S. Wood, *The Radicalism of the American Revolution* (New York, 1991), 57.

44. For a stimulating discussion of these and related problems concerning representation and the expression of consent in England, see Mark Knights, *Representation and Misrepresentation in Later Stuart Britain: Partisanship and Political Culture* (Oxford, 2004), passim. Also useful is Edmund S. Morgan, *Inventing the People: The Rise of Popular Sovereignty in England and America* (New York, 1988), chs. 8 and 9. For the debate concerning duties in the 1720s, see Matson, *Merchants and Empire,* 166–67.

45. *Journal,* 27 January 1734; Tully, *Forming American Politics,* 404.

46. *Journal,* 14 January 1734; *Journal,* 21 January 1734; James Green, "English Books and Printing in the Age of Franklin," in Hugh Amory and David D. Hall, eds., *A History of the Book in America,* vol. 1, *The Colonial Book in the Atlantic World* (Cambridge, Mass., 2000), 254.

47. For this double perspective on the role of print see, Warner, *Letters of the Republic,* 34–43. Other fictive characters included "Jack Frenchmen"—who whipped up fears of a possible attack from the north—and "John Scheme" who informed readers that "As I frequent the Coffee House . . . I there have the Opportunity of Hearing the various Sentiments of the Courtiers concerning your Journal." Scheme's intelligence regarding Cosbyite intentions to shut down the *Journal* prompted one more indignant defense of press freedom.

48. Thus wealthy landowners such as Lewis Morris railed against city merchants for keeping "money in your pockets which should have gone towards the Support of the government," and his upriver neighbor William Livingston warned of the "Dangers flowing from Luxury" to the virtue and liberty of freemen. This while both men maintained thriving trading houses in the city and stocked their homes with fine plate and the best imported French wines. See Kierner, "Traders and Gentlefolk," 347.

49. All quotes from the letters come from Timothy Wheelwright [pseud.], *Two Satirical Letters on the Election for Aldermen,* 8 and 12 September, 1734. Livingston Family Papers, New York Public Library, Rare Books and Manuscripts.

50. For the protest against Rutgers's draining of the swamp, see "Petition of Captain Anthony Rutgers to the King, December 1730," *DRCNY,* 5: 914–18; "Governor Cosby to the Lords of Trade, 15 December 1733," *DRCNY,* 5: 960–63; *MCC,* 4: 177–78.

51. Katz, *Newcastle's New York,* 120–24.

52. In addition to emitting bills of credit to finance the provincial debt and accepting a revenue bill of only twelve months' duration, Clark approved a triennial bill introduced by Lewis Morris Jr. The bill was subsequently disallowed in London, but, in 1743, a septennial bill was enacted, gained approval in England, and regularized provincial elections thereafter. Bonomi, *Factious* People, 135; Nash, *Urban Crucible*, 144–46; Katz, *Newcastle's New York*, 150–53. Adrian Howe argues that it is possible that Clark's favoring of Morrisite officeholders was a cunning attempt to sever ties between the opposition's leaders and their popular supporters: the lieutenant governor must have figured that the Philipsite council members would strike down many of his recommendations, but only after the details of offers of provincial posts had made it into the public domain. Howe, "Accommodation and Retreat," 314–16.

53. *Journal*, 27 June 1736.

54. In addition to the usual partisan appeals, the Morrisites accused Philipse of favoring merchant interests in his campaign and even resorted to spreading rumors that Philipse and his co-runner, David Clarkson, would not seek reelection forcing the two men to take out an advertisement denying the rumors in the *Gazette*, 9 May 1737; "Colden to Mrs. Colden, 11 September 1737," NYHS, Collections 51 (1918), 179; Varga, "New York Government," 263; Bonomi, *Factious People*, 133; Katz, *Newcastle's New York*, 145–54.

55. The following points concerning the breakdown of support in the Van Horne by-election draw on Adrian Howe's analysis of the Morrisite petitions signed in January 1735 and September 1737. Howe, "Accommodation and Retreat," 299, 305, 321–28, 347–67; "Petition Demanding the Removal of the Sheriff, 12 September 1737," *DHSNY*, 3: 484–86.

56. For the economic recovery, see "Lieutenant Governor George Clarke to the Lords of Trade, 15 December 1741," *DRCNY*, 6: 206–8; Nash, *Urban Crucible*, 141–48.

57. The second petition also called for the Assembly to "strike a Sum of Money pursuant to their Solemn promises, lower the Interest of Money, and moderate the Lawyers Fees which we sorely groan under." *Journal of the Votes and Proceedings of the General Assembly*, 1: 676, 709–10, 23. Also see Morris, *Government and Labor*, 183; Kammen, *Colonial New York*, 182; Berlin, *Many Thousands Gone*, 180.

58. Gary Nash notes the likely division between slaveholding and nonslaveholding artisans in *Urban Crucible*, 109. Adrian Howe's analysis indicates that seventeen coopers, representing the poorer sort, signed the petition in support of Van Horne—less than half the forty-two coopers identified in the 1730 tax assessment. Howe, Accommodation and Retreat," 358.

59. In the Assembly elections the following year, the Philipsites went so far as to publish a list of candidates they claimed had been nominated by a public meeting of freeholders and freemen—although there is no evidence that such a meeting ever took place. See Becker, *History of Political Parties*, 18. For the shift to greater focus on the Assembly and popular campaigning in the 1740s and 1750s, see Varga, "New York Government," 47–51; Bonomi, *Factious* People, 134; Tully, *Forming American Politics*, 127.

60. Between 1740 and 1760 imports to New York from Britain rose from £135,487 to £480,106. Bruce Wilkenfeld estimates that the volume of city trade increased by some 600 percent between 1747 and 1772, mostly along existing trade

routes connecting New York to its plantation customers to the south. Wilkenfeld, *Social and Economic Structure*, 139, 143; *Historical Statistics of the United States: Colonial Times to 1970* (White Plains, N.Y., 1989), part II, ser. 2, 213–26; additional figures for imports and exports in Matson, *Merchants and Empire*, 320–21. Also see Kammen, *Colonial New York*, 279, 292; Nash, *Urban Crucible*, 238.

61. Peter Kalm, *The America of 1750: Peter Kalm's Travels in North America, The English Version of 1770*, ed. Adolph B. Benson, 2 vols. (New York, 1937), 1: 131–32; Carl Bridenbaugh, *Cities in Revolt: Urban Life in America, 1743–1776* (New York, 1955), 42; Burrows and Wallace, *Gotham*, 172–74. Generally see Cary Carson, "The Consumer Revolution in Colonial British America: Why Demand?" in Cary Carson, Ronald Hoffman, and Peter J. Albert, eds., *Of Consuming Interests: The Style of Life in the Eighteenth Century* (Charlottesville, Va., 1994), 483–697.

62. Kammen, *Colonial New York*, 279. Bruce Wilkenfeld estimates that by the early 1760s, one-third of the city's shippers started out as tradesmen or shopkeepers and approximately 10 percent of urban residents had a share in one of the city's 477 vessels. Wilkenfeld, *Social and Economic Structure*, 149–50, and "New York Shipowning Community, 1715–1764," *American Neptune* 37 (1977): 61. This confirms contemporary assessments, by Cadwallader Colden and William Smith, who observed that many wealthy traders had "suddenly rose from the lowest rank of the People to considerable fortune," and "Every man of industry and integrity has it in his power to live well, and many are the instances of persons who come here distressed by their poverty who now enjoy easy and plentiful fortune." See "Mr. Colden's Account of the State of the Province of New York, 6 December 1765," *DRCNY*, 7: 796, and William Smith, *History of the Province of New York*, ed. Michael Kammen, 2 vols. (Cambridge, Mass., 1972), 1: 226.

63. T. H. Breen, "An Empire of Goods: The Anglicization of Colonial America, 1660–1776," *Journal of British Studies* 25 (1986): 467–99 and his "'Baubles of Britain': The American Revolution and Consumer Revolution of the Eighteenth Century," *Past and Present* 119 (1988): 73–104. For consumption and its connection to the cultural formation of a middle class and the development of republican politics, see David Shields, *Civil Tongues and Polite Letters in British America* (Chapel Hill, N.C., 1997), 38, 61–62; J. G. A. Pocock, "Virtues, Rights, and Manners," in *Virtue, Commerce, and History* (Cambridge, 1985), 48–51; Serena Zabin, "Places of Exchange: Race, Gender, and New York City, 1700–1760" (Ph.D. diss., Rutgers University, 2001), ch. 5; Burrows and Wallace, *Gotham*, 167–82; Robyn Davis McMillin, "Enlightened Thought in Eighteenth-Century New York: 'Fitting for a Gentleman or a Storekeeper'" (paper given at Omohundro Institute for Early American History Annual Conference, New Orleans, 2003). Also see Richard L. Bushman, *The Refinement of America: Persons, Houses, Cities* (New York, 1992); C. J. Barker-Benfield, *The Culture of Sensibility: Sex and Society in Eighteenth-Century Britain* (Chicago, 1992).

64. *New York Mercury*, 31 January 1757, cited in Wilkenfeld, "Revolutionary New York," 56. For critiques of the attachment to luxuries and public vice, see William Livingston et al., *Independent Reflector: Or, Weekly Essays on Sundry Important Subjects, More Particularly Adapted to the Province of New York*, ed. Milton M. Klein (Cambridge, Mass., 1963), 111–18, and T. H. Breen, *The Marketplace of Revolution: How Consumer Politics Shaped American Independence* (New York, 2004), 33–72.

65. Robert E. Cray, *Paupers and Poor Relief in New York City and Its Rural Environs, 1700–1830* (Philadelphia, 1988), 68–70; Nash, "Urban Wealth and Poverty," 550–52, 575–76; Wilkinfeld estimates that population grew at 1.49 percent per annum between 1698 and 1723 in contrast to 4.62 percent per annum between 1756 and 1771. Wilkenfeld, "Revolutionary New York," 44; *Social and Economic Structure*, 138–39. A third of new immigrants who came between 1732 and 1754 were slaves. Berlin, *Many Thousands Gone*, 179.

66. *New York Post Boy*, 19 March 1753, cited in McKee, *Labor in Colonial New York*, 27; Livingston et al., *Independent Reflector*, 437–38; Peter Linebaugh and Marcus Rediker, *The Many Headed Hydra: Sailors, Slaves, Commoners, and the Hidden History of the Revolutionary Atlantic* (New York, 2000), ch. 6.

67. Between 1736 and 1772 the number of inmates of the poorhouse grew from less than twenty to more than four hundred and muster rolls indicate that two-thirds to three-fourths of militia places were taken by mariners, laborers, shoemakers, weavers, and tailors. Greenberg, *Crime and Law Enforcement*, 137; Wilkenfeld, *Social and Economic Structure*, 144; Cray, *Paupers and Poor Relief*, 68.

68. "Lieutenant Governor Clarke to Lords of Trade, 2 June 1738," *DRCNY*, 6: 117. On the growth of poor neighborhoods and an informal economy see Carl Abbot, "The Neighborhoods of New York, 1760–1775," *New York History* 55 (1974): 35–74; Elizabeth Blackmar, *Manhattan for Rent, 1785–1850* (Ithaca, N.Y., 1989), 28–38; Hodges, *New York City Carters*, 46–49; Zabin, "Places of Exchange," 137–74.

69. For example, benevolent associations such as the St. Andrew's Society (established in 1756) whose membership included middling artisans made an important contribution to the costs of urban poor relief. Cray, *Paupers and Poor Relief*, 217, n. 20. In 1759, the *New York Gazette* reported that "the Company of Hatters" erected a large bonfire on the commons to celebrate the success "of his Majesty's Arms at the Battle of Quebeck." Cited in Guterman, "Ancient Freemen," 260, 265–66; also see Howard B. Rock, "All Her Sons Join in One Social Band," *Labor's Heritage* 3 (July 1991): 7–9. For fire companies in the eighteenth-century city, see Benjamin L. Carp, "Fire of Liberty: Firefighters, Urban Voluntary Culture, and the Revolutionary Movement," *William and Mary Quarterly* 58 (October 2001): 781–818. Militia service also continued to provide occasions for assertions of popular rights. In November 1747, when Clinton ordered the militia captains to "hold their regiments in readiness to march upon any emergency," the rank-and-file "unanimously refused to obey any orders from the Crown, unless an Act of Assembly" was passed confirming the instruction. "Governor Clinton to the Duke of Newcastle, 9 November 1747," *DRCNY*, 6: 410.

70. Paul Gilje, *The Road to Mobocracy: Popular Disorder in New York City, 1763–1834* (Chapel Hill, N.C., 1987), chs. 1 and 2; Lemisch, "Jack Tar in the Streets," 381–95.

71. For voters' diminishing interest and the difficulties of consensus building, see Nash, *Urban Crucible*, 228–29; Klein, *American Whig*, 184, and his "Shaping the American Tradition," *New York History* 69 (1978): 173–97; Tully, *Forming American Politics*, 365–75; Richard Beeman, *The Varieties of Political Experience in Eighteenth-Century America* (Philadelphia, 2004), 256.

72. For Delancey's career and London connections, see Katz, *Newcastle's New York*, 166–93, and "Between Scylla and Charybdis: James De Lancey and Anglo-American

Politics in Early Eighteenth-Century New York," in Alison Olson and Richard M. Brown, eds., *Anglo-American Political Relations, 1675–1775* (New Brunswick, N.J., 1970), 92–108.; Bonomi, *Factious People*, 140–79.

73. Assembly elections were held in 1745, 1748, 1750, and 1751. The Delanceyites relied on the *New-York Evening Post*, and Clinton and his supporters upon the *New-York Post Boy* to deliver their party's message, and both sides courted the artisanal vote. In 1750, the Delanceyites claimed to be running an artisanal candidate when they put up the wealthy goldsmith William de Peyster for city alderman; Clinton exempted city artisans from unpopular service on the watch and the Clintonite mayor John Cruger constructed a system of patronage within the ranks of city carters. Varga, "New York Government," 10; Bonomi, *Factious People*, 158–66; Hodges, *New York City Carters*, 62–64.

74. Smith, *History of the Province of New York*, 2: 245–47; "Governor Clinton to the Duke of Newcastle, 22 April 1748," *DRCNY*, 6: 424; Howe, "Accommodation and Retreat," 387–98.

75. The controversy centered on the funding and religious affiliation of King's College and pit a powerful group of city Anglicans against dissenting lobbies, including Livingston and the Presbyterians. Although all parties eventually agreed to support the principle of religious toleration, the controversy prompted lengthy and frequently vituperative debate concerning the established church and the dangers posed by conspiracies and arbitrary authority to the public good.

76. My view of Livingston and his political philosophy draws upon Klein, *American Whig*, ch. 8, and Bernard Friedman, "The Shaping of Radical Consciousness in Provincial New York," *Journal of American History* 56 (1970): 781–801.

77. Livingston et al., *Independent Reflector*, 143, 145, 286–87.

78. Patricia Bonomi settled on "popular" and "moderate" Whigs as the most appropriate labels for the "main rhetorical differences between the two factions." Bonomi, *Factious People*, 239. Alan Tully makes a similar distinction, retaining "popular" Whig for the Delanceyites but substituting "provincial" for their Livingston opponents. Tully, *Forming American Politics*, 233–49. Leopold S. Launitz-Schurer argues that Livingston's ideology was "unexceptional . . . and perfectly in accord with the mainstream of conventional Whig thinking" in *Loyal Whigs and Revolutionaries: The Making of the Revolution in New York, 1765–1776* (New York, 1980), 13–19. On the place of New York Whig beliefs in the broader eighteenth-century political culture, see Bailyn, *Origins of American Politics*, 128–29, and *Ideological Origins*, 53, 250.

79. The assessment of elite claims concerning popular rights as "facile and empty" is Richard Beeman's. See his *Varieties of Political Experience*, 248.

80. For the gentry's prejudicial view, see Friedman, "Shaping of Radical Consciousness," 787. For example, Cadwallader Colden lumped artisans and farmers together in the "last Rank [that] comprehends the bulk of the People and in them consists the strength of the Province. They are the most useful and the most moral, but alwise made the Dupes of the former, and often are ignorantly made their Tools for the worst purposes" in his "Account of the Condition of the Province of New York 6 December 1765," *DRCNY*, 7: 795.

81. Wood, *Radicalism of the American Revolution*, 243.

82. Stokes, *Iconography*, 4: 722; Morris, *Government and Labor*, 156–66; Guterman, "Ancient Freemen," 207, 271, 286.

83. Kammen, *Colonial New York*, 331; "Governor Clinton to the Lords of Trade, 9 December 1746," *DRCNY*, 6: 317; NYHS, Collections (1885), 507–11; Nash, *Urban Crucible*, 238–39.

84. See, for example, Esther Singleton, *Social New York under the Georges* (New York, 1902), 79, 81, 89, 177, and Rita S. Gottesman, comp., "The Arts and Crafts in New York, 1726–1776: Advertisements and News Items from the New York City Newspapers," NYHS, Collections (1936).

85. Singleton, *Social New York under the Georges*, 165; Kierner, "Traders and Gentlefolk," 370–85; NYHS, Collections (1936), 7, 17, 87, 181, 356.

86. NYHS, Collections (1936), 100, 183, 293, 295, 305.

87. Here I am paraphrasing J. R. Pole's observation that "people continue, with disarming simplicity, to believe the words they utter, they frequently imagine themselves to be governed by the forms described by a rhetoric belonging to the past." Pole, *Political Representation in England and the Origins of the American Republic* (Berkeley, Calif., 1966), 526.

88. Amy Bridges, "Becoming American: The Working Classes in the United States Before the Civil War," in Ira Katznelson and Aristide R. Zolberg, eds., *Working-Class Formation: Nineteenth-Century Patterns in Western Europe and the United States* (Princeton, N.J., 1986), 194–95; Timothy J. Gilfoyle, *City of Eros: New York City Prostitution and the Commercialization of Sex, 1790–1920* (New York, 1992), 92–117; Richard B. Stott, *Workers in the Metropolis: Class, Ethnicity, and Youth in Antebellum New York City* (Ithaca, N.Y., 1990). Generally, see Elliot J. Gorn, *The Manly Art: Bare Knuckle-Prize Fighting in America* (Ithaca, N.Y., 1986); Karen Halttunen, *Confidence Men and Painted Women: A Study of Middle Class Culture in America, 1830–1870* (New Haven, Conn., 1982); Michael Denning, *Mechanic Accents: Dime Novels and Working-Class Culture in America* (London, 1987).

89. Wilentz, *Chants Democratic*, part I.

90. Fred Anderson, *The Crucible of War: The Seven Years War and the Fate of Empire in British North America, 1754–1766* (New York, 2000), 400–09; Joseph S. Tiedemann, *Reluctant Revolutionaries: New York City and the Road to Independence, 1763–1776* (Ithaca, N.Y., 1997), ch. 2; *MCC*, 6: 336–42; DeVoe, *The Market Book*, 147.

91. The crucial role of artisans in the coming of the American Revolution in New York City has long been recognized by historians. For example, see Staughton Lynd, "Mechanics in New York City Politics, 1774–1788," *Labor History* 5 (1964): 225–46; Jesse L. Lemisch, "New York's Petitions and Resolves of December 1765: Liberals vs Radicals," *The New-York Historical Society Quarterly* 59 (October 1965): 313–26; Roger J. Champage, "New York's Radicals and the Coming of Independence," *The Journal of American History* 51 (June 1964): 21–40 and his "Liberty Boys and Mechanics of New York City, 1764–1777," *Labor History* 8 (1967): 115–35.

Chapter 7

1. For a discussion of these problems in early modern English and French historiography, see Wood, *Politics of Social Conflict*, introduction, and Sonenscher, *Work and Wages*, introduction.

2. Gareth Stedman Jones, *The Languages of Class: Studies in English Working*

Class History, 1832–1982 (London, 1983), 90–105, and his "Anglo-Marxism — Discursive Approach to History," in Alf Ludtke, ed., *Was Bliebt von Marxistischen Perpektiven in der Geschichtforschung?* (Gottingen, 1997), 151–209; Patrick Joyce, *Democratic Subjects: The Self and the Social in Nineteenth-Century England* (Cambridge, 1994), introduction, and Joyce, ed., *Class* (Oxford, 1995), 3–16. Also see William Sewell Jr., *The Language of Labor from the Old Regime to 1848* (London, 1980), 1–14, 62–86, and his "Toward a Post-materialist Rhetoric for Labor History," in Lenard R. Berlanstein, *Rethinking Labor History* (Chicago, 1993), 15–39; Jacque Ranciere, "The Myth of the Artisan: Critical Reflections on a Category of Social History," in S. L. Kaplan and C. J. Koepp, eds., *Work in France: Representations, Meaning, Organization, and Practice* (Ithaca, N.Y., 1986), 317–34. For America, see Allan Kulikoff, "The Transition to Capitalism in Rural America," in *The Agrarian Origins of American Capitalism* (Charlottesville, Va., 1992), 1–27; Clarence E. Walker, "How Many Niggers Did Karl Marx Know? Or a Peculiarity of the Americans," in *Deromanticizing Black History: Critical Essays and Reappraisals* (Knoxville, Tenn., 1991), 1–33, and Gregory Nobles, "Class," in Daniel Vickers, ed., *Companion to Colonial American History* (Malden, Mass., 2003), 273–75. Two scholars who have combined a critique of the class concept with calls for a reappraisal of the early modern Atlantic economy are Christopher Tomlins, "Why Wait for Industrialism? Work, Legal Culture, and the Example of Early America: An Historiographical Argument," *Labor History* 40 (1999): 5–34, and Marcus Rediker, "The Revenge of Crispus Attucks: Or, The Atlantic Challenge to American Labor History," *Labor* (November, 2004): 35–47.

    3. Vickers, "Competency and Competition," 3–29; Michael Merrill, "Putting Capitalism in Its Place: A Review of Recent Literature," *WMQ* 52 (April 1995), 315–26; Naomi R. Lamoreaux, "Rethinking the Transition to Capitalism in the Early American Northeast," *Journal of American History* 90 (September 2003): 437–61. Also see Craig Muldrew's excellent discussion of these issues in "Interpreting the Market: The Ethics of Credit and Community Relations in Early Modern England," *Social History* 18 (1993): 163–83, and his *Economy of Obligation*.

    4. Barbara Clark Smith, "Beyond the Vote" (paper given at Conference on Deference in Early America, at McNeil Center for Early American Studies, Philadelphia, 11 December 2004). For a controversial critique of the idea of colonial American deference, see Michael Zuckerman, "Tocqueville, Turner, and Turds: Four Stories of Manners in Early America," and the other contributions to "Deference or Defiance in Eighteenth-Century America? A Round Table," *Journal of American History* 85 (June 1998). On the difficulties of applying the term "radical" to popular politics in early modern contexts, see Gary S. DeKrey, "Radicals, Reformers and Republicans: Academic Language and Political Discourse in Restoration London," in Alan Houston and Steve Pincus, eds., *A Nation Transformed:England after the Restoration* (Cambridge, 2001), 71–100.

    5. For example, Barnet Schecter, *The Battle for New York: The City at the Heart of the Revolution* (London, 2003), 22, and Richard M. Ketchum, *Divided Loyalties: How the American Revolution Came to New York* (New York, 2002), 138–49.

Index

Abrahamsen, Jacob, 85
Abrahamsen, Pieter, 58
Ackerson, John, 112
Act of Union, 145
Adolph, Peter, 111
Agriculture, 22, 27, 64, 72–73, 75
Albany, 74, 81, 91, 93, 117, 137; female fur
    traders and tavern keepers in, 71;
    Hudson River trade, 58, 70, 72, 134, 175;
    Lutherans in, 117, 265 n.55
Alexander, James, 210, 283 n.60; likely
    contributor to *New York Weekly Journal*
    and admirer of Cato, 206, 287 n.39; and
    Van Dam affair, 199, 285 n.24
Algonquians, 19
Allair, Alexander, 196
American Revolution, 1, 3, 6; radical whig
    ideas in, 218–19, 228
Amsterdam, 4, 11–12, 32, 36, 55, 57–58;
    model for municipal and legal practice
    in New Amsterdam, 18, 20, 37–38, 43,
    45–46, 248 n.42; New Netherland
    dependent on supplies from, 13, 100
Andros, Edmund, 55, 81–82; challenges to
    and recall, 75–76; and coopers combina-
    tion, 83–84; reforms in New York, 70–73,
    149, 151, 160, 172
Anglicans, 79, 97–98, 118, 179; diminutive
    congregation in late seventeenth
    century, 139, 272 n.21
Anglo-Dutch relations: imperial, 36–37,
    51–52, 54, 69–70; regional, 18, 27–28, 62
Anthill, Edward, 180, 182
Anthony, Allard, 66
Antipopery, 7, 55, 77–79, 94, 164
Apprenticeship, 116, 175, 178; apprentices'
    rates for hire, 120, 266 n.65; decline of,

133, 149, 154–59; female apprentices and
    masters, 111; in New Netherland, 16, 19;
    predominance of poor and orphaned
    young people in, 159–60; regulation of
    following the conquest, 60, 84, 87;
    variance in terms of service of, 157–58;
    withdrawal of Dutch masters from, 156.
    See also Labor
Arenzen, Frederick, 42
Articles of Capitulation, 54–56, 62, 69–70,
    171
Artisans. *See specific occupations*;
    Tradesmen
Assembly, New York, 96, 102, 122; factional
    contests within, 197–203, 210–12, 216–19;
    increase in influence of, 132–33; retreat
    on manumission restrictions, 144.
    See also Provincial government
Atwood, William, 180

Bacon, Nathaniel, 93
Bakers, 17, 35, 108, 116; complaints against
    and regulations in New Amsterdam, 19,
    23, 25–30, 40, 42–43; after the conquest,
    63–65, 73–75, 98; in eighteenth-century
    New York City, 196, 202, 207, 220; local
    market for, 236 n.45. *See also* Bolters
Bancker, Elizabeth, 100
Barbados, 64, 75, 82, 116
Barhyt, Andries, 103, 175
Bayard, Nicholas, 60, 70, 79, 180; and
    Leisler's Rebellion, 90, 93
Beekman, Henry, 118
Beenvos, Christina, 182
Bellomont, Richard, Earl of, 112, 115, 118,
    122; death of, 136; opinions regarding
    lawyers, 173, 180, 183; provincial

Acknowledgments

It is a pleasure to be able to thank those who have helped me with the production of this book. My interest in early American history was first fired by my graduate studies at the incomparable City of University of New York, Graduate Center, where Professors Jack Diggins, Thomas Kessner, Kathleen McCarthy, Gerald Sider, and my advisor David Nasaw provided superlative guidance and counsel. At the University of East Anglia, Eric Homberger, Mark Knights, and Andy Wood have given invaluable support. John Arnold deserves particular thanks for helping me through some of the stickier moments in thinking and writing about the colonial trades. I have also benefited from the encouragement of many fine scholars of New Netherland and early New York who have read portions of the manuscript, talked through ideas, written letters in support of grant proposals, or simply inspired my efforts by their own scholarly example, including Firth Fabend, Charles Gehring, Joyce Goodfriend, Graham Hodges, Jaap Jacobs, Dennis Maika, Martha Shattuck, Russell Shorto, and David Voorhees. I also thank Edward Countryman, Christopher Tomlins, Alfred Young, and my recent collaborator on various projects, Billy G. Smith, for comments and their support. Portions of the argument have been tested out at conferences, in particular the Omohundro Institute of Early American History and Culture Annual Conferences in Glasgow (2001) and New Orleans (2003), the Rensselaerswijck Seminar at the New York Genealogical and Biographical Society (2001), the modern history seminars at Clare College, Cambridge, and Pembroke College, Oxford, and the convivial annual meetings organized by the British Group of Early Americanists. Parts of Chapters 1 and 3 draw upon material that appeared in "How It Came That the Bakers Bake No Bread: A Struggle for Trade Privileges in Seventeenth-Century New Amsterdam," *William and Mary Quarterly*, 3d ser., 58 (April 2001): 347–72, and "The World Beyond the Workshop: Trading in New York City's Artisanal Economy, 1680–1740," *New York History* 81 (October 2000): 381–416. I am grateful to the editors for their permission to reprint some of this material in the book.

I am also pleased to have the opportunity to thank the archivists and librarians at the New York Public Library and the New-York Historical

Society; Jim Folts and his team at the State Archives and Library at Albany, the Municipal Archives at 31 Chambers Street, New York City; and especially Bruce Abrahms in the Division of Old Records in the New York County Court. I am grateful to the funding bodies and prize committees that sustained the research for the writing of this book: Frank Knox Memorial Fellowship; City University of New York; Colonial Dames of the State of New York; E. P. Thompson Memorial Fellowship; Richard C. Wade Prize; Gilder-Lehrman Research Fellowship (New-York Historical Society); United Kingdom Arts and Humanities Research Board, Research Leave Scheme; University of East Anglia, School of English and American Studies Research Committee; Library Company of Philadelphia, Program in Early American Economy and Society; New York State Archives, Hackman Research Fellowship; British Academy; and New Netherland Project, Andrew Hendricks Manuscript Award. At the University of Pennsylvania Press, Daniel Richter, Robert Lockhart, Ellie Goldberg, and Erica Ginsburg have overseen the passage from draft submission to finished book.

My biggest thanks are reserved for Carol Berkin, who has been my strongest supporter since my first week in graduate school at CUNY. Long after finishing my doctoral studies, I continue to benefit from Carol's sagacious counsel and her unfailing hospitality during many research visits to the Upper West Side of New York City. Finally, thanks to Carolyn for her love and patience, our wonderful daughters, and the life we have together.